100 Pioneers

Other books by Richard Lapchick

*100 Heroes: People in Sports Who Make
This a Better World*

New Game Plan for College Sport

*Smashing Barriers: Race and Sport
in the New Millennium*

*Never Before, Never Again: The Stirring
Autobiography of Eddie Robinson, the
Winningest Coach in the History
of College Football*

*Sport in Society:
Equal Opportunity or Business as Usual?*

*Five Minutes to Midnight:
Race and Sport in the 1990s*

Rules of the Game: Ethics in College Sport

*On the Mark: Putting the Student Back
in Student-athlete*

*Fractured Focus: Sport
as a Reflection of Society*

Broken Promises: Racism in American Sports

*Oppression and Resistance:
The Struggle of Women in Southern Africa*

*Politics of Race and International Sport:
The Case of South Africa*

100 Pioneers

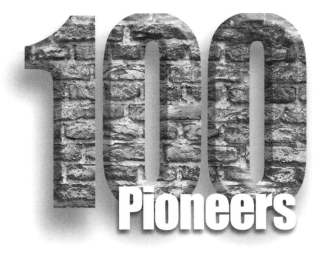

AFRICAN-AMERICANS Who Broke Color Barriers in Sport

Richard Lapchick
with
Jessica Bartter
Jenny Brenden
Stacy Martin
Horacio Ruiz
Marcus Sedberry

Library of Congress Card Catalog Number: 2007940196

ISBN 13: 978-1-885693-81-5

Cover photographs (wrapping around from back cover): C. B. Claiborne, courtesy of Duke Sports Information; Brud Holland, courtesy of Jeremy Hartigan, Cornell University; William White with the 1879 Brown University Baseball Team, courtesy of the Edward North Robinson Collection of Brown Athletics, Brown University Archives; Eddie McAshan, courtesy of Georgia Tech Sports Information; Jerry Gaines, courtesy of Virginia Tech Athletics Communications; Charlie Scott, courtesy of University of North Carolina Athletic Communications; Lester McClain, courtesy of University of Tennessee Sports Information

Production Editor: Valerie Gittings
Cover Design: Bellerophon Productions
Typesetter: Bellerophon Productions
Copyeditor: Valerie Gittings
Proofreader: Mark Slider
Printed by Sheridan Books

10 9 8 7 6 5 4 3 2 1

Fitness Information Technology
A Division of the International Center for Performance Excellence
West Virginia University
262 Coliseum, WVU-PE
PO Box 6116
Morgantown, WV 26506-6116
800.477.4348 (toll free)
304.293.6888 (phone)
304.293.6658 (fax)
Email: icpe@mail.wvu.edu
Website: www.fitinfotech.com

100 Pioneers could be dedicated to all the pioneers in this book. However, I have decided to dedicate it to Jackie Robinson, Althea Gibson, Arthur Ashe, Nat "Sweetwater" Clifton, and Eddie Robinson, the pioneers I have personally known, who are now gone but who changed my life as well as the culture in and destiny of our nation.

—*Richard Lapchick*

Contents

Foreword by John Thompson xv

Acknowledgments xvii

CHAPTER 1 • **An Introduction:**
Race and Sport in America   **1**

Part One: Professional Sport

CHAPTER 2 • **Major League Baseball:**
African-American Pioneers in America's Favorite Pastime   **9**

Jackie Robinson 14
First African-American Player in MLB
Larry Doby 19
First African-American Player in MLB's American League
John Jordan "Buck" O'Neil 23
First African-American Coach in MLB
Frank Robinson 28
First African-American Manager in MLB
Bill Lucas 31
First African-American General Manager in MLB
Bill White 34
First African-American National League President of MLB
Cito Gaston 37
First African-American Manager in MLB to Win a World Series
Bob Watson 40
First African-American General Manager in MLB's
    American League
Ulice Payne, Jr. 43
First African-American President in MLB

CHAPTER 3 • NFL Pioneers: A Story of Pioneers in Two Eras   47

Frederick Douglass "Fritz" Pollard 51
First African-America Coach in the NFL

Kenny "Kingfish" Washington 55
One of the First Two African-American Players
   in the Modern-Day NFL

Woodrow "Woody" Wilson Woolrine Strode 59
One of the First Two African-American Players
   in the Modern-Day NFL

Arthur Shell 62
First African-American Coach in the Modern-Day NFL

Ozzie Newsome. 65
First African-American General Manager in the NFL

Lovie Smith and Tony Dungy 68
First African-American Coaches to Face Off in the Super Bowl

Tony Dungy. 71
First African-American Coach to Win the Super Bowl

CHAPTER 4 • NBA: The NBA Is the Pioneer Leader   75

Nat "Sweetwater" Clifton 78
First African-American Player to Be Signed to the NBA

Charles "Chuck" Cooper. 84
First African-American Player to Be Drafted into the NBA

Earl Lloyd 87
First African-American Player to Play in the NBA

Don Angelo Barksdale 90
First African-American to Be Selected to an NBA All-Star Team

Bill Russell. 93
First African-American Head Coach of Any Major
   Professional Sport

Wayne Embry 97
First African-American General Manager and President
   of a Professional Sports Franchise

Al Attles and K. C. Jones. 101
First African-American Coaches to Face Off in a Professional
   Championship

Peter Bynoe and Robert Johnson 104
First African-American Owners of a Professional
   Sports Franchise

CHAPTER 5 • National Hockey League: African-American Players in a Traditionally White Sport   **109**

William O'Ree 113
First Black Player in the NHL

CHAPTER 6 • Tennis and Golf:
Country Clubs' Slow Integration of Great Sports   **117**

Althea Gibson. 123
First African-American to Win Wimbledon
Arthur Ashe 128
First African-American to Win Wimbledon and the U.S. Open
Charlie Sifford. 133
First African-American Golfer on the PGA Tour
Lee Elder. 136
First African-American to Play in the Masters

CHAPTER 7 • Boxing:
Champions Who Set the World Stage   **139**

John Arthur "Jack" Johnson 141
First African-American World Heavyweight Boxing Champion
Joe Louis Barrow 145
African-American Boxing Pioneer for the Human Race
Muhammad Ali 149
"The Greatest"

Part Two: College Sport

CHAPTER 8 • College Coaching Ranks Still
Show Long Way to Go in Spite of Great Pioneers   **157**

Larry Ellis 163
First African-American Head Coach in the Ivy League
Payton Fuller. 165
First African-American Head Coach in the Big Ten Conference
Fletcher Carr 167
First African-American Head Coach in the Southeastern
  Conference
Marian Washington. 171
First African-American Coach in the Big 12 Conference

Willie Jefferies. 173
First African-American Head Football Coach at a Division
    I-A University
Robert Purnell Wade 176
First African-American Coach in the Atlantic Coast Conference
John Thompson, Jr. 179
Black Coaches & Administrators
George Raveling 183
Black Coaches & Administrators
John Chaney 187
Black Coaches & Administrators
Nolan Richardson. 191
Black Coaches & Administrators
Eddie Robinson. 194
A Once-in-a-Lifetime Man
Carolyn Peck 201
First African-American Female Head Coach to Win an NCAA
    Women's Basketball Championship
C. Vivian Stringer 205
First Basketball Coach to Take Three Schools to the Final Four
Tyrone Willingham 209
First African-American Coach to Win a Division I-A Bowl Game

CHAPTER 9 • College Administrators:
African-American Athletics Directors
Who Opened the Door   213

Abraham Molineaux Hewlett and Charles Harris. 217
First African-American Athletics Directors in the Ivy League
Gale Sayers. 221
First African-American Athletics Director at a Major
    Division I Institution
McKinley Boston 225
First African-American Athletics Director in the Big Ten Conference
Gene Smith. 229
First African-American Athletics Director in the Big 12 Conference
Craig Littlepage 232
First African-American Athletics Director in the Atlantic Coast
    Conference

Damon Evans 236
First African-American Athletics Director in the
     Southeastern Conference

CHAPTER 10 • Student-Athletes Play with Courage   239

Section 1
Southeastern Conference Student-Athlete Pioneers • 245

Nat Northington 246
First African-American Student-Athlete at the University
     of Kentucky and in the SEC
Lester McClain 249
First African-American Football Scholarship Student-Athlete
     at the University of Tennessee
Perry Wallace 253
First African-American Student-Athlete at Vanderbilt University
Maxie Foster. 257
First African-American Student-Athlete at the University of Georgia
Henry Harris 260
First African-American Student-Athlete at Auburn University
Ron Coleman 264
First African-American Student-Athlete at the University of Florida
Jon Richardson 267
First African-American Student-Athlete at the University of Arkansas
Coolidge Ball 271
First African-American Student-Athlete at the University
     of Mississippi
Collis Temple, Jr. 275
First African-American Student-Athlete at Louisiana State University
Wendell Hudson. 278
First African-American Student-Athlete at the University of Alabama

Section 2
Atlantic Coast Conference Student-Athlete Heroes • 283

Lou Montgomery 284
First African-American Student-Athlete at Boston College
Irwin Holmes 287
First African-American Student-Athlete at North Carolina State
     University

Darryl Hill. 291
First African-American Student-Athlete at the University of Maryland
William Smith, Robert Grant, and Kenneth Henry 295
First African-American Student-Athletes at Wake Forest University
C. B. Claiborne 298
First African-American Student-Athlete at Duke University
Fred Flowers. 301
First African-American Student-Athlete at Florida State University
Ray Bellamy. 305
First African-American Student-Athlete at the University of Miami
Charlie Scott. 309
First African-American Student-Athlete at the University of North
    Carolina, Chapel Hill
Jerry Gaines 312
First African-American Scholarship Student-Athlete at the Virginia
    Polytechnic Institute of Technology
Eddie McAshan. 316
First African-American Scholarship Student-Athlete at the Georgia
    Institute of Technology
Craig Mobley 319
First African-American Scholarship Student-Athlete
    at Clemson University

Section 3
Big 12 Conference Student-Athlete Barrier Breakers • 323

Sherman, Grant, and Ed Harvey. 324
First African-American Student-Athletes at theUniversity of Kansas
George Flippin 327
First African-American Student-Athlete at the University of Nebraska
Johnny "Jack" Trice 330
First African-American Student-Athlete at Iowa State University
Harold Robinson 333
First African-American Student-Athlete at Kansas State University
Al Abram. 336
First African-American Student-Athlete at the University of Missouri
Prentice Gautt 339
First African-American Student-Athlete at the University of Oklahoma
Orlando Hazley 343
First African-American Student-Athlete at Oklahoma State University

James Means 345
First African-American Student-Athlete at the University of Texas
John Westbrook 347
First African-American Student-Athlete at Baylor University

Section 4
Big 10 Conference Student-Athlete Trailblazers • 353

Moses Fleetwood Walker 354
First African-American Student-Athlete at University of Michigan
Frederick Douglass Patterson 359
First African-American Student-Athlete at The Ohio State University
Preston Eagleson 362
First African-American Student-Athlete at Indiana University
Carleton W. "Kinney" Holbrook 366
First African-American Student-Athlete at the University of Iowa
Julian Ware and Adelbert Richard Matthews 370
First African-American Student-Athletes at the University
    of Wisconsin
Roy Young and Hiram Wheeler 373
First African-American Student-Athletes at the University of Illinois
Bobby "Rube" Marshall 375
First African-American Football Player at the University of Minnesota
Cumberland Posey, Jr. 378
First African-American Student-Athlete at The Pennsylvania
    State University
Gideon Smith 382
First African-American Student-Athlete at Michigan State University

Section 5
Ivy League Student-Athlete Leaders • 387

William Edward White 388
First African-American Student-Athlete at Brown University
William Henry Lewis 392
First African-American Student-Athlete at Harvard University
Matthew Washington Bullock 396
First African-American Student-Athlete at Dartmouth University
John Howard Johnson 400
First African-American Student-Athlete at Columbia University
Jerome "Brud" Holland 402
First African-American Football Student-Athlete at Cornell University

Arthur Wilson, Jr. 406
First African-American Student-Athlete at Princeton University
Jay James Swift 409
First African-American Student-Athlete at Yale University
Student-Athlete Epilogue 411
"Ball Like Paul"
Paul Robeson, The Triple Threat

Part Three: Olympic Sport

CHAPTER 11 • World Stage Pioneers: African-American Olympians   417

John Baxter Taylor 420
First African-American to Win an Olympic Gold Medal
James Cleveland "Jesse" Owens 424
First American in Olympic Track and Field History to Win Four
    Gold Medals
Alice Coachman 427
First African-American Woman to Win an Olympic Gold Medal
Wilma Ruldolph 430
First American Woman to Win Three Gold Medals
Tommie Smith and John Carlos 434
Shaking Up the Sports World
Jackie Joyner-Kersee 437
The "First Lady" of Olympic Track and Field
Vonetta Flowers 443
First African-American Woman to Win a Winter Olympics
    Gold Medal
Shani Davis 446
First African-American Winter Olympics Gold Medalist in an
    Individual Sport

CHAPTER 12 • Conclusion   449

Epilogue 453
    Floyd Keith: Keeper of the Flame

About the National Consortium 457
    for Academics and Sports

About the Authors 461

Foreword

When Richard Lapchick approached me to write this foreword, I felt a profound sense of pride to learn that I was included in the amazing list of American sport's pioneers. To be mentioned in the same breath as coaching greats Eddie Robinson, Frank Robinson, and Bill Russell is such an honor. I have been fortunate to receive many awards and win championships, but whatever contribution my work made in helping African-Americans in sports, particularly as coaches, holds a big place in my heart. To be recognized as a pioneer in such a fashion by civil rights activist Lapchick validates the challenges I have encountered and the responses I made.

In learning of Lapchick's latest book project, what stood out the most was the difficult time he and his writing team had researching the names of some of the pioneers, particularly the student-athletes at our nation's institutions of higher education. How could some schools at the very least not know the names of their pioneers, or more deservedly, celebrate their bravery to solicit change on a regular basis? Why 30, 40, 50, sometimes over 100 years later, did it take an outsider to spark the interest of some schools and make them realize that their first pioneers of color should be institutionally celebrated heroes? Although many could recall their first student of color or their first student of color to graduate, why is the first student-athlete of color not equally documented and acknowledged? In a nation that so highly regards sports and athletes, such a hole in the recordkeeping at some schools was shocking. It saddens me to try to fathom the number of pioneers who have been omitted from the history books. Worse still are the countless others who never got their chance to be the first because society fought back with ignorance. Although it is evident that many still drag their feet to accept change in our society, I am hopeful that the publication of *100 Pioneers* will help bring the most deserved attention to pioneers whose accomplishments and place in history are far too often overlooked. More importantly, perhaps its publication will bring forth the names and faces of the many more pioneers whose stories need to be told. Eventually, Lapchick can write *200 Pioneers* or *300 Pioneers* or better yet, *1,000 Pioneers*, because there is no doubt they existed.

One of the most beautiful parts of this book is the compilation of success stories that the pioneers went on to achieve. Some stayed in the athletic arena becoming coaches and administrators to help the next generation of athletes down a similarly rewarding path. Many more chose careers outside sports but surely never forgot the game they loved. As you will read, these pioneers went on to become entrepreneurs, actors, doctors, lawyers, politicians, educators, and a slue of other professions. But the path they traveled was often a treacherous road and is painful to read about. Nonetheless, each is an important piece in the puzzle of our nation's history.

It comes as no surprise to me that the National Consortium for Academics and Sports (NCAS) and The Institute for Diversity and Ethics in Sport (TIDES) are at the forefront of this project. I have personally contributed to The Institute because of the important research it does through the leadership of Richard Lapchick. While race continues to be an explosive subject in the 21st century, how will we ever achieve an equal society if we don't continue to talk about equality or how far we have to go to achieve it? Lapchick continues to push racial issues into the forefront of our minds through the media, his research, and speaking out. It is my hope this book will create a similar passion for equality in those who read it. I hope it will move the readers to stand up to better themselves, their families, their towns, their states, our nation, and the world.

When I started coaching college basketball in 1973 I looked around to see no one that looked like me and many of my players. It hurt to know that my players were receiving a message that they were good enough to play on the court but not good enough to later lead younger generations from the sideline. I know my time at Georgetown brought hope to many young African-American players that they, too, could coach at a major Division I institution. I am proud that my sons, John III and Ronny, have both been Division I college basketball coaches. Although they followed in my footsteps, each has created his own path. As you read *100 Pioneers*, I know you will admire the path blazed by these pioneers, and I challenge readers to forge their own paths of success.

—John Thompson
August 2007

Acknowledgments

It is with a profound sense of appreciation that I must acknowledge the individuals who saw *100 Pioneers* from a dream of mine into a reality for everyone to enjoy. I feel so fortunate to be working with a team of writers who share my passion for equality in sport and society. Their enthusiastic devotion allows me to breathe a sigh of relief knowing that the leaders of the next generation can, and will, make a difference. It is with great respect and adoration that I acknowledge the team members: Jessica Bartter, Jennifer Brenden, Stacy Martin, Horacio Ruiz, and Marcus Sedberry.

I must also mention Catherine Lahey who handled the arduous process of editing each and every story. She did so day in and day out with a bright smile on her face despite being told countless times, "This is the last one." Zoie Springer was always there to help me with research issues.

It would be criminal not to acknowledge the more than 100 pioneers mentioned in this book who lived lives of such valor and significance that each story deserves to be required reading in American history classes. It is with great honor that my team of writers tells their stories in hopes of showing the esteem they deserve. To all of the pioneers—thank you for the change you led.

Finally, I would like to thank everyone associated with the National Consortium for Academics and Sports (NCAS) and the DeVos Sport Business Management Program. My colleagues Keith Lee, Tom Miller, Robert Weathers, Jessica Bartter, Bill Sutton, Keith Harrison, Philomena Pirolo, and Maria Molina sustain me with their never-ending commitment to the huddle.

Most importantly, I would like to thank my family whose support did not flinch when I undertook a second book after previously vowing to take a long-awaited hiatus from the laborious process of 12 prior publications. My family fills me with strength and courage, and my heart with love and happiness each day. My wife, Ann, our children, Joe, Emily, Chamy and her husband, Michael, and grandchildren, Taylor and Emma, provide undying encouragement and understanding that still allows me to wake up motivated each morning. Their spirits brighten each day and keep me striving to leave this world better than the way I found it.

I

RACE AND SPORT IN AMERICA:
AN INTRODUCTION

Richard Lapchick

Everyone knows the story of Jackie Robinson and the way in which his joining the Brooklyn Dodgers in 1947 began to change the face of American sports. He is celebrated in virtually every ballpark, his number has been retired, and there are regular ceremonies in his honor. When Americans are asked who the greatest racial pioneer in sport is, Jackie Robinson's name will most often be mentioned.

Yet, few know names of the people who broke the barriers in the American League just a few months later, in the NFL, NBA, NHL, who were the first African-American athletes to break down the barriers of segregation at the Southeastern, Atlantic Coast, Big Ten, Big 8/Big 12, and Ivy League conference schools. Some know about Arthur Ashe and Althea Gibson in tennis but few know the names of those who led the way in other sports. Many who know Muhammad Ali might not know Jack Johnson.

Sports and race relations have traveled throughout most of history on a parallel plane. It was only with the breakthrough and courageous actions of the 100 pioneers written about in this book that sport was able to influence the perception that society had about African-Americans. In the late 19th and early 20th centuries, there were a few individuals who crossed the color barriers in MLB and the early NFL. However, those athletes were often unable to eat in restaurants or stay in hotels with their teammates due to segregation.

Then society began to impose its barriers over sport once more. Gentleman's agreements to keep African-Americans out of sports were quietly made. Sport was re-segregated.

Jesse Owens' victories in the Berlin Olympics, coupled with Joe Louis' defeat of Max Schmeling, highlighted African-American athletes once again but this time on an international stage. There were some colleges that had African-American student-athletes, including those highlighted in this book in the Big Ten and Ivy League. The early Civil Rights Movement heated up. Although tensions at some of those schools were palpable, athletics became a common bond and focus once again. The brave acts of the early collegiate pioneers began to shape the unified spirit of a team, a college, a town, and sport as we know it today. However, there were many colleges and universities that dragged their feet and integrated their teams long after MLB, the NBA and the NFL. It took Jackie Robinson and the pioneers who followed him to finally really open up sport in America.

100 Pioneers is designed to tell their courageous stories, our history, and the way in which sport positively impacted race relations in the United States. It is the second book in a series, following *100 Heroes: People in Sports Who Make This a Better World.*

The series began at the National Consortium for Academics and Sport (NCAS). Because of the work that we do in the NCAS and the DeVos Sport Business Management Program, we have become all too aware of the problems that exist in sport. Each day, it seems, we read about a rule being violated, an athlete getting in trouble with drugs, an athlete being arrested for sexual assault, steroid use in baseball, the NFL, or track and field, the threat that gambling poses to college sports, or agents recruiting young athletes with illegal monetary inducements. The list goes on and on. That is why it was so joyous for me when Dr. Taylor Ellis, the dean of undergraduate education in the College of Business Administration at the University of Central Florida, came to my office in February of 2005.

I had just put to bed a book called *New Game Plan for College Sport* and was frankly tired of writing. I vowed that I would not take up another book project for several years. Taylor changed all of that on the morning after the 2005 NCAS banquet. He came in, sat down, and said, "When I was a boy, I wasn't involved in school. I had no sense of direction or sense of purpose." He said, "Then someone gave me this book," and placed a well-worn copy of *Real Life Stories: Champions All the Way* by Barlow Meyers, published 45 years earlier, on my desk. He said, "About that time in my life somebody gave me this book about seven athletes and the obstacles they overcame to do great things in life. This book transformed my life and gave me a sense of direction and hope." Taylor continued, "Every year you honor five or six such athletes at the Consortium's award banquet. You have to write a book about them." So came the idea for *100 Heroes*.

It was a no-brainer to think about undertaking the project in spite of my vow to the contrary. This book could be, I thought, a real celebration of sport. It could portray the power of sport to transform not only individuals, but their impact on the broader society. I ran through my head the names of all the award winners I could recall and knew that their stories would inspire people collectively who could not be in the presence of these people in the halls when we honored them.

With the 20th anniversary of the Consortium exactly a year away, I knew that we would have to work hard to get this project done. I enlisted the support of Jessica Bartter, who is the assistant director for communications and marketing of the National Consortium. We began to draw all of the names and addresses together and contact the previous award winners who were still alive. Their support for the project was overwhelmingly positive. We began to collect the biographical materials and stories that were the basis for the awards. We also asked Drew Tyler, Stacy Martin, Jennifer Brenden, and Brian Wright, all graduate students in the DeVos Sport Business Management Program, to help write the individual stories.

100 Heroes was published in February 2006. I knew there was more to do.

In *100 Pioneers*, we have gathered the stories of the first African-American players, coaches, general managers, and team presidents in the various professional sports. We hoped to have the first African-American male and female student-athletes to compete in each of the SEC, ACC, Big Ten, Big 8/Big 12, and Ivy League schools, as well as the first African-American coaches and athletic directors in those conferences. We have John Thompson and Carolyn Peck, the first African-American coaches to win the NCAA men's and women's basketball championships, respectively, and Ty Willingham, the first to coach in a BCS Bowl Game. Included are Willie Jeffries, the first African-American Division I football coach, and Gale Sayers, the first African-American Division I athletics director.

We also included those icons who did not neatly fit categories, such as Coach Eddie Robinson at Grambling State and renaissance man Paul Robeson. Don Barksdale made more than one break-through. He was the first African-American to be named a basketball All-American and the first African-American to appear in an NBA All-Star Game. There are four "events" that shaped their times, in-cluding Joe Louis' 1938 defeat of German Max Schmeling, widely viewed as the victory of democracy over Nazism; the clenched fist, black glove salute of John Carlos and Tommie Smith at the 1968 Mexico City Olympics; the 1975 NBA Finals, at which two African-American head coaches first faced each other for any championship; and the 2007 Super Bowl when two African-American head coaches faced each other for the NFL title for the first time.

100 Pioneers is a mixture of historical research and interviews with those who broke down color barriers on college campuses and in cities around the country. I believe sharing the inspiring life sto-ries of those who paved the way for other people of color in the world of sports can continue to make this world a better place. Such important figures deserve a platform from which to have their sto-ries told and share what their experiences have meant to them. I am part of a team of writers and researchers made up mostly of my grad-uate assistants at the DeVos Sport Business Management Graduate Program in the College of Business Administration at the University of Central Florida. As with *100 Heroes*, the team was led by Jessica Bartter. The writers also included Stacy Martin, Horacio Ruiz, Jenny Brenden, and Marcus Sedberry. The editor was Catherine Lahey, and research support was offered by Zoie Springer. We are all proud to have played a role in publishing these stories, which include the ad-versities each pioneer conquered, the decisions each faced, and the accomplishments each achieved.

The book is organized into three parts. The first is on profes-sional sport and includes chapters on pioneers in MLB, the NFL, the NBA, the NHL, tennis, golf, and boxing. There is an introduction to each followed by the individual stories of the pioneers.

The second part is on college sport and includes chapters on college coaches, athletics directors, and student-athletes. Once again, there is an introduction to each of the three chapters, followed by the stories of the pioneers themselves. The largest chapter in the book is on student-athletes. The original goal for this chapter was to have the first African-American male and female student-athletes at each of the schools in the respective conferences. After exhaustive attempts, we found only a handful of schools that could identify their first African-American female student-athlete. In several cases, there was little or no information about the male pioneers. The next book in this series will be about women pioneers, and we hope to be able to find those female student-athletes and include their stories. Thus for this edition, we ended up with only the male student-athletes and, in some cases, only their names and a smattering of the story. This reflects so much of American history, in which the stories of some racial and ethnic groups were not recorded in writing but were passed on from generation to generation in an oral tradition.

After tireless research efforts, there are still nine schools whose male pioneers' stories remain untold. Their stories represent important threads in the quilted patchwork of our history. Although the details are unknown, the simple action of stepping forth into uncertain circumstances and forging a path for countless others to follow deserves praise and gratitude. Robert Bell of Mississippi State, Ansel "Jackie" Brown of the University of South Carolina, Nat Lucas of the University of Virginia, Clifford Evans of the University of Colorado, Curtis Mills, Sidney Chachere, and Edgar Harvey of Texas A&M University, Danny Hardaway of Texas Tech University, George Henry Jewett of Northwestern University, John Henry Weaver of Purdue University, and Howard M. Smith of the University of Pennsylvania were the pioneers identified by our research and the individual school or conference, but the stories of their experiences as pioneers remain almost unknown still today. It is my hope that the publication of *100 Pioneers* will lead to those missing stories being captured and celebrated in writing, securing their permanent place in history.

The final part of *100 Pioneers* is about the Olympics. We have included the stories of the first African-American men and women to win gold medals in the summer and winter games. One story in the Olympic section recreates the historic 1936 Olympic Games when the multi-gold medal winning performance of Jesse Owens was a crushing blow to the Nazi hype of Aryan supremacy. We also included Wilma Rudolph, the first woman to win three Olympic gold medals, and Jackie Joyner-Kersee, the first lady of Olympic track and field.

As I wrote in *100 Heroes*, sport reaches all kinds of people for all different reasons. Sport can be played competitively or recreationally, or sport can be watched and enjoyed as entertainment. We watch sports we never play and we play sports we never watch. Sport can help build friendships, families, respect, confidence, and character. Sport provides health benefits some medical professionals can only begin to understand.

Most importantly, sport is unique in the boundaries it crosses with both its participants and its audience. Differences in gender, race, physical and mental abilities, age, religion, and cultures are irrelevant in the huddle, on the field, in the gym, or in the water. Sport smashes these barriers like nothing else can. The athletes in *100 Pioneers* represent that better than anyone because of their own life experiences.

Yet many of today's young athletes do not realize how different their playing field may have looked 100, 50 or even 25 years ago. The racial history of the United States may be studied by young Americans but too many cannot relate. Young people do relate to sport. By illustrating the history of America's racial barriers through the vehicle of sport, the picture may become clearer. It can be the role of those who lived it to educate the next generation and there will be no better time to do so than now.

Young athletes who look up to LeBron James, Tiger Woods, Donovan McNabb, and Serena and Venus Williams should know of those who came before them and opened so many doors. For without these pioneers, today's heroes might still just be knocking at the doors.

PROFESSIONAL
SPORT

2

MAJOR LEAGUE BASEBALL: AFRICAN-AMERICAN PIONEERS IN AMERICA'S FAVORITE PASTIME

Introduction by Richard Lapchick

In the year *100 Pioneers* was completed, Major League Baseball (MLB) celebrated the 60th anniversary of Jackie Robinson's breaking the color barrier in a weekend of festivities at Dodgers Stadium.

Jackie Robinson had a life cut short but had an impact on sport and America that was profound and historical. The future of sport was forever changed in that electrifying moment when he took the field and all that he subsequently stood for.

My father, who was the coach of the New York Knickerbockers at the time, took my brother, Joe, to that first game. It inspired him to try to get the all-black Renaissance Five into the league that year, an attempt that proved to be unsuccessful. Three years later, my father brought Nat "Sweetwater" Clifton to the Knicks as the NBA's first African-American player to sign, one week before the NBA draft when Chuck Cooper was drafted by the Celtics and Earl Lloyd by Washington. The three became the first African-American players in October of 1950.

Students of the history of the game should note that 45 years before Jackie Robinson played, Major League Baseball was almost integrated. In 1902 John J. McGraw, the famous Baltimore Oriole's manager, signed Charlie Grant, an African-American who almost "passed" with a light complexion, straight hair, and high cheekbones. However, Chicago White Sox owner Charlie Comiskey managed to get Grant banned from MLB before the start of the season.

Denied the chance to play in MLB, African-Americans ended up developing their talents in the illustrious Negro Leagues. It was 1920 before the Negro National League completed a full season.

Among the great teams were the Homestead Grays, Pittsburgh Crawfords, and Kansas City Monarchs.

Andrew "Rube" Foster, a former player, manager, and owner for the Chicago American Giants, helped launch the effort. Other leagues formed, mainly in states in the East and South. The talent of great African-American players was showcased across the land and served as a cultural affirmation for many black communities. Players saw the country and developed as leaders in and out of sport.

Superstars included James "Cool Papa" Bell, Josh Gibson, and Leroy "Satchel" Paige. Negro League players who went on to star in the major leagues included Willie Mays, Henry Aaron, Roy Campanella, Ernie Banks, Junior Gilliam, Don Newcombe, and Joe Black.

Aaron held the all-time homerun record for three decades; Mays, Aaron, Campanella, Banks, and Newcombe were all league MVPs; and Newcombe won MLB's Holy Trinity: the Rookie of the Year, Cy Young, and MVP awards.

In September 1971, the Pittsburgh Pirates took the field with the first all-African-American lineup in the history of MLB. Pittsburgh Pirates' manager Danny Murtaugh's lineup card called for Rennie Stennett, 2B; Gene Clines, CF; Roberto Clemente, RF; Willie Stargell, LF; Manny Sanguillen, C; Dave Cash, 3B; Al Oliver, 1B; Jackie Hernandez, SS; and pitcher Dock Ellis.

Ironically, much of what was written about the 60th anniversary of Jackie Robinson was about the declining numbers of African-American players in Major League Baseball. At 8.4 percent, MLB was at the lowest percent in decades and half of where it was on the 50th anniversary in 1997, when 17 percent of the players were African-American.

By the time of this writing, African-American pitchers, who had always been rare, were even rarer. There had not been an African-American 20-game winner since 1990 when Dave Stewart starred for Oakland, becoming only the 12th African-American 20-game winner in MLB history. In 2006, there were only four African-American regular starters: Dontrelle Willis, Dewon Brazelton, C.C. Sabathia, and Jerome Williams.

There are several reasons that could have led to the decline of African-American ballplayers in MLB:

- In 1987, Al Campanis made remarks on *Nightline,* questioning whether blacks had "the necessities to do more than play the game."

- Barry Bonds, baseball's biggest African-American star, deservedly or not, is one of the most vilified athletes ever, in spite of the fact that he was chasing one of the most revered records in the history of Major League Baseball.

- The popularity of basketball and football, both at the college and professional levels, has resulted in their becoming the most desired route for African-American student-athletes at a young level to go forward.

- African-Americans are nearly 80 percent of the players in the NBA and nearly 70 percent of the players in the National Football League and also dominate statistically at the college level.

- The pipeline for African-American players to get to the major leagues is even less populated than Major League Baseball. At the college level, less than seven percent of the players are African-American, and the numbers decline at the high school and youth sport levels.

- There is a lack of playing fields in urban America where many African-Americans live and where playing basketball is easier and much less expensive. There are also a smaller number of scholarships for college baseball players than there are for college football and basketball players.

Baseball has made significant efforts to fill the void. The new Compton Academy, modeled after academies in the Dominican Republic and other places, as well as its longstanding RBI program, will be helpful. In spite of that, it appears as if baseball will virtually skip a generation of African-Americans, and if there is to be an increase, it will be in the future and not in the short term. We may have lost a generation of potential African-American players in MLB.

However, Jackie Robinson's vision for America was broader than his country's when he took his first swing in MLB. I do not think he would simply be discouraged by who he saw on the fields today. Robinson was about opportunity for all. While he would surely be frustrated by the pace of change, there would be things he would like. I believe he would like the fact that, according to the *2006 Major League Baseball Racial and Gender Report Card*, nearly 41 percent of the players were players of color, near baseball's all-time high. Robinson likely would not be satisfied but would see it as progress, too, that there were two African-American managers and four Latino managers when baseball started the 2007 season.

I am confident that he would be pleased that the New York Mets made it to game seven in the National League Championship Series with Willie Randolph, an African-American manager, and Omar Minaya, a Latino general manager. I know he would have been pleased that the 2005 World Series was won by a team led by baseball's only African-American general manager, Ken Williams, and Ozzie Guillen, a Latino manger. That was a historic first in the Jackie Robinson tradition.

I think it would please him that 37 percent of the coaches in MLB and the minor leagues were people of color. Baseball is the only sport where the percentage of players of color is nearly the same as the percentage of coaches of color.

Should Jackie Robinson have had the opportunity to visit the offices of Major League Baseball before the season began, he probably would have nodded his head toward Commissioner Bud Selig as he saw that 32 percent of the professional staff were either African-American, Latino, or people of Asian descent.

He probably would have smiled at the fact that his own team, the Los Angeles Dodgers, had Kim Ng, an Asian woman, as a finalist for its general manager position. I am sure he would be happy to know that Elaine Weddington Steward, a former Jackie Robinson Foundation Scholar, has been vice president and general counsel for the Boston Red Sox for many years—the same Red Sox team that was the last in MLB to sign an African-American player. In fact, the team signed Pumpsie Green after the Boston Bruins signed Willie O'Ree as the first African-American player in the history of the National Hockey League.

However, Jackie Robinson probably would have had an animated conversation with Selig about some of the leadership positions that still show little representation for African-Americans, including the fact that there are only two general managers of color. If he were to address the owners, I think he would chastise them for so few positions at the top of their hierarchy being held by women and people of color. He would hammer at the fact that only 13 percent of team vice presidents are people of color and 15 percent are women. He would probably shake his finger at the owners and tell them that it is unacceptable that only 16 percent of the senior administrative positions at the team level are held by people of color and 20 percent by women. Or that only 15 and 28 percent of the professional positions overall are held by people of color and women, respectively.

He might also put in a plug for the Jackie Robinson Foundation, which produces outstanding graduates among underrepresented populations, especially African-Americans. He might tell the owners that every team should sponsor at least one of these young people each year so that not only would they have more outstanding leaders in their own team pipelines but that corporate America would also have a strong group in its leadership pipelines.

I wish Jackie Robinson were here to tell us his thoughts in his own words. But his imprint is all over America and his torch is carried proudly and brilliantly by his widow and my dear friend, Rachel Robinson. What started with Major League Baseball changed sport in America forever.

Included in this chapter on Major League Baseball are sections on Jackie Robinson as the first player in MLB; Larry Doby, the first player in the American League and second in MLB; Frank Robinson, MLB's first African-American manager; Cito Gaston, the first African-American manager to win the World Series; John Jordan "Buck" O'Neil, the first African-American coach; Bill Lucas, baseball's first African-American general manager; Bob Watson, the first African-American GM in the American League; Ulice Payne Jr., baseball's first African-American team president; and Bill White, the first African-American to be a league president.

Jackie Robinson

First African-American Player in MLB

by Jessica Bartter

If his life were measured by his own quotation, "A life is not important except in the impact it has on other lives,"[1] Jackie Robinson's would be considered one of the most important of the 20th century. By the account of those who knew him, even that accolade would be an understatement.

Robinson, who was an athlete, entrepreneur, civil rights activist, actor, author, father, and husband, is remembered by many as a spectacular ball player, but it was the mere fact that he stepped onto the field in a Brooklyn Dodger uniform that had such an everlasting impact on the United States. In 1947, Robinson became the first African-American to play for any Major League Baseball team in the modern era. By donning the Dodger uniform, Robinson integrated professional athletics and broke the color barrier that had existed in Major League Baseball for decades. But Robinson couldn't do it alone. It took the foresight of Branch Rickey, president and general manager of the Brooklyn Dodgers, to recognize that Robinson was an individual with the requisite determination and willpower to effect such social change. Knowing that the abuse and threats any player of color would face would be detrimental to both his spirit and play, Rickey chose Robinson because he believed Jackie had sufficient strength and staying power to get the job done. Rickey challenged Robinson to endure the abuse in silence and instead fight back with his brilliant play on the field. And brilliant he was. In his debut season, Robinson had 12 homeruns, a league-leading 29 stolen bases, and a .297 batting average that earned him National League Rookie of the Year honors. His team was crowned National League Champions and nearly beat its archrivals, the New York Yankees, in one of the most exciting World Series ever played.

Robinson's accomplishments did not come easily. He was forced to tolerate racial insults from the stands and on the field, was the target of many wild pitches and spiked cleats, and was haunted by hate letters and death threats to him and his family. In upholding his promise to Rickey, Robinson fought back on the field, using his unselfish team play and magnificent skills to earn the respect of his teammates and eventually the nation. In particular, he was befriended by shortstop Pee Wee Reese, himself a Southerner, whose friendship helped mute the worst of the abuse. In just his third season, Robinson was named the National League's Most Valuable Player. Robinson led the league in stolen bases in both 1947 and 1949. In 1949, he won the batting title with a .342 average. From 1949 to 1952, Robinson led second basemen in double plays, and he was named to the National League All-Star team every year from 1949 to 1954.

Stardom as an athlete was nothing new for Robinson, who had lettered in baseball, track and field, football, and basketball in high school and college. Before becoming a heralded athlete at the University of California, Los Angeles, he attended Pasadena Junior College to be near his mother. Because track and field and baseball compete during the same season, Robinson had the opportunity to break his older brother's broad jump record of 25 feet and $^{1}/_{2}$ inch and star in a baseball game all in the same day. Robinson was named Most Valuable Player of the junior colleges in Southern California after leading his team to the state championships in baseball. After transferring to UCLA, Robinson earned All-American accolades for his accomplishments on the gridiron.

Unfortunately for UCLA athletics, Robinson was forced to leave college because of financial challenges. Robinson enjoyed a short stint with the Honolulu Bears, playing semipro football, leaving Pearl Harbor just two days before the Japanese attack in 1942. Shortly thereafter, he received a draft notice and joined the armed forces to put his patriotism into action. Segregation was still commonplace in the military and, eventually, Robinson felt he was fighting a war at home rather than overseas. Robinson spoke out against the racial injustices he witnessed in the military and stood up for his rights.

Jack had bone chips in his ankle from his football days, and on July 6, 1944, had gone to the base hospital to have them examined. Catching the bus on the post back to the barracks, he ran into the wife of one of his brother lieutenants, and they sat together, talking. The woman was African-American, but light complexioned. The white bus driver became incensed at a black second lieutenant talking with a woman he thought was white. He stopped the bus and ordered Jack to move to the rear. Jack, knowing that army regulations had recently been issued that barred racial discrimination on any vehicle operating on an army post, refused. The bus driver started shouting at him, and Jack, being Jack, shouted right back and said he was not budging.[2]

The bus driver reported Jack's "unruly" behavior to his dispatcher, and Robinson was taken to the military police headquarters where he eventually realized they were accusing him of being intoxicated. Although he had never had a drink in his life, the court martial was carried out. Almost one month later, Robinson was acquitted, but the court martial had prevented him from joining his outfit overseas. Robinson "was disgusted and wanted out. . . . Using the fact that Jack had bone chips in his ankle, the army gave him an honorable discharge"[3] on November 28, 1944.

Upon leaving the military, without a college degree and with little experience in the working world, Robinson began his professional baseball career with the Kansas City Monarchs of the Negro Leagues. Branch Rickey first discovered Robinson as a Monarch and called him to New York. Robinson's wife Rachel recalled that it was there, in a 1945 role-playing session, that "Rickey subjected Jack to every form of racial attack he could imagine to test his strengths and prepare him for the ordeals sure to come."[4] Robinson believed Rickey was sincere and determined to rid baseball of its social inequalities and "promised that regardless of the provocation he would not retaliate in any way."[5] After suffering through an excruciatingly painful spring training in Central Florida, Robinson spent the next year with the Dodgers' AAA team, the Montreal Royals, while he and Rickey continued to expand their relationship. Robinson scored the winning run in the seventh game of the Little World Series in 1946, leading to his debut with the Brooklyn Dodgers on April 15, 1947, changing the face of baseball forever.

After a decade of success with the Brooklyn Dodgers in which they went to six World Series and finally beat the Yankees in 1955, Robinson announced his retirement. His impact on our society in general and professional sports specifically had been etched in stone. Robinson paved the way for many to continue the journey to social equality that he initiated. He recognized the magnitude of being the first, but knew that if he was not followed into the big leagues by more players of color, his accomplishment would be insignificant. As a sign of success for "the great experiment," many other African-Americans were signed to the league, including teammates Don Newcombe, Joe Black, and Roy Campanella. The New York Giants quickly followed suit, signing Monte Irvin and Willie Mays, and the Cleveland Indians integrated the American League when they signed Larry Doby and then Luke Easter.

Robinson remained active after he finished playing. He opened a men's apparel shop in Harlem, served a radio station as the director of community activities, and was vice president of Chock Full o'Nuts. Robinson balanced his business endeavors with civic engagements. While still a ballplayer, Robinson had marched with Dr. Martin Luther King, and his involvement in the Civil Rights Movement only increased after retirement. Jackie and his wife, Rachel, organized an outdoor jazz concert on their property to raise funds to be used as bail money for civil rights activists who had been jailed for their involvement in the movement. To date, the same concert is still held the last Sunday every June, first taking place in Connecticut and recently having moved to New York City. Robinson served on the board of directors of the NAACP for eight years and was one of their leaders in fundraising. Robinson traveled the country making appearances and demonstrating his support for numerous causes, proving that one person can make a difference. In one of Robinson's last efforts to do good for others, he established the Jackie Robinson Construction Company. The company's mission was to build homes for families with low and moderate incomes.

In 1972, Jackie Robinson's jersey, number 42, was retired alongside those of Roy Campanella and Sandy Koufax at Dodger Stadium in Los Angeles. Years later, number 42 was permanently retired throughout Major League Baseball. After Mariano Rivera retires from the Yankees, no player in MLB will ever wear his number again.

Sadly, Jackie Robinson lost his life to diabetes and heart disease on October 23, 1972. Though his life was tragically short, his impact on others will last forever. Today, Rachel Robinson recognizes that, despite the progress that was made by her husband and so many others in so many hard fought battles, challenges and threats still remain. She hopes that we can look back on Jack's triumphant struggle and "recommit to equality of opportunity for all Americans."[6] Major League Baseball's 60th anniversary celebration of that day in 1947, when sport began to change, highlighted the legacy of Jackie Robinson's fighting spirit.

Notes

1. Jackie Robinson, The Jackie Robinson Foundation, http://www.jackierobinson .org/ (accessed September 12, 2007).

2. Rachel Robinson with Lee Daniels, *Jackie Robinson: An Intimate Portrait* (New York: Harry N. Abrams, Inc., 1996), 31.

3. Ibid., 32.

4. Ibid., 37.

5. Ibid.

6. Murray Chass, "Standing by Her Man, Always With Elegance," *The New York Times*, April 16, 1997.

Larry Doby

First African-American Player in MLB's American League

by Horacio Ruiz

Larry Doby walked into the Cleveland Indians clubhouse for the first time, ready to shake hands with his new teammates. Lou Boudreau, the Indians manager, took him around the locker room to formally introduce him. The first player Doby was introduced to, second baseman Joe Gordon, shook his extended hand firmly. Doby would receive no more than two handshakes in the rest of his travels around the room. And these were his teammates.

What Doby did not know was that the day before, players were considering the option to walk out rather than play with an African-American teammate. Eventually, those who did not want to play with Doby were phased out by owner Bill Veeck, the man who told those who wanted to walk away to please do so, as Doby would be better than every single one of them.

Doby was not the first black baseball player in Major League Baseball; that distinction is held by Jackie Robinson, the Hall of Famer who broke into the Majors with the National League's Brooklyn Dodgers and whose jersey number is retired by MLB. Doby came second, though, by a mere three months. As the first African-American in the American League, he exposed an entirely different audience to the concept of the African-American major-leaguer. In that sense, Doby did much for the integration of baseball. People's attitudes had not changed in the three months between Robinson's debut and Doby's debut. Nothing was easier about being second.

Veeck's online Hall of Fame biography describes him as "an inveterate hustler and energetic maverick"[1] and he was keenly aware of the racial impact Doby's signing would have on both his club and the climate of baseball. For once, Veeck wasn't interested in the hype. He signed Doby to make the Indians winners. "I'm not going to sign a Negro and send him to a farm club," Veeck once said. "I'm going to get one I think can play with Cleveland. One afternoon when the team trots on the field, a Negro player will be out there with them."[2]

The scouts in charge of finding such a player all came back

with the same name: Doby. In 1946, he batted .341 for the Newark Eagles of the Negro Leagues and caught the final out of the Negro World Series, as he led the Eagles to the title in seven games versus the Kansas City Monarchs. By July 4, 1947, the day before his call-up to the major leagues, Doby was leading the Negro National League with a .415 batting average and 14 homeruns. Veeck paid a $15,000 transfer fee to the Eagles, unlike Branch Rickey who paid nothing to the Negro Leagues for Robinson. Doby's final at-bat in the Negro Leagues was a homerun. The next day he would be in Chicago as a Cleveland Indian, ready to make his major league debut. The Eagles held an impromptu ceremony in celebration of his move to the majors, presenting him with a travel kit that included a comb and razors.

The anticipated moment came on July 5, during the top of the seventh inning, when Boudreau inserted Doby as a pinch hitter. Doby was so nervous he forgot how many outs there were and then proceeded to strike out. The next day, he would make his only start of the 1947 season. He was tabbed to play first base, but had no first base mitt as he was generally a second baseman. Boudreau asked a teammate to lend his glove to Doby, but the teammate refused. It was only when the team's traveling secretary asked the teammate to hand him the glove that he finally gave in. The secretary delivered the glove to Doby. He would finish the season with five hits in 32 at-bats in a pinch-hitting role, and Doby thought it might be the end of his career. Recognizing the strain Doby was under, Boudreau decided to conserve him for next season. He also needed to find him a new position. At season's end, assistant coach Bill McKechnie told Doby to buy a book and learn how to play the outfield because second base wasn't going to be a possibility.

Doby took the assignment seriously and bought a book by New York Yankees star Tommy Henrich to learn the basics of the outfield. By the following year, he was the starting right fielder and would later be moved to center field, tracking down virtually every ball hit his way. The 1948 season would be a historic one for Doby. After batting over .300 during the regular season, his homerun clinched game four of the World Series for the Cleveland Indians as they won the championship in six games versus the Boston Braves. He became the first African-American to play on a championship club and to hit a homerun in the World Series.

A photograph taken after game four of the Series, the one in which Doby's homerun clinched the game, shows pitcher Steve Gromek putting his arms around Doby's neck, the two players cheek-to-cheek with joyous celebratory smiles. The photo is now a seminal symbol for racial integration in sport. "That made me feel good because it was not a thing of, should I or should I not, not a thing of black or white," Doby told David Maraniss of the *Washington Post*.[3] "It was a thing of where human beings were showing emotion. When you have that kind of thing it makes you feel better, makes you feel like, with all those obstacles and negatives you went through, there is someone who had feelings inside for you as a person and not based on color."

Gromek would receive hate mail asking how he could have embraced a black man. He could not believe the reaction he received. Doby had won the game and had helped the team win the title. This social response did not go unnoticed by Doby, who was sensitive to the issues surrounding his integration. He was told by Veeck not to question any calls made by umpires, not to react to words directed at him by opponents, and to ignore the cat calls from the stands. Any outburst would give people an excuse, a pretense, for throwing Doby and Jackie Robinson out.

At times, it seemed like too much for him to handle. In a game in St. Louis, Doby attempted to climb into the grandstands with a bat to silence a fan who had been hurling insults at him all game. Luckily, McKechnie was there to stop him. Another time, a player spit in his face after Doby slid into second base. An umpire stood between the two, preventing Doby from fighting the man and possibly ruining his career. Pitchers had an unwritten rule of brushing back African-American players after another player had hit a homerun. If one of Doby's teammates hit a homerun, it would mean Doby's receiving a fastball to the head during his next at bat. Later in his career, Doby became fed up with the practice and charged the mound after being knocked down by a pitch, throwing a left hook to the pitcher's face. It was his way of standing up to a white man and showing him he was his equal, even at the expense of a bench-clearing brawl.

Early in his career, Doby would have no roommates because in every city except Boston and New York, he would have to go to a black hotel or room with black families in the area. It wasn't until

1954 that Doby and his other African-American teammates could stay in the team hotel during spring training in Arizona.

After the 1948 season, Doby cemented his star status. He would be selected to seven consecutive All-Star games and would help lead the Indians to another World Series in 1954, though they fell to the New York Giants in four games. With admiration from his teammates as a five-tool player, he could hit for average, hit for power, throw, run, and catch. He would finish his career with a .283 average, 253 homeruns, and 969 runs batted in during a 13-year span.

In 1978, he became the second African-American manager in major league history after taking over the Chicago White Sox in the midseason. He would go on to hold front office positions with the Indians, White Sox, and Montreal Expos. Doby also worked in the commissioner's office and was director of community relations for the NBA's New Jersey Nets in the late 1970s.

Doby seemed almost anonymous until 1997 when MLB celebrated Robinson's barrier-breaking integration into the league. The media remembered that Doby was not far behind Robinson and had endured as many indignities as his National League counterpart. That year, he was named honorary co-captain of the American League All-Star team as he threw out the ceremonial first pitch in front of hometown fans at Cleveland's Jacobs Field.

A year later, he was elected to the National Baseball Hall of Fame by the Veterans Committee. He joined Robinson and his former owner, Bill Veeck. Doby passed away on June 18, 2003 at the age of 79 after a long illness. Before his death, it was clear that both Robinson and Doby had fulfilled a mission beyond their individual achievements. They had summarily proven that African-American men could play the game of baseball with skill and dignity. "I thank God for giving me the ability and Mr. Veeck for giving me the opportunity," Doby once said. "All we ever asked for is an opportunity."[4]

Notes

1. The National Baseball Hall of Fame and Museum. "Bill Veeck." http://www.baseballhalloffame.org/hofers/detail.jsp?playerId=492585.

2. Andrew O'Toole, *The Best Man Plays* (North Carolina: McFarland & Company, Inc, 2003).

3. David Maraniss, "Neither a Myth nor a Legend: Larry Doby Crossed Baseball's Color Barrier—After Robinson," *The Washington Post*, July 8, 1997.

4. O'Toole, *The Best Man Plays.*

John Jordan "Buck" O'Neil

First African-American Coach in MLB

by Jessica Bartter

On July 18, 2006, John Jordan O'Neil, known to many simply as "Buck," made his mark on baseball history yet again. Although O'Neil's legendary career ranges from a Negro League star to the first African-American coach in Major League Baseball, O'Neil will also be remembered as the second oldest professional baseball player, one of only two aged in their 90s (the minor league Schaumburg Flyers signed 96-year-old Ted "Double Duty" Radcliffe to a one-game contract in 1999). At 94 years old, O'Neil signed a one-day contract with the minor league Kansas City T-Bones. O'Neil led off for the West in the top of the first inning of the All-Star Game and was walked with a count of 4-1, making him the oldest player to make a plate appearance. After running to first base, as fast as the 94-year-old was able to, he rounded the bag as if he was ready to steal second base on the next pitch. But, as planned, O'Neil was replaced with a pinch runner, thus ending his professional career for the final time.

O'Neil first made MLB history on May 29, 1962, when he became the first black coach of a Major League Baseball team. O'Neil's involvement in baseball dates back more than seven decades to when he grew up watching his father play and subsequently started his own semi-professional career at just 12 years old. The early exposure led to a baseball and football scholarship to Edward Waters College. After two years, he left college for the Negro Leagues. O'Neil moved among the Miami Giants, New York Tigers, and Shreveport Acme Giants from 1934 to 1938, prior to finding his place with the Kansas City Monarchs. In 1938, O'Neil joined the Monarchs and led them to four consecutive Negro American League titles and to the Negro World Series in 1942. The first baseman won batting titles in 1940 and 1946 with averages of .345 and .350 respectively. During the 1942 World Series, O'Neil's impressive .353 batting average helped the Monarchs sweep the Homestead Grays in four games. His 1946 batting title contributed to the Monarchs' reaching the World Series again that year. Despite

O'Neil's two homeruns, including a grand slam, and a .333 average, the Monarchs lost to the Newark Eagles in an exciting seven game series.

Of O'Neil's Negro League World Series appearances, what may be most impressive is that his play was disrupted by a two-year stint in the Navy, during which he did a World War II tour. During O'Neil's absence, the Monarchs failed to reach the World Series but succeeded the year before O'Neil left and the year in which he returned. Buck O'Neil was surely a difference maker.

Upon his homecoming in 1945, O'Neil returned to the field with the Monarchs. After four league titles, three All-Star game appearances and one World Series Championship as a player, O'Neil took over as manager for the Monarchs in 1948. He guided the team to two more league titles and managed four victorious All-Star teams for the West. Among his players were more than 20 future major leaguers, including Ernie Banks and Hank Thompson. O'Neil proved himself a highly successful manager with the premiere team of the Negro League at a time when his options were finally expanding in the world of baseball. At the beginning of O'Neil's career, his skin color, or as he called it, his "beautiful tan," limited him to the Negro League. Though the League produced great players and exciting competition and attracted thousands of fans, the segregated United States prohibited African-Americans from playing interracially in Major League Baseball. In 1956, although O'Neil's playing days had ended, he was still able to enter Major League Baseball as a scout for the Chicago Cubs, as they slowly transitioned away from segregation. When O'Neil was named coach of the Chicago Cubs six years later, he became the first African-American to do so across all major league teams. O'Neil is credited with signing Hall of Famer Lou Brock, who went on to have a long, illustrious professional career, to his first MLB contact. After two years of coaching, O'Neil returned to the realm of scouting where he remained for over two decades. In 1988, he left the Cubs to scout for the Kansas City Royals, where he was named Midwest Scout of the Year in 1998.

Although O'Neil wished he could have made the player transition to the major leagues like many of his teammates, including Jackie Robinson and Satchel Paige, O'Neil was proud to finally see integration.

O'Neil was not a stranger to segregation while growing up in rural Florida. On November 13, 1911, O'Neil was born in Carrabelle, Florida. As he got older, he was able to travel all over Florida with his semi-pro team, the Sarasota Tigers. As an adolescent, O'Neil was excited about the newly built Sarasota High School but was equally disappointed when his grandmother explained to him that the nice, new high school was for white kids only. At the time, there were only four high schools in all of Florida that African-American students could attend. After working a summer in a celery field with his father, O'Neil moved to live with relatives in Jacksonville where he could attend a black high school.

Despite the division of baseball players, not by ability but by skin color, O'Neil, the grandson of a slave, never learned to hate others. Ironically, when white America could no longer ignore the talent of greats like Larry Doby and Hank Aaron and finally integrated MLB, it ultimately meant the demise of the Negro Leagues. O'Neil described the Negro Leagues as being "an aggressive style of baseball that relied on hit-and-run squeeze plays, steals, double steals, taking the extra base and even hidden-ball tricks. The athletes, 40 percent of whom were college educated, managers and the businessmen behind the Leagues were all entrepreneurs who hustled, entertained and played for the love of the game." O'Neil also noted the innovations the League had brought to baseball since "Negro Leaguers played the first night games under lights five years before the major leagues."[1] Understandably, O'Neil was disappointed to see the end of the Negro Leagues regardless of the fact that it meant integration of baseball. At the Negro League's peak when O'Neil's salary neared $700 a month, the organization was the third largest black-owned business in the United States. Because African-Americans had been outlawed from the major leagues, they had been forced into building their own league. The undertaking had been accepted with passion and had achieved great success.

O'Neil knew MLB had much to learn from the Negro Leagues as white and black fans had long been enjoying the Negro Leagues side by side at games that attracted 40,000 fans compared to the 20,000 of some major league games. It is facts like these that drove O'Neil to establish the Negro Leagues Baseball Museum in Kansas City, Missouri. O'Neil served as the board chairman of the Museum from its inception until his death on October 6, 2006. He was a member of the Baseball Hall of Fame Veterans Committee in

Cooperstown, New York, until 2001. O'Neil continued to advocate for deserving Negro Leaguers to be inducted despite his own induction oversight, which disappointed thousands of people. O'Neil asked his disappointed fans to contribute to an Education and Research Center instead of fussing over him, because it was "more important to [him] than any Hall of Fame."[2] The Negro Leagues Baseball Museum launched a "Thanks a Million Buck Campaign" to raise funds for what they will call the John "Buck" O'Neil Education and Research Center. The Center will be part of an expansion of the Museum scheduled to be completed by early 2009 at the historic Paseo YMCA, the birthplace of the Negro Leagues. Plans for the expansion include a 45,000-square-foot area of archives, educational tools, exhibits, conference facilities and administrative offices. The Center will also provide innovative curriculum allowing students to use baseball when learning about math and science.

Despite the grueling life of barnstorming nearly 300 games a year, those years in the Negro Leagues were easily the best times of O'Neil's life. A favorite memory comes from Easter Day of 1943. That day in Memphis, O'Neil hit a single, a double, a triple and a homerun—a "cycle" as he called it, and a feat he had never seen or heard of anyone doing before. But more importantly, he met his wife that day. "That was a great day," O'Neil said. Ora, to whom he was married for more than 50 years, died of cancer in 1997.

In 1996, O'Neil coauthored a book recounting his experiences in the Negro Leagues. It was titled *I Was Right on Time*, referring to his no-regrets attitude toward missing out on playing in the major leagues. O'Neil also felt fortunate for the opportunity he had in 1994 to help narrate Ken Burns' nine-part PBS documentary called *Baseball*. Being able to keep the Negro League alive through education was a dream come true for O'Neil.

Another dream came true for O'Neil several years ago when Sarasota High School held a ceremony to give him an honorary degree. So many kids came out in support that the ceremony had to be moved to the football stadium. O'Neil recognized the irony in that many of the kids in attendance "were the great-great grandchildren of the people who wouldn't let [him] attend Sarasota High School." But he also remembered the wise words of his grandmother, who told him, "I won't live to see it. But you will. Someday, all kids will be able to go to Sarasota High."[3] Yet again, Buck O'Neil was "right on time."

Although O'Neil died from complications of congestive heart failure and newly diagnosed bone marrow cancer on October 6, 2006, at the age of 94, his 95th birthday celebration continued as planned on November 11, 2006. The guest list of about 750 included many baseball greats, celebrities, and political leaders, all of whom were inspired by O'Neil's life. The life of the great ambassador of Negro Leagues Baseball, Buck O'Neil, was celebrated instead of mourned. It was a celebration that surely will not be the last.

Notes

1. John Jordan O'Neil, U.S. Congressional Testimony, November 15, 2005.

2. Negro Leagues Baseball Museum, "Thanks a Million Buck," http://www.www.nlbm.com/buck/buck.htm (accessed September 14, 2007).

3. Harry Minium and Tony Germanotta, "The Buck Stops Here," *The Virginian Pilot*, July 21, 2004.

Frank Robinson

First African-American Manager in MLB

by Richard Lapchick

I remember the day Frank Robinson was hired by the Cleveland Indians as the first African-American manager in Major League Baseball. The NBA's barriers had been broken since 1966, when the Celtics hired Bill Russell, and the NFL was more than a decade away from hiring Art Shell as its first African-American head coach in 1989.

In fact, the NBA had eight African-American head coaches before Robinson was hired. In 1975 K.C. Jones and Al Attles had become the first two African-American head coaches to face each other in the NBA finals.

So there was so much promise when Cleveland made the announcement. Would MLB, with its much-heralded breakthrough of Jackie Robinson, now follow the NBA and open more doors for other African-American managers? For the next 15 years, the answer was a resounding no!

In the end, Robinson coached until 1977 with the Indians. By the time he got another shot, with the Giants, in 1981, only Larry Doby (1978 with the White Sox) and Maury Wills (1980 with Seattle) had had opportunities, and both were only for a single season. In fact, throughout the 1980s, there was no other African-American manager in Major League Baseball besides Robinson, who stayed with the Giants through 1984 and then got a third managerial job with Baltimore in 1988.

So while Jackie Robinson opened the door for African-Americans as Major League players, Frank Robinson opened a different door but only ever so slightly at first. A 13-time All-Star player, Frank Robinson built his name as a great baseball player, however; in 1975 Robinson became part of the history of sport when he took the job in Cleveland.

One of ten children, Frank Robinson was born August 31, 1935 in Beaumont, Texas. It is no small coincidence that the McClymonds High School basketball team in Oakland had both Robinson, MLB's first African-American manager, and NBA legend Bill Russell, the

NBA's first African-American head coach. Additionally, he played baseball with future MLB stars Curt Flood and Vada Pinson. After graduating, Robinson attended Xavier University in Cincinnati.

Just as Russell became a basketball superstar, Frank Robinson became a baseball icon. He was Rookie of the Year in 1956 and the first player to earn the Most Valuable Player in both the National League (Reds in1961) and the American League (Orioles in 1966). In 1966, Robinson won the American League Triple Crown. He hit 586 homeruns and just missed the 3,000-hit club.

Known as an intelligent and aggressive player, he seemed an obvious choice to become a manager but there was no certainty in that since no African-American had been named previously. After his great years with the Orioles, he played for the Dodgers in 1972 and the Angels in 1973 and 1974. It was during that season that he joined the Indians as a player. Just as his high school teammate started his coaching career as a player-coach with the Celtics, he was the Indians player-manager in 1975.

He stayed with the Indians until 1977. Twice voted manager of the year, Robinson managed the San Francisco Giants from 1981–84, and then he managed the Orioles from 1988–91. In 1991, Robinson took a job as the assistant general manager of the Orioles, before becoming the director of baseball operations for the Arizona Fall League and consultant to the commissioner for special projects in Major League Baseball's main office in 1997. In 2000, he became MLB's vice president for on-field operations.

When MLB took over the Montreal Expos franchise, Commissioner Bud Selig named Robinson as manager and Omar Minaya as the first Latino general manager in the history of Major League Baseball. It was also baseball's first African-American/Latino team at the top, paving the way for the Chicago White Sox to win the 2005 series with their own team of Ozzie Guillen and Kenny Williams. Robinson remained the manager when the Montreal Expos were relocated to Washington D.C. as the Nationals.

Robinson told Steve Inskeep of NPR, "I treat . . . men as equals and I don't look at the color of people's skin. I feel like if you're not doing something I feel like you should be doing, I don't care what color your skin is. I don't look at it that way. You're going to hear from me."

Robinson commented that sometimes players thought that he

singled them out because of the color of their skin, and that some didn't respect him due to the color of his skin. Frank Robinson spoke of Jackie Robinson, saying that what he did off the field was even more significant than what he had done on it, as he brought together people of all colors to enjoy the sport. Jackie Robinson proved that African-Americans are equal and could excel, which Frank Robinson later proved when he became another great pioneer.

His tenure with the Nationals ended in 2006, when he was told he was not going to return as manager. General Manager Jim Bowden said, "It's the most difficult decision because of who Frank Robinson is and what he means to the game of baseball, not just in Washington, not in Baltimore, not just in Cincinnati, for all of baseball. Frank represents playing the game the way it's supposed to be played."[1]

Robinson had spent 51 seasons in baseball, with 16 of them serving as a manager. Robinson's legacy has bettered the way the game is played. In the 2006 season, he was one of five managers of color in Major League Baseball. The others were Don Baylor (Cubs), Ozzie Guillen (White Sox), Felipe Alou (Giants), and Willie Randolph (Mets). Baseball hit its peak with 10 managers of color in the 2002 season, after Commissioner Selig had made it mandatory that a person of color had to be interviewed for each opening for manager and general manager.

It seemed fitting that in 2007 Robinson accepted an offer with ESPN to be an analyst for a two-week special in honor of Jackie Robinson's 60th anniversary of breaking baseball's color barrier. Robinson made appearances on *SportsCenter, Baseball Tonight, Cold Pizza*, and ESPNEWS. One pioneer was being saluted by another who shared the same last name.

Robinson and his wife, Barbara Ann, have two children, Frank Kevin and Nichelle.

Notes

1. Bill Ladson, "Robinson Out as Manager," *MLB.com*, October 1, 2006, http://kansascity.royals.mlb.com/news/article.jsp?ymd=20060930&content_id=1691152&vkey=news_mlb&fext=.jsp&c_id=mlb (accessed October 1, 2007).

Bill Lucas

First African-American General Manager in MLB

by Jessica Bartter

It is well known that when Jackie Robinson stepped onto the baseball field in a Dodger uniform in 1947 he instantaneously broke a color barrier that had lingered in Major League Baseball for decades. A less-known fact is that it took nearly two more decades for a man of similar boldness, valor, and aptitude to do the same for the front offices of Major League Baseball. His name was Bill Lucas.

Early exposure to baseball came to Lucas when he was a bat boy for a Jacksonville, Florida, minor league team. While handing the bat to a young Hank Aaron, Lucas too dreamt of the big leagues. And in 1956, his big league journey began. Lucas was noticed by a Milwaukee Braves scout who signed him to the team's minor league club. Lucas quickly made a mark on the organization during the Braves' training camp in Waycross, Georgia. Although unimaginable for teams today, in 1957, the players' barracks were separated by race. It was also common practice to lock the African-American players inside their barracks while they slept. In addition to the injustice of the situation, Lucas protested against its inherent danger. According to *The Atlanta Journal*, Lucas said, "No way. No one's locking me into that fire trap." The Braves organization quickly took notice of Lucas' stand toward inequality.

Lucas spent eight seasons with the minor league organization hoping to catch his break into the majors. When it didn't come, he decided to retire his glove and become a teacher in 1964.

In 1965, a break into the major leagues did come to Lucas, but it was not on the playing field as he had hoped. Instead, the Braves asked Lucas to join their front office staff. Hesitant at first, Lucas accepted the job offer after reassurance that he was not a "token hire." The Braves organization was moving from Milwaukee to Atlanta, and the executives in the front office thought Lucas could help the organization adjust to being in a different demographic area, one with a much higher population of African-American residents.

Lucas started with the sales and promotions department, quickly leaving his mark. When charged with hiring employees for the new stadium, he thoughtfully hired one black worker for each white worker. According to Mark Bowman with MLB.com, Lucas' conscientious hiring practices "forced both races to communicate and work together toward a common goal."

Lucas' climb up the Braves' corporate ladder was quick and steady. In 1966, he moved to the public relations department before a promotion to assistant farm director the next year. After five years of assisting, Lucas became the farm director in 1972, a position he held for another five years. Young players quickly noticed the genuine care and concern Lucas felt for them and their development. Lucas related easily to the ball players as he had struggled in the minor leagues himself for nearly a decade. Lucas respected his players for the employees that they were but also knew how to show them patience and respect as if each were a member of his family.

In 1976, Ted Turner, an American media mogul and founder of CNN, purchased the Atlanta Braves. He quickly came to be known as one of the most hands-on owners in MLB. The way in which Lucas built the Braves' farm team showed many, particularly Turner, how much he cared about the organization. In September 1976, Turner handed Lucas another promotion—one for the history books. Lucas was named vice president of player personnel and became the first African-American to hold such power within a major league organization. The reality was that Lucas held even more power than his title would suggest. Although owner Turner kept the general manager title for himself, he gave Lucas the GM duties. In fact, many of the players thought Lucas *was* the GM.

Because of the responsibility he acquired and the decisions he made, Lucas is widely considered the first African-American GM of Major League Baseball, without ever officially holding the title. It was almost 20 years later, in 1995, that Bob Watson became the second African-American general manager of a MLB team. Unfortunately, Lucas was not around to see this momentous and long-awaited occasion. In just the third year in his lofty position, Lucas suffered a massive stroke. He died on May 5, 1979, at the age of 43.

Lucas' legacy was easy to see after his passing. The minor league team he worked so fervently to build for a decade eventually put stars on the field, and the Braves won the National League West Division title in 1982. Many players believed the team's success was owed to the tireless work of Lucas.

Lucas is often remembered for his sense of humor, commitment to community, and remarkable character. The Braves 400 Club, the official fan club of the team, annually hands out an award to the Braves minor leaguer who best exemplifies sportsmanship and character. It is called the Bill Lucas Award.

In 2006, the Atlanta Braves hosted their 8th Annual Hall of Fame Induction. It proved to be an emotional one as Ralph Garr and the late Bill Lucas joined the class of 17 other players, owners, and broadcasters. Garr and Lucas joined Hank Aaron as the only African-American members of the Braves' Hall of Fame. Lucas' wife accepted the award for her late husband and thanked Turner for "this place in history." She said "Ted Turner saw no color. No color. No Negro. No African-American. Just a man. A man Ted saw as intelligent, level-headed and capable of doing a job."[1]

Ted Turner saw things clearly. Just as Jackie Robinson ripped through segregation on the field, Bill Lucas tore down the segregated wall that stood tall in the front offices of the major leagues. Sadly, also like Robinson, Lucas died far too early. Two great heroes, two great losses.

Notes

1. Jon Cooper, "Garr, Lucas Welcomed to Braves Hall," *Special to MLB.com*, August 11, 2006, http://mlb.mlb.com/content/printer_friendly/atl/y2006/m08/d11/c160 4489.jsp.

Bill White

First African-American National League President of MLB

by Jessica Bartter

Few could wish for, let alone achieve, the Major League Baseball debut that Bill White enjoyed. On May 7, 1956, when the rookie stepped up to plate for the New York Giants, he batted his nerves and the ball all the way over the fence. White became just the 26th player in history to belt one out of the park in his major league debut. Despite a homerun in his very first at-bat, White told *Sport* magazine in 1964, "I wasn't a great athlete, I just worked harder than anyone else." But White *was* a great athlete, sportscaster, and executive, all in the game he loved—baseball.

The Lakewood, Florida, native caught the eyes of baseball scouts from the New York Giants, who signed the former pre-med student to a professional contact when he was 22 years old. Despite a dreamlike major league debut, White spent time moving up and down between the minor and major leagues for the next three seasons. In 1959, White was traded to the St. Louis Cardinals where, just as his debut had promised, his career blossomed into one of glory. When he was finally given the chance to play, improve, and strut his skill on the field daily, White made the All-Star Team. The 1959 season was the first of five All-Star Game appearances in six years with the Cardinals. The first baseman was a seven-time Gold Glove winner for his impressive fielding in consecutive years from 1960 to 1966. The homerun hitter also made his presence felt at the plate. Pitchers feared the reputation he earned for being a dangerous clutch hitter. White's hitting streaks seemed unstoppable. In July 1961, White set a National League record, tying the MLB record set by Ty Cobb, by getting 14 hits out of 18 at-bats in two consecutive doubleheaders.

In 1964, White helped the Cardinals reach the World Series where they faced the New York Yankees. The seven-game series finished with the Cardinals earning the world championship and is remembered as a turning point for the National League's commitment to signing Latino and African-American players. David Halberstam's book, *October 1964*, chronicles the 1964 baseball season and its mark on increasing diversity on the field as well as the end of the 1950s Yankee dynasty of Mickey Mantle, Roger Maris, Whitey Ford, and Yogi Berra. In 1966, White moved to the Philadelphia Phillies for three years before returning to the Cardinals for his final season in 1969. He ended his 13-year career with 870 RBI's, a .286 batting average, and 201 additional homeruns, all as impressive as his first.

A 13-year career for a professional athlete is rare, but White is even more revered for his 18-year career in the New York Yankee broadcasting booth. His straight-shooting style of commentary was a breath of fresh air when coupled with that of his booth partner, the cheeky Phil Rizzuto. White was the first African-American to do play-by-play on a regular basis for any major league team. Although this was a pioneering effort, then-president of the Yankees, Michael Burke, told *The New York Post* it was just a coincidence. White was hired "because he was the best man for the job."

A similar situation arose in 1989, when White was hired as the president of the National League of MLB. Once again, White was hired because he was the best man for the job, but he was a trail-blazer nonetheless. Then Commissioner Bart Giamatti heard White's name often when conducting a national search for a new NL President. Giamatti and MLB wanted an individual who had a high understanding and commitment to the game and could confidently face a challenging assortment of personalities in the players, owners, and fans. Bill White had the perfect combination of savvy executive skills and a deep love for baseball that the major leagues needed. His NL presidency made him the highest ranking African-American in the history of the major leagues.

In a 1987 interview on *Nightline*, the Los Angeles Dodgers' GM, Al Campanis, responded to Ted Koppel's question of why African-Americans were virtually nonexistent in MLB's manager and general manager posts by saying, "It's just that they may not have some of the necessities to be, let's say, a field manager, or, perhaps, a general manager." Campanis suggested that African-Americans were better left to positions on the field. The one-time teammate of Jackie Robinson subsequently lost his position, but many baseball fans, particularly in the African-American community, were outraged and turned off by "America's pastime." White's achievements in the NL presidency quieted MLB critics after the 1987 incident and helped mend the bridge between white and African-American fans.

Shortly after White's hiring, he was quoted as saying, "I hope to bring to the job my experience as a player and a love of the game. I also hope to bring a little more harmony between players and owners."[1] White did just that. He was instrumental in taking Major League Baseball teams to Miami and Denver and helping to keep one in San Francisco. Always considered frank, White didn't hold back from bringing attention to MLB's lack of women and minorities in front office positions. White was so concerned with keeping the ball rolling on increasing diversity through his position that he announced his intent to resign in 1993 and gave Major League Baseball a full year to find a proper successor. Len Coleman, another African-American man, stepped into the NL presidency and filled the big shoes White left behind after his five years on the job. Coleman held the position until 1999 when it was eliminated, although Bill Giles, son of former NL President Warren C. Giles, currently holds the title of honorary National League President.

White's contributions to the game of baseball as a player, broadcaster, and league executive have had many talking about his potential induction into the National Baseball Hall of Fame. In 1997, current Yankee owner George Steinbrenner said, "White was great. He and Rizzuto had a rapport that nobody else will ever have."[2]

White has since retired to Bucks County, Pennsylvania. He remained close to baseball by sitting on the Veteran's Committee for several years. The Veterans Committee looks at players who were possibly overlooked for induction into the Hall of Fame, White among them. Hall of Famer or not, Bill White is celebrated for his lifetime of service to the game of baseball. His free time is now spent fishing, traveling and, surely, recalling his first big league hit.

Notes

1. Justice B. Hill, "White Has Enjoyed Diverse Career and Made Several Contributions to Baseball," National Baseball Hall of Fame, January 29, 2007, www.baseball halloffame.org/news/2007/election/vc/white.htm.

2. Russell Wolinsky, "Bill White: Player, Pioneer, Broadcaster, President" National Baseball Hall of Fame, www.baseballhalloffame.org/library/columns/rw_04 1117.html (accessed June 14, 2007).

Cito Gaston

First African-American Manager in MLB to Win a World Series

by Horacio Ruiz

Cito Gaston didn't receive much attention for being the first African-American to manage a team into the World Series or for being the first to win the World Series in 1992. He doesn't mind at all. While reflecting on his accomplishments prior to Super Bowl XLI, the game in which two African-American head coaches faced off for the NFL championship, Gaston was content to see the media attention given to coaches Tony Dungy and Lovie Smith. "This is the first Super Bowl I won't lose," Gaston said to writer Jim Street. "Usually, every fan has a team he wants to win. I'll be rooting for both of those guys. The way I see it, I'll win no matter who wins. It will be a great day for me—and all [African-Americans]—just to sit here in front of my TV and watch history unfold."[1]

Gaston blazed a trail throughout his managing career, becoming not only the first African-American manager to win the World Series but also the first to win a division and a league title, achieving those feats in 1989 and 1992 respectively. He then managed the Blue Jays to a second consecutive Series title in 1993, marking the first time a team had repeated as champion since the 1978 New York Yankees.

Prior to the beginning of the 1993 World Series, one rival manager said, "Just once I'd like to know how Cito would do if he had to live like the rest of us, without so many superstars in his dugout." Gaston's critics labeled him a "push-button manager," noting that his team was so skilled that he as the manager had to make few tactical decisions. The Blue Jays possessed a lineup loaded with talent, including Paul Molitor, Roberto Alomar, Joe Carter, Dave Winfield, and Devon White. Carter, who won the 1993 Series with a walk-off homerun, had this to say about his manager: "Cito knew how to work with each individual, treating everyone like a human being. He knows exactly what to say, when to say it, what to do and how to go about doing it. When you have a manager like that, it makes you want to play for the guy. We'd go to war for him. What Cito has done for the Blue Jays can't be taken lightly."[2]

It was more than coincidence that after Gaston, who had been the Blue Jays' hitting coach since 1982, took over the struggling 12-24 Toronto squad early in the 1989 season the team began an impressive turn around. The Blue Jays would post a record of 77-49 over the rest of the season, winning the American League East Division before losing in five games in the American League Championship Series. Gaston initially didn't want to accept the position of manager as he was happy with the relationships he had built with the players and was fearful of what taking the job would do to those ties. With the players' encouragement, he took the position. He became so consumed with the responsibilities of his new job that he lost 15 pounds during his first two weeks. "When I was offered the job as manager, I didn't want it. I was happy working as the team's hitting instructor," Gaston said. "The only reason I took the job was because a lot of the players just came out and asked me to do it."[3]

Prior to becoming a hitting instructor and then a manager, Gaston had a respectable 11-year major league career with the Atlanta Braves and the San Diego Padres. He was an All-Star in 1970 when he finished the season with a batting average of .318, 29 homeruns, and 93 runs batted in. When he was traded from San Diego to Atlanta, Gaston had the good fortune of rooming with Hank Aaron, baseball's all-time homerun leader as of the middle of the 2007 season. Gaston credits Aaron with teaching him how to be a man and how to stand on his own.

"Hank taught me how to handle my money and how to deal with many of those things associated with baseball off the field," Gaston said. "He even taught me how to tie a tie. He was kind of a father-figure. And when you are younger and away from home, it's good to run into those types of people. I just thank God that I ran into Hank Aaron."[4]

A lot of the advice Aaron gave Gaston was helpful when Gaston was later criticized for having the easiest job in baseball. Gaston was confident of the job he had done, although he did not have another winning season after the 1993 World Series. Gaston was let go toward the end of the 1997 season and has been a finalist for a number of open positions, but had not landed a managerial role as of July

2007. He is known around the league for having a confident, quiet air about him without any sense of pretense. Gaston gave much of his time to charity events in Toronto while he was manager, including the annual Cito Gaston Golf Classic. He still is involved with charities in Toronto, which is his primary residence.

"What I did made me part of history," Gaston said to Street. "The more I get away from it, the more I enjoy it. I'm proud of what I have done, but I don't walk around with my chest out.

"I think it changed a lot people's lives more than it changed mine. It gave other minorities a chance to coach or manage, but neither compares to what Jackie Robinson did for all of us. He gave us a chance to play in the major leagues and eventually coach and manage."[5]

Notes

1. Jim Street, "Gaston Takes Pride in Super Bowl," *MLB.com*, February 2, 2007, http://mlb.mlb.com/news/article.jsp?

2. Walter Leavy, "Cito Gaston: On Top of the Baseball World," *Ebony*, May 1994.

3. Ibid.

4. Ibid.

5. Street, "Gaston Takes Pride in Super Bowl."

Bob Watson

First African-American General Manager in MLB's American League

by Horacio Ruiz

In November 1995, Bob Watson began his stint as the general manager for the American League's New York Yankees, thus becoming the first African-American American League general manager in history. The importance of Watson's status as the only African-American general manager in baseball was not lost on him. Watson has said he encountered racism as a minor leaguer while on his way to a 19-season major league career. His position with the Yankees only further validated his role as a baseball lifer. In 1996, his first season with the Yankees, Watson brought his boss, George Steinbrenner, and the Yankees their first world title in 18 years.

Watson had a wealth of knowledge from which to work. Prior to joining the Yankees, Watson had become only the second African-American general manager in MLB history when he took the post with the Houston Astros. When he received a call from Steinbrenner to join the Yankees, the opportunity was too tempting to pass up, even though others warned him of the rigors of working in New York under an owner as demanding as Steinbrenner. The job did take a toll on Watson's health. In a 1997 interview, baseball writer Bob Klapisch noted that Watson had gained considerable weight in his year and a half with the Yankees, making his physical stature as a former major leaguer a distant memory. At the time, Watson was only a few days removed from being hospitalized for high blood pressure. Watson remained resolute, unwilling to resign a post that he felt an obligation to continue, partly because of his consciousness as an African-American.

Earlier in 1997, Watson wrote in an opinion editorial in the *Rocky Mountain News* that baseball had not done enough to integrate its management. He pointed toward himself as an African-American administrator in a senior position and then quickly pointed out that he was the only one. In his editorial, he plainly stated there were men of color being passed over for upper-level management positions who were just as qualified as white men. He went on to mention that the minor leagues didn't have many minorities or women in front office positions.

Watson figured that as Jackie Robinson had endured racist insults and obstacles when he became the first African-American player in MLB history, it was not too much for him to endure the hardships of his position. "I never got the chance to meet [Jackie Robinson]," Watson told the *Sporting News* in 1998. "But my grandparents made me very much aware of who Jackie was and all that he stood for. Al Campanis said we didn't have the 'necessities' to sit in the front office, and he was wrong. I don't think it's going to take 50 years to have another African-American general manager, but I'm still the only one around."[1]

Watson became a regular in the major leagues in 1970 as a Houston Astro and would become an All-Star in 1973 and then again in 1975. Nicknamed "The Bull," Watson finished his 19-year career with a .295 average and became famous for scoring the millionth run in Major League Baseball history, a milestone that he almost missed.

With the scoreboard in San Francisco showing the countdown to the millionth run, Watson stood on second base, after reaching first on a walk and advancing to second on a walk to a teammate. Milt May, Houston's catcher, hit a homerun on an 0-2 count that sent Watson jogging toward third base. As he rounded toward home, he heard his teammates from the bullpen down the third baseline screaming at him to run faster. Watson took off in a dead sprint to score the millionth run. He beat Cincinnati's Dave Concepcion, who had hit a solo homerun at nearly the same time as May, by a second and a half.

Watson became upset soon afterward when baseball officials took his cleats to display them in the Hall of Fame. "I wasn't going to let them take my shoes because in those days it took you a long time to break your shoes in," Watson told the *Rocky Mountain News*. "They weren't like shoes you have today where you can wear them right out of the box. I had just gotten my shoes broken in, and then they took them."

In honor of the milestone, Watson was given a million Tootsie Rolls and a million pennies. He split the candy between the Girl Scouts and Boy Scouts of America and donated the money to a fund for minor leaguers who faced financial hardship. Charitable opportunities like these helped the millionth run take on larger significance for Watson. "I was in the right place at the right time," he told the *Rocky Mountain News*. "What it really means to me is, for a long, long time, minorities were not allowed to play the game, and for me to score a significant run, it means that the game has definitely moved on."

Watson moved away from his general manager duties just before the 1998 season, subsequently moving into MLB's League Office. He currently is the chief disciplinarian for MLB and vice president of rules and on-field operations. He maintains an open phone policy, meaning anyone who wants to call Watson, including a disgruntled fan unhappy with Watson's decision on a fine or suspension, can reach him by phone and argue about why his decisions make no sense. Watson figures if people take enough time to call him, he might as well give them enough time to listen. In the meantime, Watson helped put together the 2000 baseball team that won the gold medal at the Sydney Olympics, and he was recently named the USA baseball general manager for all professional teams for the 2008 Games in Beijing. As USA baseball general manager, he is in charge of helping select players and coaching staffs and of scheduling exhibition games. He is looking to bounce back to the success he experienced in 2000, as the 2003 team whose selection he oversaw failed to qualify for the 2004 Olympics in Athens.

Being the architect for championship teams has never left Watson's blood, even as he took a position in MLB's front office. He ranks his role in building USA baseball's 2000 gold-medal-winning team as one of the top accomplishments of his baseball career. He is hopeful to relive the glory he's experienced with the Yankees and at the international level once more in Beijing.

Notes

1. David Falkner, "Yankee Pride (New York Yankees' General Manager Bob Watson)," *The Sporting News*, February 1998.

Ulice Payne, Jr.

First African-American Team President in MLB

by Jessica Bartter

When Bud Selig was hired as the ninth commissioner of Major League Baseball (MLB) in 1998, he brought with him an emphasis on diversity that was new to MLB. Under his leadership, MLB has seen significant improvements in racial and gender hiring practices, particularly in the areas under his direct influence. Unfortunately, the Commissioner's effect otherwise extends only to the tone he sets; his role does not actually authorize him to mandate change at the team level. Nonetheless, Selig's influence on equal hiring practices is undeniable. In 2002, while Selig still owned the Milwaukee Brewers, the team broke new ground by hiring Ulice Payne, Jr., as their president and CEO. Payne, a well-known lawyer and business figure in the Milwaukee area, is the first African-American to ever hold the position of president in MLB. Selig, who made it a requirement that teams interview minority candidates for key positions in baseball, was glad to see further integration in baseball, but Milwaukee residents and fans were also very pleased with the Brewers' pick.

Payne recognized the significance of his appointment; being first was a concept with which he was well acquainted. Payne's previous feats include being the first black State of Wisconsin securities commissioner and the first black minority managing partner at Wisconsin's largest law firm, Foley & Lardner. The real significance, he insisted, of being the first is that now there can be a second, a third, and so on until there is no longer a need to count. When hired, Payne expressed his desire to be remembered for his ability to run the Brewers, rather than for the color of his skin, emphasizing that he was hired for his management abilities.

Payne's athletic prowess had long been established in Milwaukee after his own successful basketball career at Marquette University. After graduating Ringgold High School near Donora, Pennsylvania, in 1973, Payne enrolled at Marquette. He played on the university's 1977 NCAA championship basketball team before graduating with his degree in business administration in 1978. Payne's performance earned him a 9th-round pick in the 1978 NBA Draft by the Detroit Pistons. Yet, the Marquette Golden Eagles held a special place in Payne's heart, and he returned to Marquette for law school in 1979. Marquette University returned the admiration to Payne in 1998 when it elected him to the university's Board of Trustees. He also received the All-University Merit Award and the College of Business Administration's Professional Achievement Award.

Payne had experience on the baseball field in high school and, after starring on Marquette's basketball court, he was asked to throw out the first pitch of the Milwaukee Brewers' 1978 season opener at County Stadium. Payne, who became a Brewers fan during college, kept a photo of the occasion as proof of the cherished memory. He earned more practical baseball experience as an attorney for the New York Mets in the mid-1990s and was later called upon to handle special cases in the MLB commissioner's office. Yet, he never would have pictured himself transitioning from the amateur on the pitching mound to the president in the front office 24 years later. Through his hard work and dedication, Payne became a highly respected lawyer and community activist in the Milwaukee area. Aside from being the managing partner of Foley & Lardner, Payne sat on the board of a number of local organizations and committees. One of these organizations, the Southeast Wisconsin Professional Baseball Park District, was given the task of overseeing the construction of Miller Park, the baseball facility that would replace the stadium in which Payne began his direct connection with the Milwaukee Brewers. As a board member and a baseball fan, Payne traveled to a number of cities, including Denver and Baltimore, in search of the best information and advice about building a high-quality baseball facility.

When Payne officially entered the Brewers organization in late 2002, he inherited a team with a rather dismal record and disappointed fans. Brewers' fans had not seen a playoff berth in 20 years and suffered through more than 100 losses with the team in 2002 alone. Payne had his work cut out for him. His goal was to develop the Brewers into a team its players and fans could be proud of after it had suffered an all-time low in attendance the previous season. To gain this support, Payne stressed the need for the community, the team, and the fans to work together and the importance of being competitive. After 10 consecutive losing seasons, Payne hoped focusing on these key objectives would help achieve the main goal of any professional sports organization—more wins in its record.

Payne was in charge of the day-to-day business decisions of the Brewers organization. He worked closely with General Manager Doug Melvin, who was in charge of running the baseball operations. Together, they encouraged fans to once again embrace the Brewers, most notably with their inaugural Brewers Fan Forum. Payne and Melvin fielded questions from more than 4,200 fans who had much to say about the 56-106 record in 2002. For two hours, frustrated fans fired questions about possible trades, prospective newcomers, ticket policies, in-game entertainment, the organization's minor league team, and more. As relatively new additions to the organization, Payne and Melvin charmed disillusioned fans with their honesty and accessibility.

In 2003, Payne hosted the 2nd Annual Brewers Fan Forum to a considerably smaller crowd. Fewer than 2,800 fans attended this forum, perhaps because there was considerably less to be upset about. In his first season as president, Payne saw his team improve by 12 games. Although they had closed out another losing season, the Brewers were moving in the right direction with a 68-94 record.

Despite the improvement, Payne was faced with a daunting challenge presented by the team's payroll. Many are familiar with the New York Yankees' infamous payroll, which topped the league in 2003 at $153 million. Less noteworthy was the Milwaukee Brewers' payroll of $40.6 million, which was the third-lowest in all of MLB at the time. Payne believed this, in part, was what kept the Brewers out of contention for the pennant. Unfortunately, rather than increase the payroll, the Brewers organization opted to cut the payroll by about 25 percent, a decision that came just one year after a 20 percent decrease. This controversy eventually led to Payne's early departure from the Milwaukee Brewers.

After leaving his mark on the Brewers and Major League Baseball as a whole, Payne didn't venture far from the sports world. Payne's professional law degree and experience have led to his providing expertise to several boards and committees. He has served as a member of the Greater Milwaukee Committee, board member of the Journal Communications, Inc., president of the Wisconsin World Trade Center, vice-chair of U.S. Department of Commerce Wisconsin

District Export Council and co-chair of American Bar Association Customs Law Committee. Utilizing his knowledge and love for sports, Payne serves as the Chairman of the Board of the Bradley Center, which is home to the NBA Milwaukee Bucks, the AHL Milwaukee Admirals, and the Marquette University Golden Eagles men's basketball team. The Center hosts an estimated two million people each year for approximately 180 events, including sporting events, community programs, family shows, and concerts. Today, the Center is considered the best entertainment destination in downtown Milwaukee.

Although his tenure with the Brewers was short-lived, Payne made a positive, lasting impression on the face of professional sports management through Major League Baseball. The residents of Milwaukee appreciated Payne as a Brewers president they could relate to and as someone they felt cared about the community, the city that carries a team on its shoulders. Brewers' fans renewed their passion thanks to Ulice Payne, Jr., a man who is best remembered as an executive who could lead in the boardroom and in the stands and not just as the first African-American president in the major leagues. The young athlete from Donora, Pennsylvania, the land of baseball greats, has become a baseball great in his own right.

3

NATIONAL FOOTBALL LEAGUE: A STORY OF PIONEERS IN TWO ERAS

Introduction by Richard Lapchick

Now that two African-American head coaches have faced off in a Super Bowl in 2007, it is easy to forget how hard it has been for African-Americans to get ahead in the National Football League (NFL).

The story of African-American pioneers has two eras. The National Football League had the great Fritz Pollard, finally inducted into the Football Hall of Fame, who played in an NFL championship in 1920 and became the first African-American head coach in the NFL a few years later.

Then the door slammed shut for more than 20 years.

Pro baseball, basketball, and football had similarities as all remained segregated during World War II, when Americans were fighting for democracy outside our own borders. There were African-American stars in all of these sports, but the greatest showcase was the Negro Leaguers in baseball. However, there were enough great college basketball and football players to let the pros know they were ready. Until the pros were ready, though, the African-American basketball and football players had to join semi-pro or all African-American teams.

Major League Baseball was a much more established and popular league so that even though football integrated first, the impact was not as great. The Los Angeles Rams of the NFL broke the racial barriers in 1946 by signing Kenny Washington and Woody Strode; the Cleveland Browns of the old All-America Football Conference signed Marion Motley and Bill Willis. By 1962 all the NFL teams had at least one African-American player. The Washington Redskins were the last to integrate.

As for other pioneers, the NFL's pace was far behind the NBA and MLB. Although both had African-American head coaches and general managers by the 1970s, the NFL did not have its first African-American head coach until the Raiders hired Art Shell in 1989, 23 years after the Celtics signed Bill Russell.

Ozzie Newsome became the first African-American General Manager in the NFL with the Baltimore Ravens in 2002, 31 years after Wayne Embry became the NBA's first GM in 1971, when he signed with Milwaukee. The NFL has never had an African-American majority owner or team president as of the publication of *100 Pioneers*.

However, the NFL did make a great deal of progress in the decade before publication under the leadership of former Commissioner Paul Tagliabue. He left the sport with an economic vitality beyond compare and seemingly secure with labor peace, loyal fans, and fabulously wealthy TV contracts.

The University of Central Florida's Institute for Diversity and Ethics in Sport released the *2005 NFL Racial and Gender Report Card* measuring the NFL's hiring practices by race and gender. Although the NFL still does poorly with women in key positions, its record on race has continuously improved over the past decade, especially in the past five years. The NFL had its highest grade ever, with a B+ for race. In fact, it came close to an A-. The report shows the NFL reached all-time highs in the key positions of head coach, general manager, and assistant coach.

In the midst of the growth of the NFL's big economic picture, the issue of race was barely mentioned when the commissioner stepped down. But it is the issue I write and speak about among other social issues in sport, so I have watched the decades of his work as commissioner more than just as a fan. When he took over on November 5, 1989, more than 50 percent of players were African-American, but there had been no African-American head coaches or general managers in the modern history of the game. I will always remember that one of his first acts was to remove the Super Bowl from Arizona because the state refused to honor Martin Luther King Day. I took it as a statement by him of a core value.

I never doubted he wanted to increase opportunities for African-Americans in league and team leadership roles off the field. But he did not control what teams did, so his lead in the NFL should have been a barometer. Early on came Harold Henderson as the head of the critical NFL Management Council. Labor peace had been elusive and previous player/management relations had been explosive. Henderson, who is African-American, helped craft the best labor relations in pro sports. In the most recent figures obtained from the NFL (from the 2002 season), 26 percent of management positions in the league office were held by people of color. Ray Anderson was hired in the league office as Senior Vice President for Football Operations and became the first African-American in that key position.

Yet on the club level, there was minimal progress. A decade into his tenure, the NFL had gone from zero to three African-American head coaches and no general managers. Major League Baseball was also moving slowly, while the NBA was way ahead at all senior levels.

More years went by and the NFL seemed stuck at the same number of African-American head coaches—three. In 1999, MLB Commissioner Bud Selig, bogged down with baseball's own slow progress, mandated a diverse pool of candidates for all manager and general manager positions. MLB went from three to nine managers of color and zero to two GM's who were either Latino or African-American.

In the fall of 2002, Washington, D.C., civil rights attorney Cyrus Mehri called me to see if I would join him and renowned attorney Johnny Cochran in using a new study about the success of African-American coaches in the NFL to pressure teams to change their woeful hiring practices in the area of head coaches. At that time, the NFL had the worst record by far when compared to the NBA and Major League Baseball. I went with Mehri to the NFL league headquarters for the first meeting.

The study showed that the small number of African-Americans who had become NFL head coaches had records in the regular season and playoffs that were better than most white NFL coaches. Along with the study came the implication that if changes were not forthcoming, Mehri and Cochran were ready to take legal action.

The pace subsequently quickened in key team positions after the NFL adopted the "Rooney Rule," which was similar to MLB's policy for hiring managers and GM's. It gave the commissioner more clout. Former players formed the Fritz Pollard Alliance to add pressure and create more momentum for change. I have no doubt the efforts of the commissioner's office, as well as the diversity groups appointed by the NFL in the past four years, have brought about a direct change. The "Rooney Rule," which was named after Steelers' owner Dan Rooney (who heads the league's diversity committee) has helped increase the number of African-American head coaches in the NFL from three to seven in the 2006 season. The season was followed by the historic Super Bowl pitting the Bears and the Colts, with both teams led by African-American head coaches (Lovie Smith and Tony Dungy, respectively).

In addition to the head coaching ranks, other examples of progress from the Report Card:

- African-American general managers increased from two in 2003 to four in 2005. As of July 2006, with the hiring of Rick Smith by the Houston Texans, the NFL reached a record high of five African-American general managers or people in the equivalent position.
- The 2005 season saw a record percentage of people of color in assistant coaching positions in the NFL: 162 assistant coaches, or 34 percent. This was up from the previous record of 33 percent in the last Report Card.

However, not all is rosy regarding race at the team level. There was a higher percentage of people of color in team professional positions in 1993 (12 percent) than in 2005 (11 percent). Both years were short of the NFL's record for team professional positions of 16 percent in 1999. People of color hold 14 percent of the team senior administrative positions, the same as in 1999 and lower than the team record high of 17 percent in 2003.

In 2006 the NFL circulated a memo urging teams to interview at least one person of color for all front-office vacancies. The "Rooney Rule" attaches a financial penalty when a team fails to include a person of color in its candidate pool for head coaching vacancies. This memo does not carry the same weight. Such a penalty would give the commissioner even more leverage with teams.

Paul Tagliabue left the NFL not only in remarkable fiscal shape but also with a new model on racial hiring practices for Roger Goodell to use in his tenure as commissioner. In the early days of his own tenure, Goodell has shown great resolve on this issue. The NFL has gone from the slowest to break barriers to being called a model for diversity. Like the other sports, it owes a debt to its historic pioneers from its early days to the modern era.

Frederick Douglass "Fritz" Pollard

First African-American Coach in the NFL

by Marcus Sedberry

If a pioneer can be described as a person who is first or among the earliest in any field of inquiry, enterprise, or progress, thus opening it for occupation and development by others, then Frederick Douglass "Fritz" Pollard was nothing less than a pioneer for African-Americans in sport, business, and society. As Floyd Keith, executive director of the Black Coaches & Administrators said, "Fritz Pollard was a pioneer, a man who excelled not only because of his magnificent athletic gifts, but also because of his wits, intelligence, and ability to lead and inspire people."[1]

On January 27, 1894, Rogers Park, Illinois, gave birth to one of America's vanguards of all time, as one of eight children. As a teenager, Pollard attended Lane Technical High School where he was a talented three-sport athlete in football, baseball, and track and field. It was in football and track that he found his most noted success. At the time of graduation, Pollard was a three-time Cook County track champion, a half-mile state finalist, and a three-year All Cook County running back. As of 1912, the Chicago suburb had fostered the beginning of a young man's quest toward becoming one of the best at everything he did.

Despite his success in baseball and track, football was the epicenter of Pollard's passion. After an impressive career as a high school star, Pollard briefly played football for Northwestern, Harvard, and Dartmouth universities, before receiving a scholarship in 1915 from the Rockefeller family to assist in his attendance at Brown University. While John Rockefeller, Sr., was on campus visiting his grandson, he heard of the clothing business Pollard had opened to pay for school. He became interested in meeting Pollard because the enterprising young man reminded Rockefeller of himself. From this relationship came a loan to aid in the financing of Pollard's education and a jumpstart to Pollard's making history.

In his freshman year at Brown University, Pollard became an immediate star. He led his fellow football team members to an outstanding 1915 season that ended in a heartbreaking loss to Washington State in the Rose Bowl. His presence as the first African-American to play in the Rose Bowl was merely the beginning of many firsts for Pollard. After a splendid football season, Pollard headed to the track. To few people's surprise he had a stellar showing on Brown's track team. Pollard not only qualified for the Olympic Team, but also set a world record in the low hurdles.

The subsequent year, as part of the Brown football team, Pollard led his team to an 8-1 record with 12 touchdowns. In a game against Yale he gained 144 yards rushing, 74 yards on kickoff returns, and 76 yards on punt returns. Pollard did not stop there. During the same season, he led Brown to a first of its own, defeating Harvard for the first time in school history. This first made Brown the first college to defeat Yale and Harvard in the same year during the two Ivy League powerhouses' premier years. In beating Harvard, Pollard rushed for 148 yards with 44 punt return yards and 51 receiving yards. In addition to all of the successes Pollard had accomplished thus far, he became the first African-American in the backfield to be named to Walter Camp's All-American first team. With such achievements, it is only fair to speculate that had this been 10 years later or had there been the Heisman Memorial Trophy Award, Pollard would have received a number of votes for consideration as the best collegiate athlete of his time.

Following his collegiate career, Pollard served in World War I before eventually making it back to continue his success on the football field. From 1919 to 1926 Pollard was a part of the American Professional Football Association (APFA). In 1920, the league officially became the APFA, adopting the name National Football League (NFL) in 1922. In 1919 Pollard began his professional career with the newly formed Pros of Akron, Ohio, a team that became a part of the APFA in 1920. This marked another pioneering act for Pollard as he became one of the first African-Americans to play professional football. With Pollard in an Akron uniform, the Pros found immediate success, going unbeaten in the first 19 games Pollard played. That season, with a record of 15-0-4 and having outscored their opponents

236 to 7, the Akron Pros won professional football's first national championship. The 1920 season proved to be just as successful, to the tune of an 8-0-3 season, with Pollard leading the team in rushing, receiving, scoring, and punt returns.

The following year started with the same skillful play by the Pros, but now Pollard was leading the team as both the head coach and star player. The team won its first seven games with a defense that completely shut out all opponents. Although they started strong, the Pros ended their season with a record of 8-3-1, after suffering losses of several key players including Pollard. Nonetheless, this proved to be another first for Pollard as he became the first African-American head coach in the NFL. Even more impressive was that Pollard still managed to lead the 1921 team in rushing, scoring, and punt returns while serving as the head coach, because sideline or bench coaching was not allowed. In ensuing years, Pollard played and sometimes served as coach for the Milwaukee Badgers in 1922, the Hammond Pros from 1923 to 1925, and the Providence Steam Roller in 1925. During this time, Pollard recorded yet another first as the first African-American quarterback in the NFL, a position he played with the Hammond Pros. Pollard is also credited with organizing the first interracial all-star game in Chicago to showcase African-American players. Pollard also spent time in 1923 and 1924 playing for the Gilberton Cadamounts, a strong independent pro team in the Pennsylvania Coal League, making him the first African-American to play in that league.

In essence, Pollard truly paved the way for African-Americans in sports, particularly in the NFL. During the following years, however, the number of African-Americans in the blossoming National Football League decreased drastically until the final injustice in 1933. The teams' owners made a "gentlemen's agreement" completely banning African-American athletes from the NFL. Like the rest of Pollard's life, this setback was a way for him to step up and accomplish more by blazing new paths. Despite the NFL's effort to limit African-Americans in professional sports, Pollard persevered. In 1935 he became the coach and owner of the Brown Bombers, a professional football team that played in Harlem for three successful seasons. Pollard also organized the Chicago Black Hawks, an All-Star African-American football team. Pollard's mission to expose the many talents of African-American athletes was realized through the Browns as he recruited prominent African-American athletes, including stellar basketball, baseball, and former NFL players.

Unfortunately, the Depression crushed many pro sports and ended the career of Fritz Pollard and the Brown Bombers in 1938. Although his football years were over, Pollard's pioneering spirit constantly moved him forward. In 1954, Pollard was elected into the National College Football Hall of Fame, making him the first African-American to garner such an honor. He was also elected to several other halls of fame, including the Rhode Island Heritage Hall of Fame in 1967, the Brown Athletic Hall of Fame in its inaugural year of 1971, and the National Black Hall of Fame in 1973. The most anticipated and perhaps most deserving hall of fame recognition Pollard achieved was his 2005 election and induction into the prestigious National Football League Hall of Fame.

Although Pollard is known to the world primarily for his athletic ability, he has also made many notable strides in the world of business. Pollard did not allow himself to be quieted by his hardships. Instead, he continued to press forward. Pollard founded the first African-American investment firm, F.D. Pollard & Co. He also established the first weekly black tabloid, the *N.Y. Independent News*, and founded coal delivery companies in Chicago and New York. While in Harlem, Pollard managed Suntan Movie Studio and served as a theatrical agent. He booked African-American talent in white clubs in New York, counting Dizzy Gillespie, Ella Fitzgerald, and Paul Robeson among his contacts. A community man, Pollard was a member of Alpha Phi Alpha Fraternity, Inc., the first intercollegiate Greek-letter fraternity established for African-Americans.

Sorrowfully, on May 11, 1986, Pollard passed at the age of 92, but not before leaving this world a better place than when he entered it. Pollard, at 5 foot 9 inches and 165 pounds, accomplished things far greater than his stature or statistics could ever imply. Although he was not the biggest on the field, Pollard was a man who lived and led a large life, paving the way for others in football and business. His perseverance was immeasurable and will never be forgotten—Frederick Douglas "Fritz" Pollard, a true American pioneer.

Notes

1. Brown University, "Brown University and the Black Coaches Association Establish Annual Fritz Pollard Award," http://www.brown.edu/Administration/News_Bureau/2003-04/03-078.html (accessed September 3, 2006).

Kenny "Kingfish" Washington

One of the First Two African-American Players in the Modern-Day NFL

by Marcus Sedberry

Once upon a time, the University of California, Los Angeles, had two barrier-breaking pioneers on campus and on the same football and baseball teams. Most people know of the late, great Jackie Robinson, who after a successful career at UCLA in football and baseball became the first African-American to play for any Major League Baseball team in the modern era. On the other hand, Kenny Washington was another UCLA athlete who went on to be one of the first African-Americans to play in the modern day National Football League (NFL).

Kenneth S. Washington was born August 31, 1918, in Los Angeles, California. As the son of Edgar "Blue" Washington, Kenny inherited great athletic ability. Edgar Washington played professional baseball as a part of the Negro League's Kansas City Monarchs and Chicago American Giants. Kenny's father also was an actor and had small roles that included a part in *Gone with the Wind*. Both the Negro League and his acting career began to take over his life and consequently took him away from home and his family for a substantial part of Kenny's youth. Subsequently, Kenny was raised by his father's brother, Rocky Washington, whom Washington considered to be his real father. Rocky Washington ended up being a great influence on Kenny's life. Rocky Washington was the highest-ranking black officer in the Los Angeles Police Department at that time.

Growing up, Washington played football at Abraham Lincoln High School in Los Angeles. Although his primary role was as a running back, Washington verified his multiple abilities on the field throughout his years at Lincoln High. In his junior year at ALHS, Washington threw a 60-yard touchdown pass. He graduated the following year, 1936, and entered UCLA as a highly touted running back at a time when African-American football players were rarely found in universities outside of historically black colleges. Nonetheless, Washington played a valuable role on the team. Racial hostility on American campuses was prevalent at UCLA as well. African-

Americans during this time were not allowed to attend any student events except for those sponsored by the African-American club, the Sphinx.

Washington earned the role of left halfback, a position of the single-wing offense where the player in that role was both a runner and a passer. In 1939, Jackie Robinson joined the team as a receiver, and Washington's numbers increased even more. By the end of his UCLA career, Washington had accumulated 1,914 rushing yards, which was the school record for 34 years, and 1,300 passing yards, which also stood as a long-time record for UCLA. He led the nation in total offensive yards with 3,206 in the 1939 season. During this season, Washington also played 580 out of the possible 600 minutes, a feat in which he took much pride, as he played both offense and defense. Washington was quoted by *USA Today* as saying, "Records are made to be broken, but when somebody breaks my endurance record, let me hear about it."[1]

One of the most famous and most noted games in UCLA history was a game in which Washington ran juking and jiving and then passing the ball for 62 yards in the air for a 73-yard touchdown, to take the Bruins to a close final score against their cross-town rival, USC. At UCLA, he also played baseball and had batting averages of .454 in 1937 and .350 in 1938, numbers even his fellow teammate Robinson would have trouble keeping up with. Washington was regarded by his teammates as one who was tough on the field but jovial off of the field. Teammate Ray Bartlett is quoted as saying Washington "could smile when his lip was bleeding."[2]

Washington was tough, but the end of his playing career would not be the end of his hard times. Despite his wonderful athletic career, overt racism still existed for Washington. As a result, he was named to 2nd team All American honors instead of first and was omitted from selection to the East-West Shrine Game, which was a game for top senior football players. At that time; no African-American player had ever played in the game. A *Liberty* magazine poll then asked college players themselves to select an All-American team. Out of the 664 nominees, Washington was the only one to receive votes from every player who had played against him. He won the Douglas Fairbanks trophy, was named the Helms Foundation Athlete of the Year in 1939, and was also dubbed "the Kingfish" due to his 6-foot-1-inch, 200-pound stature.

The next step for Washington was the NFL; however, the NFL was not ready for Washington or for any African-American for that matter. In 1933, the National Football League's team owners made a "gentlemen's agreement" completely banning African-American athletes from the NFL. Therefore, Washington would have to wait for his chance because of his race. Immediately following Washington's graduation, he played for a local semi-pro team, the Bulldogs, for a few years. In 1940, he was part of the college all-star team that played in an exhibition game at Chicago's Soldier Field against the NFL champion, Green Bay Packers. In that game, Washington played well and sparked some team owners to question the rule. He then joined the Hollywood Bears of the Pacific Coast League in the 1940, 1941, and 1945 seasons, where he became a popular player. While playing in the Pacific Coast League, he worked as a Los Angeles police officer. Although two serious knee operations slowed Washington down and kept him out of World War II, in 1944 he played for the San Francisco Clippers of the American Football League.

Following the war, Washington would finally get his opportunity to play in the NFL. In 1946, Cleveland Rams owner Dan Reeves moved the franchise to Los Angeles. The commissioners of the LA Coliseum, following a city anti-discrimination ordinance, threatened not to allow the Rams to play in the Coliseum if the team was not integrated. As a result, Washington played on September 26, 1946, thereby reintegrating the NFL. He took the field along with Woody Strode, one of Washington's African-American teammates at UCLA. As might have been expected, Washington's transition did not go over well, and white players made things worse with mental attacks as well as physical attacks, especially on his already battered knees. Washington's NFL career did not last long, as he retired after three seasons. During that time, however, he averaged six yards per carry and led the NFL with an average of 7.4 yards per carry in 1947. Before retiring in 1948 from the Rams and the NFL, he tallied nearly 860 yards rushing; including a 92-yard run that remains the record for the longest run from scrimmage.

In 1950, his raw talent resurfaced when he was given an opportunity to try out for Major League Baseball's New York Giants. He later became a skillful golfer. In 1956, Washington was inducted into the National Football Foundation's College Football Hall of Fame. In this same year, his jersey number 13 was retired at UCLA and he was inducted into the College Football Hall of Fame. Kenny "Kingfish" Washington passed away on June 24, 1971, after years of circulatory problems. His story of being a legend and pioneer for African-Americans and for Americans in general, however, will forever live on.

Notes

1. "Kenny Washington Biography," http://biography.jrank.org/pages/2544/Washington-Kenny.html (accessed March 17, 2007).

2. Denicke, Dave. "Constructing a Legacy," http://www.dailybruin.ucla.edu/db/issues/00/02.24/sports.washington.html (accessed March 16, 2007).

Woodrow "Woody" Wilson Woolwine Strode

One of the First Two African-American Players in the Modern-Day NFL

by Marcus Sedberry

In the early half of the 20th century, there were no multi-million-dollar football contracts or million-dollar signing bonuses. Millions of dollars were not spent on endorsements, nor was any revenue generated from national television broadcasts. It was simply football—just pigskin, a few pads, and men blocking, running, throwing, catching, and tackling on a field. In addition to the lack of a financial revenue stream that exists today, when the NFL was in its infant stage there was very little diversity. In fact, in 1933, the NFL team owners made a "gentlemen's agreement" to ban African-Americans from playing in the league. It wasn't until 13 years later that the modern-day NFL became integrated.

One of the men who reintegrated the modern-day NFL was Kenny "Kingfish" Washington who was born on August 31, 1918. The other was Woodrow "Woody" Wilson Woolwine Strode, born on July 28, 1914. Both natives of Los Angeles, they were favorites of the city and were followed throughout their careers. Even though they went to opposing high schools, Abraham Lincoln High School and Thomas Jefferson High School respectively, they joined forces at the University of California, Los Angeles (UCLA) and later in the NFL.

In 1945, the Cleveland Rams won the NFL Championship and soon moved to Los Angeles, California. The owner of the team at the time, Dan Reeves, was particularly interested in Los Angeles because of the opportunity to be in a major U.S. city, and he hoped playing off of the Hollywood atmosphere would be a positive for his team. Another perk of interest to Reeves was the famous publicly owned LA Coliseum. The NFL and the Rams were both utterly white organizations at this time and this rubbed African-American sportswriters Halley Harding, Herman Hill, and Abie Robinson the wrong way. They felt it totally unacceptable for the Rams and the NFL to play in a publicly owned stadium while segregated. The three sports-writers even gained the support of LA County Supervisor Leonard Roach, who also did not support a racist team playing in the publicly owned facility. Thus the Rams' contract with the LA Coliseum stipulated that they integrate the team.

The next year, local favorites Washington and Strode were the first to reintegrate the NFL. Washington was signed on March 21, 1946 and played for three seasons with the Rams. Strode signed with the LA Rams shortly after, on May 7, 1946 at the age of 31. Strode played only the 1946 season with the Rams. Later that year, guard Bill Willis and running back Marion Motley were signed with the Cleveland Browns of the competing league, All American Football Conference (AAFC), on August 6 and August 9 respectively.

Football was not Strode's only love, so playing in the NFL for just that one year was not the end of the world for him. He played for a couple more seasons in 1948 and 1949 with the Calgary Stampeders of the Canadian Football League. However, he did not stop there. In fact, some would say that football was only the beginning of Strode's true and most noted career. In addition to his wonderful career as a track and field decathlete, in which he came within six inches of the world record at the time, 6 feet 10 inches, and his professional wrestling career, which included fighting the likes of Gorgeous George from 1950 to 1955, Strode was an actor.

For the next few decades, Strode would play in a variety of movies on the big screen and in live shows. Strode's impressive physique made him desirable for roles either as a vicious villain or a gallant hero. Many of his roles were in westerns. Strode made his screen debut in 1941 in *Sundown*. He had dual roles, an Ethiopian king and a slave, in the *Ten Commandments* (1956). In 1959, Strode portrayed Private Franklin in *Pork Chop Hill*. Strode began to gain the respect and friendship of film director John Ford, who led Strode to other meaningful roles. Ford was so impressed with Strode, he gave him the title role in *Sergeant Rutledge* (1960) as a member of the Ninth Calvary falsely accused of murder and rape. He had other parts in *The Last Voyage* (1960), *Two Rode Together* (1961), and *The Man Who Shot Liberty Valance* (1962). One of Strode's biggest awards as an actor was his Golden Globe nomination for Best Supporting Actor for his role as gladiator Draba in the 1960 film *Spartacus*. Strode played in numerous other films throughout the 1960s,

'70s and '80s, including three Tarzan films. The last film Strode shot was released in 1995, a year after his death, entitled *The Quick and the Dead*.

Strode was inducted into the Stuntmen's Hall of Fame and the UCLA Hall of Fame in 1992. Five years prior, he was awarded the Golden Boot Award. Strode was also a proud member of the first-intercollegiate Greek-letter fraternity established for African-Americans, Alpha Phi Alpha Fraternity, Inc. In 1990, Strode finished his autobiography, *Gold Dust*.

Strode's accolades and accomplishments were very impressive athletically as well artistically. Throughout his lifetime he faced society's racism. He was not allowed to eat at certain restaurants or stay at certain hotels, and he was frequently treated poorly in other ways as well. Strode took it in stride. For him, there were no boycotts and protests. Strode was a silent warrior in the truest sense. Although his contribution to the NFL may be overlooked by many, his legacy of pioneering into the NFL and the big screen live on as a testament to his unique role as a pioneer.

Arthur Shell

First African-American Coach in the Modern-Day NFL

by Jessica Bartter

During a 45-minute self-guided tour of the Professional Football Hall of Fame in Canton, Ohio, the night before a Hall of Fame Game, Art Shell found himself captivated by a video that was set to repeat continuously in the Hall. The video told a story Shell had never heard before about football legend Fritz Pollard, the first African-American coach of an NFL team. As the Los Angeles Raider was eager to learn the history of African-Americans in the National Football League, he listened intently, not knowing he would later follow in Pollard's footsteps.

At the time of Shell's Hall of Fame tour, neither Shell nor Pollard was a Hall of Fame member—a fact which later changed for both of them. This was one department in which Shell preceded his elder, Pollard. Shell's Hall of Fame career started and finished with the Raiders, first in Oakland in 1968, then in Los Angeles in 1982. Shell was picked 80th in the third round of the 1968 draft. The left tackle from the University of Maryland Eastern Shore was named to eight Pro Bowls during his 14-year career. Offensively he helped the black and silver get to 24 playoff contests, including two Super Bowls. The South Carolina native was named to the NFL's 1970s All-Decade Team and South Carolina's Sports Hall of Fame. Six years after his retirement, Shell was elected to the Pro Football Hall of Fame in 1989. Pollard would follow 16 years later. Even seven years post-playing, Shell was named 55th on *The Sporting News'* list of the 100 Greatest Football Players in 1999.

Although he hung up his no. 78 Raiders jersey in 1983, Shell did not leave the locker room. He remained with the team as an offensive line coach until he was named head coach in 1989. With such responsibility, Shell continued the legacy Pollard started by becoming just the second African-American head coach in the NFL. Shell is considered the first African-American coach of the modern-day league; his appointment was separated from Pollard's by 68 years, part of which time a "gentlemen's agreement" had barred African-Americans from the NFL. The Hall of Fame player continued to be a driving force behind the Raiders, except now the players called him "Coach." In his first season at the reins, the Raiders won the AFC West Division with a 12-4 record, earning Shell AFC Coach of Year honors for 1990. Shell was also named 1990s Coach of the Year by *Pro Football Weekly*, Maxwell Football Club, and United Press International. Over the next three years he garnered 42 wins and 34 losses, bringing his overall coaching record to 54-38. Dissatisfied with the Raiders' 9-7 record in 1994, Owner Al Davis let Shell go at the conclusion of the season.

Shell spent a year as the Kansas City Chief's offensive line coach and three years in the same position with the Atlanta Falcons before stepping off the field and into the NFL's front office. Shell's first league office responsibility included trips to college campuses, particularly the Historically Black Colleges and Universities of the Southeast, including his alma mater. Shell would visit with their football players to help paint a realistic picture for those dreaming of a professional football career. Shell wanted the young athletes to know what to expect and helped them cultivate realistic aspirations.

Shell traveled during the off-season, offering his expertise on the world of professional athletics, but during the season he was needed in the league office. In 2003, Shell was named the NFL's Appeals Officer. When a player is fined on the field, the player is allowed to appeal the fine, a course of action which, according to Shell, happens 99 percent of the time. Shell was charged with hearing the appeals and deciding on the subsequent action. He could choose to affirm, reduce, or rescind the fine based on each player's story and corresponding video footage. Shell's final rulings were generally quietly accepted because players knew they were talking to a respected former player who had seen and heard it all during his own time on the field. Shell knew firsthand what could happen in "the heat of the moment" and supplied the players with fair, clear, and appropriate decrees.

Shell's experience on the field brought him back to the Raiders in 2006 after working as the NFL's executive vice president. Owner Al Davis admitted he had long regretted his decision to fire Shell in 1994. The black and silver had suffered tremendously, winning just 13 games in the previous three seasons combined and going through five coaches in the 11 years since Shell's departure. Davis wanted a coach who could instill intensity in the floundering Raiders' franchise.

The typical fire and will to win associated with the Raiders had appeared to fade, and Davis could not handle the recent lack of respect his players showed for division rivalries with the Broncos, Chiefs, and Chargers. Who better fit for the challenge than a former player and coach who had led the Raiders to winning seasons as both?

Shell's second stint as head coach was brief. With problems beyond the realm of what a head coach could control or fix, the Raiders went a dismal 2-14, scoring just 12 touchdowns all season. Shell left the Raiders at the conclusion of the 2006–07 season.

Nonetheless, encouraging news came from Shell's last season regarding the NFL's hiring practices, thanks in part to his pioneering efforts. At the start of the 2006 season, Shell was one of seven black head coaches of the NFL's 32 teams. The NFL had certainly come a long way since his inaugural coaching stint. This time, though, NFL fans did not have to wait another 68 years to see an African-American run a team on the field. The progress in the NFL had been so extensive that Shell's firing in 2007 did not cause a media heyday like his original hiring in 1989. Instead, the 2006–07 season culminated with a highpoint of NFL history. For the first time in the 41 years of the Super Bowl, two African-Americans led their teams to the illustrious game. Just hours after the Chicago Bears beat the New Orleans Saints, sending Lovie Smith to Super Bowl XLI, the Indianapolis Colts beat the New England Patriots behind the leadership of Coach Tony Dungy. Before the Super Bowl started, the real winner was already crowned; diversity in the NFL coaching ranks had finally taken a giant leap after the small, but arduous, steps forged by Pollard and Shell.

Ozzie Newsome

First African-American General Manager in the NFL

by Marcus Sedberry

Growing up in Muscle Shoals, Alabama, during the late 1950s and '60s would have been difficult for any black youngster. Ozzie Newsome was born March 16, 1956, eight years before the civil rights act was passed, exposing him to the painful trials and tribulations of being an African-American in the South. In spite of the institutionalized racism and hard times, Newsome persevered and began setting the stage for his rise to stardom as a barrier-breaking pioneer.

As far back as Little League baseball, Newsome remembers breaking barriers as one of the first African-Americans to play in his town. That pioneering spirit has carried on throughout his life. On November 25, 2002, Newsome became the first African-American general manager of a National Football League franchise.

In 1975, Newsome enrolled at the University of Alabama to gain an education and to pursue an athletic career. He excelled in both areas. Off the field, Newsome graduated with a degree in recreation administration. On the field, Newsome was extremely successful as he recorded 102 receptions for a total of 2,070 yards. The legendary coach, Paul "Bear" Bryant of the University of Alabama, recalls, "He was a total team player, fine blocker, outstanding leader, great receiver with concentration, speed and hands."[1] Coach Bryant's opinion was shared by many as Newsome was named a two-time All Conference selection in the 1976 and '77 seasons, as well as an All-American in 1977. He averaged 20.3 yards per reception, which was a Southeastern Conference record that now places him second in the SEC All-Time record books for athletes with more than 100 receptions. Newsome's leadership also shined as the Crimson Tide rolled to 11-1, 11-1, 9-3, and 11-1 records during his career, as well as to three SEC conference championships.

After graduating from the University of Alabama, Newsome entered into the National Football League draft. In 1978, he was drafted as the second of two first round picks by the Cleveland Browns. During his professional athletic career, Newsome accumulated numerous awards in addition to gaining respect across the nation as one of the best tight ends to play the game of football. In his rookie season, Newsome was named the offensive player of the year for the Browns. The following season, he was named All-Pro and garnered the same honor in 1984. Although tight ends were seldom used in the NFL, Newsome was a vital part of the Browns' offense. Before retiring after his 13th season with the Browns, Newsome caught 662 receptions for 7,980 yards and 47 touchdowns. He had three pro-bowl appearances (1981, 1984, and 1985) and was a four-time winner of the Cleveland Touchdown Club's Offensive Player of the Year Award (1978, 1981, 1983, and 1984). Newsome retired as the all-time leading tight end receiver and fourth among all receivers. He also went 150 games in a row with at least one reception, second in NFL history. As a result of the magic he created on the field and the unbelievable feats he accomplished, Newsome gained the nickname "Wizard" and subsequently became known to some as the "Wizard of Oz."

His wizard-like mentality and work ethic carried over to his professional administration career. Immediately following Newsome's historic career for the Browns in 1990–91, he was hired as a special assignment scout for the Browns. Two years after his initial hire, Newsome was promoted to the position of assistant to the head coach/offensive/pro personnel and in 1994 was named the Browns' director of pro personnel.

In 1996, Newsome was invited to join the Ravens as the vice president of player personnel, as the team had recently moved to Baltimore. Almost immediately, Newsome began to work his "wizard" magic for the Ravens. As his first draft with the Ravens came to a close, Newsome found himself with two future pro bowlers: Jonathan Ogden and eventual Super Bowl XXXV MVP and 2000 and 2003 NFL Most Valuable Defensive player, Ray Lewis. The trend of drafting well has continued throughout Newsome's career. In his first 10 drafts as a Raven, he and his staffs have selected first-round picks who have earned pro bowl selections a combined 28 times. Newsome has had tremendous success in free agent signings as well. With acquisitions of players like Rod Woodson, Michael McCrary, and Shannon Sharpe, Newsome has been able to gain veteran players who are willing to help the team remain competitive year in and out. In November of 2002, Newsome was named the general manager and executive vice president of the Baltimore Ravens.

The Wizard's abilities have been recognized not only by players and coaches, but by the entire sports world. In 1990, Newsome was the winner of the Byron "Whizzer" White Award as the NFL's top community volunteer. He also serves on several committees throughout the NFL, including the NFL Competition Committee and the NFL Diversity Committee. Newsome holds positions in several halls of fame as well. In 1994, he was inducted into the National Football Foundation's College Hall of Fame and the NCAA Hall of Fame. The following year, he was inducted into the State of Alabama Hall of Fame. Newsome was also introduced as a new inductee into the NFL Pro Football Hall of Fame in Canton, Ohio, in 1999 by NFL great Calvin Hill.

Newsome had wonderful and historic collegiate and professional athletic careers. He set the stage for many tight ends and receivers to follow. During his life he has had many prestigious moments; however, trailblazing through the many barriers to becoming the first African-American NFL general manager is truly a magical accomplishment.

Note

1. National Football Foundation's College Football Hall of Fame, "Ozzie 'The Wizard of Oz' Newsome," http://collegefootball.org/famersearch.php?id=70017 (accessed November 27, 2006).

Lovie Smith and Tony Dungy

First African-American Coaches to Face Off in the Super Bowl

by Richard Lapchick

Right in the middle of Black History Month 2007 we found a sports event making history. The fact that the 2007 Super Bowl Sunday marked the first time two African-American head coaches led their teams against each other in a Super Bowl was widely discussed and extensively covered in the media. Lovie Smith and Tony Dungy, the two coaches, were so gracious and humble that their frequent references to their families and their faith seemed to further endear them to the nation. There is a separate story in this section on Tony Dungy winning the big game.

Will we forget? Most were surprised when I mentioned that having two coaches of color in the NBA finals had only happened once and that it had never happened in a World Series, a men's or women's national championship, or in any BCS bowl game. Not one person I spoke to remembered which coaches (Al Attles' Golden State team defeated K. C. Jones' Washington Bullets in a four-game sweep) or when (the 1975 finals) the two African-American NBA coaches faced each other. Not many could name all the coaches of color whose teams won the NBA championship (Attles, Bill Russell, Lenny Wilkens, and K.C. Jones), the World Series (Lou Piniella, Cito Gaston, and Ozzie Guillen). Or the three African-American coaches (John Thompson, Nolan Richardson, and Tubby Smith) who won the men's Division I championship.

So why was it important if we eventually lose count of the facts, including the who, when, and how? Let's take the NBA to see exactly why. Before Attles and K. C. Jones faced off, there had been five African-American coaches in the history of the league. After the collision of their teams, there have been 46 more. We no longer notice when an African-American has been hired or fired in the NBA. The same is true in college basketball. There had only been a few African-American head coaches in Division I basketball before John Thompson's Georgetown team won the Big Dance. As of the publication of *100 Pioneers*, African-Americans now hold more than 25 percent of the Division I positions. Like the NBA, we rarely notice when an African-American is hired or fired. Unlike the past, both the NBA and college basketball feature fired African-American coaches getting rehired elsewhere. That was rare before championships were carved out.

Okay, so we might not remember the specific facts, but a championship has mattered in the past. What lessons then emanated from this Super Bowl for college sport? Before the game, the NCAA had all but dropped the idea of a Rooney Rule for colleges. Will it be reconsidered now? The Black Coaches & Administrators has been threatening Title VII lawsuits against colleges that Executive Director Floyd Keith hoped would follow the successes of Title IX lawsuits for women when colleges finally began to comply more effectively after a series of successful Title IX suits in the courts.

I believe that who coached in the Super Bowl and how they carried themselves will become more important than threatened lawsuits in the NFL or the Rooney Rule. However, the threatened suits and the Rooney Rule played important parts in getting us to the point where there were seven African-American head coaches in the 2006 NFL season. Johnnie Cochran and Cyrus Mehri, two attorneys, threatened to sue the NFL in 2002, leading to the adoption of the Rooney Rule, which mandated that African-Americans be included in the interview process for every head coaching position. The NFL went from two to seven African-American head coaches in a short period of time. Now Tony Dungy stands as a humble Super Bowl Championship coach.

The Super Bowl has forced leaders to look at college football, which has the worst record for hiring practices for head coaches in any pro or college sport. There were seven coaches of color out of 119 at the Division IA level in the 2007 season, fewer than there were a decade before!

However, we do have a visionary leader on the issue in Dr. Myles Brand, the NCAA president. His role at the top has been unique for an NCAA leader. Brand has been outspoken on the issue of how few African-Americans have been head coaches in Division IA football. Moreover, his actions in the creation of the NCAA Office for Diversity and Inclusion, the hiring of Charlotte Westerhaus as vice president for Diversity and Inclusion, the work of a high-powered Diversity Leadership Strategic Planning Committee he created, his support for the Black Coaches & Administrators, and the funds invested by the NCAA targeted for improving the hiring records, are testaments to Dr. Brand's desire for meaningful change. I am hopeful that, as the work of the Strategic Planning Committee is implemented, bigger changes will come soon. However, for college football it cannot come soon enough.

As with the NFL five years ago, lawsuits contemplated by the BCA are on the horizon. The NFL short-circuited legal action by adopting the Rooney Rule. The results in the NFL are Black History Month-worthy. College sport desperately needs a similar rule. College administrators are trying to avoid it, but surely they do not want lawsuits. There have been congressional hearings on the issue. I believe that the effects of both threatened lawsuits and sustained congressional hearings will be avoided if colleges adopt the rule and hiring processes become more open. Five years ago the NFL was being criticized even more than the colleges for its poor record of hiring practices for coaches. Now the NFL is being called a model for diversity for corporate America.

The ball is in the air. It is up to the NCAA members to catch it and make a college football moment Black History Month-worthy in the future.

Tony Dungy

First African-American NFL Coach to Win a Super Bowl

by Horacio Ruiz

The polite coach had finally won the Super Bowl. On stage during the Vince Lombardi Trophy presentation, Indianapolis Colts Coach Tony Dungy eagerly awaited his chance to hold the prize, reaching for it three times before Colts owner Jim Irsay relinquished the hardware. Finally the trophy was Dungy's, silencing those who questioned his ability to conquer the biggest game in sports. Dungy was proud of his players, the organization, the city of Indianapolis, and the fact that he had just become the first African-American coach to win the Super Bowl. With Dungy leading the Colts and his counterpart Lovie Smith leading the Chicago Bears, Super Bowl XLI marked only the second time in the four major American sports leagues that the two teams playing in a championship game were led by African-American coaches.

The presence of Smith and Dungy in the championship game was a validation for African-American coaches in all sports, confirming their professionalism and skill as team leaders. The match-up was also a validation of the National Football League's Rooney Rule, requiring that every team with a head coaching vacancy must interview at least one person of color for the open position.

After the Super Bowl, Dungy paid tribute to the African-American coaches who preceded him, those who didn't get the same opportunities he did when he took his first head coaching position in 1996 with the Tampa Bay Buccaneers. "Great coaches," Dungy would say about them, "that I know could have done this if they'd been given the opportunity. I feel good I was the first one to do it and represent the guys who came before me. I dedicate the game to them."[1] He told Smith of the pride he felt in sharing the moment with him. In true Tony Dungy fashion, he assured Smith that in due time the Bears would have their grand winning moment.

Prior to becoming the Colts' head coach, Dungy spent six seasons as head coach of the Tampa Bay Buccaneers. He turned a franchise once thought to be doomed to perpetual failure into a yearly Super Bowl contender. In his six seasons at Tampa, Dungy helped lead the team to four winning seasons, one more than the franchise had achieved in its first 20 years, and to three double-digit totals in wins, a feat accomplished by a Tampa team only once from 1976 to 1995. Even while lifting a franchise from the NFL's junk yard, Dungy became a victim of his own success when he could not guide the Buccaneers to the Super Bowl. After his sixth season in Tampa, one in which the team reached the playoffs, Dungy was let go by owner Malcolm Glazer. Eight days later Dungy became the head coach of the Indianapolis Colts.

As of the beginning of the 2007 NFL season, Dungy has compiled a 67-24 record, including the playoffs, in his five years with the Colts. His success and ability to coach in the regular season were never questioned, but Dungy had acquired his share of doubters. Some said he was too nice, not intense enough, lacking the killer instinct to motivate his players for the big games. The polite coach persevered and came away with a Super Bowl title. There was nothing anybody could say.

Although Dungy appeared joyful with the Lombardi Trophy in his hands, he had faced a devastating personal tragedy just two years prior. Late in the 2005 NFL season, with the Colts contending for the Super Bowl after beginning the season with a 13-0 record, Dungy's oldest son, James, committed suicide. Dungy was very hesitant to speak about his family's loss, preferring to keep that segment of his life private. Those whose lives he touched not just as football players but as men had something to say. "Whether I'm playing on his team or not, he's forever my coach," Edgerrin James told *USA Today* about his coach of four years.[2]

Not only was James outspoken, but he also attended the funeral. All those in attendance were blown away by Dungy's strength, character, and candor. "At the funeral, do you know who he thanked?" James said. "He thanked the owner of the Tampa Bay team (Malcolm Glazer). This is the guy who let him go. That's letting you know, 'It's cool. I'm not sweating stuff.' That stood out. Through all that drama . . . he put that past him. He thanked the dude for everything he had done for his son."

Another former player, Warren Sapp, was also at the funeral. He could not believe that Dungy would be reading his own son's eulogy. "I'm thinking, 'There's no way,'" Sapp told *USA Today*. "But he got up there and laughed, cried and talked. It just left more of a stamp on me. You stand up like that, and you're burying your son? C'mon. That just shows what the man is made of." When the service was over, Sapp embraced Dungy, the person he's called "the greatest man I've ever met in my life," and broke down.

Dungy had always done things differently, refusing to be the coach who spent countless hours in the office, even running some of his assistants out of the football offices late at night telling them they all should go home and spend time with their families. His style of coaching is different, he doesn't berate his players or ridicule them; he maintains a cool composure on the sideline, watching the game at times with arms crossed under an extremely successful and watchful eye.

"I think Lovie runs his program the same way [I do], with respect for his players, with the idea he wants his players to be part of their city," Dungy said to an ESPN writer after winning Super Bowl XLI. "You want to do things the right way."[3]

"I can coach with no profanity, no violations of the rules, anything like that," Dungy said. "And I hope that gets across to owners, maybe athletic directors in college football, that hey, look at maybe a different set of people than you always looked at."

"There's a lot of African-American men that can do the job." Hopefully, they're given the chance.

Notes

1. Greg Garber, "Colts Coach Stands Alone in History," ESPN.com, http://sports
.espn.go.com/nfl/playoffs06/news/story?id=2754582 (accessed June 27, 2005).

2. Jarrett Bell, "Tragedy Forces Dungy to 'Live in the Present,'" *USA Today*, http:
//www.usatoday.com/sports/football/nfl/colts/2006-08-31-dungy-cover_x.htm (accessed
June 27, 2005).

3. Garber, "Colts Coach Stands Alone."

4

NATIONAL BASKETBALL ASSOCIATION: THE NBA IS THE PIONEER LEADER

Introduction by Richard Lapchick

When we dissect the racial issue about things of consequence, the NBA has more African-American pioneers than any other sport. There are African-Americans in the category of minority team owner, majority team owner, team president, general manager, coach, and, of course, player. These seven categories are almost double the next best league, which is Major League Baseball with four (team president, general manager, coach, and player).

The Institute for Diversity and Ethics in Sport at the University of Central Florida published the *2006–07 NBA Racial and Gender Report Card* in the spring of 2007. I was the author, along with Horacio Ruiz and Marina Bustamante.

The reality is that the NBA, from the day David Stern became commissioner, has been the model for doing things right on the issue of race in professional sports. It is the only men's professional sport that has ever had an African-American owner (Robert Johnson of Charlotte). It had pro sport's first African-American head coach, Bill Russell, in 1966 (he was also pro sport's first African-American head coach to win a championship) and pro sport's first African-American general manager, Wayne Embry, in 1971 in Milwaukee. Embry also became the first African-American team president in 1994, with Cleveland.

100 Pioneers is being published in an era when everybody is correctly lauding the progress made by the NFL and Major League Baseball in hirings of head coaches/managers. However, the NBA, with 40 percent of its head coaches being African-American, has more than double the percentage of any other league. At the end of the 2006 season, the NFL hired another African-American general manager, giving it a total of five. As its 2006–07 season ended, the NBA had eight African-American general managers.

Many celebrated the fact that two African-American head coaches faced each other in the 2007 Super Bowl with the Colts being led by Tony Dungy and the Bears by Lovie Smith. The NBA can point back to the 1975 Finals with pride, the first time two African-American NBA head coaches faced off. K. C. Jones and Al Attles led the Washington Bullets and the San Francisco Warriors in the NBA Finals. The NBA has had four African-American head coaches win NBA championships (Attles, Jones, Bill Russell, and Lenny Wilkens). Through the end of the 2006–07 season, there have been 53 African-American head coaches. Major League Baseball is a distant second with 25 managers of color.

So, as we look around and see baseball and the NFL making their progress to better opportunities for people of color in front offices and on the field, we need to remember that the NBA has been the industry leader for nearly two decades and has been a great model for the other sports. David Stern once said to me that his goal is that "when an African-American coach is hired and, more importantly, when a team fires an African-American, nobody will notice." It is clear that the NBA has reached that stage with so many of its top executive positions being held by African-Americans.

That is why, in the *2006–07 NBA Racial and Gender Report Card*, the NBA got the first ever A+ for racial hiring practices with all-time records for people of color in the positions of league office professionals, team vice-presidents, assistant coaches, and team senior administrative and team professional positions.

Among the other highlights in the Report Card:

- 15 percent of the NBA's team vice president positions were occupied by people of color, three percentage points higher than last year and the highest in the Report Card's history, as well as the highest in the history of any professional sport.
- In the NBA, almost 79 percent of the players were people of color. The percentage of African-American players increased to 75 percent from last year's 73 percent mark.
- Professional opportunities for people of color in the NBA League Offices—at 34 percent—increased by two percentage points from the previous Report Card. This was the highest

percentage in the NBA's history and the highest in the history of any professional sport.

- At the beginning of the 2006–07 NBA season, there were 12 African-American head coaches. This number remained the same as in the 2005–06 season. The NBA continues to have the highest percentage in all pro sports history at 40 percent of the total. This season matched the second-highest in NBA history, equaling the 40 percent in the 2004–05 season.
- At 41 percent, the NBA achieved its highest percentage of assistant coaches of color ever.
- There were four African-American CEO/presidents in the NBA and two additional African-American presidents of basketball operations during the 2006–07 season. They are the only African-American CEO/presidents in the history of men's professional sports. Susan O'Malley was the only female president in the NBA.
- In the 2006–07 season, the NBA had eight African-American general managers. The 27 percent was the highest for African-Americans since the 1997–98 season. This was also higher than any other men's professional league in any previous Report Card.
- The percentage of people of color holding NBA team senior administrative positions remained constant at 20 percent, matching the 2005–06 all-time record for the NBA. The percentage of women holding these positions increased from 23 percent to 25 percent during the same period.
- The NBA remained constant in its percentage of people of color holding team professional administrative positions at 26 percent. This matched last year's all-time record for the NBA for race. The percentage of women holding these posts decreased to 41 percent from last year's 42 percent.

With its best-in-sport contemporary record, the NBA may have more reason to be thankful for the pioneers depicted in the following pages. It all started when Nat "Sweetwater" Clifton, Early Lloyd, and Chuck Cooper became the NBA's first African-American players, in October of 1950.

Nat "Sweetwater" Clifton

First African-American Player to Be Signed to the NBA

by Richard Lapchick

Although I did not know it at the time, my earliest memories as a child involve Nat "Sweetwater" Clifton. Then five years old, I looked outside my bedroom window in Yonkers, New York, one afternoon and saw my father's image swinging from a tree with people under it picketing. Over a period of several years I would occasionally pick up the extension phone upstairs and overhear calls directed at my father. Often the message was "nigger-lover, nigger-lover." For years I had no idea what this was all about except that there were people who disliked my best friend.

The connection to Clifton was that my father, as coach for the New York Knicks, had signed Nat "Sweetwater" Clifton as the first African-American basketball player to be under official contract with the National Basketball Association, and there were a lot of people who did not welcome that. It was 1950, and the Celtics drafted Chuck Cooper and Washington drafted Earl Lloyd. Together they took the courts and the NBA was never the same. Six decades later, basketball is the most integrated sport in America both on and off the court.

Personal Collection of Richard E. Lapchick.

Nat "Sweetwater""Clifton and Joe Lapchick, Coach of the New York Knicks from 1947 to 1957.

Opening the door for African-American athletes, Nat "Sweetwater" Clifton was in the first of what would become generations of great African-American stars in the NBA. Clifton embraced the public. Because of that characteristic, coupled with his ability to perform on the court, many believe that Clifton would have been a wealthy man in the modern-day NBA.

He was reportedly born on October 13, 1922. (He never acknowledged his age.) Clifton spent the first eight years of his life in England, Arkansas. His real name was Clifton Nathaniel and he earned the nickname "Sweetwater" because of his boyhood love of soda pop. Born poor, he could not afford to buy soda pop, so he often mixed water with sugar to make "sweetwater." Clifton and his family moved to Chicago when he was eight, and it became his adopted home. It is where his love for playing basketball began. When he was becoming a star in high school, he bowed to a media request that the order of his name be changed so it would fit in the newspaper headlines.

While playing at DuSable High School in Chicago, Clifton dominated his opponents. He stood at over 6 foot 7 inches tall, weighed more than 235 pounds, and had hands that spanned 10 inches. In the city championship game in his senior year in 1942, Clifton shattered the tournament's previous record of 24, scoring 45 points in a single basketball game. According to the *Chicago Daily News*, he was one of the two greatest basketball players in the state's history.[1] Clifton played on a local softball team called the Gas House Gang but then picked up a love for baseball.

Clifton enrolled at Xavier University in New Orleans in 1944. However, like many people his age, he was drafted into the United States Army, and he served for three years in Europe.

Bob Douglas was the owner of the New York Rens, which was the great all-black team that had started in the Renaissance Casino Ballroom in Harlem in the 1920s. In 1947, Douglas and my father presented a case to the new professional basketball league board to admit the Rens and break the color barrier. My Dad and Douglas waited outside the board room for the decision. When Ned Irish, the Knicks owner and my father's boss, came out, he told them the league had rejected the proposal.

My father told Bob Douglas that he was considering resigning, but Douglas told him he had to stay because he might get another chance. That chance was a few years away and it came as Nat "Sweetwater" Clifton returned from the Army and started his professional basketball career.

Clifton was the first African-American ball player to join the Dayton Metropolitans. Following Dayton, Clifton played briefly for the Rens. In 1948, Clifton, who knew how to play an entertaining style of basketball, joined the Harlem Globetrotters and received $10,000, the highest salary ever paid to an African-American player at the time. The Rens played the game straight, while the Globetrotters were more of an attendance draw with a fast-paced, razzle-dazzle game. Some said the Trotters were so popular because they portrayed themselves as stereotypical blacks, thus making white audiences feel comfortable. Clifton and the Globetrotters traveled the world, showcasing their skills on the court and often defeating all-white teams. While Clifton spent three years with the Globetrotters, he also played baseball for an AA-team in Pennsylvania. He was constantly being sought by baseball scouts, who were impressed by his 86 runs batted in and his .304 batting average.

Despite being a successful athlete in both basketball and baseball, his chance to become a major league athlete didn't arrive until the summer of 1950. Globetrotters owner Abe Saperstein saw the opportunity to capitalize on the situation and was ready to sell Clifton's contract to the Knicks. The "chance" that Bob Douglas told my father he might get was about to present itself. Nathaniel Clifton made history when he signed with the New York Knickerbockers in the summer of 1950, becoming the first African-American under official contract with the NBA.

Clifton was initially upset that "Abe got $10,000 for me, I think. I got $2,500. But for me, that was a lot of money. And I didn't worry about that. I just liked to play the game. We played for the sport of it." Clifton maintained the positive attitude that he was known for and moved forward with his career. He even managed to play for Saperstein and the Globetrotters during the NBA off-season.

His NBA debut took place on November 3, 1950, and he quickly made his mark on the court. During his rookie year, he averaged 8.6 points, and by his second year had reached the double digits. He was a fundamental to the team, serving as a forward for a highly powerful squad. According to former Knickerbockers player Al McGuire, Clifton "had the body of a power forward of today but he never looked much to score. He was the first guy to really cuff a ball without the stickum. He even cleared his rebounds with one hand most of the time."[2]

As an individual, Clifton had a positive working relationship with his team. He went to church with his teammates and played cards with them. He was congenial toward his white teammates. He said, "Around Chicago and in the army, I was used to playing with white players, and I could get along. I figured everybody had to make a living and nobody gave me dirt. [The Knicks] were a great bunch of guys."[3]

Gus Alfieri, who was a former player for my father at St. John's and who became his biographer with *Lapchick: The Life of a Legendary Player and Coach in the Glory Days of Basketball*, wrote, "When Sweetwater Clifton came to the Knicks, Lapchick was able to apply the same chemistry that I mentioned that he did with us (later at St. John's). With Clifton, Lapchick did everything that was necessary to make things flow. Clifton was someone who you respected; he was a big, strong guy. Lapchick tried to prepare him for the NBA. In one situation, he told him, 'Sweets, you have to defend yourself out there; otherwise, these guys are going to run you out of the league even though you are a very strong player.' So Lapchick encouraged Clifton to defend himself. Once, Lapchick asked him if he could fight and Clifton said, 'A little.' Lapchick kind of rolled his eyes and thought that Clifton was going to get hurt out there but what Lapchick didn't know was that Clifton had fought with fighters like Joe Louis and Bob Satterfield—he used to spar with them in Chicago. So he was very familiar with handling himself and he had huge hands. There was a famous incident with the Boston Celtics when a guy (Bob Harris made a racial slur toward Clifton) threatened Sweetwater Clifton and Clifton decked him. The Celtic team just kind of ran away from him because they realized that he could really hurt them.

"I mentioned that Lapchick didn't like to pin himself down by making a lot of rules and he did that with Clifton, too. The team very often traveled by plane but some guys traveled on their own. Ernie Vandeweghe was a doctor and he would often get there right before the game because he was just getting done with his work as an intern. Lapchick let Sweetwater drive up to Boston by himself and didn't make regulations that would tie him up in a knot. He made it very flexible for him and I think that that helped the integration of the NBA, too. What really made the whole thing work for Lapchick is that he didn't try to do anything that would limit Clifton from doing what he would have to do. When they got to a city, if it was a segregated city then sometimes the team would say that we don't have to stay in this hotel. . . . Sweetwater had been traveling on the road for years as a baseball player and Harlem Globetrotter and he really knew how to handle himself. When he got to a city he had millions of friends and he didn't need the Knickerbockers to watch over him. His ability to do that helped make his transition to the NBA a smooth one."[4]

Although Lapchick's coaching style and Clifton's playing style were very different, Clifton understood that he was in an incredible position. His razzle-dazzle playing style was suited for the Globetrotters, while Lapchick played with a more controlled game. His teammates included Max Zaslofsky, Ernie Vandeweghe, Vince Boryla, Carl Braun, Connie Simmons, Harry Gallatin, and Dick McGuire. They went to the NBA Finals three times and never missed the playoffs.

Clifton's best season was in 1956–57. During that season, he averaged over 13 points a game and played in the NBA All-Star game at Madison Square Garden. During that game, he had 11 rebounds and proved his position as a great player.

After the 1956–57 season, Clifton was traded to the Detroit Pistons. He left the NBA after that season due to the lack of playing time he was given by the coach. He continued playing until the mid-1960s when a knee injury convinced him to put away his basketball shoes. In his seven-year NBA career, he averaged 10.3 points per game.

Clifton decided to remain in his hometown, Chicago, with his wife. His playing death preceded union-driven pensions, so Clifton searched for a job to support his family. He was a people lover and most of the people in his neighborhood knew him. As a well-known figure in Chicago, he probably could have gotten a city job, but he liked his freedom and became a taxi-driver.

Every time I landed in Chicago, I hoped Sweets would be in the driver's seat. When I asked the other cabbies, they all knew Sweets and admired him. Finally on one trip in the late 1980s, I got in a taxi and saw him up front. We took a lot of extra time to get where I was headed so we could talk. He had not known about the attempt to get the Rens in the league or about what my father had faced as my dad never made that public. He told me, "Joe always treated me like the other players. That is how I wanted it but I am not sure how many other coaches would have done that. Chuck [Cooper] told me Red

[Auerbach] was like that also." He was proud that he was inducted into the Black Athletes Hall of Fame in 1978.

Clifton told me he was comfortable and enjoyed driving. He passed away at the wheel of his cab on August 31, 1990, near Chicago's Union Station, where he had picked up so many of his fares.

I was glad he lived to see his induction into the Hall of Fame but know he would have been even more proud that in 2005 the New York Knicks renamed their City Spirit Award as the Sweetwater Clifton City Spirit Award. It honors local heroes who have made a significant difference in the lives of others in New York, New Jersey, and Connecticut. The recipients of this award have included such as the Tuskegee Airmen and FDNY Paramedics. Recipients are honored at the last home game of the month at Madison Square Garden.

Sweetwater Clifton will be remembered as a great athlete who made a difference in the lives of many African-American athletes, helping to open the opportunities for them in professional sports. By his entry into the NBA, he unknowingly launched me into a life of work on the issue of race in sport in particular and as a human rights activist outside of sports. Thank you, Nat Sweetwater Clifton. Your life has made the lives of so many others sweeter.

Notes

1. James M. Manheim, "Nathaniel "Sweetwater" Clifton Biography" http://biography.jrank.org/pages/2338/Clifton-Nathaniel-Sweetwater.html (accessed on October 1, 2007).

2. Ibid.

3. Ibid.

4. David Friedman, "Part IV of an Interview with Gus Alfieri, Author of *Lapchick*," September 25, 2006, http://20secondtimeout.blogspot.com/2006/09/part-iv-of-interview-with-gus-alfieri.html (accessed October 1, 2007).

Charles "Chuck" Cooper

First African-American Player to Be Drafted into the NBA

by Jessica Bartter

When Boston Celtics founder Walter Brown said, "I don't care if he's striped, plaid or polka dot, so long as he can play," he was referring to Chuck Cooper. That was Brown's response when another owner remarked, "Don't you know he's a colored boy?"[1] after Brown selected Cooper in the second round of the 1950 NBA draft, thus helping to break the color barrier in the NBA.

By definition, a pioneer is one who starts or leads others in the development of something new or an early settler of an unknown or unclaimed territory. The word *pioneer* is rooted in the French term *pion*, meaning "foot solider." *Pioneer* originally referred to a solider whose task was to prepare the way for the troops marching to a new area. Therefore, *pioneer* can be used to describe anyone who ventures into an unknown region. In the case of Chuck Cooper, the region was the National Basketball Association, but in this exploration, Cooper did not work alone.

Oftentimes, it takes more than one individual to break down the walls of exclusion. In fact, it took many to enact the drastic societal change that took place in the NBA in 1950. In that case, three pioneers led the way, supported by several key owners, executives, and coaches who stood behind their efforts. Chuck Cooper was the first African-American to be drafted by the NBA; Earl Lloyd was the second, but the first to step on the court and play; and in the same year, Nat "Sweetwater" Clifton became the first African-American to sign an NBA contract. Each was equally important. One man *can* make a difference, but one man does not always make *the* difference alone.

Cooper had graduated from Pittsburgh's Westinghouse High School in 1944 and went to West Virginia State. Soon thereafter, he was drafted by the Navy where he remained until after World War II ended. By 1946, Cooper had less than one semester of college under his belt, but he was determined to complete his education. This time he chose a school closer to his hometown—Duquesne University.

Duquesne had temporarily ceased basketball operations during the last two years of the war but reestablished its program in 1946, coincidentally Cooper's first year with the school. Despite the youth of the team, the 6 foot 5 inch guard averaged 10.5 points per game, leading the Dukes to 19 straight wins and an overall record of 21-2. One of those wins was easily earned but hard to swallow. Duquesne was scheduled to play the University of Tennessee, but the all-white university refused to take the floor because of Cooper. The game date, December 23, 1946, preceded the 1954 *Brown v. Board of Education* case; therefore, such overtly segregationist policies were still allowed.

Cooper's four years brought a 78-19 record to the Dukes and two National Invitation Tournament (NIT) appearances. The NIT was the most prestigious event of college basketball in the 1940s. Cooper was named All-American as a senior, catching the attention of NBA scouts.

In 1949, the Basketball Association of America (BAA) and the National Basketball League (NBL) merged to become the 17 teams of the National Basketball Association, the NBA as we know it today. In 1950, the NBA consolidated to 11 franchises, at which it remained until 1954, when the league shrank to its all-time low, eight franchises. After the end of a four-year, league-wide ban that kept African-Americans out of the NBA, three of the league's eleven teams integrated their rosters. For many years, the white professional teams would play exhibition games against the all-black professional teams like the New York Renaissance and Harlem Globetrotters, but the teams remained segregated. Whether the separation was based more on financial security or racial prejudice is unknown. Surely, it was some combination of both. The owner of the Harlem Globetrotters, Abe Saperstein, threatened to boycott NBA cities if NBA teams signed any black players. The threat was taken seriously at first because the Globetrotters were big revenue drivers when their exhibition games preceded NBA competitions. Eventually, owners recognized that the segregation was excluding some of the country's best basketball players from professional basketball simply because of the color of their skin. Walter Brown helped end such practices.

After Brown picked Cooper in the draft, Cooper enjoyed six seasons in the NBA, four with Boston, one with the Milwaukee Hawks, and one with the Fort Wayne Pistons. He averaged 6.7 points and 5.9 rebounds per game.

After retiring from basketball, he wed Irva Cooper. He earned his master's degree in social work from the University of Minnesota in 1961. Eventually, he and Irva returned to his hometown of Pittsburgh. Cooper became Pittsburgh's first African-American to head a city government agency when he was named Director of the Parks and Recreation Department. At the time of his death, he was working at the Pittsburgh National Bank.

When Cooper died of liver cancer on February 5, 1984, at the age of 57, his death went largely unnoticed. *Chicago Sun-Times* writer, Rich Hoffer, described it best in his 1986 article titled "NBA black pioneers all but forgotten." Referring to Cooper, Lloyd, and Clifton, respectively Hoffer commented that "the men who paid the most are largely forgotten, the game's considerable debt to them apparently written off. Consider that of the three men to break the color line in 1950, one has passed so unheralded that his death may yet be unreported in some parts. Another, his whereabouts unknown even to the team for which he once played and coached, counsels quietly for a school district. A third, perhaps the best of them, drives a cab." Nonetheless, the 75 percent of today's players who are African-American are eternally indebted to Cooper, Clifton, and Lloyd. The "early settler," Chuck Cooper, prepared the way for troops of all colors to march in the NBA, claiming territory for change in the league's racial make-up of players, coaches, executives, and staff, change that makes the NBA almost unrecognizable when compared to the 1950s version of itself.

Note

1. Milan Simonich, "Chuck Cooper: The Pioneer Spirit," *Pittsburgh Post-Gazette*, February 1, 2004.

Earl Lloyd

First African-American to Play in the NBA

by Jenny Brenden

In his early playing days, fans would often yell harsh, derogatory words at Earl Lloyd, hoping that their mind games would negatively affect his performance. Lloyd's detractors significantly underestimated the mental and physical strength that allowed him to play through all the name calling and to focus on the game. For Lloyd, the constant barrage of racist commentary made the physical aspect of basketball seem easy. The disparaging words that were yelled at him from the fans on the sidelines only motivated Lloyd to run faster, jump higher, and play harder. He used those fans' hate to elevate his game instead of mirroring their rage and ignorance.

Lloyd played a crucial role in integrating the game of basketball. After graduating from West Virginia State College in 1950 with a laundry list of accolades, including three-time CIAA All-Conference selection (1948–50) and two-time All-American honors (1949 and 1950), as well as leading his team to two CIAA conference and tournament championships (1948 and 1949) and an undefeated season in 1947–48, Lloyd went on to make history at the next level. Following his senior basketball season, Lloyd was the second African-American to be picked in the 1950 NBA draft; the Boston Celtics had selected Charles Cooper only a few picks earlier. He was one of three African-Americans to integrate the NBA in 1950. The New York Knicks had signed Nat "Sweetwater" Clifton from the Harlem Globetrotters shortly before the college draft. Although behind Cooper in the draft, Lloyd still beat Cooper to the playing floor. Of the three pioneers, Lloyd was the first African-American to actually play in an NBA game, beginning his career with the Washington Capitols. On October 31, 1950, Lloyd debuted on an NBA court, one day ahead of Cooper and four days ahead of Nat "Sweetwater" Clifton of the New York Knicks. Lloyd's rookie year was cut short when the Capitols folded in early January of 1951, after only seven games. After a short stint in the army, Lloyd proceeded to play for the Syracuse Nationals from 1952 to 1958 and for the Detroit Pistons from 1958 to 1960.

Lloyd spent the better part of a decade in professional basketball (1950–1960). The period of Lloyd's professional basketball career spanned a time in history when racism was rampant in American society; hate and violence often found their way into the world of sports and the game of basketball. Lloyd's integration into the NBA closely followed Jackie Robinson's breaking of the color barrier in MLB in 1947. The relative newness of this barrier-breaking phenomenon meant that individuals like Lloyd faced little tolerance and much hostility from fans.

African-American players were forced to encounter a great deal of hate and volatile behavior, all the while resisting the urge to retaliate. Lloyd remembers racist remarks coming largely from fans and not from teammates and opponents. Just because Lloyd chose not to retaliate against spectators does not mean he never fought on the court. He threw a few punches in his career, and he certainly never backed down from a challenge, but the altercations were usually instigated by rough play on the court or by choice words that players said to one another.

Although he was nicknamed "the Big Cat," his moves on the court were anything but smooth and cat-like. The 6-foot-6-inch, 220-pound power forward enjoyed throwing his weight around. Lloyd was very strong and loved to hit people, not with the intention of hurting them but just because he enjoyed the rough play. He relished fighting with an opponent over a rebound or setting a solid pick to help a teammate get open. Lloyd's toughness came from honing his skills on the rugged courts of inner-city Washington, D.C., during his youth. The rules of basketball on the playground generally are a little different from those used in an official, regulated game. It is quite possible that the old adage, "No blood, no foul," held true on the playground that Lloyd frequented. No competitor wanted to be called weak, wimpy, or soft for calling a foul on the opposing team or for stepping down from a fight.

Lloyd carried this playground mentality with him throughout his entire career. In light of this background, it's hardly surprising that one of Lloyd's favorite players to watch in the NBA today is Shaquille O'Neil. Lloyd was a very unselfish player, an attribute he associates with Shaq as well. Lloyd's strengths were his great fundamental basketball skills. He was not a prolific scorer, with his highest scoring season earning him an average 10.2 points per game. That same season, his average, along with his hard work, helped him lead his Syracuse Nationals past the Fort Wayne Pistons in the 1954–55 NBA Championships. Lloyd and teammate Jim Tucker were the first African-Americans to win an NBA title. Lloyd's career average was a little over eight points, but he did so much more than score; his presence on the floor simply made an impact. Lloyd knew the game and he knew how to be good at it.

This knowledge enabled Lloyd to make a smooth transition from player to coach. In 1968, he became the first African-American assistant coach in the NBA with the Detroit Pistons. He moved up to the position of head coach with the Pistons for the 1970–71 season.

Lloyd still enjoys being a fan of NBA basketball. He was inducted into the Basketball Hall of Fame in 2002, joining the collection of basketball's greatest players and coaches. Earl Lloyd, a basketball pioneer and brave barrier-breaker, should be remembered and applauded forever.

Don Angelo Barksdale

First African-American to Be Selected to an NBA All-Star Team

by Jenny Brenden

Does it seem right for an All-American collegiate basketball player to be rejected by the National Basketball Association? Among all of the discrimination and prejudice that existed in the mid-1940s, this unfair situation is exactly what Don Barksdale had to endure. He had proven to be one of the elite players coming out of college, but his athletic prowess was not enough to earn him a spot on an NBA roster. At that time, the NBA had constructed very strict rules prohibiting African-Americans from entering the league. Today, NBA teams would be strategizing how to obtain a player of Don Barksdale's status. Despite such a setback, Barksdale persevered in many ways and went on to succeed not only in basketball, but also in life.

Barksdale wasn't just an All-American. In 1947, he was the first African-American collegiate men's basketball player to be named a consensus All-American. Although his college prowess makes it difficult to believe, Barksdale had trouble making his way onto a basketball team when he was younger. He graduated from Berkeley High School in 1941 without ever having been a member of the basketball team. Lack of skill and effort were not the reasons he did not make the team. Barksdale was barred from the team because he was African-American. When Barksdale's buddy, who also happened to be African-American, made the team, the head coach told Barksdale, "One black is enough."[1]

Barksdale did not try to fight this very obvious display of a quota system, but instead fought for himself in a much more graceful way. The class that he exhibited in this situation is one of his defining characteristics as a role model. He could have easily hung up his sneakers and called it quits on basketball, but instead he continued to play the game that he loved. He worked hard to develop his skills and by the time he graduated from high school he had become good enough to play basketball in college.

Because it is difficult to obtain a scholarship without playing in high school, Barksdale began his collegiate basketball career at Marin

Junior College where he played for two years. After his tenure at Marin, he received a scholarship to play basketball at UCLA. Barksdale received his consensus All-American honor in 1947. Any doubts about whether he was worthy of this award evaporated soon enough; he was chosen as the first African-American to be a member of the USA Olympic men's basketball team, who competed and won a gold medal in London at the 1948 Olympic Games. Barksdale received significant playing time from Adolph Rupp, the well-known Kentucky Wildcat head basketball coach who wouldn't even begin recruiting African-Americans for his own college team until 20 years later. Barksdale was transforming the way basketball was played. Although people had trouble disregarding his skin color, they eventually recognized his amazing talent and his ability to change the game in more ways than one.

In the year he graduated from college, 1947, the color barrier was just being broken by Jackie Robinson in the MLB. Sadly, the NBA was still a few years away from that milestone. Although an NBA team did not pick him up right away, he did continue playing basketball for the Oakland Bittners in the Amateur Athletic Union (AAU), winning a national championship in 1950. Finally, in 1951 he had the opportunity to play in the NBA. He signed a two-year contract for $60,000 with the Baltimore Bullets, becoming one of the NBA's highest paid players. He joined other African-American pioneers in the NBA, such as Nat "Sweetwater" Clifton, Chuck Cooper, and Earl Lloyd. Coincidentally, Barksdale was a 28-year-old rookie in 1951, the same age that Jackie Robinson was in his rookie season with the Dodgers. Barksdale had no problem keeping up with the youngsters on the court as he was the first African-American to be selected to play in the NBA All-Star game in 1953. When asked about the experience, he stated, "I was extremely happy I was chosen because the coaches choose you. It wasn't like today when the fans choose. I didn't touch the ball much in the game, but at least I was on the team. I was very proud of it."[2] Shortly thereafter he was traded to the Boston Celtics, where his career was cut short by ankle injuries.

Even when Barksdale was starring at UCLA, he had a bigger picture in his mind of what he was capable of. He opened a record store while he was a student-athlete at the university, which was only the beginning of his entrepreneurial career. After his college years came to a close and he was playing AAU basketball locally, Barksdale became the San Francisco Bay Area's first African-American disc jockey. He also became the host of a popular television variety show featuring African-American entertainers. In addition, he opened up his own advertising agency and entered the beverage industry as the first African-American owner of a beer distributorship in northern California. At the conclusion of his NBA career, he reverted back to his entrepreneurial/musical roots. He started his own record label, Rhythm Records, and opened up two nightclubs in the Bay area, the Showcase and the Sportsman.

In addition to Barksdale's athletic prowess and his business savvy, he became a philanthropist later in his life. In 1983 he founded the Save High School Sports Foundation for the Bay Area high schools that were struggling to maintain proper athletic programs for their students. In the 10 years that Barksdale operated it, until his death in 1993, the foundation raised over one million dollars for local high schools.

A former professional basketball player named Doug Harris is bound and determined to keep Don Barksdale's memory alive and to remind everyone that this special man had a vital role in basketball history. He believes Barksdale is deserving of a spot in the Basketball Hall of Fame, and he has said, "Don Barksdale left a positive impact on just about everyone he came in contact with in both the sports and entertainment world. His presence in the Basketball Hall of Fame would be a breath of fresh air for sports enthusiasts who appreciate true sports heroes and treasure our history."[3]

Although Barksdale has not yet been inducted into the Hall of Fame, Harris has written, produced, and directed a documentary on Don Barksdale called *Bounce*, so that basketball players and enthusiasts, as well as young people, have the opportunity to learn about and be inspired by a true basketball pioneer. Don Angelo Barksdale was a great man who deserves to be honored and remembered.

Notes

1. Dave Newhouse, "Do You Know Black History? *The Oakland Tribune*, February 22, 2007, http://www.insidebayarea.com/oaklandtribune/ci_5279822 (accessed April 15, 2007).

2. "Don Barksdale, 1st black NBA All-Star, dies at 69—obituary—Brief Article," *Jet*, March 29, 1993, http://findarticles.com/p/articles/mi_m1355/is_n22_v83/ai_13 558316 (accessed February 5, 2007).

3. Dave Zirin, "Resurrecting Don Barksdale: Basketball's Forgotten Pioneer," March 8, 2007, http://www.zmag.org/content/showarticle.cfm?ItemID=12285

Bill Russell

First African-American Head Coach of Any Major Professional Sport

by Horacio Ruiz

The man who stepped into his battered home one day in 1971 was far removed from the hardwood floors, champagne celebrations, and celebratory cigar smoke to which he had become accustomed. In that moment, as he discovered that vandals had broken into his home, destroying basketball trophies and mementos, going so far as to defecate on his bed and spread it on the walls, he felt a pain that was all too familiar. The man who had won an Olympic gold medal, two national college basketball championships, and 11 NBA titles was again forced to confront a harsh reality. He was African-American, and some people did not like him because he was.

What's more is that this man is one of the most successful figures in the history of sport, one who transcends time. On April 18, 1966, Bill Russell became the first African-American coach or manager of any major professional sport since before the Great Depression. Legendary Boston Celtics coach Red Auerbach, retiring from the game as the leader of the great Celtic dynasties of the 1950s and '60s, handpicked Russell to succeed him. Auerbach was shrewdly aware of the dynamics involved—he, the great Jewish coach, choosing the centerpiece of the Celtic dynasty, the African-American player, to continue conquering the basketball world in racially charged Boston. Russell would win two championships in his three seasons as a player/coach, the two titles coming in his last two years before what some considered a premature retirement in 1969.

As much as that reverberated throughout the sports world, Russell was making history long before his appointment as coach of the Celtics. The coaching appointment was merely icing on the cake. Russell was a different type of athlete—by all accounts an undeniably brilliant man who refused to let his status as a person of color affect the way he lived his life. No apologies needed to be made for his appearance; he would be damned if he had to apologize for his genetic make-up. Simple as it may seem, he wanted to live life on his own terms. The fact that he was an African-American man dominating his sport like never before did not mean that he had to act polite or be nice in the way others tried to force upon him. He did not seek preferential treatment, nor, understandably, did he seek to be treated as an inferior.

After being refused service at a highway diner, Russell was quoted as saying, "Some [black] entertainers try to show whites that they are nice people. All of us are nice people, but this isn't a popularity contest. I don't care if the waitress likes me when I go into a restaurant. All I want is something to eat."[1]

It did not matter to Bill Russell what waitresses or others thought about him. It was not in his nature. Even as he was winning 11 world titles in the NBA during his 13-year career, including a run of eight consecutive titles, Russell would rarely oblige fans by signing autographs, because he didn't feel comfortable doing it. Every autograph he signed made him feel like he was giving away a tiny piece of himself without much interaction with the fan, and he found no joy in that.

Even before his time as a national basketball star, Russell was no stranger to racism. As much as his parents tried to shelter young Russell from the prejudices he faced growing up in Oakland, California, he was acutely aware of what others wanted him to feel about himself. He was no better and no worse than anybody else, his mother would say, a lesson that he took to heart.

The character and qualities of Bill Russell in the 1960s differed from other outstanding athletes of his time. Unlike boxing great Joe Louis who felt pressured to act "proper" and "polite" for the mass of white audiences, Russell brought on a little bit of the persona of Jack Johnson, the boxing giant who did not change his behavior to comply with how people wanted him to act in the early 1900s. Russell did what he wanted when he wanted, speaking and acting in the way he felt he needed to for himself. Other black teammates felt safe when he walked with them in the streets of Boston, a city where they often did not feel so safe. The relationship between a great champion and his city is usually one of admiration, and there was no mistaking the respect Russell garnered in Boston. There were also the break-ins and refusals of service at local hotels and restaurants. It is hard to understand how a man who brings so much glory to a city can be the target of so much ignorance and hatred, but Russell understood that he was viewed as one man on the court and a completely different entity off of it.

By 1971, he was two years removed from his playing career and still the target of blind racism and vandalism in his Reading, Massachusetts, home. Only a few months before the break-in, the town held a dinner in his honor, celebrating his part in the community. A friend of his, who had entered the league with him in 1956, said the gesture meant so much to Russell that it was the first time he had seen him cry.

It has long been debated whether or not Russell is the greatest basketball player of all time, with those who played against him swearing he is nothing less than the absolute best. There is certainly no denying that Russell is the greatest winner of all time. His college and professional careers include 13 total championships, plus an Olympic gold medal along the way. He literally altered the way the game was played defensively; the college game changed the width of its lane from six to 12 feet because of Russell.

In 1968, he was named *Sports Illustrated* magazine's "Sportsman of the Year" after he was awarded the Most Valuable Player award five times, including four times from 1961 to 1965. In 1972, Russell declined a public ceremony for his jersey retirement. Only a handful of friends and family attended, and when he later took his courtside position as an announcer, he did not acknowledge the applause he received from the Boston Garden crowd. In 1975, he publicly stated that he did not want to be elected into the Naismith Basketball Hall of Fame, but even his own sentiments could not get in the way of his election. A Hall of Fame without Russell would have been like the Louvre without the *Mona Lisa*. In 1980, Russell was named the greatest player in NBA history by the Professional Basketball Writers Association of America. Then in 1996, in honor of the NBA's 50th anniversary, Russell was recognized as one of the league's greatest 50 players of all time, joining a list of players who were stars, pioneers, and founders of the game. Russell encompasses all three. Slowly, the bitterness melted away, and Russell would soon become known for his big smile and infectious laugh, one that echoed a deep and joyful satisfaction of life.

On May 26, 1999, Russell consented to have his jersey retired once again, this time in public. His tribute helped raise funds for a youth mentoring program he had become involved with and finally allowed the city of Boston to show Russell a token of appreciation. He also began signing autographs, but not before spending a small amount of time getting to know each person for whom he was signing. The man had changed, but his principles had not. Despite the hardships he was forced to endure, Bill Russell's legacy in sport history is forever cemented.

Notes

1. Tony Kornheiser, "Nothing but a Man," in *ESPN SportsCentury*, ed. Chris Berman and David Halberstam, 179–189 (ESPN-Hyperion, 1999).

Wayne Embry

**First African-American General Manager and President
of a Professional Sports Franchise**

by Jenny Brenden

Wayne Embry cherishes every minute and every involvement he has
with the sport of basketball. He is very fortunate to have had the opportunity to have worked where his passion lies, for the better part of
his life. Embry believes the sport has taught him lessons that span
far beyond the court. In his biography, *The Inside Game*, he specifically refers to these lessons as the keys to success.

These lessons, as stated in his book, are: preparation through
education, practice, hard work and dedication, perseverance through
developing mental toughness, perception of opportunities and obstacles that are presented, pride in achievement, persistence in never
giving up your dream, and passion for that which you seek to accomplish. These are not characteristics that are exclusive to sports or
the NBA. In fact, anyone could strive to obtain these qualities in any
aspect of his or her life. Embry wanted his message and his book to
appeal to the masses, not just to basketball fanatics. He didn't want
to have an impact only on the world of sports; he wanted to change
the world as a whole. As Wayne Embry's basketball career is revis-
ited in this story, the role of his outlined success factors will become
apparent in both his on-court and off-court achievements, as well as
in his position as a pioneer in professional sports.

Embry has certainly proven to be successful on the court, both
in college and during his tenure in the NBA, much of that success
coming within his home state of Ohio. He attended Miami University in Oxford, Ohio, from 1954 to 1958, becoming a high-scorer,
team captain, and team MVP in 1957 and 1958. In his post-collegiate
career, Embry went on to play for the Cincinnati Royals (1958–66),
the Boston Celtics (1966–68) and the Milwaukee Bucks (1968–69).
He was a five-time NBA All-Star (1961–65), and he won an NBA
championship in 1968 with the Boston Celtics. Embry also established himself as a leader on his teams by being named captain of the
Cincinnati Royals from 1962 to 1966 and the Milwaukee Bucks from
1968 to 1969. Embry was enshrined in the official Basketball Hall

of Fame in 1999 as a contributor, which is someone who has contributed in a very special way to the history of basketball. His accolades followed him into his post-playing days, as he was named NBA executive of the year in 1992 and 1998.

After his playing days were over, he found himself working for the Milwaukee Bucks, quickly ascending the corporate ladder. The first question Embry was asked by the media after having been named the general manager of the Milwaukee Bucks was, "How does it feel to be the first African-American general manager in professional sports and do you think that it is significant?" Embry's response was, "It is significant only if others think it is significant." Many people did believe Embry's achievement to be significant based upon his race; however, an article written the day after the press conference read, "Embry's ability, not his color, earned him this job, and Embry's ability will determine his success in it."[1]

This momentous event took place in 1972 in Milwaukee, Wisconsin, which was a city at least a step behind in the area of race relations when compared to many cities across the country. The worries Embry had surrounding this ground-breaking step in sports pertained more to the reaction that he would get from others, rather than whether or not he was capable of doing the job well. There was added pressure for Embry because he was representing the African-American community, and if he failed to succeed in this position, it might have been perceived by some that all African-Americans were unfit for such high-level opportunities. Many white people had failed to succeed as general managers, but most critics still perceived that white people could thrive in such jobs. This double-standard is an issue African-Americans continually face.

One of Embry's biggest trades came before he stepped into the GM position with the Bucks. In 1971, he negotiated to bring Oscar Robertson to the Milwaukee Bucks to play with Kareem Abdul-Jabbar. This deadly duo teamed up to bring the NBA Championship to Milwaukee that year. Although the Robertson trade was an unquestionably good move, Embry also made some questionable decisions, such as trading Kareem Abdul-Jabbar to the Los Angeles Lakers in 1975. This may have seemed like a poor choice, but those outside the organization can only guess as to its motivations. More important, whether this was a good decision or not, Embry continued to follow his passion for many, many years.

In serving as general manager, one of Embry's jobs was to put the best possible team together in order to make the franchise successful. He had to know players' strengths and weaknesses, personalities, team chemistry, and the nature of their competitors. What Embry looked for specifically when he was recruiting players was character. Having a player with character certainly never meant having the "nicest" players, as Embry understood that nicety was not equivalent to character. In his biography, Embry describes character as strength, courage, fortitude, moral fiber, integrity, and the will to win. He says that players with character don't make excuses, they play with injuries, they practice self-discipline, and they respect themselves and their teammates. Embry has been criticized for not simply going after the players with the most talent and instead looking for players who had character, but he firmly believed that "talent may win games, but it is character that wins championships."

Embry made history in 1972 when he accepted the position of general manager for the Milwaukee Bucks franchise, a post he would hold for the next eight years. He eventually made history again as pro sports' first team president with Cleveland. He joined the Cleveland Cavaliers organization in 1985, and over the years he held positions of vice president, executive vice president, team president, chief operating officer, and general manager. He saw the Cavs through some of their most successful seasons. Embry was replaced as general manager in 1999 by Gordon Gund. Subsequently, Embry served as a consultant for several years before becoming a senior advisor for the Toronto Raptors.

In recent years, Embry has been asked if he thought there would ever be a day when the discussion of race won't be necessary. He replied that he hoped that day would come someday, but it was a little discouraging that race still is such a hot topic in sports these days. Embry recognizes that he was a pioneer in professional sports, being the first African-American general manager and team president of a professional sports team, and that professional sports have continued to evolve over the years. It is a slow process. Embry remembers that in 1986 when he was interviewing for the general manager position in Cleveland, he was asked whether, if he became the GM, he would be compelled to hire a black coach. He replied, "I hope that you would want me to hire the best qualified person. That is what I've been taught and believe. Isn't that the way it should be?" In further responding as to whether or not there would be a time when a discussion of race wouldn't be necessary, Embry said, "I think that eventually we're gonna have to reach back and disregard the color of one's skin and other biases to rely entirely on the content of one's character, in the words of Dr. King."

Note

1. Wayne Embry with Mary Schmitt Boyer, *The Inside Game* (Akron: The University of Akron Press, 2004), 193.

2. Meyer, Bruce. "Wayne Embry: I knew I had to suceed." HoopsHype.com-int erviews. July 30, 2004.

Al Attles and K. C. Jones

First African-American Coaches to Face Off in a Professional Championship

by Horacio Ruiz

In 1975 when Al Attles and K. C. Jones were the first African-American coaches to compete head-to-head for a professional title, it seemed nobody, not even the coaches themselves, noticed that both were African-American. Attles' Golden State Warriors were the underdogs heading into the 1975 National Basketball Association Finals against Jones' Washington Bullets. All that either remembers thinking was how much they each wanted to win. Neither coach recalls race in any of their conversations. It would not be until 2007 that two African-American coaches again would again face each other for a professional title, when Tony Dungy and Lovie Smith led their teams to Super Bowl XLI. Thirty-two years later, it seemed everyone noticed both coaches were African-American.

Looking back more than three decades later, what stands out for both Attles and Jones is that it took so long for it to happen again. "People have to ask why is it that two African-American coaches in the Super Bowl is something that should be all over the media," Jones said in a *Boston Globe* interview.[1] "I'm happy they're there with their teams, but does a double standard still apply?"

Attles' Warriors swept Jones' Bullets 4-0 to win Golden State's only basketball title. According to Attles, the dynamic of his team was especially significant given that it was comprised of 10 African-American and two white players. Attles gives much of the credit to former Warriors owner Franklin Mieulis for giving him an opportunity to coach and then to construct the team as he saw fit. "There weren't many Franklin Mieulis' back then," Attles told the *Oakland Tribune*. "We had situations where I went to him for input because of our racial makeup. Franklin said, 'Al, you take the best 12 players available to you, and I don't care what they look like.' That was a statement to me. I was going to do what I thought was best regardless, but if you get the backing of the person who's paying—I don't know if that happens very often, even now."[2]

Both coaches believe there was a different attitude in the NBA at the time of their meeting in the 1975 Finals. They believe Bill Russell's success as a player-coach when he won back-to-back championships in 1968 and 1969 and the emergence of Lenny Wilkens, the NBA's all-time leader in coaching victories, were factors in the lack of media attention they received in 1975. Wilkens would go on to win the 1979 Finals with the Seattle Supersonics. In the 12-year span between Russell's '68 championship and Wilkens' '79 title, African-American coaches were involved in five NBA Finals, winning four of them. By comparison, the NFL was still 14 years away from hiring its first African-American coach, when Oakland Raiders owner Al Davis would hire Art Shell in 1989. In 1975, the Cleveland Indians hired Frank Robinson, making him the first African-American manager in Major League Baseball history.

With all the successes of African-American coaches pointing in the direction of improved opportunities for minority coaches, at one point in 1992 the NBA was composed of 72 percent African-American players with only two African-American coaches in the league. That prompted Attles to advise that "the NBA has to take a hard look at itself."[3] Recently, the statistics have improved as black head coaches in the NBA have hovered between 37 percent and 48 percent the past five seasons.

Attles finished a 14-year coaching career with a 557-518 record, including six postseason appearances. After his coaching career he took a position with the Warriors' front office, where he currently serves as Golden State's community relations ambassador.

Jones, like Attles, gives credit to Washington owner Abe Pollin for hiring him and recognizing his ability as a coach. Though Jones would lose his first Finals appearance, he would go on to coach the Boston Celtics from 1983 to 1988. In his five years with the Celtics he would win NBA championships in 1984 and 1986 and would win the Atlantic Division in all five seasons. He was enshrined in the Naismith Memorial Basketball Hall of Fame in 1989. He is the last African-American coach to win an NBA title and while Attles led a team made up primarily of African-American players, the 1986 Celtics are the last NBA champion to have a majority of white players on their roster and a majority in the starting lineup. In 1973, Jones hired future basketball head coach Bernie Bickerstaff even though Bickerstaff had never played or coached beyond the Division II college level. Years later, Bickerstaff paid Jones the biggest compliment during a *USA Today* interview. "Whatever I have in the NBA, I owe to K. C. Jones," Bickerstaff said. "I got respect from him immediately and our friendship never swayed from that. He taught me a lot of things that transcend just being a basketball coach."

More than 30 years later, with the NFL's two best teams led by African-American coaches, Attles and Jones received great recognition for a feat first accomplished in the NBA in 1975. The fact that there was so much media coverage such a long time from when it first happened speaks volumes for Attles. "It says very simply that for as far as we've come, we haven't come very far," Attles said to the *Oakland Tribune*. "It says we still have to continue to work to make the playing field a lot more level."[4]

Attles believes that, although the coaching successes of African-Americans have created a different impression on front offices, it would be dangerous to stop and think everything is fine now, just as some may have thought in 1975. "People are now saying, 'Whoa, I can't believe this,'" he said. "I say, don't stop here. We can't rest on laurels. Keep going. It goes to what Dr. King said about being judged on the content of their character."

Notes

1. Derrick Jackson, "A Bittersweet Celebration," *The Boston Globe*, January 24, 2007.

2. Carl Steward, "Attles, Jones Have Been Where Smith, Dungy Now Sit," *The Oakland Tribune*, January 30, 2007.

3. David Steele, "In Minority Hiring, NBA Has Always Led the Way," *Baltimore Sun*, January 28, 1997.

4. Steward, "Attles, Jones."

Peter Bynoe and Robert Johnson

First African-American Owners of a Professional Sports Franchise

by Jenny Brenden

The ownership position is the highest position on the organizational chart, the one from which leadership and organizational culture trickles down. It has been and continues to be a struggle to create equal opportunity for all people within the workforce, within corporate America, and within professional sports organizations. Women and people of color face a constant uphill battle in their quest to rise to the top of an organization.

Peter Bynoe took a big step in the right direction in 1989 when he became the first African-American owner of a professional sports franchise by being a part of the Denver Nuggets ownership group. The presence of an African-American in such a leadership position in sports was long overdue. African-Americans were integrated into the world of professional sports in 1947 with Jackie Robinson crossing the color barrier in MLB. The NBA followed suit three years later in 1950. African-Americans further integrated the NBA over time; the first African-American coach graced the sidelines in 1966. Thirteen years after Bynoe, Robert Johnson went one step further, becoming the first African-American majority owner of a franchise when he was awarded ownership of the Charlotte Bobcats expansion franchise.

Both of these men have been successful many times over in their lives. Beyond their ownership stories, Bynoe and Johnson have quite a bit in common. Although they have traversed different roads, their paths to success have been extremely similar. Both men are Ivy League-educated and both were successful very early in their careers. They each have created their own thriving companies as well as each serving on several boards and committees within their respective industries and communities.

Peter Bynoe loves making deals, and one of his many successful deals was the acquisition of the Denver Nuggets to become part of the first African-American ownership group of an NBA franchise.

Attaining bachelor's, master's and law degrees from Harvard

sounds like a formula for success, and that is exactly what it has proved to be for Peter Bynoe, who currently serves as a lawyer for the Chicago-based firm Piper, Marbury, Rudnick, and Wolfe.

Bynoe achieved success at a very young age. After working as an executive intern at Citibank for one year after completing his law degree, he became a vice president of James Lowery and Associates and five years later went on to be the founder of a business consulting firm.

In 1989 Bynoe put together his most renowned deal, leading a collective that included Bertram Lee, Arthur Ashe, and Ron Brown to become the first African-American ownership group of a NBA franchise. In his entire experience with the Denver Nuggets, he reports that the most exciting part was actually consummating the purchase after a tough deal creation and finalization process. Bynoe admits that he devoted six months of his life to negotiating the deal, putting together the finances and the group and actually gaining ownership of the asset. This was a $65 million acquisition of the Denver Nuggets. Bynoe helped with the restructuring of the organization and was very focused on turning a loser into a winner, both on the court and within the organization.

Bynoe was very aware that he was making history when he became the owner of the team, making a huge advance for minorities in sport management. He didn't, however, enjoy the fact that, in his three-year tenure as an owner, the media always focused on his history-making deal, as opposed to focusing on what he and his partners were trying to accomplish with the organization.

In his post-ownership career, after joining Piper, Marbury, Rudnick, and Wolfe, Bynoe continued to make deals in sports, gearing his interests toward negotiating stadium deals. He was a key player in the development of the new Comiskey Park for the Chicago White Sox, and he negotiated deals for stadiums for the Washington Redskins, San Francisco 49ers, and Milwaukee Brewers.

Bynoe believes sports are a great platform to improve race relations and promote the advancement of African-Americans, but his deal-making and leadership skills extend far outside the realm of professional sports. Within his firm, he manages clients such as Bank of America and the City of Chicago. Bynoe contributes to the community of Chicago by serving as the director of the Chicago Economic Club, chairman of the Chicago Planning Commission, director of the Illinois Sports Facilities Authority, and director of the UniRoyal Technology Corporation.

Peter Bynoe's business success has made him a very highly regarded individual in the city of Chicago, in the sport business industry, and in sports history. He will continue to hold that position of influence as long as there are deals to be made.

Much like his counterpart Bynoe, Robert Johnson is a phenomenal businessman who is in the business of making money. "Anything that has to do with money, I want to be in that business," he has said.[1] Although his entrepreneurial goals have always been focused on the bottom line, he realizes that the success he has had and his career path have put him in a position to be a role model and to contribute to changing social perceptions and creating opportunity for others.

Johnson was the first African-American in history to be the majority owner of a professional franchise. Although this was a big deal in the world of sports, Johnson's dealings go far beyond the sports realm. Johnson was a successful businessman prior to becoming the first African-American owner and he continues to be successful in his ventures after his NBA acquisition.

Being the grandson of a freed slave, born in Mississippi and then moving to Illinois as a child, Johnson is well aware of the past and where he came from, but he chooses to focus more on the future, particularly looking for his next great business venture. Johnson has been a first-mover in several different categories, the initial one of them being that he was the first child in his large family to attend and graduate from college. After graduating from the University of Illinois in 1968, he went on to receive his master's degree from Princeton in 1972.

In 1979, with $15,000 of his own money and $500,000 loaned by a venture capitalist, he founded Black Entertainment Television (BET). BET was original because it was the first network targeting an African-American audience, and it would eventually become the leader in providing music, entertainment, and news to its target audience. When the company went public in 1991, he was the first African-American owner of a company on the New York Stock Exchange (NYSE). In 2000, Johnson sold BET to Viacom for a $3 billion price tag, which was the biggest deal ever made with an African-American-owned company, and which also made Johnson America's first African-American billionaire. There is no plateau for Johnson; there is no endpoint in sight when it comes to his business ventures. He continues to move up and out, always looking for ideas to expand his already impressive portfolio. Even after the billion-dollar sale he made with Viacom, he did not show signs of slowing down in his business dealings. If anything, it only inspired him to go out and make another huge sale or create another brilliant venture.

Next, Johnson set his sights on owning a professional sports franchise. He attained this goal in December of 2002 when he bought the newest NBA expansion team for $300 million and became the first African-American majority owner of a professional franchise, the Charlotte Bobcats. There were other interested parties with whom Johnson was competing, but in the end, he beat out his competition, which was an ownership group that included Larry Bird and other former Boston Celtic executives. His optimistic attitude, passion for the game of basketball, and commitment to making the Bobcats a successful franchise were the attributes that made him a good fit as an owner. The selection committee that made the decision remarked that the fact that Johnson was African-American was not a determining factor. Although this was a positive byproduct of awarding the team to Johnson, he certainly had the goods and the business savvy to make this transaction successful. Also, Johnson was willing to be the liaison to connect the city of Charlotte with another NBA franchise. Many basketball fans were distraught at past management's decision to move the Hornets to New Orleans. Gaining the love and loyalty of the fans promised to be a challenge, but Johnson was up to the task. The Bobcats' inaugural year in the league was the 2004–05 season.

Johnson is currently the chairman of RJL companies, which employs several hundred African-Americans and aims to work with African-American-owned vendors. RJL has ventures in several different industries, such as real estate, and several businesses in the gaming, restaurant, and music industries. Johnson is also the biggest African-American hotelier in the country. Very recently he announced that he was going to start a bank called Urban Trust. The bank will be geared mainly toward African-Americans and other minorities, providing mortgages, investment opportunities, student loans, and other banking options. Johnson and Dwight Bush, the CEO of the bank, want to focus on increasing the minority home-ownership rate. Johnson has also been involved in convincing those who run universities and state pension funds to be more racially inclusive.

Johnson cherishes the fact that he has been a pioneer in the business world and in the world of sports. He is also very proud that through his business dealings he has been able to give back to the African-American community, as well as provide wealth, both monetarily and through opportunity, to African-Americans. He is someone to be looked up to by everyone. Ultimately, regardless of skin color, Johnson hopes to be remembered as an innovative businessman and a successful owner.

Notes

1. CBS News, "Second Act for Robert Johnson: Self-Made Billionaire Continues to Break Ground for African Americans," http://www.cbsnews.com/stories/2006/02/26/sunday/main1346193.shtml (accessed March 20, 2007).

5

NATIONAL HOCKEY LEAGUE: AFRICAN-AMERICAN PLAYERS IN A TRADITIONALLY WHITE SPORT

Introduction by Richard Lapchick

The smallest section in *100 Pioneers* is African-Americans in hockey. The same would be true if we included African-Canadians. While we can report on the first African-American owner, team president, general manager, coach, and players in the NBA and for most of those categories in the other professional sports covered in this book, there has never been an African-American owner, team president, general manager, or coach in the history of the National Hockey League (NHL).

Although the NHL did not integrate its players until 1958, it claims that it never had any restrictions. Strongly rooted in Canada, the NHL claims that it shared the Canadian tradition of racial fairness and open-mindedness and if there ever were black hockey players good enough to play in the NHL, they would get their chance. In the 1950s, Canada had a black population of less than one tenth of one percent. There was only one non-Canadian in the league in the mid-1960s. As the NHL opened up to non-Canadians, the influx was primarily from the United States, where few African-Americans played hockey, and later from Russia, Sweden, the Czech Republic, and other European countries.

Arthur Dorrington became the first black American to sign a pro hockey contract on November 15, 1950. He signed with a New York Rangers farm club in 1950 but decided to play for the Atlantic City Seagulls of Easter League instead. An injury ended his career and he never made it to the NHL.

Willie O'Ree was the first black player in 1958 when he joined the Boston Bruins. Ironically, the Bruins integrated before the Boston

Red Sox signed their first African-American player, Pumpsie Green. O'Ree, who was nicknamed "King of the Near Miss," played his first game for the Boston Bruins on January 18, 1958. The "near-miss" label referred to his supposed inability to score goals despite his great speed. While playing, O'Ree told the press, "They've called me the Jackie Robinson of hockey, and I'm aware of being the first, and of the responsibilities, but I'm also aware that there have not been, and are not many colored players able to play hockey, that there has never been the discrimination in this game there was in baseball, and that I didn't face any of the very real problems Robinson had to face."[1] O'Ree did face racial taunting and a serious hit in the mouth from a Chicago Black Hawks player. When a fight broke out, Chicago fans were reportedly shocked that a black man would fight back.

O'Ree's arrival hardly opened the floodgates for other players of color. Mike Marson, who joined the NHL in 1974, was the first of the contemporary black hockey players to enter the league after O'Ree's career. Marson did not have an easy time and recalled playing in Chicago, where he may have been the only black person among the 20,000 fans in the arena. "A lot of people have never been faced with that type of difficulty or awareness. They miss the whole concept of what it's like to be the minority in a situation like that and the psychological setup you have to put yourself through going out on the ice night after night and the opposing teams are calling you whatever, and the guys are spitting in your face and then you're dealing with whatever goes on in the dressing room with your team-mates."[2] According to the NHL, only 18 black players got to the league between 1958 and 1991. In the 2007 season, there were 14 African-American or African-Canadian NHL players.

Grant Fuhr is considered to be the most successful black player in NHL history. As goaltender on the Wayne Gretzky-led Edmonton Oilers of the late-1980s, Fuhr was in ninth place in all-time wins for goalies as of this writing. Fuhr was the first black to have his name on the Stanley Cup and was the first black inducted into the Hockey Hall of Fame, in 2003.

Like the Negro Leagues in baseball in the United States, there was a Colored Hockey League in Atlantic Canada. The written history from that period does not make it clear (and thus does not contradict the NHL claim that it never banned black players) whether the CHL was formed because of racial exclusion or if players felt, like other minorities in Canada, the necessity to have their own association for self-identity and pride.

There has never been a black NHL head coach, although Ted Nolan, who is of Native American descent, did coach in the NHL. John Paris from Windsor, Nova Scotia, was the first black head coach in professional hockey. He led the Atlanta Knights to the International Hockey League championship in 1994. Less than one percent of the assistant coaches in the NHL were African-American as recently as 2003.

Tony McKegney is considered to be the NHL's first African-Canadian star. McKegney had a 40-goal season in 1987–88 with the St. Louis Blues and scored nearly 350 NHL regular season and play-off goals. He said, "Sometimes I would wonder why I was trying to be a pro player when there were none to look up to. I'm proud of the fact that I was the first black to establish myself in the NHL. Now there are a few. I hope that helps youngsters who need someone to emulate."[3]

Like Major League Baseball's RBI program, the NHL has a Diversity Task Force. It is "designed to introduce children of diverse ethnic backgrounds to the game of hockey. The program's mission is to help and enable local youth hockey programs to teach hockey and other life skills to economically disadvantaged children, creating a fun experience for boys and girls of all age levels."[4] There are more than 30 programs in various stages of development that receive support from the National Hockey League.

According to the *2003 Racial and Gender Report Card*, while the NHL has never had a African-American or African-Canadian owner, the New York Islanders were the first professional sports team that had people of color as majority owners. Charles B. Wang of Shanghai, China, and Sanjay Kumar of Colombo, Sri Lanka, became the co-owners of the team.

African-Americans held just over two percent of the vice president positions in the 2003 season. In that season, 97 percent of senior administrators were white, while African-Americans, Latinos, and Asian-Americans each held one percent. Five percent of NHL League Office professional staff in 2003 were African-American.

The NHL League Office, in addition to trying to increase players of color in the league, has expressed a commitment to a more diversified league and team front offices.

Notes

1. William Humber, "An Historical Overview," special to NHL.com, February 1, 2001, http://www.nhl.com/blackhistory/history.html (accessed October 1, 2007).

2. Ibid.

3. Ibid.

4. Richard Lapchick, "2003 Racial and Gender Report Card" (Orlando, Florida: April 28, 2003).

William O'Ree

First Black Player in the NHL

by Jessica Bartter

Jackie Robinson's Major League Baseball debut was on the front pages of newspapers everywhere, but when Willie O'Ree joined the National Hockey League as the first black player, it barely was noticed in any papers. O'Ree wasn't interviewed for the nightly news or *The New York Times*. Perhaps it was because O'Ree was not born in the United States or perhaps because more than 10 years had passed since Robinson broke the color barrier in MLB. Either way, much of O'Ree's deserved attention and recognition came four decades later—four decades too late.

One of 13 children and the youngest of six boys, O'Ree was born into competition and excelled as a youngster in hockey, rugby, soccer, basketball, track, and baseball. Born in 1935, O'Ree was raised in Fredericton, New Brunswick, of hockey-loving Canada. He starting skating in nearby arenas, on frozen ponds, rivers, creeks, and in his backyard as early as age three, on the rink his father built with water from a garden hose. By the time he was five, he was playing in a league like most youngsters during the Canadian winters. As a high school student, O'Ree joined a junior team so skilled that many compared the team's level of play to that of an American collegiate team.

Although hockey was his first love, O'Ree attracted much attention for his baseball talent. At the age of 14, his Little League team won a trip to watch the Brooklyn Dodgers play. Not knowing that he would one day be called "the Jackie Robinson of hockey," O'Ree seized the opportunity to meet the pioneer player. He took a moment to talk to Robinson and told him of his love for baseball and hockey. Surprised, Robinson fired back, "There are no black kids in hockey,"[1] never knowing he was talking to the young man who would one day change all that. But his future in hockey would come later. In 1956, O'Ree was invited to Major League Baseball's Milwaukee Braves' training camp in Waycross, Georgia. O'Ree had no intention of pursuing a professional baseball career. He saw baseball more as a way to keep in shape during hockey's off-season. In addition, the unwelcoming segregated bathrooms and racial hatred he was subjected to in Georgia quickly drove him away from baseball and back to Canada.

In the same year, O'Ree suffered an injury that could have meant the end of his hockey career before it officially started. While playing in a junior league game, O'Ree was hit in the right eye with a puck. The impact shattered his retina and caused him to go legally blind in his right eye, thus forcing a position change. O'Ree had been a left wing but began to lose sight of the puck and starting getting checked more often after the injury. Keeping his loss of sight a secret, O'Ree moved himself to right wing and managed a successful career passing with his backhand.

O'Ree first turned pro when he signed with the Quebec Aces the following year. The Aces were a minor league team affiliated with the Boston Bruins of the National Hockey League. O'Ree signed for $3,500 with a $500 bonus and helped lead the team to their league championship in his first professional season. O'Ree's skill was quickly noticed by the Bruins. During the 1957–58 season, the Bruins' roster suffered injury after injury, forcing them to call up talent from their minor league team, a series of events which led to O'Ree's debut in the NHL. While O'Ree was preoccupied with how he would handle the puck in his first NHL game, players, executives, and officials fully recognized the significance of O'Ree's name on the roster, and many had nerves of their own about the repercussions of what was about to take place. One by one, each of O'Ree's teammates offered him encouragement before the game, but O'Ree's nerves related only to the realization of his NHL dream coming to fruition. O'Ree made history as the first black to play in an NHL game as his team won 3-0 over the eventual Stanley Cup Champions, the Montreal Canadians. O'Ree played in one more Bruin game before returning to the minors.

Although many had anticipated a tidal wave of reaction from NHL fans, O'Ree's presence barely caused a ripple. The historical and political significance seemed to be ignored or overlooked. Until, that is, O'Ree made a more permanent return to the NHL in 1961. During his second season, O'Ree played in 43 games, making his presence widely known and seemingly less widely accepted. Fans heckled him with hateful words and actions, throwing bananas, cotton balls, and once even a black cat onto the ice. Many opponents refused to ease his transition as well. He was subjected to more racial slurs and cheap shots than he thought he could handle. During his first game in Chicago, the 5-foot-10-inch, 180-pound O'Ree was blindsided by a 6-foot-4-inch, 235-pound opponent who maliciously hit him in the face with the butt end of his stick, knocking out two teeth, cutting his lip, and breaking his nose. As the opponent made racial remarks and laughed at O'Ree lying on the ice and gushing blood, O'Ree felt he had to retaliate. The ensuing brawl caused both benches to clear and led to both players being kicked out of the game. As O'Ree paced in the locker room for the remainder of the game, he made a deal with himself. He refused to be driven out of the NHL by hatred. O'Ree kept his focus on hockey. He denied his opponents' future instigations to fight over their racial insults and would defend himself only when under a physical, rather than verbal, attack. O'Ree also made a promise to himself to leave hockey only when his skills were no longer adequate, rejecting the possibility that he could not handle the racial bigotry.

Such hatred was new to the Canadian-born O'Ree, yet he handled it with professionalism and respect. In Fredericton, along the St. John River, O'Ree's family had shared the community with mostly white families. The family was prominent and accepted, and Canada did not suffer from the same racial segregation as the United States. O'Ree's only previous experience with racial injustices had come from Georgia when he attended the Braves' training camp.

After the 1961 season, the Boston Bruins traded O'Ree to the Montreal Canadians, where he was quickly relegated to their minor league team. The Bruins never told O'Ree of the trade or its reasoning. He first learned the bad news from a sportswriter calling to get his opinion on the trade. O'Ree's surprise quickly turned to disappointment. He suspected the Bruins had discovered his vision disability or perhaps they could not handle the ramifications of having the only black player in the NHL. Either way, it was the end of O'Ree's NHL career. He spent the remainder of his 21 seasons as a professional hockey player in the Western Hockey League (WHL). O'Ree spent six seasons with the Los Angeles Blades of the WHL before they folded in 1968. The San Diego Gulls quickly picked up O'Ree's contract, and he played on that team until his retirement in 1980.

O'Ree's love for San Diego had blossomed, and he decided to remain there after retiring from his professional hockey career. The two-time scoring champion of the WHL became a supervisor for a security company of the San Diego Chargers. He later worked security at the prestigious Hotel del Coronado in San Diego's harbor. O'Ree's passion for hockey remained, and in 1990 he began promotional work for the International Hockey League's San Diego Gulls. In 1996, the NHL enlisted O'Ree's help and support for an All-Star Game that would celebrate hockey's growing diversity. It was named the Willie O'Ree All-Star Game in honor of his pioneering career. The game allows selected boys and girls between the ages of 14 and 16 from NHL Diversity programs throughout North America the opportunity to interact with NHL players, attend an NHL game, and compete in an East vs. West game.

At a particularly special All-Star Game, on the 40th anniversary of O'Ree's NHL debut, he was announced as the Director of Youth Development for NHL Diversity. Since January 18, 1998, O'Ree has worked with the NHL's Diversity Program, supporting almost 40 inner-city programs as well as the All-Star Game, "Hockey is for Everyone" Month, the Hockey Scholarship Program, and the Equipment Bank. Since the program's inception, more than $500,000 worth of equipment has been donated by the general public and hockey manufacturers and delivered to at-risk youth through the Equipment Bank. Great strides have been made in the NHL since its development of a diversity task force. Since O'Ree skated through the barriers in 1958, more than 35 blacks have played in the NHL. O'Ree continues his work with the NHL Diversity Program at the age of 70 to ensure that the number keeps growing. As they do, so will his legacy and opportunities for others like Willie O'Ree.

Note

1. Glenn Hibdon, "Breaking Barriers: Prejudice Couldn't Keep O'Ree from the Sport He Always Loved," *Tulsa World*, February 17, 2006.

6

TENNIS AND GOLF: COUNTRY CLUBS' SLOW INTEGRATION OF GREAT SPORTS

Introduction by Richard Lapchick

Watching the Williams sisters pound tennis balls and Tiger Woods dominate golf, it is easy for some to forget that golf and tennis have long been considered country club sports. Many of those country clubs were completely segregated, which of course meant that African-American athletes were unlikely to participate. Where they did, they faced inferior facilities, equipment, and teachers. The pioneers who made it in these sports deserve so much credit for not only breaking through America's racial barriers but also our class barriers.

Tennis

African-Americans playing tennis faced the same barriers as golfers, although tennis had superstar champions in Althea Gibson and Arthur Ashe who smashed many barriers between the 1950s and 1970s. But Gibson was hardly the first great African-American female tennis player just as Ashe was not the first great male African-American player. As had happened in America with so many great African-American athletes, others were hidden from the bigger stage.

According to Howie Evans, the long-time columnist for the *Amsterdam News*, "Before Althea and Arthur Ashe, the greatest tennis players in the world were black, ignored and left out of the mainstream of the sport. In 1916, a group of the sport's top black players founded the American Tennis Association (ATA) in Washington, D.C. Ora Washington, Lucy Slowe, Isadore Ballard and Flora Lomax were the best women's tennis players in the world. Washington won the ATA women's singles eight of nine years beginning in 1929. On the men's side, great players like Talley Holmes, Edgar Brown,

Reginald Weir and Jimmy McDaniel year after year were turned down to play in major tournaments around the country. Eyre Saitch, who played with the Harlem Renaissance, was another great one."[1]

Leslie Allen became the first African-American woman to win a major tournament in the 1981 Avon championship, 23 years after Gibson's last win. In the 1990s Zina Garrison and Lori McNeil were mounting successes while the men's side was bare. Things were so bad that Congress investigated charges of discrimination in the United States Tennis Association's junior programs in 1988.

It took public pressure and media scrutiny about the lack of African-American players, coupled with the dramatic arrival of Venus and Serena Williams, to bring us to a point where we can now see hope. But the pioneers stand out like giants.

In 1956, Althea Gibson became the first African-American player to win a Grand Slam title, winning the French Open. Gibson was to win a great deal more, including Wimbledon in 1957 and 1958 and the U.S. Championship in 1957 and 1958. In 1957, she earned the No. 1 ranking in the world and was named the Associated Press Female Athlete of the Year in 1957 and 1958. She was the first African-American female to win the AP award.

Arthur Ashe was the first African-American member on the United States Davis Cup team, won the NCAA title, and had victories in the U.S. Open, the Australian Open, and Wimbledon. To this day, Arthur Ashe is the only African-American male to have won Wimbledon and the U.S. Open.

In 1996, Mal Washington became only the second African-American male to reach the Wimbledon final. He later became the first African-American man to represent the United States in Olympic tennis.

If the Williams sisters may be the real successors of Althea Gibson, James Blake may finally be a legitimate on-the-court successor for Arthur Ashe. Only history will tell that story. He reached a No. 4 ranking in 2006 and has nine career titles. This came after he suffered from a broken neck and a severe case of shingles in 2004, the same year his father died. He took up the game because Arthur Ashe was his role model.

The story of the Williams sisters, however, is more secure. Both have achieved number one in the world status. On September 11, 1999, Serena became the first African-American woman to claim a Grand Slam singles title since Althea Gibson in 1958. The next day, Serena and her sister Venus won the U.S. Open doubles title. Serena has won eight other Grand Slam singles and an Olympic gold medal as of this writing.

Older sister Venus has won six Grand Slam singles, six Grand Slam doubles, and two mixed doubles events as part of her collection of 47 career titles as of this writing.

One can argue that the Williams sisters are tennis' Tiger Woods or that Tiger Woods is golf's Williams sisters. But the sisters and Tiger Woods would readily agree that the pioneers written about in this section made their journeys possible.

Golf

Being a country club sport, golf was often seen as the property of the rich and famous. Augusta National may be America's most hallowed golf course. When Tiger Woods was still dreaming about playing in the Masters, it was annually taking place where African-Americans could not be members. Although he has now had historical victories on those links, at the time of this publication his wife and the mother of his child could not be a member.

Even when his fellow African-Americans could not play on many of America's courses, Dr. George Grant helped straighten out the games of all golfers. Himself an avid golfer, Dr. Grant was also an inventor and received a U.S. patent in December 1899 for an improved golf tee. In 1870, Dr. Grant was also another kind of pioneer, as he was one of the first two African-American graduates from Harvard Dental School where he later taught.

As in others sports, there were many fine African-American players in golf whose names rest mainly in the memories of those who knew them. In this chapter we will go into depth about the pioneering roles of Charlie Sifford, who became the first African-American PGA Tour member in 1962, and Lee Elder, who was the first African-American to play at the Masters Tournament at Augusta National in 1975.

Among those who never got the opportunity for fame and fortune were Teddy Rhodes, James Black, Bill Spiller, Nathaniel Starks, and Joe Roach.

In addition to Dr. Grant's invention of the wooden tee, the model of which is still in play more than 100 years later, African-

Americans' involvement in golf has included others like John Bartholomew of New Orleans, who built courses. Bartholomew knew whites who recognized his skills and sponsored his education to study architecture in New York. The reality of segregation was once again put in his face when he was not allowed to play on the course he designed in New Orleans.

John Shippen, Jr., was an African-American laborer who helped in the construction of the Shinnecock Hills Golf Course in New York. It was the site of the 2nd U.S. Open, and he was allowed to play in it, finishing in fifth place.

The PGA was all white and intended to keep it that way until public pressure forced open the PGA for Sifford. Prior to that, as in other sports, African-American players in golf formed their own association. They played out of the bigger public lens on courses that were less than magnificent and for purses that would not support them. But their love of the game kept them at it.

In 1925 a group of African-Americans interested in golf met in Washington, D.C., to form the United States Colored Golfers Association. A young golfer named Harry Jackson won the UGA-sponsored first National Colored Golf Championship at the Shady Rest Golf Club in Westfield, New Jersey. He beat Shippen, then past his prime in his fifties, by three strokes and claimed the $25 purse and recognition in the African-American community. The National, as it became known, became the big annual event for African-American golfers.

In the meanwhile, segregation meant that many of the African-Americans who wanted to play learned how as caddies. Fifteen years after the UGA was formed, estimates were that only 20 of the 5,000 private and public courses allowed African-Americans to play.

A year after Jackie Robinson broke sports' biggest color barrier, three African-American golfers filed a civil lawsuit to open the PGA: Theodore "Rags" Rhodes, Bill Spiller, and Madison Gunther. The PGA avoided the bullet at the moment and altered its tournaments to be "invitation only" in an effort to avert any legal and moral obligations to break the PGA's color barrier. However, Rhodes, Spiller, and Gunther had laid down the gauntlet. Charlie Sifford became the first African-American PGA Tour member in 1962.

One year after the *Brown vs. the Board of Education* decision, in a far less heralded case, the same Court ruled against Atlanta Georgia's "separate but equal" formula for public golf courses. It was November 7, 1955.

The case was called *Holmes vs. Atlanta*. The Holmes family was one of prominence in post-war Atlanta. Dr. Hamilton M. Holmes, Sr., had a family practice in Atlanta. His son, Oliver Wendell Holmes, was a respected minister. Alfred (Tup) Holmes was the outspoken sibling who served as union steward. The three joined with Charles T. Bell to make a stand against segregation. All four loved golf and they all belonged to black-owned and run Lincoln Country Club.

The group attempted to play on the all-white Bobby Jones Golf Course, one of seven public courses in Atlanta. The only African-Americans on Bobby Jones at that time were the caddies.

Charles Bell said, "The head pro told us straight out we couldn't play, that they didn't allow no niggers at Bobby Jones."[2] Two years later they filed the lawsuit that sought to desegregate public golf courses and parks in the city. They lost in the U.S. District Court and again in appeals court.

The NAACP sent the chief counsel of its legal defense team, a promising lawyer named Thurgood Marshall, to present its case to the U.S. Supreme Court. This time they won. The Supreme Court ruled in favor of the African-American golfers.

Whites' resistance was strong as most whites were hardly ready. Georgia Governor Marvin Griffin simply said, "Co-mingling of the races in Georgia state parks and recreation areas will not be tolerated."[3] Atlanta's then-mayor William B. Hartsfield urged the city to sell its courses to individuals and make them open to private membership only.

However, Atlanta's public courses were officially desegregated without incident. "It's gratifying to know that I participated in something so meaningful,"[4] said Bell.

The PGA was also tough in its fight. In 1990, the story about the PGA Championship at Shoal Creek in Birmingham, Alabama, grabbed the headlines when it was revealed that Shoal Creek did not allow African-American members. Investigations by the media revealed that 17 of the 39 PGA Tour events in 1990 were scheduled for segregated clubs. Shoal Creek founder Hal Thompson said the club was private and would not change; the PGA backed him and the other 16 courses. That changed quickly when IBM, Toyota, Anheuser-Busch, and Delta withdrew their PGA Tour sponsorships. Further media reports showed many private clubs that had no Tour connections excluded African-Americans and Jews. The withdrawal of corporate support lifted the veil and started to open up golf forever. But for all the years in between, African-American golfers who won and played on the Tour did so in the face of mass resistance.

Sifford won the Long Beach Open in 1957 and the Alameda Open in 1960, but the PGA made them "unofficial" events. Pete Brown became the first African-American golfer to win an official PGA event in the 1964 Waco Open. Lee Elder had moderate successes in the 1970s and 1980s, and Calvin Peete and Jim Thorpe had the same in the 1980s and 1990s. Although you could call that progress, victories for African-American golfers had been elusive until Tiger Woods changed everything. And even his wins are solitary, as a decade after his first Masters victory, there is not another African-American golfer on the PGA Tour.

Notes

1. Howie Evans, "Althea Gibson Was a Role Model for the Ages," *New York Amsterdam News*, October 8, 2003.

2. Holmes v. Atlanta ruled, The African American Registry, http://www.aaregistry.com/african_american_history/1392/Homes_v_Atlanta_ruled (accessed October 1, 2007).

3. Ibid.

4. Ibid.

Althea Gibson

First African-American to Win Wimbledon

by Richard Lapchick

We honored Arthur Ashe when I was director of Northeastern University's Center for the Study of Sport in Society. After tennis luminary Bud Collins rightly extolled all of Arthur's accomplishments and virtues, the first thing Arthur Ashe said in his acceptance speech was, "I would not have had the chance to do what I have been able to do if Althea Gibson had not blazed the way for me."

This daughter of a sharecropper titled her autobiography *I Always Wanted to Be Somebody*. By the time the book was released in 1958, she definitely *was* somebody. It came out two years after she won her first Grand Slam event with victories in both the singles and doubles in the French Championship. Her doubles partner was Angela Buxton, who was Jewish. Buxton and Gibson had confronted anti-Semitism and racism, respectively. They repeated their doubles victory at Wimbledon. Buxton was the first Jewish champion at Wimbledon and Gibson was the first African-American champion. An English newspaper reported their victory at Wimbledon under the headline "Minorities Win."

Gibson was to win a great deal more, including Wimbledon in 1957 and 1958 and the U.S. Championship in 1957 and 1958. In 1957 she earned the No. 1 ranking in the world and was named the Associated Press Female Athlete of the Year in 1957 and 1958. She was the first African-American female to win the AP award.

She suddenly retired from amateur tennis in 1958 in her prime, at age 31. There was no prize money and were no endorsement deals for women in that era. Male tennis players had to give up their amateur status, but there was no pro tour for women, so Gibson could earn money only in exhibition matches.

Gibson was driven to succeed and became an historical figure in and out of sport. Having grown up in an impoverished Harlem, Althea Gibson would change tennis. She became the first African-American tennis star to be hailed internationally and seemed to be opening the door during an era when sexism and racism were abundant. The door was slow to open wider for others. The successes of

Serena and Venus Williams, while so important, have been but faint knocks on the door at the elite level of tennis.

Although hopes were high when Gibson won at Wimbledon, it took 42 years for a repeat by an African-American woman. Other women of color to win that coveted crown were Australian Yvonne Goolagong Cawley (1971 and 1980), Maria Bueno (1959, 1960, and 1964) and Conchita Martinez (1994).

Gibson was born in 1927 in Silver, South Carolina. In 1930, her family moved to Harlem in New York City, where they lived on welfare for most of her youth. Gibson often skipped school and ran away from home.

Developing her early skills through table tennis in public recreation parks, she won Police Athletic Leagues and Parks Department-sponsored tournaments. Musician Buddy Walker gave her the first opportunity to play tennis and helped her to become a member of the Harlem Cosmopolitan Tennis Club, a group of all African-American athletes. In 1942, Althea Gibson played and won her first tournament, which was sponsored by the American Tennis Association (ATA). Later, Gibson was introduced to a physician from Lynchburg, Virginia, Dr. Walter Johnson. He mentored her and gave her the opportunity to play more and better tennis. Dr. Johnson would later be an influential person in the life of Arthur Ashe. In 1946, Gibson decided to further pursue her tennis career and moved to Wilmington, North Carolina, to work under Dr. Hubert A. Eaton while attending high school in North Carolina. Honing her great skills through steady practice, Gibson won her first of 10 straight ATA National Championships in 1947.

Her tennis career continued to rise fast while she was a student at Florida A&M University in Tallahassee, from which she graduated in 1953.

Tennis was virtually a 100 percent segregated sport. In 1949, Gibson competed against white tennis players for the first time. Alice Marble, a dominant women's tennis champion in the 1930s, wrote an editorial for the July 1950 edition of *American Lawn Tennis Magazine*. Marble noted, "Miss Gibson is over a very cunningly wrought barrel, and I can only hope to loosen a few of its staves with one lone opinion. If tennis is a game for ladies and gentlemen, it's also time we acted a little more like gentlepeople and less like sanctimonious hypocrites. . . . If Althea Gibson represents a challenge to the present crop of women players, it's only fair that they should meet that challenge on the courts." Marble further stated that if Gibson were not given the opportunity to compete, "then there is an ineradicable mark against a game to which I have devoted most of my life, and I would be bitterly ashamed." Gibson played in the U.S. Championships in 1950 for the first time.

In 1953, Gibson competed on a goodwill tennis tour to Southeast Asia sponsored by the U.S. State Department. When she returned from the tour, the big victories piled up and she won the 1956 French Championship.

Althea Gibson won 56 singles and doubles titles during her amateur career in the 1950s and won 10 major titles after the 1956 French Championship. She was inducted into the International Tennis Hall of Fame, the International Women's Sports Hall of Fame, the International Scholar-Athletes Hall of Fame, and many others.

After her retirement from amateur tennis, she released a record album, *Althea Gibson Sings*, and later appeared in the film, *The Horse Soldiers*. Her "pro" tennis career included her tour with the Harlem Globetrotters playing exhibition tennis, for which she reportedly made $100,000 in matches before the Globetrotters games. In 1964, Gibson began playing professional golf on the Ladies Professional Golf Association tour.

She married Will Durben. In 1971, Gibson again tried to play professional tennis but was far past her prime at the age of 44 and could not compete with many of the younger players.

She became a tennis professional and taught instead. In 1975, Gibson was named the manager of the East Orange, New Jersey, Department of Recreation and held the position for 10 years. She was also the New Jersey State Commissioner of Athletics from 1975 to 1985. Althea Gibson then served on the State's Athletics Control Board until 1988 and the Governor's Council on Physical Fitness until 1992 when she retired.

Althea Gibson began experiencing health problems in the 1990s and suffered from a stroke in 1992. She also had two cerebral aneurysms. These health problems caused a significant financial burden on her, and she became a recluse rarely seeing people or being seen in public. Again living on welfare, Gibson was unable to pay for her medical or living costs. Eventually Gibson called her old doubles partner, Angela Buxton, and told her she had contemplated suicide. Without informing Gibson, Buxton arranged for a letter requesting support to appear in a tennis magazine. Nearly $1 million poured in from around the world.

I attended the funerals of both Arthur Ashe and Althea Gibson. Arthur, who hailed her as his champion and role model, drew thousands from across the globe to his funeral in Richmond. After nearly a decade of Gibson's being a recluse, hundreds came but did not quite fill the Trinity St. Phillip Cathedral in Newark, New Jersey, for her services.

Alan Schwartz, president of the United States Tennis Association, told those gathered that, "She simply changed the landscape of tennis. . . . Gibson was no less a trailblazer than baseball great Jackie Robinson or tennis champion Arthur Ashe, although she received less recognition for her accomplishments. Arthur Ashe's job was not easy, but if he had to climb a hill, Althea Gibson had to climb a mountain. She was the original breakthrough person."[1]

Zina Garrison was the next African-American woman after Gibson to reach the finals of Wimbledon, 32 years later, when she played Martina Navratilova in 1990. Garrison eulogized that Gibson was her inspiration: "Althea used to say she wanted me to be the one who broke her barrier, to take the burden off of her (as the only black woman to have won Wimbledon). She showed me the stall where she dressed and where she popped the champagne when she won. She knew she opened the door for all of us, and she was so excited about all the women who followed her."[2]

Venus Williams released a statement after Gibson passed away saying she had been a role model for her tennis career. "I am grateful to Althea Gibson for having the strength and courage to break through the racial barriers in tennis. Althea Gibson was the first African-American woman to rank number one and win Wimbledon, and I am honored to have followed in such great footsteps."[3]

Her legacy is being carried on by the Althea Gibson Foundation, which was founded "for the primary purpose of identifying, encouraging and providing financial support for urban youth who wish to develop their skills and talents in the sports of tennis or golf, and have decided to pursue a career as a student-athlete at the post-secondary level. . . . The Foundation will continue her work to encourage young people to utilize sports to help improve upon the social condition of urban America and to promote global unity."[4]

Gibson once said, "I hope that I have accomplished just one thing: that I have been a credit to tennis and my country."[5] She was a credit to all of humanity.

Notes

1. Alan Schwartz, Eulogy, Funeral of Althea Gibson, Trinity St. Phillip Cathedral, Newark, New Jersey, http://qp1.quepasa.com/english/news/sports/197008.html (accessed October 2, 2007).

2. Zina Garrison, Eulogy, Funeral of Althea Gibson, Trinity St. Phillip Cathedral, Newark, New Jersey, http://qp1.quepasa.com/english/news/sports/197008.html, (accessed October 2, 2007).

3. Venus Williams, "Tributes Pour in for Tennis Legend Althea Gibson, Dead at 76," September 29, 2003, http://qp1.quepasa.com/english/news/sports/197008.html (accessed October 2, 2007).

4. Althea Gibson Foundation, http://www.altheagibson.com/AGFoundation.htm

5. Jone Johnson Lewis, "Althea Gibson Quotes," About.com: Women's History, http://womenshistory.about.com/od/quotes/a/althea_gibson.htm (accessed October 2, 2007).

Arthur Ashe

First African-American Male to Win Wimbledon and the U.S. Open

by Richard Lapchick

That day in Richmond stays with me more than a decade later. A rainbow of 11,000 people gathered to pay tribute to Arthur Ashe in the most integrated scene I had ever witnessed. Now, in a post-September 11th era when we have redefined the word *hero* in sports to take on the meaning of an athlete who has served his community, Arthur Ashe remains a giant. The people came to Richmond from across the nation and around the world, knowing that they were saying farewell to a genuine hero.

Arthur was born in Richmond, not far from where he was buried. It was, of course, a segregated city during his childhood. When he started playing tennis at age seven, Arthur was so small that he was considered "skinny as a straw." In 1953, Ashe met Coach Ronald Charity, who worked with Arthur on his game. Coach Charity arranged for Ashe to spend the summer in Lynchburg practicing under Althea Gibson's coach, Dr. Walter Johnson. Dr. Johnson became Ashe's mentor. In 1960, Ashe decided that he had to get away from the segregation in Richmond and moved to St. Louis for his senior year of high school. Arthur continued playing tennis and his star power was recognized by UCLA as he excelled on the court. He won a National Championship at UCLA and earned a bachelor's degree in business administration.

Ashe gave up two years in his prime by serving as a 1st lieutenant in the United States Army from 1966 until 1968. Things other than being a tennis champion were taking more of Arthur's time after he won the U.S. Open in 1968. While on a goodwill tour in Africa in 1971, Ashe met the young, charismatic, and talented African player, Yannick Noah. Ashe helped him go to France to develop his tennis game. He did that and more, including winning the French Open. Later, Noah's son, Joachim, would lead the University of Florida to two consecutive NCAA basketball titles in 2006 and 2007.

In the mid-1970s Arthur Ashe pleased his loyal fans by returning his own focus back to the tennis world. Ashe regained the number-one-in-the-world ranking after he won Wimbledon by defeating Jimmy Connors. Ashe was the first in 1968 and remains the only African-American to ever hold that ranking.

I first got to know Arthur Ashe, as an opponent, in the early 1970s, when he was competing in South Africa, believing that this was the way to break down the structure of the apartheid government. I had become the American leader of a coalition of more than 50 groups that had come together to boycott South African sport. Arthur Ashe was our most visible and striking opponent. He was a great African-American tennis player maintaining that the boycott was wrong, saying that competing and being an example of the result of integration was the way to bring about change in apartheid South Africa.

In 1977, we were holding our first protest against South African tennis players at the United States Open. Dick Schaap, the legendary sportscaster, came over to tell me that Arthur Ashe was going to address the small band of protestors that had gathered. I was more than anxious, because I believed that if he expressed his opposition to those demonstrating, some might change their minds and leave.

After all, by that time he had played as the first African-American member on the 1963 United States Davis Cup team, received the Johnston Award in 1964 as the American tennis player who demonstrated good sportsmanship and character and helped the growth of the sport, and had the NCAA title, as well as victories in the U.S. Open, the Australian Open (1970), and Wimbledon. To this day, Arthur Ashe is the only African-American male to win both Wimbledon and the U.S. Open. As he approached the crowd, there is no doubt that he *was* the man.

Arthur came out and, much to my surprise, told the crowd that he had been wrong all those years. He had realized his error after trying to purchase tickets for some young Africans for a tennis match in South Africa. He was told to go to an "Africans only" ticket counter. Arthur then knew the boycott was the only way. Two things happened that day. First, the boycott got an enormous boost by being joined by one of the most prominent African-American athletes in the United States. Second, I saw the enormous courage of Arthur Ashe up close.

I had always thought his going to South Africa was based on principle and never doubted that he believed he was doing the right thing. I knew he was a man with such commitment and passion. That day in 1997, he taught me the power of being able to say that you have been wrong and changing direction. Arthur was with us when we protested the South African Davis Cup Team one year later. It was an event that would be described as the turning point of America's history of cooperating with South Africa in sports. Finally, we began to join the world in isolating South Africa. Arthur never stopped protesting injustice in America, South Africa, Haiti, or anywhere else people were oppressed.

I will always remember holding a different opinion about John McEnroe than the public had as a result of an action by Arthur and McEnroe's response to it. McEnroe had just agreed to play tennis in Bophuthatswana, a South African "homeland" that South Africa was using to try to mislead the world about the nature of apartheid by proclaiming these "homelands" as free when they remained part of South Africa. He was to receive a virtually unheard-of payday of $1 million. Former U.S. Ambassador Franklin Williams and I met with McEnroe's father, and Arthur met with John. Within 24 hours John McEnroe cancelled his $1 million match and became the first prominent white athlete to reject the apartheid government's gold.

I was on an ESPN special, *Seasons of Change*, in 2003. It marked the then-upcoming 40th anniversary of the March on Washington. Among those on the roundtable with me were Coach John Thompson, Reverend Jesse Jackson, NFL Hall of Famer Bobby Mitchell, Tennessee Titan Eddie George, and Michael Jordan Brand creator, Howard White. Host John Saunders kept coming back to the question of whether or not athletes, especially African-American athletes, have the responsibility to speak out on social issues.

I could not get Arthur Ashe out of my mind as so many of us there bemoaned the inactivity of today's pro athletes. He would have been speaking out on President Bush's assault on affirmative action, teaching younger athletes to understand what it has done for women and people of color in our nation. You couldn't listen to Arthur and not think, if he challenged your beliefs. The power of changing direction and changing your opinion was part of his life.

He would have been very public about the Bush Commission on Athletic Opportunity's pending moves to soften the teeth of Title IX. He would not want to lose the opportunity for his daughter,

Camera, to be an athlete if that is what she would choose. He would tell us that the Commission on Athletic Opportunity is, in fact, a commission designed to remove athletic opportunity from women under the guise of creating more chances for male student-athletes.

A product of a time when there were tennis courts on which he could not play, Arthur would have been up there informing us why Augusta National cannot continue to exclude women. He knew that sport is such an important symbol in our nation and the world that what we do in our "private lives" that becomes public, such as holding the Masters at this private club, is unacceptable if we exclude anyone.

I don't know if Arthur thought he could keep his having AIDS as a private matter until the end. He did not have the chance to make such a decision when *USA Today* broke the story in 1992. Ashe received the news that he was HIV positive during his third brain surgery. He had most likely contracted the virus during a transfusion in his second surgery. On April 8, 1992, Arthur Ashe announced that he was HIV positive. Arthur was simply Arthur when he seized the reality of having the disease to help educate the American people that HIV and AIDS were not restricted to gays and intravenous drugs users. He founded the Arthur Ashe Foundation for the Defeat of AIDS. On World AIDS Day in December 1992, Ashe spoke at the United Nations General Assembly about the need for further research and funding toward AIDS. Always educating, always shedding light on the hard issues. There would be more American athletes speaking out today if Arthur was still here to guide them, to urge them to stand up.

Ashe retired from tennis in 1980 with a record of 818-260. He had won 51 titles. Ashe served as a commentator for HBO Sports and ABC Sports, and as a columnist for *The Washington Post*. In 1985, Ashe was arrested in the midst of an anti-apartheid protest.

Ashe showed his intellectual side as the author of a three-volume history of African-American athletes titled *A Hard Road to Glory*, which was published in 1988 and eventually adapted to television, winning an Emmy. Ever the activist, he founded several organizations including the Safe Passage Program, the National Junior Tennis League, and the Athlete Career Connection. In 1991, Ashe, along with 30 other African-American delegates, returned to

South Africa to monitor the political changes being made in the country where he once was denied entrance. He was elected into the International Tennis Hall of Fame in 1985.

I appeared on programs with Arthur for 15 years, learning lessons of life from my friend. I knew no person who better understood than Arthur Ashe that all battles for human rights are fought on the same plane. If I ever got discouraged, I thought of his determination and courage to engage both global and personal battles of heroic proportions. I thought of him as a husband and father, often on the road, missing his wife, Jeanne Moutoussamy, and daughter, Camera. He was a man unafraid to talk of the gentle love he had for his family.

One of the best days of my life was a little bit sad. On May 10, 1994, I was a guest of Nelson Mandela at his inauguration in Pretoria, South Africa. It was a great day that showed that anything and everything is possible if we work to end oppression and racism. The sadness came because Arthur, who had worked so hard for this moment to happen, was not with us. I looked up to the bright African sky, nodding to Arthur, because his life and his work had hastened the day that apartheid was smashed and democracy launched under President Mandela.

Athletes today should read about Arthur because they would realize that their voices could be amplified and their lives inspired by that of Arthur Ashe.

I have been fortunate to receive some wonderful awards. The two I treasure most are the Arthur Ashe Voice of Conscience Award in 1997 presented by Jeanne (the same year that the U.S. Tennis Association named its stadium the Arthur Ashe Stadium) and one in 1999 when I was in inducted into the Commonwealth Nations Sports Hall of Fame. In its twentieth year, these nations created a humanitarian category. I was one of the first three inductees. The others were Nelson Mandela and Arthur Ashe. His legend and inspiration continue unabated.

Charlie Sifford

First African-American Golfer on the PGA Tour

by Jessica Bartter

Although Charlie Sifford's Hall of Fame golf career did not make him millions of dollars like those of many of his professional counterparts, his impact on golf made his life's journey rich. Sifford blazed a trail that saw him start as a caddie and end, almost 70 years later, with a World Golf Hall of Fame induction.

Golf in the United States has often been considered a sport as white as the ball used to play it, largely rooted in its "members only" club houses and golf courses owned and operated largely by whites. There have always been minority-run courses and tournaments in which minorities shot par as often as whites, but the Professional Golfers Association (PGA) of America and the PGA Tour refused to recognize such tournaments and talented players simply because of skin color. That mentality was the unapologetic bottom line until a determined and talented golfer named Charles Sifford set himself on the path for change.

Born and raised in Charlotte, North Carolina, Sifford began working as a caddie when he was just 13. At this age, Sifford could already shoot par. Even after becoming an experienced and knowledgeable caddie, Sifford still made less than $1.00 a day, most of which he gave to his mother. The passion he had for golf was easy to see, and his talent was hard to ignore. But to dream of a professional golfing career was just that, a dream, for someone who looked like Sifford. The professional opportunities for people of color were minimal during Sifford's adolescence and nonexistent in the PGA. The PGA had an article in its bylaws stating that it was "for members of the Caucasian race," thereby automatically denying Sifford and other minorities the opportunity to compete on the best platform afforded to golfers and the opportunity to earn tournament purses that could have made Sifford millions of dollars in his prime. Instead, Sifford resorted to working as a caddie, hustling players on different courses during his travels and playing with the United Golfer's Association (UGA). The UGA was a league for African-

Americans that offered professional golf tournaments during the era of racial segregation.

While golfing with the UGA, Sifford met and played with world heavyweight boxing champion Joe Louis and Major League Baseball's (MLB) first African-American, Jackie Robinson, among other great African-American athletes. Sifford spoke with Robinson about his hope to break the color barrier of the PGA and received firsthand advice from the legend himself, shortly after he had done the same thing for MLB in 1947. Robinson warned Sifford of the obstacles but encouraged him to take the challenge as long as he wasn't a quitter. Then and there, Sifford made up his mind. He was determined to show that African-Americans could play golf at the highest level, and that meant on the PGA Tour.

The battle proved to be as difficult as Robinson had warned when Sifford softly knocked at the door of the PGA. He first attempted to qualify for a PGA Tour event in 1952 at the Phoenix Open. He used an invitation offered to Joe Louis but was unsuccessful in being allowed to play, instead being subjected to threats and racial abuse. While making noise on behalf of African-Americans, Sifford competed the only way he knew how, with the UGA. He spent his best years with the UGA and won the National Negro Open five years in a row, from 1952 to 1956. While Sifford was working as a private golf instructor for Billy Eckstein, Eckstein paid for Sifford and his friend Teddy Rhodes to enter the 1955 Canadian Open. The Open was Sifford's first professional tournament outside of the UGA. Remarkably, Sifford shot a course record 63, edging out Arnold Palmer's 64. A lifelong friendship between Sifford and Palmer started on that course and was the ultimate reinforcement of Sifford's lifetime commitment to golf.

In 1957, Sifford won the Long Beach Open. Although it was co-sponsored by the PGA and Sifford beat some well-known white players, the tournament was not officially sanctioned by the PGA. Therefore, Sifford did not earn an invitation to the Masters like a white winner probably would have. With the help of columnists and the California attorney general, Sifford kept the pressure on the PGA. In 1960, the PGA dropped its "Caucasian only" membership clause. At the age of 39, Sifford was finally awarded a player's card. His first PGA invitation came from Greensboro, North Carolina.

Despite the fact that playing his first PGA event in the South frightened him, the encouragement and support he received from his wife drove him to accept the invitation. Sifford led the field the first day with a 68, but pressures from the crowd caused his performance to suffer for the remainder of the tournament.

Sifford had passed his prime, but his determination never floundered. In 1967, he became the first African-American to win a PGA event. He shot a 64 in the final round to secure the Greater Hartford Open Invitational title. Two years later, at the age of 46, Sifford won another official PGA event, the Los Angeles Open. In 1975, Sifford won the Senior PGA Championship and became a member of the Champions Tour where he also won the Suntree Classic.

When Sifford first started to dream of being a professional golfer, he set five very ambitious goals for himself. He wanted to play in the PGA, win a tournament, play in the National Open, play in the Masters, and get inducted into the Hall of Fame. Sifford considered 1947–1960 his best playing years, and despite the fact that he did not receive his PGA player's card until after that time, he managed to accomplish four of his five goals. The only one he did not achieve was a Masters' appearance, although he believes he earned the right. Sifford has no regrets, because his World Golf Hall of Fame induction in 2004 completed his career vision. The induction, which made him the first African-American among the 100 existing hall-of-famers, validated his golfing ability in addition to honoring the first African-American to play on the PGA Tour and the first to win a PGA event. Seeing other African-Americans succeed on the tour makes all his pain and sacrifice worthwhile. In part because of Sifford's perseverance against segregation, Lee Elder became the first African-American to be invited to play in the Masters in 1975. In that same year, Tiger Woods was born and has since dominated the Masters Tournament.

It puts a smile on Sifford's face to see such opportunities for minorities, but he knows that true privilege lies in the will to achieve. If only every child could dream as big as Charlie Sifford did.

Lee Elder

First African-American to Play in the Masters

by Jessica Bartter

In 1975, it had been 29 years since Kenny Washington and Woody Strode integrated the National Football League, 28 years since Jackie Robinson and Larry Doby integrated Major League Baseball, and 25 years since Nat "Sweetwater" Clifton, Chuck Cooper, and Earl Lloyd integrated the National Basketball Association. In each case, their historic achievements could not have been possible without help from others. Dan Reeves signed Washington, Branch Rickey signed Robinson, and Joe Lapchick signed Clifton. No one with sufficient power had spoken out enough against the injustices of country club practices, which had allowed the game of golf to remain segregated. In 1962, Charlie Sifford became the first African-American to play on the Professional Golfers' Association (PGA) of America Tour. But golf remained a game of tradition and invitation-only events. The officials of the most prestigious tournament, the Masters, excluded whomever they wished, especially African-Americans. The Masters has been held at the Augusta National Golf Course in Georgia since 1934 and was kept all white for more than 40 years, until a man named Lee Elder stepped up to the tee box for the first time, leading the way for change.

Elder was introduced to golf as a nine-year-old when he began caddying to earn money for food. His love for golf grew as a teenager when he got a job as a caddy for Alvin C. Thompson. Although Thompson had the skills to succeed on the PGA Tour, the possible earnings were not nearly as high as the amounts he earned challenging golfers on courses across the country. As a black man, Elder was not permitted in many of the country clubs where he caddied, so he negotiated competitions for Thompson with other caddies out in the caddyshack. Often, Thompson would bet that he and his caddy could beat any two golfers at a club, and they usually did. Elder picked up many pointers from Thompson and could drive the ball a long way. He even snuck onto the back holes of a segregated course in Dallas, Texas, where he caddied, to practice with clubs he had borrowed from a course manager. Despite Elder's ability to drive long distances, he believed he could make more money as a caddy than as a golfer with the United Golf Association, the all-black golf tour.

Elder later joined the Army where he earned acclaim for his golf skills. In 1961, in his late 20s, Elder finally joined the United Golf Association and dominated the tour, making a name for himself. Six years later, Elder joined the PGA to compete on the tour. Pete Brown and Charlie Sifford had won on the tour, yet neither were invited or voted by past champions to play in the most prestigious golf event, the Masters. Presumably, the lack of opportunities was upholding the long-standing tradition of whites only at Augusta National. Finally in 1972, the Masters Tournament began automatically inviting all PGA Tour winners, opening the door for a new face in the game of golf.

Ironically, Elder was able to integrate golf in South Africa, a country built on apartheid, before doing so in the United States. In 1971, Elder was invited to play at the South African PGA Tournament, the first integrated tournament in South Africa. Although Elder wanted to make history, he wanted to make sure that it meant more than just a golf game. Elder agreed to play in South Africa only after being assured that the gallery would be integrated and that he and his wife would be permitted to stay and go wherever they chose. Elder was not content with the social change he instigated in South Africa and was intent on seeing the same in the United States. And change he saw on April 21, 1974, when he sank an 18-foot putt on the fourth hole of a sudden death playoff to win the Monsanto Open in Pensacola, Florida, qualifying him for the Masters, the first African-American to do so. Elder was 40 years old in his first Masters Tournament when he shot a 74 and 78 on opening day, missing the cut by five shots. Yet, Elder won with the significance of the event. Elder made history just by walking onto the course in 1975. He returned to the Masters Tournament again in 1977 and every year until 1983. During that time, he made the cut twice. Although he never walked off the course with the prized green jacket, Elder carved a path for others to follow. At the time, Augusta National Golf Club had no members of color and did not for more than a decade following Elder's inaugural competition. Elder also became the first African-American to golf with the American team in the Ryder Cup in 1984. The Ryder Cup matches up the best American golfers with those of Europe in a competition that has been played every year since 1927.

Elder left the PGA Tour and in 1984 joined the Senior Tour where he dominated for years. Elder won the Suntree Senior Classic and the Hilton Head Seniors International in 1984; the Denver Post Championship, the Merrill Lynch/Golf Digest Commemorative, the Digital Seniors Classic, and the Citizens Union Senior Golf Classic in 1985; the Merrill Lynch/Golf Digest Commemorative in 1986; and the Gus Machado Classic in 1988.

Elder has been witness to too many injustices in his lifetime and does his best to take a stand whenever possible. He has spoken out against the lack of opportunities for women and minorities in golf. The Lee Elder National Junior Golf Program was started to promote the game to minority youth. The junior program teaches basic instructions and golf etiquette to youth who most likely would not otherwise have the opportunity to play golf. Elder remains troubled by the lack of people of color playing golf. Indeed, a lack of awareness and opportunity in golf for inner-city children keeps the percentage of those young people involved disturbingly low. Elder's program was developed to help lead the way and to increase the number of African-Americans teeing up on courses across the country. Lee Elder fought tirelessly to earn his spot in golf's history. The path he paved was long overdue, but this pioneer's best reward is to see it followed over and over.

7

BOXING:
CHAMPIONS WHO SET THE WORLD STAGE

Introduction by Richard Lapchick

The sport of boxing, perhaps more than any other, has been identified with various racial and ethnic groups seeing the sport as a way out of poverty and a way to fame and riches. There have been great Jewish, Italian, Irish, and Latino boxers.

However, for many, the issue of race and boxing, particularly when it comes to whites and African-Americans, has been a dominant theme in boxing. It was usually not a pretty sight when it became black vs. white. The term "great white hope" came from boxing. The "hopes" of the race for white people were there at the turn of the century trying to rid white America of whatever evils they thought Jack Johnson had introduced to threaten American society. Jim Jeffries, a former champion, carried the hope of many white Americans into the ring against Johnson, who won easily. As African-Americans celebrated across America, race riots broke out.

Sometimes it twisted the other way, as when Joe Louis represented the nation against Max Schmeling, who hailed from Hitler's Germany. Their two fights became international social events because of their racial and ideological implications. Schmeling won the first bout in New York, defeating a previously unbeaten Joe Louis in 1936. At that point, most of Louis' followers were African-American. Louis became the champ in 1937 and took on Schmeling at Yankee Stadium in 1938. With the American entry into the war on everyone's mind, Louis represented all Americans and became a hero when he won by a TKO in the first round.

Sometimes fights between black and white boxers were used for marketing hype more than for racial politics. Gerry Cooney had fights against Ken Norton, Leon Spinks, George Foreman, and Larry

Holmes. The Holmes fight came after Cooney beat former champ Norton and was marketed in 150 countries worldwide.

Then there were overt racial moments like those when John L. Sullivan refused to fight African-American boxers.

Although we chose to highlight Jack Johnson, Joe Louis, and Muhammad Ali as the pioneers for this book, there were clearly many great African-American boxers, including the current female champion, Laila Ali, the daughter of "the Greatest," who became even better known as a humanitarian and leader after his career ended. Louis and Holmes have been noted but then there were also George Foreman, Joe Frazier, Archie Moore, Rubin "Hurricane" Carter, Tommy Hearns, Sugar Ray Robinson, Sugar Ray Leonard, Evander Holyfield, and Marvin Hagler. So many more could be mentioned and written about, but for now, enjoy the accomplished lives of Jack Johnson, Joe Louis, and Muhammad Ali.

John Arthur "Jack" Johnson

First African-American World Heavyweight Boxing Champion

by Jessica Bartter

Words like "clever," "quick," "agile," and "champion" were used to describe Jack Johnson's white counterparts in boxing at the turn of the century. Although Johnson boxed with a similar style in the same era, the press chose to describe him with words like "cowardly," "devious," and "flashy." In fact, Johnson received heavy criticism for his patient style of fighting that often had him playing defensively from the start, waiting to capitalize on an opponent's mistake. Even while his technique was greatly scrutinized by the press, Jim Corbett, a white world heavyweight champion, was praised by the same press as "the cleverest man in boxing" for his comparable style. Corbett was even nicknamed "Gentleman" Jim Corbett. This double standard was not limited to boxing. Rather, it described the inequalities that African-American athletes had faced for centuries in all sports. Many Americans had a hard time accepting Jack Johnson, but the history books cannot deny that he truly was a champion.

Widely known as Jack Johnson, he was born John Arthur Johnson in Galveston, Texas, in 1878. Standing 6 feet 1$^{1}/_{2}$ inches tall, he was eventually nicknamed the "Galveston Giant." Born to former slaves, Henry and Tiny Johnson, Jack Johnson was one of six siblings. Henry and Tiny taught Jack and his brothers and sisters how to read and write. Johnson had just five years of formal education. Watching his parents work so tirelessly to raise six children taught Johnson at a young age that he had to fight for what he wanted. He refused to listen to anyone who said he wasn't good enough or anyone who told him he couldn't be the best. Johnson didn't hesitate to go after what he wanted. In particular, Johnson knew change had to be made in American society in regards to race relations, and he decided to use his boxing skills to make that change. Surely, he was a difference maker.

After boxing for fun as an amateur for a few years, Johnson decided to go pro when he was 18 years old. He quickly understood that he could earn more money in a single fight than his blue-collar father could in a week. Early in his professional career, a heavy-weight named Joe Choynski began training Johnson in Galveston. Johnson realized he had much to learn from Choynski after the trainer knocked him out in the third round of a match. Their training soon took an interesting turn. Because boxing was illegal in most states, including Texas, both Johnson and Choynski were arrested for boxing against each other and spent 23 days in jail. In testament to his determination to be the best, Johnson continued to train with Choynski while they were locked up.

After being released from jail, Johnson soon left Galveston. Of his 27 fights on record before being incarcerated, 23 of them took place in Galveston. Over the next 37 years, Johnson traveled the United States and the world, boxing close to 100 more fights. Only once did he return to fight in Galveston.

Johnson's worldwide journey started in Colorado and stretched from California to Pennsylvania, from Mexico to Spain, and dozens of stops in between. Johnson's first title came in 1903 after he beat "Denver" Ed Martin in Los Angeles in the 20th round to win the Colored Heavyweight Championship.

Although he had boxed both African-American and white opponents, a gentlemen's agreement prohibited African-Americans from competing for the top titles, including the world heavyweight championship. Johnson not only had the talent to compete for the title, he had the talent to win. His superior skills drove even more resistance Johnson's way. Boxing is a sport that requires stamina and endurance, both physically and mentally. Boxers rely on their intelligence as much as they do on their strength. In accordance with popular sentiment, many did not want to see an African-American take a white boxer down in the ring. In fact, it frightened many. For an African-American to beat a white boxer would have challenged the notion of black inferiority.

Johnson was smart enough to recognize the anxiety his talent created in others and was bold enough not to back down. He tried to challenge world heavyweight champion James J. Jeffries, but the fellow American refused to face him. Instead, Johnson earned a fight with former champion, British Bob Fitzsimmons, in 1907 and was able to knock him out in just two rounds. Johnson knew that at some point the boxing world would take him seriously.

Although the press did not often write about Johnson with an open mind, he was able to use the press to finally earn his World Championship bout. In 1908, he followed the world heavyweight champion Tommy Burns around the world, ending up in Australia. Johnson taunted the Canadian through the media until Burns finally agreed to fight him. Johnson performed as his critics had feared. After 14 rounds, the police broke up the fight, but Johnson was handed the match after the referee decided it as a TKO. As opposed to a knockout (KO), in which a fighter is unable to get off the mat for a certain period of time, a technical knockout, or TKO, is a situation in which the referee decides a fighter cannot continue a match. On December 26, 1908, an African-American was awarded the world heavyweight champion title for the first time. Sadly, news cameras stopped rolling just as Johnson was finishing Burns off, so that no one could actually witness an African-American man defeating a white man.

Unwilling to accept Johnson's superiority, boxing promoters threw a series of fighters in the ring hoping he would relinquish his title. Over and over, the fighters were each deemed the next "great white hope," but all proved inferior to Johnson. The media and boxing fanatics everywhere began criticizing Johnson's title by belittling Burns' talent. This drove Jeffries, who had previously refused to fight Johnson, out of retirement. The public convinced Jeffries he was finally ready to face an African-American in the ring, but first he had to lose the 100 pounds he had gained since his last fight six years earlier. The boxing world was so ecstatic at the prospect of the two Americans finally meeting that a ring was built in Reno, Nevada, for that very occasion. Before there was Joe Frazier and Muhammad Ali in the 1970s, the Jeffries-Johnson match-up was termed the "fight of the century." On Independence Day, 1910, in front of more than 20,000 spectators, Johnson's performance dismayed many white fans. Jeffries was knocked out in the 15th round, allowing Johnson to retain his world heavyweight title.

Still, white fans refused to accept Johnson, and race riots broke out following his victory. Certain states even banned the film that proved Johnson beat Jeffries. It was not until 2005, almost a century later, that the U.S. National Film Preservation Board recognized the fight for its historical significance. The footage now rests safely with the National Film Registry.

According to boxing records, Johnson did not accept another

challenge for two years until he met "Fireman" Jim Flynn in a Las Vegas ring. Flynn reportedly fought dirty by repeatedly head-butting Johnson and throwing racial epithets at him until the sheriff had to step in the ring to end the fight. Johnson retained his title.

Over the next three years, Johnson fought two boxers in Paris and one in Argentina before meeting his match in Cuba. A 45-round fight was scheduled for Johnson and challenger Jess Willard, but Johnson was knocked out in the 26th round and forced to surrender the championship title he had defended for nearly five years.

Johnson's mission to challenge the social norms that pitted whites against blacks did not stop at the boxing ring. Johnson was married three times, all to white women. Johnson never hid who he was or whom he represented. He proudly lived the life of a famed athlete—endorsing products, driving fast cars, dressing in the finest clothes, and dating a long line of women. He never backed away from the disapproving public, often appearing on the radio and even in the movies. Johnson's fast life caught up to him in 1946 when he died in a car crash in North Carolina. He was just 68.

Johnson's battle to the top forced many eyes open to the reality of racial inequality. His legacy opened the doors for other boxing greats like Joe Frazier, Muhammad Ali, and George Foreman. It was 22 years before another African-American regained the world heavyweight championship title when Joe Louis beat Lou Braddock in 1937. Although slower than the fancy vehicles he drove, Johnson's journey shows the power sport can have as a vehicle for social change.

Joe Louis Barrow

African-American Boxing Pioneer for the Human Race

by Marcus Sedberry

During the 1920s and '30s many youth throughout the world grew up wanting to replicate the tremendous demonstration of athleticism they saw at boxing matches and heard about through radio broadcasts. Some of these young people were born with the natural toughness and determination of a boxer. A rare few had the innate knack and instinct of a true fighter.

Many say Joe Louis was one of the few who were born with all the right elements of a great boxer. Some ascribe his nature to growing up in the South during a time when African-Americans were racially discriminated against, oppressed daily, and even lynched. Joseph Louis Barrow was born on May 13, 1914, in Chambers County, Alabama, to Munroe and Lillie Barrow. His father, Munroe, was a sharecropper, and the Barrow family struggled for much of Louis' childhood. His father was admitted to an asylum when Louis was two years old and died two years later. Louis' mother remarried when he was seven years old and eight new people were added to his already large family. In the mid-1920s, the family moved to Detroit, Michigan, in hopes of a better life.

While in Detroit, Louis attended Duffield School and Bronson School, a vocational training school, until he was 17 years old. Before school, Louis worked at Eastern Market and after school at Pickman and Dean, a neighborhood ice company. Myth has it that Louis developed his initial physique through those young years working at the ice company, lifting blocks of ice that weighed up to 50 pounds.

When he was 16, Louis' mother gave him money to take violin lessons. Instead, Louis used the money for a locker at the local recreation center, Brewster's East Side Gymnasium, where amateur boxers trained. In order to keep his mother from finding out about his interest in boxing, Joseph Louis Barrow shortened his name to Joe Louis. She eventually figured out his secret. Although this initially disappointed his mother, she told Louis and the other children that if they wanted to do something badly enough, she would support them and try to make a way for them to do it. The "violin lesson" expenditure proved to be a very wise investment.

In his first amateur match, Louis was knocked down seven times. This was symbolic of his first few years in amateur boxing. In 1933, Louis began to work with the manager of the Detroit Athletic Club, George Slayton, and later made it to Golden Gloves. The national light-heavyweight division of Amateur Athletic Union (AAU) boxing fell victim to the hands of Louis. Just three months later, he became a professional boxer. In his first professional fight versus Jack Kracken, Louis won $50, but within a year Louis had knocked out Primo Carnera and earned $60,433. After his first eight fights, he became known as the "Brown Bomber." Louis experienced immediate success in the professional ranks as he went 27-0 with 23 knockouts, including former heavyweight champions. At the age of 21, Louis had accomplished what many other professionals could not do in their entire careers. He had knocked out Primo Carnera, Kingfish Levinsky, Max Baer, and Paolino Uzrudum in a total of 12 rounds. In fact, in September of 1935 Louis married his first of three wives, Marva Trotter, just two hours prior to his bout against Max Baer.

Because of his success, Louis began to become the face of the African-American community. In years prior there had been an extensive separation between white and African-American boxers. On June 19, 1936, Louis would become the face of the only race—the human race. In the months preceding June 19, Louis slowed down with his training efforts, possibly in a state of complacency. Rather than placing all of his efforts on his match against German boxer Max Schmeling, Louis began to take up golf. The United States and Germany were going through many differences at the time as German dictator Adolf Hitler had begun to force his anti-Semitic ideology on his citizens. The tension between the two countries grew. In the boxing world, the same held true, as Schmeling had already beaten an American world heavyweight champion, Jack Sharkley, by disqualification. Although Schmeling held the title, he was considered by the world as merely a stepping stone for the rising star Louis, a bump in Louis' road to becoming world champion.

When June 19, 1936, came, the pounding was set to begin in favor of Louis. However, to the surprise of many, the outcome was much different. Schmeling had studied the style and tendencies of Louis and was able to identify flaws in Louis' approach. Although many felt Schmeling was simply bluffing prior to the fight, in the fourth round, people saw the upcoming star experience something he had not experienced in years as he fell to the canvas. Louis attempted to fight back, but the German proved too much for Louis. He was knocked out in the 12th round.

Louis went on to become world champion as expected, when he knocked out James Braddock in the eighth round of the 1937 bout. This win made Louis the first African-American to hold the heavyweight title since Jack Johnson had beat Tommy Burns in 1908. Louis refused to pronounce himself world champion, though, and asked others to do the same until he beat Schmeling.

The 1930s were a tough time for the American people as they suffered from the Depression and looked for any way to build hope. During this same time, Hitler continued to press his genocidal campaign as he began invading other countries across Europe. The U.S. government did not sit well with Nazi power gaining size and economic status. Considering war to help silence the propaganda of the Germans, the U.S. issued anti-Nazi material. For Hitler, Schmeling represented the racial superiority of Aryans. For much of the world, the rematch of Louis and Schmeling would be symbolic of good versus evil.

Louis and Schmeling were set for a rematch on June 22, 1938, exactly one year after Louis had won the world championship, at the same place the previous Louis vs. Schmeling match had been held, Yankee Stadium, and with the same referee, Arthur Donovan. As an antagonist to Hitler's belief of white supremacy, the United States began to promote Louis as a representative of the U.S. A few weeks prior to the bout, President Franklin D. Roosevelt was quoted as saying, "Joe, we need muscles like yours to beat Germany."[1] Louis was determined to send a message to the world and came roaring out of his corner in the first round. The once-confident Schmeling became lost in the variety and abundance of punches thrown by Louis. After being knocked down three times within two minutes and four seconds of the fight, Schmeling found himself on the canvas without means of getting up as Louis redeemed himself. The entire country celebrated Louis' and America's victory.

Louis' terrorizing of opponents and boxing dominance continued for 12 years, and he held the title of heavyweight champion of the world longer than anyone before him. His rise to glory included beating notables Lou Nova, Tony Galento, Gus Dorazio, Buddy Baer, Johnny Paycheck, and perhaps most memorable, Billy Conn. In 1942, Louis entered the Army and as a result did not defend his title again until 1946, when he defended it four times prior to 1949.

In 1949, Louis retired as the undefeated heavyweight champ but returned to the ring a year later versus Ezzard Charles, and the year following versus Rocky Marciano. By points, Charles was given the victory in their bout and Marciano handed Louis another loss, knocking him out in the eighth round. Following the Marciano fight, Louis decided to retire for good.

Louis' reign was one of impressive stature before his death in 1981. To become a heavyweight champion, cheered for by thousands of Americans in a time when many of the people who looked like he did were being treated horribly, is an amazing feat. Louis' victories briefly showed the world that the only race that matters is the human race. They showed the world not only the power sport has to bring together countries and people with different views, but also the power it has to barge through social injustices to create awareness and change. Louis' life was one of perseverance and determination that resulted in his status not only as an African-American pioneer but as an American hero as well.

Note

1. International Boxing Hall of Fame, "Louis Destroys Schmeling in Rematch," http://www.ibhof.com/ibhfhvy5.htm (accessed July 17, 2007).

Muhammad Ali

"The Greatest"

by Richard Lapchick

Muhammad Ali accepting his Hall of Fame induction from the National Consortium for Academics and Sports in 2000.

Considered brash and bold when he was young, Muhammad Ali later became a messenger of peace for the United Nations. He was considered to be the athlete who most divided the races after he proclaimed allegiance to the Black Muslims and announced that he would not go to Vietnam to fight. And yet, Ali has undoubtedly become *the* public figure who helps unite people across racial groups and makes people feel comfortable when they are in the presence of people who do not look like themselves.

I have been to more than 125 countries over the course of my 61 years. Whatever nation I was in, as soon as it was discovered that I had anything to do with sports, someone would ask me if I knew Muhammad Ali. Even the first time I visited Nelson Mandela in Johannesburg, he asked me if I knew Ali. When I told him yes, he smiled wryly and said, "I do, too!"

Ali turned 65 in 2007. I doubt if there is another living American whose birth would be hailed more universally than Ali. I met him for the first time at Kutsher's Country Club in Monticello, New York, in the early 1960s, when his political side had not yet emerged in public view. He was still Cassius Clay, having been named Cassius Marcellus Clay after the famous Kentucky abolitionist.

Ali is a presence of such magnitude that a 96,000-square-foot Muhammad Ali Center was opened in the fall of 2005 to commemorate the life of this giant. Ali captured the public's attention with his great athletic skills. By the time he was 18, he had won six Kentucky Golden Gloves Championships, two National Golden Gloves Championships, and two National Amateur Athletic Union titles. Barely 18, he won the gold medal in the 1960 Rome Olympics. In coming home, Ali faced the ugly reality of racism in America. After a public parade welcomed him back to Louisville (which would later become the site of the Ali Center), Ali went into a restaurant and was refused service.

With that as the backdrop, Ali trained hard to try to win the world heavyweight championship. Facing a menacing Sonny Liston as a seven-to-one underdog, Cassius Clay upset the champion and took the title in 1964. Within 24 hours he announced that he had become a member of the Nation of Islam and was changing his name from Cassius Clay to Cassius X. His polarization from the media and white America had begun. He was soon renamed Muhammad Ali.

On August 23, 1966, Ali applied for conscientious objector status with the Selective Service, on religious grounds. He said he refused to fight because, "I ain't got no quarrel with them Vietcong."[1] That action seemed to erect concrete barriers. He soon lost his boxing licenses all across America. Stripped of his championship, Ali was unable to fight for nearly three years. He became a spokesperson on college campuses against the war in Vietnam. The war became more and more unpopular.

I marched against the Vietnam War, but Ali was willing to give up a lucrative boxing career to stand behind his principles. He did more for the anti-war movement than so many of the hundreds of thousands marching against the war. He became our hero while many white Americans and most of the American media saw him as being racially divisive and unpatriotic. To those around the globe who opposed the war, he helped them see that America was not a monolith. To those who saw injustices to people of color across the globe, he became a giant who stood up for justice.

He had also become what many would call the greatest athlete of the 20th century. That gave him the platform.

Ali won his case in the Supreme Court and in 1970 beat Jerry Quarry. The next year was his first fight with Joe Frazier, which Frazier won. Both had been unbeaten. Frazier lost the heavyweight title to George Foreman in 1973, and then Ali faced Frazier again in 1974 in New York City for the right to face Foreman. They battled for 12 rounds, and Ali won a unanimous decision.

"The Rumble in the Jungle," the most heralded match of Ali's career, was staged in Kinshasa, Zaire. George Foreman came in as a three-to-one favorite. It was in this fight that Ali invented his famous "rope-a-dope" strategy that tired Foreman out and allowed Ali to re-claim the championship. This fight and the weeks leading up to it were featured in the 1996 Academy Award winner for best documentary film, *When We Were Kings*.

In 1975, Ali defeated Frazier in the "Thrilla in Manila," and he retained his world heavyweight champion title between 1976 and 1978.

He had been dancing on top of the world when he was upset in a stunning match by Olympic champion Leon Spinks. Ali won the rematch, becoming the only heavyweight to win the championship three times. Ali closed his long career, which started at age 12 and ended at 39, in 1981 with only five defeats and 56 victories. It had all started when a policeman told the young Clay to take up boxing after his bicycle had been stolen.

In his retirement, Ali tirelessly traveled the world, winning friends and working for peace, serving as an ambassador for presidents working for the release of hostages. He helped secure the release of 15 U.S. hostages during the Gulf War, was part of efforts to feed over 232 million meals to people in need around the world, and has been active with the Special Olympics and the Make-A-Wish Foundation.

Muhammad Ali has won the admiration of generations of people, even those who never saw him box. During his retirement, he met his fourth wife, Lonnie, who had lived near Ali when she was a child in Louisville. She has been his angel.

I have to relate some personal experience with Ali, whom I first met in the 1960s.

I had just taken a job at the United Nations in 1978. The Vietnam War was over, the Civil Rights Movement had gone quiet, and the Anti-Apartheid Movement was under way. There were trade, bank loan, oil, and sports boycotts of South Africa. Ali had already refused to fight there. There was a branch of Chemical Bank, a lender to South Africa, in the U.N. I got together with a staff member from Ghana and another from New Zealand to try to figure out a way to get Chemical out of the building. The man from Ghana asked if I could get Ali to speak to the General Assembly to help our efforts. A few months later, Ali spoke for an hour in the GA Hall, usually empty but then packed to hear the global hero that Ali had become. That day started a real friendship with Ali that lasts to this day.

We have been together with our families on many occasions, often several times a year. Lonnie has been a dear friend. Their youngest son, Assad, has played with our daughter Emily. When Emily introduced her then boyfriend, Steven, to Ali in 2006, Ali playfully reached his arm out to have his fist rest on Steven's chin and told him to be good to Emily. Howard Bingham, his best friend and a world renowned photographer, has become a good friend of ours. I consider the friendship with the Ali family and Howard to be one of sport's biggest gifts to my family.

Some two decades after Ali spoke to the UN, Kofi Annan, the man from Ghana who had suggested having Ali speak to the General Assembly, became the first UN staff member to be named Secretary General. He asked me to help get Ali to be his Messenger of Peace. Ali was a logical choice for the position because he had worked the globe, traveling to more than 200 cities annually. His message was always about healing.

Ali was in Boston in 1997 when the verdict in the civil case of O. J. Simpson was rendered. America's odyssey with and against O. J. Simpson may be finally faded from view now. But then it was red hot and ugly. Almost simultaneously, the continued resurgent star of Muhammad Ali, which began with the opening ceremonies of the Atlanta Olympics, seemed very much on the sports horizon. It is ironic that we have dealt in such personal depth in such different ways with two of our nation's greatest African-American athletes.

The publication of *Healing*, Ali's book with Thomas Hauser, took Ali to city after city to talk about racial healing. In most cases, Lonnie Ali talked to the students assembled at schools. Gyms were packed with young people from elementary school through high school. They had all been prepared so they could understand what Ali had done to make their principals and teachers so excited about Ali coming to their schools. I was informed that students were drilled about his artistic boxing career, his stand against the Vietnam War, and his work for civil rights of African-Americans. The preparation of the students was true and provided great perspective.

Whenever Muhammad Ali was sighted entering a gym, pandemonium broke out. Even children who didn't know the history were simply swept away by the stature and charisma of this man who has been slowed by Parkinson's syndrome but whose mind was as sharp as ever.

Moments built on one another to create a momentum of enthusiasm that few students or their teachers had ever experienced. The first school was the Hennigan Elementary School. The students had gifts for Ali and one fifth grader had written a poem that he was "the greatest and not Ali." Ali called him forth and did an unexpected Ali Shuffle. His battle with Parkinson's Syndrome led many to believe he could no longer move like this. He has so many things inside, which he mostly expresses without words.

We went to dinner with the Ali family on the second night of his stay in Boston. Present were Muhammad, Lonnie, their son Assad, my wife, Ann, our daughter, Emily, noted photographer Howard Bingham, and Henry Louis Gates of Harvard's Afro-American Studies Department. We were the guests of the LoConte family at their great Italian eatery in Boston's North End.

It was early on the same evening as President Clinton's State of the Union Address. The evening was so special to be with the Ali family that no one thought of trying to hear the President. Then a waiter came to our table to say that the jury was coming back with the O. J. Simpson verdict. Professor Gates asked if there was a TV to watch the verdict. An old set was brought out. Ali watched intently but without expression as to what he hoped for in a verdict. Everything went against O. J. this time. We turned off the TV and resumed the conversations around the table.

Ali drew a picture for Emily. She made him a valentine. Emily and Assad sent notes to each other. It was one of those nights that I know I will always remember.

I listened to the news on the way home. Commentators speculated that this new verdict would further divide the races in America as they said it already had in the criminal case. I wondered how commentators were still blind to how huge the racial divide has been, with or without the O. J. Simpson case.

I thought long and hard that night about these two African-American men. Both had incredible athletic careers. Both became beloved by the public and crossed over racial lines. O. J. seemed to spend his life trying to prove that there was no divide between the races. Ali's legacy included standing up as a proud black man, emphasizing boldly that race does matter, as no other athlete has so forcefully before or since. It seems ironic that one now roams free but lives in disgrace in the eyes of the majority of Americans, accused of dividing the races. The other, who once was accused of dividing the races because he stood so tall as a black American, now brings people of all racial groups together by preaching "healing" and appealing to everyone, irrespective of race, religion, or age.

After September 11, an unprecedented wave of hate against Muslims swept through American communities. In a fundraising concert seen around the world, Ali stood up and told the world that he was a Muslim, too, and that his Allah was a God of peace and justice. I do not think anyone else could have slowed down the bandwagon of hate rolling through our cities. Ali again stood tall to stop the hate.

Slowed by Parkinson's, Ali nonetheless continues to tirelessly travel the world, winning friends and working for peace. After the ceremony with Annan, Ali was asked to meet a march of 500 children who had walked from Harlem to the United Nations Plaza to commemorate International Children's Day. It was organized by Annan's wife. UN Security was petrified as Ali walked into this crowd without guards surrounding him. They did not know he loves to be with people, especially children. These children, who didn't know the history, were simply swept away by the stature and charisma of this man. I bet that close to 100 ended up in his arms.

The scene rang true and reminded me of the night our then-five-year-old, Emily, first met Ali. She was painfully shy. Emily was standing with my wife, Ann, when Ali caught her eye from the other side of a table. This girl, who at that age took 15 to 20 minutes to warm up to friends she hadn't seen for a week, flew across the room and jumped into his open arms. That was 1994.

Muhammad Ali called himself "The Greatest" as he put down Liston for the first time. Most people thought it was clever or funny but hardly true in February of 1964. Four decades later the world calls him "The Greatest" matter-of-factly.

Ali has given the world so many gifts of himself. How perfect it would be if our gift to Ali was to stop the hatred against Muslims and realize this peacemaker better represents the millions of Muslims around the world than the small band of terrorists who use the name of Allah to spread hate and destruction. I love you, Muhammad. And I am hardly alone.

Note

1. Esther Cooper Jackson and Constance Pohl, eds., "Muhammad Ali, The Measure of a Man," *Freedomways Reader: Prophets in Their Own Country* (Boulder, Colorado: Westview Press, 1967), 176.

COLLEGE
SPORT

8

COLLEGE COACHING RANKS STILL SHOW LONG WAY TO GO IN SPITE OF GREAT PIONEERS

Introduction by Richard Lapchick

The pioneers who broke the barriers as college coaches must look at the college coaching ranks today with sadness as they take note of the small number of African-American head coaches outside of men's Division I basketball.

The hiring of Randy Shannon as head football coach by the University of Miami at the end of the 2006 season made the headlines in college football. It was announced a few days before the *2005 College Sport Racial and Gender Report Card* was released on December 13, 2006. I was the co-author of that Report Card along with Jenny Brenden. It was published by The Institute for Diversity and Ethics in Sport (TIDES) at the University of Central Florida. Although college sport received a B- for race and a B for gender hiring practices, it received an F for college football coaches with only 5 percent of the Division IA coaches being African-American compared to 45 percent of the players.

Those concerned about the lack of opportunity for African-American head coaches were elated that the number of black head coaches had increased, even if only by one, to six. That was still below the all-time high of eight nearly a decade ago.

Floyd Keith, the Executive Director of the Black Coaches & Administrators (BCA), said "College athletics directors and search firms are paying attention to the fact that they won't go unnoticed if they don't have an equitable hiring process."[1] Keith was referring to the Football Hiring Report Card published for the third time this fall by the BCA.

When the BCA started the Report in 2004, there were three African-American head coaches. In year one, there was no change.

Presidents and athletic directors did not know how to react to the fact that a vocal and influential organization was watching. In the second year of the report, the number of African-American head coaches went from three to five with the hiring of Turner Gill at Buffalo and Ron Prince at Kansas State, who joined African-American head coaches at UCLA, Mississippi State, and Washington. Less noticed was what happened at the Division IAA level. When the report was first published there was only a single African-American head coach. As of this publication, there are now five in the head coaching ranks in Division IAA at Valparaiso, Southeast Missouri State, Northern Arizona, Indiana State, and Columbia. Keith said, "Nobody's happy that we only have six head coaches in Division I and five in IAA, but we are happy that there is progress. Universities are bringing in capable candidates who are black and the result has been hires in schools where that may not have happened previously."[2]

But football was really a microcosm for the lack of head coaching opportunities in the other college sports outside of men's basketball. Here are some of the highlights from the coaching section of the *2005 College Sport Racial and Gender Report Card*:

- In men's Division I basketball, 25.2 percent (up 2 percent) of all head coaches were African-American, an all-time high percentage.
- Opportunities for people of color in men's sports other than basketball remained poor.
- Only three of 119 Division IA head coaches were African-American during the 2005 collegiate football season. The 2006 season had five African-Americans leading Division IA football programs. Randy Shannon was hired by the University of Miami after the 2006 season making him the sixth African-American head football coach as of December 10, 2006.
- Barry Alvarez at the University of Wisconsin, Madison, stepped down from the position of head football coach after the 2005 football season to focus solely on being athletic director. Florida International hired Mario Cristolbal, and he was the only Latino head coach heading into the 2007 season.
- Only 4.1 percent of Division I head baseball coaches were people of color, with 2.6 percent Latino.

- In fact, African-Americans were so underrepresented as head coaches that, once again, the percent of women coaching men's teams actually exceeded that of African-Americans in Division III (4.3 percent versus 3.7 percent). In Division II, the percentage of women coaching men's teams almost matched the percentage of African-Americans (3.5 percent versus 4.2 percent).
- More than three decades after the passage of Title IX, women coaching women's teams still do not represent the majority of coaches in the women's game. In addition, this year's numbers show a decrease in women coaching women's sports in several different sports. Women continue to lose ground when coaching their own gender, as women head coaches in Division I basketball dropped to 64.3 percent, from the 67.5 percent that was reported in the last report card. Head coaches of Division I track/cross country, which combines the head coaches of cross country, indoor track, and outdoor track, saw a decrease in female head coaches from 21.7 percent down to 20.6 percent.
- The percentage of African-American women head coaches of women's Division I basketball teams was 9.3 percent, a 1.6 percent jump from 7.7 percent. Nonetheless, the 9.3 percent stood in stark contrast to the 43.7 percent of the student-athletes playing women's basketball who were African-American. The disparity is what compelled the BCA to initiate a women's basketball hiring report card for 2007.
- Whites held the overwhelming percentage of the head coaching positions on the women's teams in each division.
  - Whites held 89.6 percent, 89.9 percent, and 92.9 percent of all head coaching positions in Divisions I, II, and III, respectively.
  - African-Americans held 6.6 percent, 4.3 percent, and 4.2 percent of the women's head coaching positions in the three NCAA divisions, respectively.
  - Latinos held 1.6 percent, 2.9 percent, and 1.3 percent of head coaching positions for women's teams in the respective divisions.
  - Asians held 1.1, 1.2, and 1.2 percent of head coaching positions for women's teams in the respective divisions.
  - Native American representation was very minimal.

- These figures accounted for male and female head coaches of women's teams. It should be noted that the high percentage of whites coaching women's teams decreased at every level.
- Whites dominated the head coaching positions held on men's teams at each level. These figures included male and female head coaches for men's teams:
  - Whites held 90.6, 89.5, and 93.4 percent of all head coaching positions in Divisions I, II, and III respectively.
  - African-Americans accounted for 7.3, 4.4, and 4.1 percent respectively in each division.
  - Asians represented 0.4, 0.7, and 0.6 percent at each level.
  - Latinos held 1.1, 3.6, and 1.5 percent of the positions in each division.
  - Native Americans accounted for less than 1 percent of total head coaches at each level.
- On the men's teams, whites held 79.2, 82.7, and 88.5 percent of the assistant coaching positions in the three divisions, respectively. African-Americans held 17.6, 11.6, and 8.3 percent, respectively.
- Among the women's teams, whites held 81.6, 82.4, and 90.5 percent of the assistant coaching positions in Divisions I, II, and III, respectively. African-Americans had 13.2, 9.4, and 6.5 percent, respectively.
- As assistants, women held slightly more than half of the jobs on women's teams with 51.5 in Division I, 51.4 in Division II, and 54 percent in Division III.

The best news in the *2005 College Sport Racial and Gender Report Card* continued to be for Division I college basketball coaches, where we no longer even notice if an African-American coach is hired or fired. We simply have been hiring the best people for those positions and now, for the first time, more than a quarter of the head coaches are African-American.

As we look across the spectrum in college sport in Divisions I, II, and III, we see that although there is improvement, there is a long way to go. Myles Brand, the president of the NCAA, continues to emphasize the need for more opportunity for people of color and women in coaching and athletics department positions. In Division

III, some might feel sport is more pure and opportunity greater. Perhaps the most telling is the statistic in the *2005 College Sport Racial and Gender Report Card* is that for both head and assistant coaches in Division III, there are more women coaching men's teams than there are African-Americans. The percentage of women coaching men's teams in Division II is nearly the same. The Black Coaches & Administrators cannot do a hiring report card in every sport, but I believe that their report in football hiring practices has made a huge difference and that their new reports will do the same in women's basketball and athletic directors' positions.

Floyd Keith, who is featured in the Epilogue as "the keeper of the flame," said, "Other tools are necessary. There is the possibility of Title VII lawsuits against schools that don't have open hiring practices as well as the implementation of a Rooney Rule in college sport."[3] The NFL and Major League Baseball both have rules mandating that people of color be interviewed for head coaching and managerial positions, respectively. The results have been dramatic in both the NFL and Major League Baseball.

The NCAA may be resisting such a rule, because so many seem to think that college member institutions may not support it. It may be that ultimately the colleges have to adopt such a rule in order to do better in future *College Sport Racial and Gender Report Cards* and, more importantly, in the halls of higher education where we proclaim our support for democratic ideals and equal opportunity for all.

Until then, too many new African-American head coaches outside of men's basketball may themselves continue to feel like pioneers. The basketball pioneers included here are John Thompson, John Chaney, George Raveling, and Nolan Richardson. Their willingness to speak out and risk their careers really has not been matched in any other sport. Thus the story of pioneering African-American college coaches has only just started to be written.

Nonetheless, we salute the first African-American head coaches in college football (Willie Jeffries), the SEC (Fletcher Carr), the ACC (Bob Wade), the Big 12 (Marian Washington), the Big Ten (Payton Fuller), the Ivy League (Larry Ellis), as well as the first to win a Division IA bowl game (Tyrone Willingham), an NCAA men's basketball championship (John Thompson), and women's championship (Carolyn Peck). This chapter also includes the stories of

Vivian Stringer, who was the first basketball coach to take three different schools to the Final Four, and Eddie Robinson, an extraordinary football coach and HBCU (historically black colleges and universities) pioneer. They are all a distinguished part of the history of college sports.

Notes

1. Floyd Keith, interview with author, April 6, 2007.
2. Ibid.
3. Ibid.

Larry Ellis

First African-American Head Coach in the Ivy League

by Marcus Sedberry

On September 29, 1929 in Englewood, New Jersey, a star was born. His name was Larry Ellis. Throughout his life, Ellis would shine as a dynamic athlete, astounding coach, and inspiring individual. Ellis, who was raised in the Bronx, New York, attended DeWitt Clinton High School, winning numerous cross country and mile titles. He moved on to become an All-American track star at New York University. In 1950, Ellis won the 1,000-yard Canadian Indoor title, and in the 1951 NCAA Championships, Ellis placed third in the 880 yards, now 800 meters. He also spent time running for the New York Pioneer Club, where his success continued. His love for the sport didn't end there. Upon graduation in 1951, Ellis became a track coach at Jamaica High School, where he spent 13 years creating an impact on New York youth. Among those New York youth was Bob Beamon, whose world-record-breaking long jump of 29 feet 2½ inches won a gold medal in the 1968 Olympics in Mexico City.

In 1970 Ellis transitioned to the collegiate level, accepting a position as head track coach at Princeton University and becoming the first African-American head coach of any sport in the Ivy League. Under his direction, the Princeton Tigers, never having won a cross country title prior to Ellis' arrival, successfully earned eight heptagonal cross country championships between 1975 and 1983. Ellis also led the track teams to their first victories since 1938, winning seven outdoor titles and four heptagonal indoor titles between the years of 1981 and 1990. His ability to motivate and encourage student-athletes earned him Coach of the Year honors for 1981–82.

Ellis coached student-athletes to great success and left a lasting impact on their lives. One of the athletes who unintentionally followed in his footsteps was Craig Masback. Masback entered Princeton University as a star soccer recruit as well as a track athlete. Soon thereafter, Ellis helped Masback realize that his potential was greater on the oval than on the pitch. Masback recalled Ellis as much more than a coach—as a mentor and an inspirational leader. "He was the one that said to me that anything was possible in track and field and in life. He gave me belief that I should pursue my dreams. I'll forever thank him for that."[1]

Masback did just that. After a collegiate track and field career as one of the top milers in the country, what he valued most were the team victories. Coach Ellis led Masback and his three counterparts to two NCAA Championship relays. Masback said, "I appreciated his manner, his commitment to the team concept and his view of track as a larger part of life . . . If I had never run again after Princeton I would still have felt that I had an idyllic experience on the team."[2] Ellis retired from Princeton in 1992 after 22 years as head coach, and Masback later became the CEO of USA Track & Field.

In addition to his endeavors at Princeton, Ellis was a force on the national track and field level as well. He was the coach of the 1984 Olympic team that included Carl Lewis, who won four gold medals at the Los Angeles Games. He also coached USA men's teams at four other international meets, including the memorable dual meet against the Soviet Union in 1978. In 1992, Ellis began a stint as the USA Track and Field president. His presidency saw many changes and challenges, including a corporate name transformation from The Athletics Congress to the current name, USA Track and Field. During his stint as president, Ellis underwent a heart transplant. However, he returned to lead the organization until 1996.

Larry Ellis died suddenly on November 4, 1998, leaving behind his wife Shirley and four children, as well as a legacy of hard work and commitment. In his memory, student-athletes lace up their shoes and put on the Princeton uniform in pride as they compete at the Larry Ellis Invitational track meet in Providence, Rhode Island. He is remembered for his dedication to the young people he coached and is quoted as saying, "It's kind of a two-way street. You give an awful lot of yourself, but on the other hand, you get a lot back in return."[3] Ellis was a star who shed new light on the lives he touched.

Notes

1. United Press International, "Track Official Larry Ellis Dies," November 4, 1998, http://www.highbeam.com/doc/1P1-17970740.html.

2. Ivy League Sports, "Ivy @ 50." http://www.ivyleaguesports.com/article.asp?intID=5637 (accessed December 6, 2006).

3. Mary Caffrey, "Funeral Service Set for Larry Ellis, Retired Track and Field Coach at Princeton," Princeton University Office of Communications, http://www.princeton.edu/pr/news/98/q4/1106-ellis.htm (accessed June 1, 2007).

Payton Fuller

First African-American Head Coach in the Big Ten Conference

by Jenny Brenden

It is an amazing opportunity to be a collegiate student-athlete. Student-athletes have the ability to represent their university in a way that others could not possibly experience, creating a special bond that lasts forever. For those athletes who later become coaches, it is often the ultimate fantasy and privilege to coach at one's alma mater. This situation provides the opportunity for an athlete to continue to represent and give back to his or her school through the mentoring of the next generation of student-athletes. Payton Fuller, a Michigan State University soccer star, was one of those lucky athletes who had the chance to coach a program that had turned him into an All-American just a few years prior.

A 1964 All-American selection, Fuller became the head men's soccer coach at MSU in 1970. Although his tenure was short, lasting only until 1973, he made a big impact, not only at Michigan State, but on sports history as well. He represented not just MSU, but also the conference as the first African-American coach in the Big Ten. At that point in time, Michigan State was an official member of the Big Ten, but soccer was not yet officially sponsored by the conference. Fuller became the second coach in the history of Michigan State men's soccer, succeeding Gene Kinney, who had coached the team since the program's inception in 1956. Ed Rutherford followed Fuller as head coach for a short stint before Ed Baum, another former player, took the position in 1977. Baum has acted as head coach ever since. In Fuller's four seasons as head coach, he led the Spartans to a combined record of 20-8-9.

Many of the other Big Ten Conference schools followed Michigan State's lead and hired African-American coaches in the years following. Pam McKinney became the first female African-American coach in the Big Ten when she was named the head women's tennis coach at Wisconsin in 1974. Progress has not always been so quick to come. Indiana University became the last Big Ten institution to hire an African-American coach in the year 2000.

No matter the pace, forward progress is positive movement. Payton Fuller was one of the pioneers in Big Ten coaching history, jumpstarting a movement that is still evolving today. He will always be remembered for his contributions to both Michigan State and the Big Ten.

Fletcher Carr

First African-American Head Coach in the Southeastern Conference

by Jessica Bartter

In the 2006 Hollywood blockbuster *Glory Road*, Coach Orlando "Tubby" Smith's hiring in 1997 is wrongly depicted as the first African-American head coach at the University of Kentucky. The "road" was actually paved 25 years earlier by Coach Fletcher Carr.

Even before the movie's suggestion, many already believed Tubby Smith held the title of first black coach at UK, but the university would like to set the record straight. Despite the myths and confusion, it was Fletcher Carr, who came to UK in 1973, who became the university's first African-American head coach of an intercollegiate team. With his hire, Carr also integrated the Southeastern Conference (SEC) and was, as far as he knew, the only coach of color in the South at the time.

Born and raised in Erie, Pennsylvania, Carr first made an impact in the sports arena at Erie East High School. Carr was one of nine brothers and seven sisters, all of whom were athletic and several of whom were major college and Olympic wrestlers. After discovering wrestling in seventh grade, Carr wrestled with the high school varsity team for four years and also competed with the track and football teams. Coach Fran Curci recruited Carr south to the University of Tampa in Florida for football and wrestling in 1969. Carr started every football game for four consecutive seasons during which he earned All-American honorable mention honors.

But Carr's success on the field paled in comparison to his success on the mat. In four years, Carr compiled a career dual meet wrestling record of 73-1. He was a four-time All-American and two time NCAA Division II Champion in the 190-pound division. Carr dominated the Georgia Tech Invitational, taking home the trophy four years in a row. In 1970, Carr finished fourth place in the 177-pound class of the NAIA Tournament and the Olympic Trials. In 1971, he finished second place in the 198-pound class of the AAU Nationals, finished second place in the 198-pound class of the Pan American Trials, and finished fourth place in the 198-pound class of the Greco Roman Championships.

Carr was a true all-around athlete, and one of his first loves was karate. Much like everything else he does, Carr gave his full attention and effort to karate and reached its pinnacle, the prestigious black belt.

Upon college graduation, Carr planned to continue competing and was ready to leave the college wrestling arena. But his former coach at Tampa, Coach Curci, had other things in mind for his stand-out athlete. Although it took a while for Carr to see its worth, he caught a big break when the University of Kentucky hired Coach Curci as its head football coach in 1973. Curci insisted he wanted Carr to join him at UK, but racial tensions in Kentucky left Carr apprehensive. In fact, as he recalled during our interview in April 2007, he turned Curci down and told him to stop wasting his time. Carr simply "didn't want to coach."[1] Curci's persistence eventually paid off when Carr agreed to be interviewed. As Carr disembarked the plane in Lexington wearing an old t-shirt and raggedy jeans, he was bombarded by reporters who acted as if he had already accepted the job. Although he thought his mind was already made up, once there, Carr realized the difference he could make in the South, so he accepted Curci's challenge to assist the football team and head the wrestling program. And challenging it was. In addition to having no previous coaching experience, Carr faced another tremendous obstacle: there was no wrestling team. Carr was hired to build the program from the ground up.

Carr searched the campus and grabbed bodies out of the general student body to fill his newborn team. Mainly, they were architects and engineers—"non-athletes." He filled in a few holes on the team with athletes from the football team, and the wrestling program at UK was born. Other coaches in the SEC told him it would be 10 years before he could win in their conference, but Carr put together a dedicated, hard-working team that was not afraid of sacrificing. Despite Carr's lack of coaching experience and the team's lack of funds, the Wildcats finished their first season with a 7-11-0 record.

Carr had proved his critics wrong in just one season. But he knew recruiting was key for the program's future success. Carr believes the opportunity to travel was a tremendous attraction that assisted his recruitment process. He did not skimp on funds when it came to his team's travel budget. He knew that for many young men being a member of an intercollegiate team would be their only opportunity to travel and see the country. After all, the people were the reason Carr remained in coaching for so many years. More than winning matches, he enjoyed "developing young boys and watching them grow into men."[2]

With the help of actual recruits, Carr's program improved to earn second place in the Southeastern Conference and even included one wrestler who earned All-American honors in just the second year of the program's existence. Carr owes some of his early coaching success to the level of his familiarity with his recruits, younger brothers Joe and Jim Carr. Joe Carr transferred from Ashland College to join the infant squad because of the confidence and respect he had in his brother Fletcher. Fletcher coached Joe to be UK's first All-American. Joe had a decorated career under his big brother with two more All-American honors, three SEC titles, and two finishes as third in the nation. Younger brother Jim was the top-recruit in country when Carr recruited him to Kentucky. Jim was the youngest member of the 1972 Olympic team and went on to earn All-American honors as a Wildcat.

Carr and "the Mat Cats" quickly garnered national attention and local support. The Wildcats wrestling team became a perennial top 20 program under Carr's leadership. Following the first developmental year, the program finished in the top 20 five times out of the next eight seasons.

Carr was not just a champion on the mat; he was a champion when it came to managing race relations. Looking back, Carr offers, "I think one of the reasons that UK hired me was for my ability as a student-athlete to keep peace between my black and white teammates." Despite the racial tensions he felt at Kentucky and the schools his team traveled to for competitions, Carr "ignored those issues and stayed focused on what [his] mission was, and that was building a program and people."[3]

One may have thought the odds were stacked against Carr, with racial barriers to bash during a stressful time period in society and with a lack of coaching experience to overcome. But Carr proved he could do more than meet the challenge. He led the program to a decade of dominance, a feat most coaches can only dream about. And perhaps the dominance was cut short prematurely when the program was cut in 1983. Carr and his wrestlers had much more fight in them but could not compete with Title IX. Title IX is a prohibition of sexual discrimination that pertains to educational programs or activities and that protects both males and females. It does not pertain to sports or females specifically, as is often misinterpreted. Because of Kentucky's unequal offering of athletic opportunities to males and females, some programs were cut. Despite their self-sufficiency, after a decade of winning, the Mat Cats had finally met their match.

As the University of Kentucky left the wrestling world, so did Carr. Or so he thought. Carr briefly moved back to Tampa, finally joining the business world as he had previously planned. In 1985, Carr relocated to Phoenix where he now owns a collection agency.

In recent years, Carr has made brief, yet highly prominent, appearances in the coaching world, sometimes paid, sometimes as a volunteer. Shortly after Carr moved to Phoenix, a longtime friend and former foe, Arizona State University head coach Bobby Douglas, encouraged Carr to volunteer with his program a few times a month. Carr welcomed the idea of a wrestling involvement that called for less stress and responsibility, but before he knew it, he was the assistant head coach and right back to the high pressures of collegiate coaching. It is no wonder Douglas so fiercely sought assistance from his former opponent. Carr was with the program for just three years but managed to help the Sun Devils earn a National Championship in 1988. Yet again, Carr left the wrestling world a champion.

Notes

1. Fletcher Carr, interview with author, April 10, 2007.
2. Fletcher Carr, e-mail message to author, April 9, 2007.
3. Ibid.

Marian Washington

First African-American Head Coach of the Big 12 Conference

by Horacio Ruiz

She was in her 31st year as head coach of the women's basketball team at Kansas when, in late January 2004, the venerable head coach Marian Washington took a medical leave of absence. Because of unspecified health issues that were not life-threatening, Washington effectively finished one of the most accomplished coaching careers in the history of women's basketball. Washington's accomplishments go far beyond women's collegiate basketball, as she was the first African-American head coach in any sport of all the schools in the Big 12 Conference.

In 1973, Washington was 25 years old and three years removed from her college graduation when she suddenly found herself leading the Kansas women's basketball team. Just a year later, while still completing her master's degree in biodynamics and administration, she was named the school's first and only director of intercollegiate athletics for women's sports, a post she would hold until 1979, when she began concentrating on basketball full-time. The 1973 season would bring the coach an 11-8 record. By 1978, she had notched her first 20-win season, and the next year Kansas won its first of three consecutive Big Eight championships (the Big 12 Conference was formed in 1994 by a merger of the Big Eight Conference with four schools that had been members of the Southwest Conference).

While she was relatively inexperienced as a coach, Washington would watch coaches like Bob Knight, John Chaney, and John Thompson to gain inspiration for leading her team. She also drew from a number of people who had influenced her life up to that point, including a ninth-grade teacher and her international coach, Alberta Lee Cox. In 1969, under Coach Cox, Washington became one of the first two African-American women to make an American international team. Washington didn't stop there. In 1982 she was the first African-American woman to be the head coach of a U.S. team in international play when she guided the U.S. Select Team to a silver medal in Taiwan.

As Washington developed her coaching style, the accolades and successes began to pour in. In 1994 Washington was presented with the Giant Steps Award, given by the Center for the Study of Sport in Society at Northeastern University in conjunction with the National Consortium for Academics and Sports, for her role in developing women's sports and women's basketball specifically. In 1996 she guided her team to the last Big Eight conference title and advanced to the Sweet 16 for the first time in school history. She also was an assistant coach on the 1996 U.S. women's basketball team, which won the gold medal in Atlanta. She finished her career with 560 wins and 17 seasons with 20 wins or more. In the year she retired, she was inducted into the Women's Basketball Hall of Fame.

Washington's impact on others was most evident upon listening to the reactions to her sudden retirement. One of the most heartfelt expressions came from former player Kathleen Hickert who said of Washington's retirement: "It's a huge, huge loss. I cannot emphasize that enough. I hurt, and my heart aches. My first concern is her health because I want her to get well, but I wanted her to get well and come back." Jennifer Jackson, also a former player, said, "She's given of herself for 31 years and done so much for so many women, and for the game of basketball itself. For so long she has been Kansas basketball, and I think that's really telling in the way that everyone who has played for her feels about her."[1]

Apart from her accomplishments as a coach, Washington held a number of positions outside of basketball where, again, she became the first in several areas. In 1993 she was the first woman to serve as president of the Black Coaches & Administrators, later becoming the first person to serve consecutive terms as president. In 2003 she was honored with the BCA Lifetime Achievement Award and earned the Outstanding Black Women in Sports Award from *Ebony Magazine*. Upon her retirement, Washington stated: "My mission in life has been to make a difference, especially in the lives of young people, and to use the arena of athletics to help develop good character as well as athletic talent."[2] Certainly, her mission has been accomplished.

Notes

1. Ryan Malashock, "Kansas Women's Coach Marian Washington," *The Topeka Capital-Journal*, March 11, 2003.

2. Marian Washington Biography, http://www.hitrunscore.com/marian-washington-biography.html (accessed June 3, 2007).

Willie Jefferies

First African-American Head Football Coach at a Division I-A University

by Marcus Sedberry

In 1960, Lancaster Barr Street High School hired an aspiring, young football coach named Willie Jefferies, a recent graduate of South Carolina State University with a degree in civil engineering. The following year, Jefferies moved to Gaffney, South Carolina, as he was appointed the new head coach of Granard High School. Few people in Gaffney knew what to expect from the youthful leader. However, Jefferies delivered excellence in spite of the wavering expectations. In six years Jefferies coached Granard High School to a record of 65-7-2 with three consecutive state championships. At the end of those six years, it was time for him to step up to a new challenge, as a coach in the collegiate ranks.

Jefferies had much success on the college level, where he became a pioneer for future generations of coaches to follow. Jefferies became an assistant coach at North Carolina A&T University in 1968. There he was groomed and developed by head coach Hornsby Howell. In 1972, Jefferies took a position for one year as an assistant coach under the direction of Johnny Majors at the University of Pittsburgh. The following year, he began what would become a long-term relationship with South Carolina State University. His first stint with the Bulldogs lasted five years. During those five years Jefferies experienced great success, helping South Carolina State to a record of 50-13-4. He also led SCSU to five MEAC titles and one National Black Championship in 1976.

Although he loved his time with the Bulldogs, Jefferies accepted a position as the head coach of the Wichita State University Shockers in 1979. This move made Jefferies the first African-American head football coach at an NCAA Division I-A university. At the time, Jefferies was not aware of his significance. He simply wanted to do the very best job possible and transform young people's lives through football.

The love he had for his student-athletes and his desire for them to succeed on and off the field is still remembered years later. Former receiver Reuben Eckels of WSU explained, "He believed that excellence was one thing that could overcome racism, so he demanded that his players be the best they could be on and off the field."[1]

At the end of the first year at Wichita State, Jefferies was quoted as saying he saw a "bright future." In spite of his confidence, many people felt differently after a grueling 1-10 season. The following two seasons proved the Shockers were on the right path as they finished with records of 5-5-1 and 4-6-1, respectively. In 1983, Jefferies and the Shockers made their presence felt with a record of 8-3. This season was one with many memories. It was not only the first eight-win season in years, but it was also the season when they shocked in-state rival, the University of Kansas Jayhawks. The game-winning play—a play action, 50-yard touchdown pass by Prince McJunkins to tight end Don Dreher down the right sideline—is one Jefferies remembers vividly and replays frequently. In fact, one of his most prized possessions is a picture of former WSU's Athletic Director Ted Bredehoft hugging him immediately after the game with a backdrop of overjoyed student-athletes.

The 1983 season proved challenging for the Shockers as they again struggled, posting a 3-8 record. On January 27, 1984, Wichita announced Jeffries' resignation from WSU and his decision to take the head coaching job at Howard University. Jefferies left the Shockers with the third-highest winning percentage of any head coach in its history. Upon his arrival, Howard was coming off a 1-9 season. Jefferies elevated the team to 2-8, 4-7, 8-3, 9-1, and 7-4 seasons, including a league championship in 1987 before leaving the Bison to return to South Carolina State University as the head coach.

Upon his homecoming, Jefferies continued with his exceptional coaching, leadership, and success on the field. In 1994, he led South Carolina State to a 10-2 record and defeated legendary coach Eddie Robinson and Grambling State University in the Heritage Bowl. The 31-27 victory gave Jefferies and the Bulldogs the 1994 Black College Football National Champions crown. In 2004, Jefferies joined Grambling as the new athletic director, replacing Al Dennis who had served in the position for four years. One year later, Jefferies resigned from Grambling and moved back to South Carolina. There he is actively involved with committees and organizations as he is a member of the American Football Coaches Association, the NCAA Football Rules Committee, and Kappa Alpha Psi Fraternity, Inc.

Jefferies influenced people on several different levels. From having a 35-year coaching career to being a part of service organizations and committees, he has touched lives and has led by example for his peers and athletes. As a head coach, his overall record was 178-132-6, and the hearts he touched are countless.

Notes

1. Wichita State University Alumni Association. "Breaking Through," http://webs .wichita.edu/dt/shockermag/show/features.asp?_s=136 (accessed May 26, 2007).

Robert Purnell Wade

First African-American Head Coach in the Atlantic Coast Conference

by Jessica Bartter

With a record of 341-25 over a 10-year span, including a run of 119-1 from 1981 to 1985, Bob Wade built a basketball powerhouse at Dunbar High School in Baltimore, Maryland. Wade created a dynasty that was founded not just on wins, but equally on discipline and academics. Such focus and success quickly caught the attention of collegiate athletic departments. Wade turned down the vying schools for years because of the fulfillment he found assisting adolescents, preparing them for life in college and in the real world through the lessons he taught in the locker room and on the court. Wade's influence carried beyond the basketball court because he also served Dunbar High as the athletic director and found equivalent success on the field as head football coach.

Wade's Dunbar ties dated back to his own high school days since he himself attended Dunbar, where he played football before earning a scholarship to Morgan State University. Wade was a 15th-round selection in the 1967 NFL draft. He spent four seasons playing for the Baltimore Colts, Denver Broncos, Pittsburgh Steelers, and Washington Redskins as a cornerback and safety.

Eventually, in 1986, Wade received a collegiate offer he could not refuse. At age 41, Wade signed a five-year contract with the University of Maryland, making him the first African-American head coach in the history of the Atlantic Coast Conference (ACC). Obviously, this distinction made him unique at the University of Maryland and he was not fully received with open arms by the College Park community.

The color of his skin was just one of many disadvantages others placed on Wade. He had inherited a basketball team riddled with controversy and scrutinized by the media. Wade was replacing 17-year veteran Lefty Driesell, who resigned after the untimely death of former player and All-American forward Len Bias. After being picked second overall by the Boston Celtics in the 1986 NBA draft, Bias was found dead in his Maryland dorm less than 48 hours later, from a cocaine overdose. His death brought a world of questions to Maryland's basketball program and relentless media focus that Wade had not been accustomed to during his high school experiences.

While Driesell remained under investigation by the state grand jury and the university under investigation by the NCAA, Maryland looked to Wade to rebuild the disgraced basketball program. Chancellor John B. Slaughter thought Wade was just the man for the job. Slaughter, who was a rare African-American head of a major university, had met Wade the year before and quickly took notice of Wade's emphasis on education and discipline for his players. Right away, Slaughter thought that Wade had the character, coaching knowledge, and life skills focus that would cut it in the collegiate coaching ranks.

Wade faced yet another challenge by stepping into the program just two days before practices began. He had no time for recruiting and barely any time to plan practices, as he was still finishing out a high school football season that would overlap with college basketball for nearly two weeks. Bias' death and the persistent media put excessive pressure on the Terrapins during Wade's first season. The mentally drained and emotionally scarred team had a 9-17 record, going 0-14 in ACC games. Yet, Wade was determined to prove all his naysayers wrong. His first season had been riddled with hate mail and unsupportive fans, some of whom were all too happy to see Wade's squad go winless in conference play.

College coaches are often given just four years to build a strong program, regardless of the preexisting circumstances. Wade wasted no time leaving his mark. After he had had a year to recruit and establish his authority in the program, the Terrapins had a much improved second season under Wade. The 1987–88 team had an 18-13 record, with the Terrapins even making the second round of the NCAA Southeast regional tournament. The highlight of the season may have come when they upset basketball powerhouse Duke University, 72-69, in Durham, North Carolina. Although still posting a losing ACC record, the Terrapins saw a drastic improvement from 0-14 to 6-8 in conference contests.

Wade made changes on the court but was determined to make changes in the classroom as well. After all, his focus on academics had been one of the most compelling reasons for Chancellor Slaughter to hire him. Slaughter had noticed that Wade stayed in touch with his players after they went away to college and even insisted many of them call him after each college test. Wade genuinely cared about their potential as people. Elzee Gladden, Dunbar's principal, told William Gildea of the *Washington Post* that Wade's academic "discipline" enabled several players to complete college who otherwise might not have. She had a plaque outside her office that read the "Bob Wade Award" for "leadership, academics, and athletics." The order of the words placed the appropriate emphasis on each. Following suit, the Maryland athletic department decided to enforce a minimum GPA for athletes the following season. The minimum requirement gradually increased each year, forcing fourth- and fifth-year seniors to have a cumulative 2.0 GPA to be eligible.

Wade stayed with the Terrapins for one more season, but the atmosphere in which he had been hired was unrelenting, and Maryland asked him to resign after the 1988–89 season in which his team went 9-20. Chancellor Slaughter had left Maryland for Occidental College in California, leaving Wade without his biggest supporter.

Nonetheless, Baltimore's love for Coach Wade remained. Baltimore remembered Wade as the inspirational coach who led Dunbar High School to a boy's basketball national championship in 1982–83, the same year he was named National Coach of the Year. Baltimore welcomed Wade's return and hired him in 1995 as the assistant director of the department of recreation and parks in Baltimore and later as the city schools' athletic director. Wade continued to stress academics to the Baltimore high school athletes by establishing study hall at Dunbar High School and academic camps at both the University of Maryland Baltimore County (UMBC) and the University of Maryland at College Park. In early 1997, the first academic camp was held, offering academic courses, a basketball mixer, cultural enrichment, and service learning opportunities. Course topics have included SAT prep, rites of passage, college admissions, health, computers, substance abuse, and banking.

Even though Wade's reputation was built largely on his success as a basketball coach, Dunbar High School named a football game on October 20, 2006 the Bob Wade Classic. School officials hoped honoring Wade would bring back the hundreds of Dunbar alumni who had been influenced by Wade during their high school careers. Wade had brought so much to the lives of his young football players because he could speak from their perspectives.

John Thompson, Jr.

Black Coaches & Administrators and First African-American Head Coach to Win an NCAA Men's Basketball Championship

by Jessica Bartter

Personal Collection of John Thompson.

John Thompson is widely known for a basketball career that includes an NIT Championship and All-American honors at Providence College, two years in the National Basketball Association, a winning high school coaching record, a successful, three-decade coaching tenure at Georgetown University and a professional radio and television sports commentating job. What many are not familiar with is his compassionate side. Recently, when asked by columnist Jon Saraceno, "Had you been white and handled your Georgetown team the same way—" Thompson abruptly responded, "I would've been called a humanitarian."[1]

Saraceno was referring to Thompson's abrasive relationship with the media while conducting closed practices, his philosophy that taught each of his teams it was them against the world, his boycott and name-calling against the NCAA, and his signature white towel draped over the shoulder of his suit during each game, an accessory onlookers felt had symbolic meaning. Thompson was referring to his ability to take a 3-23 Georgetown team to the NCAA Tournament within three seasons, his ability to keep student-athletes focused on graduation, the fact that 26 of his players were drafted by the NBA, and his concern for shielding players from media pressure.

Thompson's commitment to basketball started at John Carroll High School in Washington, D.C., where he led his team to 55 consecutive victories and two city championships. Thompson then graced Providence College, becoming an All-American player and leading the Friars to the 1963 NIT Championship. In 1964, Thompson and his teammates made an appearance in their first NCAA Tournament. Thompson graduated at the top of the school's points, scoring average, and field goal percentage lists and finished his career second in rebounds. Thompson went from the Providence Friars to the Boston Celtics and in just two years was a member of an NBA championship team.

In 1966, Thompson hung up his jersey for the last time and embarked on a career as a social worker and teacher. He earned a master's degree from the University of the District of Columbia before coaching at St. Anthony High School. By amassing an impressive 122-28 record, Thompson attracted the attention of Georgetown University's basketball program. In 1972, the Hoyas went 3-23, and Georgetown went on the hunt for a leader who could improve the future of Hoya basketball. Problematically, few coaches were willing to accept the challenge of reversing the Hoyas' fortunes. John Thompson gladly accepted the job and dared to try to do an about-face with the team.

Thompson's coaching skill quickly put the Hoyas in the forefront of basketball headlines. Within three short seasons, Georgetown made the NCAA Tournament, largely due to Coach Thompson. First and foremost though, Thompson was an educator. Regardless of how good or bad his players' skills were, Thompson treated them as *students* and athletes. He encouraged them to stay their full four years to graduate rather than leave for millions of dollars in the NBA. Not until 1996 did he lose a player to the draft. With two years of eligibility left, Allen Iverson became the first student-athlete to leave early in Thompson's 24 years. Iverson was picked number one by the Philadelphia 76ers in the NBA draft. Of those student-athletes who did remain four years, Thompson boasted a graduation rate of 97 percent.

As one of only a handful of African-American coaches in college basketball, Thompson quickly gained a reputation for voicing his opinion. Although his 6-foot-10-inch, 300-pound build intimidated players, coaches, and members of the press, Thompson felt an obligation, as he hoped all citizens did, to take a stand against injustice.

As one of the premier collegiate coaches in the country, Thompson saw firsthand the lack of diversity in college coaching. In 1984 when Thompson won the NCAA Tournament, he celebrated two victories. In addition to achieving the ultimate prize in college basketball, Thompson was the first African-American to win a Division I Championship. Thompson set himself on the path to ensure that he would not be last.

Thompson became an outspoken advocate for people of color, although the media often dismissed his statements as the rants and raves of an angry black man. Eventually Thompson found his voice with the Black Coaches & Administrators (BCA), formerly known as the Black Coaches Association. Thompson had always stood up for players, students, and coaches, but it was his passion for diversifying collegiate coaching positions that led to his involvement with the BCA. The BCA is a non-profit organization whose primary purpose is to foster the growth and development of people of color at all levels of sports. The BCA's mission is to address significant issues pertaining to the participation and employment of people of color in sport in general and intercollegiate athletics in particular, to assist people of color aspiring to have a career in athletics through educational and professional development programming and scholarships, and to provide youth and diverse communities the opportunity to interact positively with the BCA as a corporate citizen and community builder through a variety of alliances.

In 1987, the issue of opportunity and advancement was being discussed simultaneously by two separate but significant African-American coaching groups, the assistant basketball and football coaches. With the help of John Thompson, John Chaney, George Raveling, Nolan Richardson, and others, the two groups merged to form a unified voice through one organization. The organization became known as the Black Coaches Association in 1988 and membership was extended to all coaches. In July 2007, the BCA announced its name change to the Black Coaches & Administrators.

In 1989, Thompson boycotted two games in protest of NCAA legislation known as Proposition 42. Prop 42 prevented student-athletes from receiving scholarships if they did not meet the minimum requirements of the already controversial Prop 48, which required student-athletes to earn 700 on the SAT and have a 2.0 GPA to compete as a freshman. Thompson and other BCA members believed the proposition, relying heavily on standardized tests, resulted in fewer scholarships for African-American student-athletes. Many educators were convinced then that standardized tests were biased against people of color and women.

Thompson was an advocate for gender equality as well as racial equality. Although he often spoke publicly about his confidence in women's ability to coach men's sports teams, Thompson knew that actions would speak louder than words. In 1972, Thompson was the first to put a woman on the bench with the hiring of Mary Fenlon as an athletic advisor. Five years later, he was the first to hire a female trainer, Lorry Michel.

The college basketball world lost a legendary coach in 1999 when Thompson resigned from Georgetown University. Upon his departure, colleague Nolan Richardson reflected upon Thompson's impact. Richardson said, "John Thompson is to black basketball coaches what Martin Luther King was to his people during his time. He was a leader, a trailblazer and someone who made a lot of things possible for us. He went down the path first to get the rest of us there."[2]

Despite his departure, Thompson's impact is still being felt on the coaching community. Since 1995, African-American head coaches have more than doubled in college basketball. In 2005, African-American coaches peaked at 25.3 percent after representing only 11.3 percent in 1995. Since 57.8 percent of basketball players were African-American in 2005, much work remains to achieve a coaching staff whose diversity mirrors that of its players. Nonetheless, the progress represents one more victory for John Thompson, Jr., and his colleagues to celebrate. One of America's top collegiate head coaches is his son, John Thompson III at Georgetown, who led his team to the 2007 Final Four. The legacy lives on in college sport.

Notes

1. Jon Saraceno, "Q&A with Former Georgetown Coach John Thompson," *USA Today*, March 24, 2006.

2. Associated Press, "Arkansas Coach Praises Thompson," AP Online, January 9, 1999.

George Raveling

Black Coaches & Administrators

by Jessica Bartter

Courtesy of the University of Southern California, Sport Information Office.

On August 28, 1963, under a scorching hot sun, Dr. Martin Luther King addressed a crowd of more than 200,000 in front of the Lincoln Memorial in Washington, D.C. Just to the side of him on stage stood a tall but skinny ex-basketball player who, just hours before, had volunteered to serve Dr. King as a security guard. The speech left the security guard inspired beyond any locker room message or civil rights speech he had heard before, and he could not have predicted the power of those four immortal words: "I have a dream." The untapped, future inspirational speaker inside him drove him to follow Dr. King after the conclusion and request a copy of his speech. Without hesitation, Dr. King stretched out his hand, giving the typed speech to his volunteer security guard, a young and impressionable George Raveling.

Although Dr. Martin Luther King was among the first famous public figures Raveling stood proud with, there were many more to follow. Raveling shared coaching responsibility with Bob Knight and Lefty Driesell. He coached superstars like Michael Jordan and Patrick Ewing. After years of being watched as he paced the bench with Villanova, Maryland, USC, Iowa, and the men's national team, Raveling remained in the public eye by commentating on college basketball games on television.

Raveling once joked that it was his high school coach who got him into basketball. "When I went to Catholic high school in Philadelphia, we just had one coach for football and basketball. He took all of us who turned out and had us run through a forest. The ones who ran into the trees were on the football team."[1] Raveling's light-hearted personality combined with his extensive basketball knowledge made him a vibrant commentator for television viewers. Raveling's basketball knowledge stems from his experiences at the college level, both as a player and as a coach.

After his father died when Raveling was nine years old, his mother suffered a mental breakdown and could no longer care for him. The Washington, D.C., native was shipped to an orphanage in Hoban Heights, Pennsylvania, where he excelled in basketball. Although he was skilled, basketball was not his only focus. In high school, Raveling decided he wanted to be a pilot in the Air Force.

Unaware that colleges gave scholarships to students to play basketball and other sports, Raveling spent most of high school dreaming of a career in the Air Force until his senior year, when he was summoned by college recruiters. Villanova University eventually won Raveling's talent. After starting for three years, Raveling finished his career third on the school's all-time rebounds list. Despite being drafted in 1960 by the Philadelphia 76ers, Raveling took his life down a different path by becoming a marketing analyst. His marketing genius later assisted his recruiting efforts when he returned to basketball as a coach.

Raveling's love for basketball was deep-rooted and could not be washed away with the responsibilities of a job in the "real world." He wanted to be a part of basketball so much that he accepted a part-time, unpaid position at his alma mater. Raveling moved on to assist Lefty Driesell at the University of Maryland before earning the head coaching position at Washington State University in 1972.

The WSU Cougars, under Raveling's guidance, returned to the NCAA tournament for the first time in almost 40 years in 1980. Raveling brought them back in 1983. After amassing a 167-136 record and seven winning seasons in 11 years, Raveling headed east to the University of Iowa where he earned two more NCAA tournament berths in just four years. Many were happy to see Raveling return to the Pac-10 Conference in 1986 when he was hired by USC. In keeping with his trend, the Trojans earned two more NCAA tournament berths as well as two NIT invitations in the early 1990s.

In the midst of his college success, Raveling was called upon by several national team coaches for his assistance. He served the

USA team as assistant coach at the 1979 Pan American Games, as the west regional coach at the 1979 USA Olympic Trials, and as the assistant coach for the USA Olympic team in 1980. Raveling also served the 1984 USA Olympic team as the assistant coach when it won the ninth Olympic gold medal for men's basketball.

This high-profile coach was forever changed by his moment in passing with Dr. Martin Luther King. With the gift of Dr. King's speech, Raveling inherited a commitment to equal rights. Raveling applied most of his energy to the coaching world, a world that remains unbalanced even today in its representation of people of color. After years of experience coaching in the college basketball world, Raveling helped lead the charge for change with the Black Coaches & Administrators (BCA).

In 1993, Raveling was among the faces of the BCA boycott against an issues summit that was sponsored by the National Association of Basketball Coaches (NABC). Although the NABC had offered Raveling its executive director position, he felt the BCA needed his support to stand against several changes and issues that the NCAA was proposing and that the NABC supported. The BCA and Raveling felt minorities were being ignored and suppressed. Raveling brought several key questions into the public eye, culminating in increased pressure on the NCAA. Of the NCAA and the media, Raveling asked for more to be done about the NCAA's perceived long-standing indifference to the lack of minority coaches and student-athletes. Among other things, Raveling brought attention to the lack of minorities in high-level NCAA and USA basketball positions, as well as the miniscule number of minority females coaching women's basketball.

Raveling was at the forefront of the BCA charge to boycott the three-day summit that brought together college sport's top coaches, administrators, and conference commissioners. Raveling and other black coaches demanded respect and recognition from the NCAA before they would give their attention to other college sport issues. Raveling's willingness to request "a greater sensitivity [be] given to all ethnic groups"[2] led to a change in the faces of the NCAA. Although the percentage of African-Americans has increased in vice president, chief of staff, director, and support staff positions in the NCAA since 1997, the percentage of administrators still calls for improvement. Raveling, John Thompson, John Chaney, and Nolan

Richardson propelled the BCA into a powerful voice for change in the mid-1990s.

In 1994, Raveling's car was blindsided by another vehicle; the accident left him with serious injuries, ending his coaching career and almost ending his life. He suffered nine broken ribs, a collapsed lung, and a fractured pelvis and clavicle. Bleeding in his chest cavity kept Raveling in the intensive care unit for two weeks. Feeling lucky to be alive, Raveling decided to devote his full energy to what appeared to be a long road to recovery. Citing his rehabilitation needs, Raveling retired from the Trojans' coaching responsibilities at age 57.

Youth and basketball remain his passions, evidenced by his recent work with Nike, as its global basketball sports marketing director, where he has worked since his USC retirement. Raveling has cemented his coaching brilliance in writing by publishing two books on rebounding called *War on the Boards* and *A Rebounder's Workshop*. The books just strengthen a coaching legacy already cast.

Notes

1. George Raveling, The Free Online Library, 2005, www.thefreelibrary.com/George+Raveling-a0130570602 (accessed September 16, 2007).

2. Gene Wojciechowski, "Black Coaches' Group Vows Season of Action," *The Sporting News*, October 25, 1993.

John Chaney

Black Coaches & Administrators

by Jessica Bartter

John Chaney was not like any typical college basketball coach. He didn't model himself after other coaches. He didn't pride himself on wins versus losses. He didn't stress athletics over academics. He didn't measure his success by the number of NBA players he coached. And now, in his retirement, he doesn't consider a basketball championship as his proudest career moment. Instead, this Hall of Fame basketball coach reveres Paul Robeson, preaches education, feels blessed for the numerous athletes he's coached that have touched his life, and counts being honored with the Pennsylvania Distinguished Faculty Award as his greatest career achievement.

Known as a tough, outspoken, controversial, in-your-face type of coach, Chaney was often deemed confrontational and abrasive. But, like Paul Robeson, Chaney is simply the type of person who refuses to be a silent bystander to daily injustices against poor, disadvantaged, or minority populations. Chaney chose his battles wisely and has never shied away from righting a wrong, even when it meant he would have to apologize later. As Temple University's Athletic Director Bill Bradshaw put it upon Chaney's retirement in 2006, he is "a rebel with many causes . . . who would rather teach a lesson than win a game."[1]

Chaney's commitment to social justice came from his early exposure to poverty.

Growing up in Jacksonville, Florida, Chaney recalls his mother cooking in the kitchen while sloshing through standing water on her floor. Whenever it rained, a frequent occurrence in Florida, the rain water flooded their home, ushering in rats, cockroaches, frogs, and an immeasurable amount of dirt. Chaney could never have imagined that he would one day slosh around with the likes of Red Auerbach, Dean Smith, and John Thompson in the Naismith Hall of Fame. It is an understatement to say he has come a long way.

When he was in high school, Chaney's mother and stepfather moved him and his stepbrother and stepsister north, settling in South

Philadelphia. Four years later, Chaney graduated as the Public League Player of the Year. Such honors still didn't garner Chaney any local attention from college recruiters.

By simply graduating high school, Chaney exceeded the expectations of his mother, who never passed the seventh grade. Given this background, college was a far reach for both of their imaginations. Seeing his lack of motivation for a college education, Chaney's high school coach, Sam Browne, convinced Chaney and his family that college was his key—his key out of South Philly, to an education and to a better life. Coach Browne connected Chaney with Bethune-Cookman College, returning the young man to his home state of Florida.

Although he was caught up in the idea of continuing to play the game he loved, he took longer to digest the educational aspect of college. In the end, college did allow Chaney to continue playing basketball, but more importantly, it allowed him to earn his degree. Once he finally realized its value, Chaney always remained focused on the importance of education. He later forced it down the throats of his own players, never letting them believe that they attended college just to play basketball. He made it clear to his players that they needed to make education their first priority.

After brief stints with the Eastern Professional Basketball League and the Harlem Globetrotters, Chaney first applied his educational theory to middle school kids at Sayre Junior High, where he coached basketball and gymnastics. The next stepping stone in Chaney's road was Philadelphia's Simon Gratz High School, where he coached his young athletes to a 63-23 record. Chaney then leaped to the college level at Division II Cheyney State College, now the Cheyney University of Pennsylvania.

Chaney spent a decade building Cheyney into a basketball powerhouse and infusing his name in the minds of college basketball fans across the country. Chaney took his team to the NCAA Division II Tournament eight out of 10 years while amassing a 225-59 record. In 1978, Cheyney was crowned National Champion, and Chaney garnered National Coach of the Year honors. In order to practice what he preached, Chaney also taught at Cheyney University and, in 1979, earned the State of Pennsylvania Distinguished Faculty Award, his proudest honor.

At the age of 50, Chaney took the last step in his path to the peak of his basketball career when he moved to Division I Temple University. Chaney led the Owls to a 516-252 record on their way to 17 NCAA Tournament appearances. In 27 years at Temple, Chaney never reached the apex of collegiate basketball, winning a Division I title. In fact, the Owls went to the regional finals five times but were blocked out of the Final Four in each attempt. That did not prevent the Honors Committee, made up of Hall of Famers, basketball executives, media members, and other contributors to the game of basketball, from voting Chaney into the Naismith Basketball Hall of Fame in 2001. His demand for excellence on and off the court earned him that honor.

Although Chaney was the face of Temple University basketball for nearly three decades, his start in the sport came many years prior when he was just a young boy. As the child who loved the game grew into a powerful public figure in the basketball arena, he never lost sight of his roots or his determination to stand for those without a voice. He found his voice to be particularly influential through the Black Coaches & Administrators (BCA).

With the BCA, Chaney was able to use his basketball stature and recognition for a more important victory. In 1994, Chaney led a charge against the NCAA when basketball scholarships were decreased from 15 to 13. Chaney, Nolan Richardson, John Thompson, and George Raveling put themselves in the forefront of the competition for equality. The coaches believed the scholarship reduction would prevent more African-American student-athletes from obtaining entrance to college, thereby decreasing opportunities for education in the African-American community. The BCA coaches uniformly responded by voting to boycott NCAA basketball games. The Department of Justice stepped in to mediate and, subsequently, the NCAA formed a special committee to listen specifically to the complaints and concerns of the BCA. Consequently, the boycott was prevented and the committee made recommendations and amendments in response to the BCA's requests. Thanks to John Chaney and his fellow BCA leaders, the voice of black coaches was heard.

In March of 2006, Chaney announced his retirement, but once a teacher, always a teacher. Chaney still offers his signature advice: follow the rules, be responsible, have respect for others, define yourself every day of your life, and learn to say no. Chaney has defined himself as a successful basketball coach who never hesitates to use the power and respect he has earned to stand up for justice for those who might not be able stand up for themselves. When their voices cannot be heard, John Chaney makes sure his voice is loud and clear.

Note

1. Jimmy Golen, "Hall Exhibit Gives John Chaney a Pulpit," AP Online, August 8, 2006.

Nolan Richardson

Black Coaches & Administrators

by Jessica Bartter

Nolan Richardson is no stranger to integration. Brick by brick, Richardson has torn down wall after wall using basketball as his means and determination as his way. The first wall to crumble came at the community college national championships when Richardson's players took home the title. Richardson flattened the next hurdle by winning the National Invitational Tournament (NIT) before winning the ultimate crown, an NCAA Championship. Most importantly, Richardson was the first African-American coach to win at all levels, a feat that smashed down invisible barriers so many others had faced. Long before his NCAA title, Richardson helped integrate other facets of basketball as a player and a coach.

Richardson first helped integrate basketball as a high school student. The El Paso native integrated Bowie High School as a basketball player in the 1950s. His athleticism extended beyond the court as Richardson emerged as a four-sport standout. In 1957, he was the only African-American student on a baseball team that earned a spot in the district championships. Despite being the best player on the team, his coach had to tell him that he would not be able to stay in the same hotel as his teammates, or in any hotel for that matter. Instead, Richardson was going to be put up at a local black woman's house on the other side of the train tracks from the hotel. Richardson was crushed by the inequality of the accommodations and decided he did not want to go. Hearing this, Richardson's grandmother, his main caregiver after his parents died, enlightened Richardson about the power of sport. She encouraged him not to back away but to fight for his right on the field. She knew his standout performance at the plate and on the mound would be enough to show his equality. Richardson took his grandmother's powerful and insightful words of wisdom with him to Texas Western College and still references them today, some 50 years later.

Although Texas Western College, now known as the University of Texas at El Paso (UTEP), was about one percent African-American at the time, Richardson decided to continue his basketball career there in order to be close to home. Richardson was the only African-American on the team. He was prohibited from interacting socially with his teammates outside of school. He could not go see a movie with them or even stay in the same hotel when the team traveled. During his sophomore year, the team traveled to a tournament in Shreveport, Louisiana, without Richardson because the host school, Centenary College, did not allow African-Americans to play on its court. Without their leading scorer, Texas Western went 0-3.

Richardson played his senior year under legendary Coach Don Haskins. Coach Haskins went on to recruit the best players regardless of skin color and won an NCAA national championship with five African-American starters, a statement that previously had never been made.

In 1965, Richardson turned to coaching to apply his basketball skill to many fortunate young athletes by returning to his alma mater, Bowie High School. As a result, he became the first black coach in the city of El Paso. After several years, Richardson moved on to coach the student-athletes at Western Texas Junior College. Together, they had a remarkable run.

In Richardson's first year as a junior college head coach, Western Texas won its conference. The next year, it captured the conference title again and made it to the Final Four of the NJCAA Championships. In just his third year, Western Texas achieved the pinnacle of junior college basketball when it finished the season 37-0 and became NJCAA Champion. Richardson was the first African-American coach to win the junior college tournament.

To no one's surprise, Richardson became a legend in El Paso, Texas. A school, a street, and a recreation center have all been named in his honor, but after his 1980 championship with Western Texas, the local legend received an offer to leave El Paso that he could not refuse.

Richardson's success attracted attention from college programs. Despite the fact that the Southwestern Conference had never had an African-American coach, the University of Tulsa hoped Richardson would be the man to turn their troubled program around. Richardson quickly proved he was up to the task. In just his third game as head coach during the 1980–81 season, the Hurricanes stunned the defending national champions, the University of Louisville. That season, Tulsa went on to capture the NIT title.

Richardson became only the second coach in NCAA history to win either an NCAA or NIT title in his first season as head coach.

During his five seasons at Tulsa, where he was widely noted for his polka dot shirts and cowboy boots, Richardson led the Hurricanes to three NCAA Tournament appearances and two NIT appearances. He became the first coach in NCAA history to win 50 games in his first two seasons as his teams went on to earn a 119-37 record (.763 winning percentage).

Successes generally lead people on to bigger and better things. For Richardson, this meant the University of Arkansas. Richardson took the Razorbacks to the Final Four three times. In 1990, they lost to Duke in the semi-finals. After eight seasons under Richardson, Arkansas won the 1994 NCAA Tournament Championship. Nicknamed "40 minutes of hell," Richardson's intense style of defense earned him National Coach of the Year honors in 1994. The Razorbacks returned to championship competition in 1995 but lost to UCLA in the finals.

In 2002, Arkansas let Richardson go. Many thought the issue of race was in play with the decision. Nolan Richardson had a history of speaking out for opportunities for other African-Americans to coach and for better chances for young African-Americans to get college scholarships. As a leader of the Black Coaches & Administrators along with John Thompson, John Chaney, and George Raveling, Richardson was a visible presence and clearly audible voice for change. Although all four are no longer active with the BCA, all still speak out. Richardson testified in Congress in 2007 on the issue of college racial hiring practices.

Richardson never let go of basketball. In 2005, he coached the Panama National Team. Under Richardson, they earned a berth at the World Championships for the first time in 19 years.

Richardson's name reaches near and far, locally and internationally, from a small high school program to a big-time college community. His influence has been felt nationwide, and Richardson has a long list of firsts under his name. Most importantly, he hopes he is not the last when it comes to successes for African-American coaches. Meanwhile, Nolan Richardson will always be a pioneer for his stellar coaching career and dedication to using basketball to help young men develop into winners on the court of life.

Eddie Robinson

A Once-in-a-Lifetime Man

by Richard Lapchick

When Eddie Robinson passed in the spring of 2007, 7,500 people viewed his body in the State Capitol in Baton Rouge and 9,000 attended his funeral.

Eddie Robinson's coaching career at Grambling in deep, rural Louisiana lasted through 11 presidents and three wars. Grambling was the home to Coach and his wife, Doris, for 59 years. They were married that long, and he coached for 56 years—all at the same institution! When he retired in November of 1997, many people in America stood up and took note for the first time of the winningest coach in the history of college football. In the African-American community, he was very likely the best-known coach in America and was surely the most beloved. However, institutionalized racial barriers kept Robinson a secret from most of white America outside of the world of sports.

Initially a coach in a segregated society, Eddie Robinson helped football transcend race in the America he loved and treasured. I coauthored his autobiography in the hopes that it would help Americans of every color and in every corner of our country discover the full meaning of the life of this great son of America. We called the autobiography *Never Before, Never Again* because there never was nor will be another man, coach, husband, or American like Coach Robinson.

At a time when so many coaches and players seem ready to extol their own virtues, Robinson was always reluctant to discuss any of his victories or records. He was so humble. I had to drag game stories about himself out of him, because he wanted to talk about his players and fellow coaches as men. He wanted to talk about life and philosophy, which was a pure pleasure for me to listen to. Nonetheless, getting him to talk about himself was very difficult.

In *Never Before, Never Again*, Coach Robinson wrote, "They said I would never be able to reach my third grade dream of coaching football. I saw a coach then, he looked so good and his boys seemed to worship him. The fact that he was their hero was written all over their faces. That was the life I wanted. Seventy years later I ended a 56-year ride as a college head coach!"

After achieving one of sports' most incredible records with his 400th win in 1995, Coach Eddie Robinson said, "I wish I could cut up all of these victories into 400 pieces and give them to all the players and assistant coaches I have had. They are the ones who truly deserve the credit."[1] Now that I know him I see that these words were coming straight from his heart.

The stories about his retirement brought new exposure for Coach in communities where his messages of tradition, loyalty, family, and racial understanding are desperately needed. Eddie Robinson began to become a household name after every major newspaper and TV station featured him on multiple occasions throughout the 1997 season. Viewers and readers caught glimpses of his wisdom and his wit, finally completely opening American's consciousness to this great American leader who happened to be a coach and happened to be African-American. The extent of the TV and media coverage after his death was equal to that when he retired. His life's accomplishments were again before the American public. Seeing the news coverage after his passing filled with tributes made me smile through my sadness. America does know Eddie Robinson.

In 1941, he assumed the role of mentor, role model, father, and counselor to his student-athletes both on and off the field. Grambling and college coaching have never been the same, nor have the thousands of young men who played for Coach Robinson. He guided the once-obscure Grambling State Tigers to national and international acclaim while helping to produce championship teams and players.

Yet the career-related accomplishment of which Coach is proudest is that 80 percent of his players graduated, in a sport in which the national average during his tenure had been less than 45 percent. Most head coaches today delegate caring for student-athletes to assistants, but Coach Robinson spent 54 years personally going into the athletic dorm with his now famous cow bell at 6:30 A.M. each weekday to be sure his men were awake and ready to go to class.

Coach has proven the power of an individual to make a huge difference in the lives of young people.

Coach Robinson helped motivate men at Grambling to succeed on and off the field. Under Robinson's leadership, Grambling became one of the most productive training camps for professional football; more than 300 of his players went to pro camps. More than 200 made the active rosters in the NFL. Three have been inducted into the NFL Hall of Fame. Many of his former players have become coaches themselves. Several players were, like their coach, pioneers for African-American athletes: Tank Younger was the first player drafted from an historically black college; Buck Buchanan was the first African-American to be selected as the NFL's number one draft choice; James Harris was the first African-American starting quarterback; and Doug Williams was the first African-American quarterback to start and win a Super Bowl.

But it was never just about training athletes. Robinson believed that as a coach he had many more responsibilities than just teaching the mechanics of football. Not only did 80 percent of his players graduate but many have gone on to become public servants, lawyers, and doctors. Joseph B. Johnson became Grambling's president. Raymond Jetson became a Louisiana state representative.

Of all of his accomplishments, he maintains that his greatest achievements are that he has had only one wife and one job for over 56 years. Robinson came to Grambling in 1941 just months after marrying Doris, who had been his sweetheart since he was 14! The marriage was still going strong when he passed.

They still held hands 65 years after they first met. I saw it, and it was moving. I was told on many occasions, "Listen, Rich, I have to go now to have lunch with Doris," or, "It's time for dinner with Doris." At first I thought he might just be tired from hours of talking to me. But then we would always pick it up at 10:00 P.M. and go until 1:00 A.M. For years I believed I didn't know any man who loved his wife as much as I did. I may have met him that first night with Coach.

In spite of the racial barriers that surrounded his life, Coach somehow maintained a positive attitude about opportunity in America for people of all colors. Coach believed: "We are in a position to do a lot of good and that's the real importance of this work. America offers more opportunity to young people than any other country in the world."[2]

Legendary Penn State Coach Joe Paterno said of Robinson's historic contributions to the game of college football, "Nobody has ever done or will do what Eddie Robinson has done for this game. Our profession will never be able to repay Eddie Robinson for what he has done for the country and the profession of football."[3]

Muhammad Ali said, "They call me the greatest. I know that the greatest football coach who ever stepped foot on the field is Coach Robinson. I have admired what he has done in turning boys into men. He is a credit to sport and to humanity."[4]

I flew to Monroe, Louisiana, and drove to Ruston, right outside of Grambling, to meet Coach for the first time in April 1997. In my phone call setting up the meeting, Coach told me, "No one goes to Grambling unless they plan to go there." I understood what he meant when I arrived at the Holiday Inn in Ruston deep in the Louisiana countryside.

It was the night Major League Baseball gave its tribute to Jackie Robinson on the 50th anniversary of his breaking baseball's color barrier. We watched the lobby TV and then went to my room to start the interviews. At 2:30 A.M., the then-78-year-old was still going strong, but I suggested we pick it up again the next day.

I will always remember that I called my wife at that late hour and told her she would meet someone so much like my own dad, Joe Lapchick. Dad had himself been a legendary basketball coach. He had died before I met my wife. Not only did she get the chance with Coach, but we also became good friends with Coach's wife, Doris, who reminded us so much of my mom. We enjoyed 10 years of treasured family friendship.

I realized that night that these two men named Robinson had helped to change America.

In the course of the next year, Coach Robinson told me more than 50 stories about his amazing life. We decided to stop the interviews and write the book, which was finally published in 1999. I was in touch with Coach and Doris every couple of weeks after the publication. Before the Alzheimer's started to wear on him, Coach told me another 20 plus stories that were book worthy.

I did nearly 100 hours of interviews on the phone. I would take notes and tape his words for three hours at a time. My wife, Ann, is not a big sports fan but she often sat on the floor in the home office listening to Coach talk, mesmerized by his wisdom and philosophy. He talked around four themes.

The first was his love for Doris. They always held hands, even after nearly seven decades of marriage. He wanted his players to see a happy home so it could be envisioned as the center of their future lives. He wanted them to see it was okay for a man to show affection for a woman he loved. This was a real life love affair.

The second theme was the role he played in American race relations. Never a public crusader for civil rights, Coach courageously challenged racism in his own way by proving that a black man could be a great football coach and, simultaneously, build the tenacity and determination of those in his charge as he led adolescents into manhood. I think of Coach Robinson as every bit the barrier breaker that Jackie Robinson and Muhammad Ali were.

Looking back at the issue of race, Coach said in *Never Before, Never Again*, "We made extraordinary statements to break stereotypes: Buchanan was the first Grambling player picked in the first round of the NFL draft in 1963. Grambling won 17 SWAC championships and nine National Black Championships. The Howard Cosell documentary on Grambling in 1968 had black and white sports fans calling me a 'great football coach.' As we traveled across the South, we tried to use Grambling green [dollars] to quietly integrate hotels and restaurants. None of my players or coaches were seen at demonstrations in the 1960s. We made our own. The Civil Rights Movement was helping to change the laws. Our goal was to help to change attitudes."

The Reverend Jesse Jackson told me, "Eddie Robinson has always been a hero in my eyes. Without question, he is an ambassador for our people, not only African-Americans, but all Americans. That's why I have such respect for Coach Robinson."

The third theme was Eddie Robinson, the coach. His career at Grambling was all over the news after he passed. In spite of having more wins than any other coach, sending more than 300 players to NFL camps, having a graduation rate of 80 percent when football graduation rates were around 50 percent, and never having a player get in trouble with the law until his 56th year of coaching, Eddie

Robinson was never even offered an interview for a Division I-A university head coaching job. I do not think he ever would have left Grambling, but he told me he would have liked to have been asked. When I met him in 1997, there were eight African-American head coaches in Division I-A football. When he passed in 2007, there were only six African-Americans in that role.

The fourth theme was that Eddie Robinson was a proud American. That night in the Holiday Inn, there was a table filled with six older white men about Coach's age. They kept coming by us, shaking his hand, hugging him, asking how Doris was. These same men were raised in a racist, segregated South that Ruston, Louisiana, was surely part of, in their younger days. But Eddie Robinson had regularly walked that part of the earth and forced them to see a great American who happened to have black skin. He broke big barriers and smashed stereotypes along the way.

Coach Robinson told me he had never been called "an American" until he took Grambling to play in Japan in 1976. He had confronted segregation in his life. But Eddie and Doris Robinson would stand still for the national anthem, their eyes fixed on our flag. Often you would see tears in his eyes when the singer hit "the land of the free." He was proud of his country and always tried to make it better.

He was a proud American, even though as a high school student in Baton Rouge he could not buy a ticket to see LSU play football. Yet seven decades later he became the first African-American to lie in state in the state capitol of Baton Rouge.

Coach proved the power of an individual to make a huge difference in the lives of young people. He tried to prepare a new generation of coaches to help today's youth, because he knew that life had changed dramatically in America. Coach said to me, "I know life isn't easy for young people now. They face all these challenges that my generation didn't have. When I was growing up in Jackson and Baton Rouge, children weren't killing each other, crack didn't exist, I never heard of steroids, most families had a mother and father. Many of today's student-athletes were raised in poverty and despair. They know that some white people will decide who they are just because of what they look like. Yes, indeed, life is hard today."

That is why he assumed the role of mentor, role model, father, and counselor to his student-athletes both on and off the field.

Grown men who are leaders across our nation called each other after his passing, remembering this man who helped change their lives. I am lucky to be one of them, a better person for having known Coach Eddie Robinson.

Coach ended the book with, "If I had the chance, I would call for an instant replay of my entire life—in slow motion—so I could savor every second as I continue to work on the next stage of my life. If I could have created a game plan for my own life, I'd want to be born in America to my same parents, marry Doris, go to work for Grambling and have Eddie and Lillian as our children, their children as our grandchildren, and their children as our great grandchildren. I have a great life."

He certainly did.

Notes

1. Eddie Robinson with Richard Lapchick, *Never Before, Never Again: The Stirring Autobiography of Eddie Robinson, The Winningest Coach in the History of College Football* (New York: St. Martin's Press, 1999), 217.

2. Ibid.

3. Ibid., back cover.

4. Ibid.

Carolyn Peck

First African-American Female Head Coach to Win an NCAA Women's Basketball Championship

by Jenny Brenden

"Absence makes the heart grow fonder" is the lesson that Carolyn Peck learned when she stepped away from the sport of basketball after her college graduation. Peck was a shot-blocking machine in high school, averaging six blocks per game. She went on to have a great collegiate basketball career at Vanderbilt University, averaging 10.6 points and 5.8 rebounds per contest. When her college career drew to a close in 1988, Peck thought she was ready to walk away from the game and start anew.

Three years later Peck found herself playing professional basketball abroad in Japan from 1991 to 1993, where she was the league's leading rebounder for two years and also led her team to the league championship in her final season. She realized what many people working in sports already knew. "It is such a privilege to be around the game," Peck says. "It is such a special feeling to work in sports."[1] Distance from the game gave Peck insight into her own heart and her true desires for the future.

Peck had the opportunity to work with the best in the game when she became an assistant coach at the University of Tennessee under legendary head coach Pat Summitt. Summitt has not only evolved into the best in the women's game, but the men's game as well, surpassing Dean Smith as the winningest coach in NCAA history with her 880th win in 2005. Needless to say, coaching at Tennessee was a wonderful learning experience for Peck. She then moved on to serve as an assistant at the University of Kentucky for the 1995–96 season, followed by a season at Purdue University as an assistant with the Boilermakers.

Transition is typical in the life of a young, assistant collegiate coach, and Peck was certainly living up to that expectation. She learned from each of her coaching experiences and from each head coach that she worked under. In these years, Peck developed her coaching philosophy in preparation for when she would be beckoned to a head coaching position. That opportunity arose when Purdue head coach Nell Fortner stepped down to focus on USA Basketball. Fortner went on to lead the USA National team to an Olympic Gold medal in 2000. Peck became the head coach of the Purdue Boilermakers women's basketball team for the 1997–98 season.

Peck's coaching philosophy, whether drawn from those with whom she had coached or construed on her own, is certainly a good one. Peck sees coaching as a way to help players become the best they can be, on and off the court. She says, "My job is to make them the best young women that they can become: to show them that they can have a great basketball career, maintain being a lady and get a great education on the way."[2]

This philosophy brought her immediate success, as she led the Purdue Boilermakers to a 62-45 victory over Duke to win their first NCAA Championship in 1999, in only her second year as head coach. With this win, Peck put herself in the record books as the first African-American female coach to win a NCAA women's basketball title. That same season she was named the Associated Press National Coach of the Year, the WBCA Coach of the Year, and the Big Ten Coach of the Year—quite a lot of hardware for just one year.

Although it would be wonderful to see other African-American collegiate basketball coaches achieve the same success, the chances are slim, not because these coaches aren't qualified or capable of bringing home a championship, but simply because of the low representation of African-American head coaches at the Division I level. In the 2004–05 season, 24 of the 325 Division I women's basketball programs—excluding historically black colleges and universities (HBCUs)—had African-American, female head coaches. Of the 64 teams in the NCAA tournament that same year, only four were coached by African-American women and one of those schools was an HBCU.

Another interesting statistic is that in a sport in which 41.6 percent of the players are African-American, less than eight percent of the coaches are African-American women. By comparison, 58.2 percent of men's college basketball players and nearly 25 percent of coaches are African-American. "I think, other than college football, the worst situation as far as opportunities for people of color as both head and assistant coaches is women's college basketball,"[3] said

Richard Lapchick, who has compiled the *Racial and Gender Report Card* since the late 1980s.

Peck did not attempt to repeat her team's championship performance the next year. She had been tagged as a coaching prospect for the WNBA and had actually been named head coach and general manager of the WNBA expansion franchise, the Orlando Miracle, even before she began her championship season with Purdue.

On April 1, 1999 Peck officially became a part of the WNBA and three years later, almost to the day, on April 3, 2002, Peck was introduced as the eighth women's basketball coach in Florida Gator history. Just as she had followed her heart back to basketball so many years before, she had now followed it back to the collegiate level. As excited as Peck was about the move, many others were absolutely thrilled to see Peck return to the helm of a collegiate program. "Carolyn Peck was the first person who came to mind," the athletic director at UF, Jeremy Foley, said. "Carolyn's coaching and basketball pedigree is second to none, having worked with some of the most highly respected coaches in the game."[4]

Peck worked hard to live up to some very high expectations, and she delivered results in a short time period. In the four years she coached the Gators, she nurtured 27 Southeastern Conference academic honor roll selections, three post-season bids, including NCAA tournament bids in 2004 and 2006, and some very historical victories. During the 2005–06 season, Peck's Gators defeated No. 2 LSU and later, her squad upset the fifth-ranked Tennessee Lady Vols in Knoxville. However, Peck announced during the 2006–07 season that she was stepping down from the position at the University of Florida.

A former player of Peck's, at both the collegiate and professional levels, Katie Douglas, says Peck is a player's coach. "She is very people-oriented," Douglas says. "The WNBA is more business-oriented . . . even though she has shown she is very good at doing both."[5] She has made her mark as a college sport pioneer.

Notes

1. Oscar Dixon, "Once Fatigued, Peck on the Move in Hoop World," *USA Today*, May 10, 2002, http://usatoday.com/sports/preps/basketba/2002-05-01-all-usa-girls-peck.htm (accessed May 1, 2007).

2. Ibid.

3. Cathy Orton, "Black Female Coaches Few and Far Between," Washingtonpost .com, March 3, 2005, http://www.washingtonpost.com/wp-dyn/content/article/2005/ 03/26/AR2005032600511_pf.html (accessed May 2, 2007).

4. "Official Website of Carolyn Peck: Florida Gators Women's Basketball Head Coach," Gatorzone.com, http://www.gatorzone.com/carolynpeck/?sub=carolyn (accessed May 1, 2007).

5. Dixon, "Once Fatigued, Peck on the Move."

C. Vivian Stringer

First Basketball Coach to Take Three Schools to the Final Four

by Jenny Brenden

A 35-year career in Division I basketball is an amazing feat in itself, but C. Vivian Stringer also has 35 years of coaching accomplishments and records to complement her lengthy tenure. She has been a leader in her profession for many years and she is a coach who many of her peers ardently admire.

In 2000, when Stringer took her Rutgers Scarlet Knights to the Final Four, she became the first coach in either men's or women's collegiate basketball to take three different schools to the Final Four. This was not the first situation that placed Stringer in the position of pioneer. At a very young age Stringer wanted to be involved in athletics, but there were no sports offered for girls at her high school. With no other options, she fought to become the first African-American on the cheerleading squad, the only activity available for girls. Her dad told her, "It might not be about you but about future generations of young women. If you don't stand up for something, you'll fall for anything."[1] These words gave her the strength to fight for what she wanted and what she deserved. Stringer did make that cheerleading squad, and she hasn't stopped fighting ever since. Stringer continues to live by the meaning of her father's wise words by standing up for her beliefs.

She has been an outspoken advocate for more head coaching jobs for African-American women in college basketball. Her tremendous success on the court in the 2006–07 season, coupled with the class and dignity with which she handled the offensive racial remarks of shock jock radio host Don Imus, opened the door for a class of new African-American women who will lead their teams in the 2007–08 season

Stringer has been referred to as the "master builder" of collegiate basketball. Her stellar coaching skills and ability to build a good basketball program were in her track record right from the beginning of her career. Stringer spent 10-plus years at each of the schools at which she has coached, and each school eventually made a trip to the Final Four. This type of success is certainly not achieved by every coach in the NCAA. Some of the more well-known women's programs, like Tennessee and UConn, have coaches who have been at the same school for most of their careers and have created basketball dynasties. It is much easier to continue building a program that has a strong foundation. Stringer, however, started from scratch at three different schools and was still able to be successful with each program. The success Stringer has had with her programs can be directly attributed to her talent as a coach and as a leader.

Stringer's first year of coaching was in the 1971–72 season. A decade later she was leading her squad from Cheyney State, an historically black college located outside of Philadelphia, Pennsylvania, to the Final Four in the inaugural year of the NCAA-sponsored women's basketball tournament. She spent 11 seasons at Cheyney State before moving west to face a new challenge at the University of Iowa in the 1983–84 season. She took the Hawkeyes to the NCAA tournament nine seasons out of 12, including a Final Four appearance in 1993. Two years later, in 1995, Stringer took the head coaching job at Rutgers, remaining there ever since. The Scarlet Knights made their first of two Final Four appearances under the tutelage of Stringer in 2000 and again in 2007.

Each trip to the Final Four is special to Stringer, but each is also remembered by other events that happened in her life at the time of previous Final Four appearances. Stringer has said, "My heart has never been light in going to a Final Four."[2] Just prior to her 1982 appearance, Stringer found out that her infant daughter, Janine, had been diagnosed with spinal meningitis, a condition that caused brain damage and paralysis. When she made it to the Final Four in 1993 with her Iowa team, she was still grieving the death of her 47-year-old husband, Bill, who had died from a sudden heart attack the previous year. Shortly after the second Final Four appearance, Stringer decided it was too difficult being somewhere that held so many memories of her late husband. She wanted to stop feeling sorry for herself and she wanted others to stop feeling sorry for her as well. She needed to make a fresh start for herself and for her family, which included her daughter and two sons, David and Justin. Stringer made the move to Piscataway, New Jersey, and to Rutgers University. Although Stringer could get away from the school that held so many bittersweet memories, she couldn't stay away from the event that held the same. As a coach, Stringer must have found it difficult to have such wonderful and painful memories simultaneously attached to the Final Four, one of the greatest events in collegiate sports.

Stringer faced criticism early on at Rutgers as her salary was reportedly the highest of any women's basketball coach, higher even than all other coaches at Rutgers, male or female. This was a focal point for the media and for the fans. Some were leery as to whether Stringer was worth such a salary. However, those fighting for gender equity were pleased that she was paid more than the male coaches. It did not take long for Stringer to prove herself and her abilities. She was able to silence all of the questions when she brought the Scarlet Knights to the Final Four in 2000.

In her trip to the Final Four in 2007, Stringer and her Rutgers team had to deal with racial slurs directed at the student-athletes. The day after the team lost to Tennessee in the national championship game, talk show host Don Imus made a racially and sexually charged comment on the air directed at the young women of the Rutgers team. The incident created a media frenzy. Stringer and her team did accept an apology from Imus, but it was still a scarring event. Imus was fired from CBS radio for the comment, which set an example that this sort of language is unacceptable. Unfortunately, the idea conveyed by Imus' words is far too common, at times coming from the media, the music or film industry, or from the streets. Stringer had said in conversations with the media, "Don't we realize that it is time as Americans to all hold ourselves to a higher standard?"[3] Once again, she followed the advice of her father, standing up not only for herself and for her team, but for all those offended by the insensitivity of Imus' comment. Stringer also wanted this situation to serve as a learning experience for everyone.

One of the Rutgers players has said about Stringer, "She has brought up many things that have happened to her in her life to show us that no matter when you're struggling, or how much you're struggling, there's still light at the end of the tunnel."[4] With all of the struggles that Stringer has faced, she has always fought her way through it and found the light. She may encounter more tough situations in her career and in her life, but her strength, determination, and passion will enable her to survive and thrive.

On top of making Final Four history, Stringer has received additional accolades, including being named one of the "101 Most

Influential Minorities in Sports" by *Sports Illustrated*. She was inducted into the Women's Basketball Hall of Fame in 2001 after bringing her third school to the Final Four. She is one of only three women's coaches to accrue 750 wins. She is third on the list of total wins, behind veteran coaches Pat Summitt and Jody Conradt. Stringer has been given Coach of the Year honors three different years and she also has extensive international coaching experience, including earning a gold medal in the 2004 Olympic Games in Greece as an assistant coach to the USA women's basketball team.

Stringer recently signed a contract to write her autobiography. A publishing executive had described the future publication by saying, "It's about an incredible woman with an extraordinary life story. She's a pioneer, a legend, an icon and a role model."[5]

Stringer represents a severely underrepresented group of people in NCAA women's basketball. In 2005–06, 12 percent of the NCAA Division I women's basketball coaches were African-American, and women accounted for only nine percent of that figure. A great role model in this area, Stringer is very much in favor of more opportunities for other African-American coaches. "[Stringer] has such an incredibly rich background, and she's so elegant and articulate that I believe she'll find a way to make this something people should be paying attention to," Richard Lapchick told Black-AmericaWeb.com, stressing that it's now time for people to demand that changes be made. Regardless, Stringer will continue to stand up and fight for what she believes in. She is a woman who will continue to make history by following a fundamental lesson of her childhood.

Notes

1. Kelly Whiteside, "Rutgers Coach Has History of Standing Firm," *USA Today*, April 10, 2007, http://www.usatoday.com/sports/college/womensbasketball/2007-04-10-stringer_N.htm (accessed June 4, 2007).

2. Ibid.

3. Bill Brubaker, "Rutgers Team Accepts Imus's Apology," WashingtonPost.com, April 13, 2007, http://www.washingtonpost.com/wp-dyn/content/article/2007/04/13/AR2007041300884.html (accessed June 15, 2007).

4. CNN.com, "Rutgers Coach Builds Winners Despite Life Full of Adversity," CNN.com, April 10, 2007, http://www.cnn.com/2007/US/04/10/pysk.stringer/index.html (accessed June 15, 2007).

5. Michael David Smith, "Rutgers Coach Parlays Don Imus Flap into Book Deal," AOL Sports, April 17, 2007, http://sports.aol.com/fanhouse/2007/04/17/rutgers-coach-parlays-don-imus-flap-into-book-deal/ (accessed June 15, 2007).

Tyrone Willingham

First African-American College Coach to Win a Division I-A Bowl Game

by Richard Lapchick

Tyrone Willingham is included in this book because he was the first Division I-A African-American coach to lead his team to a victory in a bowl game. But he has broken barriers throughout his carrier, including by being named as head coach at the University of Washington. That appointment made him the first African-American head coach who was fired and then got another chance to lead a Division I-A program.

One of sports toughest racial barriers was cracked when Tyrone Willingham was hired at Notre Dame as its head football coach to start coaching in the 2002 season. Although there had been a few other African-American head coaches in college football, this was and still is sports' most segregated major position. And Notre Dame was the most storied program in the history of the game. Athletics Director Kevin White made the courageous decision to hire the best available coach for America's most prestigious football program. Legendary Coach Eddie Robinson had told me that Tyrone Willingham was the best young coach in America.

All of these things made me deeply disappointed when Notre Dame made the decision to let Willingham go only three years later. At the time I wrote that it may have been the saddest day in the history of college football; there had been so much promise at Notre Dame. If I had been an aspiring African-American football coach, the decision at Notre Dame would suggest to me that my chances of getting a Division I-A job had been all but shut down.

He came to Notre Dame full of hope that he could propel the Fighting Irish back into the elite list of college football and keep them there. He had an amazing start in reversing the tide of the Irish program, leading Notre Dame to a 10-2 regular season record in 2002 and a trip to the 2003 Gator Bowl in Jacksonville, Florida. It was a spectacular and dramatic beginning. He had four All-Americans, and seven players were in selected in the 2003 NFL Draft. Ten players made the dean's list and one was an Academic All-American. The feeling of great things to come was palpable on campus.

In the process, Willingham became the only first-year coach in Notre Dame history to win 10 games in his initial campaign. He was recognized for his efforts by being named the ESPN/Home Depot College Coach of the Year, the Scripps College Coach of the Year, and the Black Coaches & Administrators Male Coach of the Year.

Willingham also made history when he became the first college football coach to earn *The Sporting News* Sportsman of the Year award in 2002. He was also named the sixth most influential minority in sports by *Sports Illustrated.*

All the expectations were complicated by one of the most demanding schedules in the nation, and the Irish slipped to a disappointing 5-7 in 2003, although they won three of their last four games. Brady Quinn, a promising quarterback broke passing yards and completion records for a freshman.

In 2004, Willingham led the Irish to a 6-5 overall record. The Notre Dame season included several big victories over top-10-ranked teams. The Irish knocked off then-number 8 Michigan, 28-20, September 11, at Notre Dame Stadium and beat then-number 9 Tennessee, 17-13, in Knoxville on November 6. The season also included wins over a bowl-bound Navy squad, Michigan State, and Pac-10 teams Washington and Stanford.

In the 2004 season, in spite of a difficult loss to top-ranked University of Southern California, Notre Dame was still 6-5 and had played what was arguably the most grueling schedule in college sport. The Irish earned a berth in the Insight Bowl and had beaten top-10 powers Michigan and Tennessee. Willingham had a strong recruiting class coming in for the 2005 season, but he was terminated because of pressure from powerful alums. Both the athletics director and the president later said they had wanted Willingham to stay. Notre Dame had a record of honoring the full length of contracts for football coaches. Willingham's .583 winning percentage was equal to or better than Bob Davie and Jerry Faust, two of the three previous Notre Dame coaches whose contracts were honored in their entirety.

The University of Washington hired Willingham at the conclusion of a dismal 2004 football season when they went 1-10. He led them to a 5-7 record in 2006.

In his last seven years at Stanford, his teams went to four bowl games, he was Pac-10 Coach of the Year twice, and had a top-10 Bowl Championship Series ranking year in his last year there. His student-athletes had a high graduation rate and represented the university as leaders, not troublemakers as sometimes happens in top-10 programs.

As an African-American, Willingham has faced a skeptical group within the alumni ranks. As with other African-Americans who broke barriers as coaches or general managers, when they won big, the fans joined the parade. When they lost, the parade got rained out no matter what color the coach was.

Few athletics directors have had the courage to hire the best head football coach available irrespective of color. Although it has been significantly better in college basketball, the record in college football has been scandalous. In his third year at Stanford, there were eight African-American head coaches in Division I-A football. In his third season at Washington in 2007, Willingham was one of only six African-American head coaches in college football. Instead of a movement toward more opportunities for black coaches, the number of black head coaches in Division I-A football has actually been reduced, thus making Tyrone Willingham even more rare. This is in spite of the fact that 46.4 percent of the Division I football scholarships go to African-Americans.

A 1977 graduate of Michigan State University, Willingham coached under Dennis Green for six seasons, three at Stanford and three with the NFL Minnesota Vikings. He worked hard to get ahead in the game, starting as a graduate assistant at MSU in 1977 under head coach Darryl Rogers. From 1978 to 1979 he was the defensive secondary coach at Central Michigan University. Coach Muddy Waters brought him back to MSU for the next three years as the defensive secondary and special teams coach. He spent the next three years (1983–85) at North Carolina State University for three seasons coaching in the same role. From 1986 to 1988, Willingham coached receivers and special teams at Rice. It was then that he teamed up with Dennis Green at Stanford (1989–91) and with the Vikings (1992–94), where he was the running backs coach. On November 28, 1994, he was named as the successor to the legendary Stanford coach, Bill Walsh.

Throughout his coaching career, Willingham was a role model

for both campus and community leaders. As such, Willingham was honored with the 2000 Eddie Robinson Coach of Distinction Award. The award, presented to a college football coach for career achievement and outstanding service as a role model, came as no surprise to those who knew Willingham from his playing days at Michigan State, where he was named the team's most inspirational player in 1976. A year later, he was awarded the Big Ten Conference Medal of Honor as the outstanding scholar-athlete in the conference.

Tyrone Willingham is also a devoted family man. He and his wife, Kim, have three children. His parents taught him well. He was born on December 30, 1953, in Kinston, North Carolina, the oldest of the four Willingham children, and was raised in the segregated South. His father, Nathaniel, had left school after the fifth grade but, along with his wife, Lillian, was able to support their four children by buying and maintaining rental properties. Lillian broke barriers herself by earning a master's degree from Columbia University. She taught elementary school and was a leader in Kinston as a member of the school board and the Kinston city council.

While facing segregation, the Willinghams taught their children to excel in the classroom and in sports. Tyrone Willingham has done that all of his life.

9

COLLEGE ADMINISTRATORS: AFRICAN-AMERICAN ATHLETICS DIRECTORS WHO OPENED THE DOOR

Introduction by Richard Lapchick

In terms of hiring practices and pioneers in college sport, most of the attention goes to head coaches in football and men's and women's basketball. The national media rarely looks at the race and gender of conference commissioners, university presidents, or athletics directors. It was not easy to research that Gale Sayers was the first African-American Division I athletics director. Yet among this grouping of positions are the real decision makers in college sport.

Perhaps the most critical in terms of potential other hires is the athletics director. There has been significant progress at the Division I-A level, where 12 African-Americans, three Latinos, and one Native American led their departments in the 2006–07 academic year. However, when you go deep and look at all of Division I, II, and III, those athletics directors posts are overwhelmingly held by whites at 94, 92, and 96 percent, respectively.

Keith Tribble, who at the time of publication of *100 Pioneers* was the most recently appointed Division I-A athletics director who is African-American, leads the University of Central Florida's department. Tribble said, "It's not about hiring African-Americans, Latinos or Asians. It is about hiring the most qualified people. Get everyone into the room for an interview and let the committee pick the best person. We just have to make sure that a diverse pool of candidates is considered."[1]

Starting in 2007, the Black Coaches & Administrators will now prepare Hiring Report Cards for Division I-A athletics director positions.

As was said in the previous chapter on college coaches, the *2005 College Racial and Gender Report Card* was released in December

2006. I was the co-author along with Jenny Brenden. It was published by The Institute for Diversity and Ethics in Sport at the University of Central Florida. What follows is from that report's highlights section. The report paints a bleak picture of how few opportunities African-Americans have for leadership positions in college sport.

- All Division I-A conference commissioners were white men. Excluding the historically black colleges and universities, all Division I conference commissioners were white. Two conference commissioners were women and four other women were commissioners of sport-specific conferences.
- In Division I-A, 94.1 percent of university presidents were white, 3.4 percent were African-American, and 2.5 percent were Latino. There were no Asian or Native American university presidents. There were 15 females in this position, which is 12.6 percent.
- As stated above, whites held the overwhelming percentage of positions of athletics directors with 93.3, 92.3, and 96.1 percent of the athletic director jobs in Divisions I, II, and III, respectively. African-Americans held 5.5 percent, 3.8 percent and 1.9 percent, respectively in Divisions I, II, and III. Latinos accounted for 0.9, 2.7, and 0.3 percent of the ADs at Division I, II, and III. Asians and Native Americans had very minimal representation at each level.
- Women had gained ground as athletics directors in all three divisions since the last Report Card. In Division I there was an increase from 7.3 to 7.8 percent, in Division II there was an increase from to 16.2 to 18.7 percent, and in Division III there was an increase from 27.1 to 27.3 percent.
- There are other key posts in athletics departments, including the associate athletics director, the senior woman administrator, and the faculty athletics representative. All three are startlingly white in all three divisions.
- The pipeline for the athletics director position may be the associate athletic director. Whites made up 89.5 percent, 94.0 percent, and 95.3 percent of the total population at Division I, II, and III respectively. African-Americans held 8.2 percent, 4.0 percent, and 3.6 percent of the positions at each level. The per-

centage of women filling associate athletics director positions was 28.4 percent in Division I, 48.7 percent in Division II, and 49.7 percent in Division III.

- Women held 97.7, 99.4, and 98.9 percent of the Senior Woman Administrator jobs in Division I, II, and III, respectively. White women continued to dominate the SWA position, holding 84.3, 90.6, and 95.7 percent in Division I, II, and III, respectively. African-American women represented 10.2, 5.3, and 2.2 percent at each respective level.

- Whites filled the majority of the faculty athletics representative positions with 92.4, 92.2, and 95.5 percent in Division I, II, and III, respectively.

NCAA President Myles Brand is very supportive of creating opportunities for women and people of color within the NCAA headquarters and at the member institutions that compose the NCAA. In his State of the NCAA address in January 2005, he called the lack of opportunity for people of color in football head coaching positions "appalling." He also said the situation was bad for women and people of color as athletics directors and for women as head coaches.

The NCAA made a major commitment to the issue of diversity by creating a new position for a vice president for diversity and inclusion. In May 2005, the NCAA hired Charlotte Westerhaus for this position. As of July 1, 2007, the NCAA headquarters had three African-American vice presidents and three women vice presidents. Westerhaus reports directly to NCAA President Myles Brand and co-chairs the NCAA's Diversity Leadership Strategic Planning Committee.

Representation of women and people of color at the high levels of NCAA headquarters increased at the vice president/chief of staff position, where the number of people of color increased from two to three, up 6.3 percentage points to 18.8 percent. The number of women increased from three to four and jumped 6.2 percentage points to 25 percent.

Outside the NCAA headquarters, college sports has a dismal record, with almost all the positions examined here being 90 percent or more white in all three divisions. For now, too many new African-American senior department leaders are likely to continue to feel like pioneers. Few are as outspoken or controversial as basketball pioneers like John Thompson, John Chaney, and Vivian Stringer. Thus, like the story of pioneering African-American college coaches, that of African-American athletics directors and top administrators is just now being written.

However, we salute the first African-American athletics director (Gale Sayers), the first African-American athletics director in the SEC (Damon Evans), the ACC (Craig Littlepage), the Big 12 (Gene Smith), the Big Ten (McKinley Boston), and in the Ivy League (Abraham Molineaux Hewlett and Charles Harris). They stand tall as a rich part of the history of college sports.

Note

1. Keith Tribble, interview with author, March 15, 2007.

Abraham Molineaux Hewlett and Charles Harris

First African-American Athletics Directors in the Ivy League

by Jessica Bartter

Upon its opening on October 16, 1859, Abraham Molineaux Hewlett was appointed director of the Harvard Gymnasium, a position much like today's director of athletics position. "A fair gymnast and remarkably good teacher of boxing,"[1] Hewlett was Harvard University's first director of physical education culture and the first African-American to hold such a position at any Ivy League institution. Hewlett's trailblazing is still celebrated by the Ivy League Office almost 150 years later. The 2003 *Sports Illustrated* edition of the 101 Most Influential Minorities included 12 Ivy League connections. Without the pioneering actions of Hewlett and Harvard University, the Ivy League may not have been able to celebrate those dozen *Sports Illustrated* selections.

Perhaps more widely regarded as the Ivy League's first modern-day African-American director of athletics is Charles Harris. Harris just so happens to be the first African-American director of athletics in the Pacific 10 and USA South Athletic Conferences as well. Harris' landmark appointments range from 1979 to 2004—25 years of groundbreaking work in athletics.

Charles Harris

Courtesy of Sam Ferguson/Averett University Department of Athletics.

Harris' journey of transforming the face of university athletics began in 1973 at the University of Michigan, where he served the Wolverines in the sports information office before moving to operations, facilities, and marketing and promotions. He worked his way up to an assistant athletics director position, which he held until he moved to the University of Pennsylvania in 1979. As AD at Penn from 1979 to 1985, over 100 years after Hewlett served at Harvard, Harris became the first modern–day African-American AD of the "great eight" Ivy League schools. Harris' work in athletic departments is character-ized by his ability to build strong foundations combining academ-ics and athletics. When Arizona State University had six sports on probation and three under investigation by the NCAA, the athletics department looked to Harris to turn their program around. Among other things, ASU entrusted Harris to improve the Sun Devils' grad-uation rate, which had bottomed in the teens in the 1980s. At the time of Harris' departure from ASU 10 years later, the graduation rate exceeded 60 percent.

His focus on education, compounded with highly effective fundraising skills, made Harris a hot commodity in the arena of col-lege athletics. At Penn, he helped negotiate the school's first televi-sion contract. In his five years, he led the charge of Quaker fundrais-ing that increased annual giving from less than $100,000 to over $600,000. At ASU, Harris so successfully managed an annual oper-ating budget of $15 million that the NCAA utilized him to negotiate a $1.7 billion television agreement with CBS. After ASU, Harris be-came the commissioner of the Mid-Eastern Athletic Conference (MEAC) from 1996 to 2002. In that short time, he helped increase annual conference revenue from $150,000 to $1.5 million, in part, thanks to his selling of the MEAC's first full-season television pack-age for football. Had Harris not been known for his integrity and leadership, such funds would not have been afforded to his programs.

Harris is also regarded for his commitment to the advancement of women and minorities. He instituted and oversaw the earliest sup-port program for women's intercollegiate athletics at the University of Pennsylvania. Upon his move to Arizona State, he created the Wings of Gold program. Wings of Gold was a fundraising campaign specifically for the women's athletics programs at ASU and stirred up an additional $100,000 each year. In 1996, Harris accepted the MEAC position to help build pride in the conference's 10 histori-cally black colleges and universities (HBCU's). A graduate of Hamp-ton University, where he earned his bachelor's degree in media arts, Harris knew firsthand the benefits of an HBCU. Harris believed that the MEAC was "a very undervalued asset"[2] and hoped to help pro-mote the value of sports and education at its 10 member institutions.

As Harris led the charge for change in five different conferences, his presence always came with a price. He received hate mail but refused to be discouraged. Instead, he said he believed that "those who understand dynamic change in society and support it will ultimately outnumber those who are stuck in the past."[3] Humbly, Harris credits his ability to integrate college athletics for being "at places where there was a combination of vision, leadership and a willingness to effect positive meaningful change on the decision making end." Harris mentioned that on his end "there was the responsibility for preparation and execution if given the chance." The unpretentious Harris forgets to credit himself with the ability to repeatedly carry out an ambitious vision for success in college athletic departments across the country.

In the span of a quarter of a century, Charles Harris was able to integrate three different conferences stretching from California to Virginia. Why wasn't more progress achieved by other schools and individuals in that time? How could so much responsibility fall on one man's shoulders? Luckily, Harris did not mind, but he doesn't doubt more change and progress could have been made. He says, "To effect change means taking risk and moving beyond the status quo." To put the action behind his words, Harris is currently a partner in Excel Development Systems, Inc. Excel is a consulting group that focuses principally on developing strategies to maximize performance and outcomes through leadership and diversity training for corporations, the public sector, and colleges and universities. Harris hopes colleges and universities, as well as conferences, come out from behind the empty "words on their websites" and make clear commitments to diversity.

In addition to his work with Excel Development Systems, Harris is the director of athletics at Averett University in Virginia, a position he accepted in April 2004. Harris' acceptance as the third AD at Averett also happened to make him the first African-American to fill that position. Averett's 14 intercollegiate teams compete in the NCAA's Division III. In his first three years at the helm of Averett athletics, the Cougars moved from sixth to third place in conference rankings. Harris is particularly proud that his athletes have won the Conference Sportsmanship Trophy for men and women in each of the past two academics years, "an affirmation," in his view, "that you can be a smart and a good citizen." Harris demonstrates this principle every day.

Notes

1. Iowa Health and Physical Readiness Alliance, Chapter 3, www.ihpra.org/chapter_3.htm (accessed April 27, 2007).

2. Jack Chevalier, "New MEAC Commissioner: Charles Harris Can Answer All the AD's," *The Philadelphia Inquirer*, August 9, 1996.

3. The remaining quotes in this article are by Charles Harris, in an e-mail message to the author on May 19, 2007.

Gale Sayers

First African-American Athletics Director at a Major Division I Institution

by Jessica Bartter

The former NFL star, Gale Sayers, is often referred to as a great athlete, business professional, community leader, and friend. Sayers' friendship with Chicago Bears teammate Brian Piccolo was so admired that a movie was produced based on their true story; a story so powerful that 30 years later, the movie was reproduced by Disney and ABC to inspire yet another generation of viewers to embrace friendships across the color line.

Although Sayers' NFL career was relatively short-lived due to injuries, he made sure it was a memorable five seasons. The quick and graceful running back became the youngest player elected to the Professional Football Hall of Fame in 1977 at the age of 34. Sayers did so by tying the NFL record for the most touchdowns in a game with six in his rookie season. His season total of 22 touchdowns was a rookie record, too, earning him 1965's Rookie of the Year Award. Sayers ducked, dove, and ran by his opponents proving to be a worthy first round pick. In his second season, he led the league in rushing with 1,231 yards. Sayers was invited to the Pro Bowl in 1965, '66 and '67 and earned the Pro Bowl MVP Award the latter two years. In 1968, Sayers suffered the first of two career-threatening injuries. During the ninth game of the season, Sayers ruptured the cartilage and tore two ligaments in his right knee. He was sidelined for the remainder of the season.

After having left college early for the NFL draft and feeling like football was all he had, Sayers was emotionally devastated by his injury. Teammate Brian Piccolo stepped in to help him. As depicted in the movie they inspired, *Brian's Song*, Piccolo, who had been vying for Sayers' starting spot since their rookie year, would not accept the position due to Sayers' injury. Although Piccolo stepped in for the remainder of the season gaining 450 yards in the last six games, he would have rather earned the starting spot from Sayers by ability outright. The only way Piccolo believed that would be possible was to get Sayers back on his feet and 100 percent healthy. So Piccolo offered Sayers no pity and pushed him back into training and forced healing upon him, thus changing Sayers' outlook on his career and life. Luckily for Sayers, his rehabilitation got him back on the field. Unfortunately for Piccolo, Sayers was once again the Chicago Bears' starting running back. Fortunately for both, a friendship was born.

Though Piccolo and Sayers had been forced to room together by the Bears' organization it was not until Sayers' injury that the friendship truly blossomed. Before they were even friends, Piccolo and Sayers made history by being the first black and white teammates in the NFL to be roommates. The change came at the height of the Civil Rights Movement when the Bears decided to room by position rather than by race. It is a practice that is commonplace for many teams in today's league.

When Sayers returned to the Bears in 1969, he led the league in rushing once more and was invited to the Pro Bowl where he again earned MVP honors. In addition to having lost his starting position as running back, Piccolo received more bad news when he went to visit his doctor for chest pains. The doctors told Piccolo he had embryonal carcinoma.

During the 1969-70 season when Sayers demonstrated his brilliant comeback, Piccolo was in and out of hospitals fighting for his life. Sayers' performance on the field earned him the George Halas Award as the league's most courageous player for his inspirational comeback. During his emotional acceptance speech, Sayers accepted the award on behalf of his dear friend, Brian Piccolo. Sayers told the audience, "He has the heart of a giant and that rare form of courage that allows him to kid himself and his opponent, cancer. He has the mental attitude that makes me proud to have a friend who spells out the word courage 24 hours a day of his life. . . . You flatter me by giving me this award but I tell you here and now that I accept it for Brian Piccolo. . . . It is mine tonight, it is Brian Piccolo's tomorrow. . . . I love Brian Piccolo, and I'd like all of you to love him, too. Tonight, when you hit your knees, please ask God to love him."[1] Sayers' request of the audience could not save Piccolo. Just like Piccolo lent a helping hand to Sayers during his time of need, Sayers returned the support to Piccolo during his battle with cancer, which he lost on June 16, 1970. Sayers lost his best friend.

During the 1970 season, Sayers was knocked down again when he faced another knee injury. Sayers utilized his rehabilitation time, on his left knee this time, to return to school. He took classes that helped him become a stockbroker. This time, without Piccolo, Sayers was right to worry about his NFL career coming to an end. Although he returned to the Bears for the 1971 season, he did not make it past the preseason with his loss of speed and agility. But by now, Sayers had a backup plan, his education.

Gale Sayers made the NFL's All Star Team of the First 50 Years, ranked 21st on *The Sporting News'* list of the 100 Greatest Football Players, set seven NFL records and 23 team records, and still holds the career kickoff return average for the NFL. Sayers holds other records, too, outside the NFL. Sayers placed his mark on college administration as he topped the list of African-American athletics directors as the first at any major university.

Sayers was just 29 years old when his NFL career ended. He utilized his working experience from Paine, Webber & Co., where he had served as a stockbroker in the off-season, to venture on a new career path. Sayers was the first African-American stockbroker in the company's history. From 1970 to 1972, he hosted a talk show on a black radio station in Chicago. For an hour and a half every day, Sayers and his guests would discuss issues arising out of the African-American community. His guest list included Jesse Jackson and James Earl Jones. In the 2001 re-release of his 1970 autobiography, *I Am Third*, Sayers remembered how much he enjoyed his radio gig. "It helped me discover truths about life as an African-American, both the good and the not-so-good."[2] Then, in 1973, he got his big break in college athletics.

"The Kansas Comet," as he was nicknamed during his college playing days, was welcomed back to his alma mater, the University of Kansas, with open arms upon his NFL retirement. While at Kansas, Sayers completed the final semester of classes that he was missing and received his bachelor's degree in physical education. He was even able to earn a master's degree in educational administration during his short return to the Jayhawks. After a few years as assistant athletic director at Kansas, Sayers became the athletic director at Southern Illinois University, thus becoming the first African-American athletic director at any major university. After five years in his pioneering role, Sayers left collegiate athletics again.

When Sayers and his family left Southern Illinois and returned to Chicago, he and his wife searched for a field of opportunity. They quickly took notice of the computer industry and jumped in, despite their limited knowledge of the field. Sayers and his wife, Ardie, opened a small computer supplies store selling discs, paper, ink, and other computer accessories. During that first year, Sayers was also called upon by a friend, Roy Peterson, who was the president of Tennessee State University. Despite Sayers' new commitment to the computer industry, his friend was able to convince him to be interim AD until Peterson was able to find a replacement. Sayers traveled between Tennessee and Illinois every week for a year until he left collegiate athletics for the last time. Meanwhile, Ardie had the computer store up and running. The initial supplies store eventually turned into a company of several stores and three offices, called The Sayers Group, that sells computers, printers, and software in addition to its original supply inventory. Sayers serves as CEO to the company that has become a world-class provider of technology products and services and a premier minority-owned business enterprise since 1984.

As a teenager, Gale Sayers received over 100 offers to play college football. Without knowing better, he signed 17 letters of intent to play at different schools. Since officially picking Kansas weeks before the fall season of his freshman year, Sayers intent has been nothing but precise. A man of integrity and distinction, Sayers offers tribute to the life of his lost friend with a life of honor during each day of his own.

Notes

1. Gale Sayers with Al Silverman, *I Am Third* (New York: Penguin Group, 2001), 77.

2. Ibid., x.

McKinley Boston

First African-American Athletics Director
in the Big Ten Conference

by Horacio Ruiz

Courtesy of Minnesota Athletic Communications.

"Whether you want to or not," Dr. McKinley Boston says, "you tend to assimilate to what you're surrounded by."[1]

Yes and no. In a time when there were few athletic directors of color to look up to, Boston became the first full-time African-American athletic director in the Big Ten when he returned to his alma mater, the University of Minnesota, on December 17, 1991. Boston was not assimilating to his surroundings, he was changing them. Yet, his willing assimilation in the mid-1960s as an African-American student-athlete on the University of Minnesota campus was one of the biggest learning experiences of his life.

As a football player growing up in the segregated North Carolina town of Elizabeth City, Boston learned how to adjust at Minnesota. He had never played with or against a white athlete until he arrived at Minnesota as a freshman. As a prep player, Boston was told he was one of the best, but that meant one of the best among African-American players. In his senior year, Boston was named an All-State selection not by the state's athletic association, but by the North Carolina Negro Athletic Association. That did not stop Boston from arriving on the Minneapolis campus full of confidence that he was one of the best—regardless of race. As Boston developed into an All Big Ten selection as a defensive tackle, he learned to respect the athletic ability of others along the way. In that sense he was assimilating, but his biggest challenge was in what he terms "remaining black."

In Elizabeth City, Boston was accustomed to listening to R&B and dressing a certain way, but he soon started listening to the Beatles and bands that were a part of the European invasion. He wore penny loafers and Levi jeans. The Civil Rights Movement of the 1960s, however, made sure that all African-Americans became aware of the issues affecting their daily lives. It was difficult not to remain black when people of his own race were fighting for equal standing in a society that begrudgingly gave them a spot to stand on.

After a successful football career in Minnesota, including being a member of the 1967 Big Ten championship team, Boston played professional football for four years. He played two years in the National Football League with the New York Giants and two years with the British Columbia Lions of the Canadian Football League. Boston would have enjoyed playing for as long as his body would allow him, but a knee injury brought him to the reality that he quickly needed to go down another path. In 1973, he went back to school at Montclair State College in New Jersey, where he completed his undergraduate degree and earned a master's degree in 1974. At the same time, he served as director of student services while also serving as an assistant football coach. Through those experiences, his career path in college athletics took off. In 1986 he was named athletic director of Division III Kean College in Union, New Jersey. In 1988 he became athletic director at Rhode Island. Throughout his playing career, he made sure that sport was a means to an end, not an end itself. The people he met while playing in New York and as a student-athlete at Minnesota were invaluable in helping Boston launch his career and then move up. While he worked, he received his doctorate in education in 1987 from New York University, a year later serving as a visiting scholar at Harvard University.

In 1991 he became the first full-time African-American athletic director in the Big Ten's history. "The one thing I never lacked was confidence in my abilities across the board," Boston said. "To be as good as was not enough or to be in a position where people could say no. My credential building was designed so that if you said no, it was because someone was better or if you were racist."[2]

No one was better. As athletic director at Minnesota, Boston described himself as chief executive officer of a $50 million company where expectations were high and, to his good fortune, they were most often met. Boston erased a $2 million deficit at Minnesota, and graduation rates increased to an all-time high during his tenure. His success was such that in the winter of 1995, Florida State University interviewed Boston for the athletic director position. The position was his for the taking and would have made him the first African-American athletic director at a predominately white institution in the South.

"Being a product of the South, I knew the symbolic nature of the position, and it weighed heavily on my mind," Boston told Debra Blum of the *Chronicle of Higher Education.* "It would have made the statement that the opportunities for African-Americans in college sports are not limited to certain parts of the country. African-American athletes who play in the South can dream of being a coach or an athletics administrator at their own school. It's easier to set goals when you see they can come true."[3]

But upon his arrival back to Minnesota at the airport, just as he took a step off his airplane, he was greeted by the governor of Minnesota, the school president, regents, and boosters in an impromptu pep rally intended to keep him at his school. Boston had wanted to be a college president, and his position at Minnesota allowed him to remain on the path toward achieving his goal. As athletic director his responsibilities were multi-dimensional, and he continued to teach. In an effort to further expand Boston's responsibilities and groom him to be Minnesota's next president, the school created a vice presidential position for him that had oversight of men's and women's athletics, residence halls, student-health center, and other campus services. He held the position of athletic director until 1998 and continued as vice president for Student Development and Athletics until 2000.

Boston then went on to become president/CEO of his own company, McKinley Boston & Associates (MB&A), a consulting company providing services that assist colleges and universities in the development of strategic business partnership planning. He worked in the corporate world for four years, and although he was making great money, he felt like something was missing. He missed not being as involved in creating an agenda as he had been as an athletic director. He also missed the interactions he had had with student-athletes. Three and a half years ago he received another opportunity to get into collegiate athletics when New Mexico State University was looking to hire a new athletic director. A search firm identified

45 potential candidates for New Mexico State, including Boston, who ultimately received the position.

Today Boston is intent on upgrading the football stadium and making NMSU one of the better mid-major programs in the country. He drives his philosophy through the message that he used: sport is simply a mean to an end. His student-athletes are required to complete 15 hours of community service every year, an initiative he brought with him from Minnesota. "We are part of an experience for our student-athletes," Boston said. "We represent the first point for which many of our alumni look at the program."[4]

Boston cites that there are 13 African-American athletic directors in Division I-A, the highest level of collegiate athletics. Recently, 11 of the 13 athletic directors were able to meet in Los Angeles, where they agreed to create a consortium and become mentors for young African-Americans eager to jump into collegiate athletic administration. He also cited the importance for all of them to back the diversity and inclusion agenda set forth by the National Collegiate Athletic Association. "Social justice has always been a part of me," Boston says, "and as long as I've remembered I've always been a mentor."[5]

Notes

1. McKinley Boston, interview with author, June 14, 2007.

2. Ibid.

3. Debra Blum, "Athletics Director Looks to Bigger Playing Fields," *The Chronicle of Higher Education*, June 9, 1995.

4. McKinley Boston, interview with author, June 14, 2007.

5. Ibid.

Gene Smith

First African-American Athletics Director in the Big 12 Conference

by Marcus Sedberry

Work ethic and listening are both traits Gene Smith vividly remembers learning at a young age. As he grew from a boy into a man in Cleveland, Ohio, Smith worked with his father, an electrical contractor, and developed unique relationships with the skilled individuals who were his father's co-workers. These people would soon be the most influential people in his life. Smith joined his father and fellow workers in leaving for work sites before sun up and returning home after sunset, while learning how to enjoy work. Often, his co-workers would pass time by telling stories of their upbringing, incorporating important life lessons. Smith carries these lessons with him still today.

Although he primarily idolized his father and the employees with whom he worked, Smith also looked up to the professional, civic, and social leaders of the 1960-70s for the way they pioneered through the hardships and changes of life to pave the way for those to come. Perhaps having these examples provided Smith a road map to becoming a pioneer in his own right.

Many years later, in 1993, Smith was named the director of athletics at Iowa State University, making him the first African-American in that role in what is now the Big 12 Conference. Prior to his successful move into athletic administration, Smith began his path to achievement at all-male and previously all-white Chanel High School, where he faced academic challenges and racial opposition. He did not allow these barriers to deter him. Instead, he persevered and grew through the experience.

Smith attended the University of Notre Dame on an athletic scholarship for football. During his four years as a defensive end for the Fighting Irish, Smith experienced hardships but also triumphs as a member of the 1973 Associated Press national championship team. Smith went on to attain his bachelor's degree in business administration from Notre Dame in 1977. Directly following his senior year, he became an assistant football coach at his alma mater and found immediate success as the Irish won the 1977 national championship.

Since then Smith's achievements have only grown. After his stint with Notre Dame, Smith became a marketing representative for IBM and then moved to Eastern Michigan, where he became the assistant athletic director overseeing nine men's sports, facilities, event operations, and event marketing. Smith was eventually promoted to the position of athletics director at Eastern Michigan in 1985 overseeing non-revenue sports, a position he kept until 1993. He then found a home in Ames, Iowa, at Iowa State University for seven years before becoming the director of athletics at Arizona State. While at Iowa State his athletic department led the Big 12 Conference in graduation rates his last three years, as well as designed and developed ISU's first athletic marketing department and first corporate partnership program for athletics. While Smith was with the Sun Devils, the graduation rates of his student-athletes improved to record numbers, 13 percent higher than the university average. In addition, Smith oversaw the completion of a $30 million capital campaign. As of 2005, Smith was named The Ohio State University's director of athletics, making him the first African-American to hold that position. At OSU, he oversees the nation's largest Division I-A athletics program.

Smith's attitude is one that is evident throughout his track record. He prides himself on the initiative of "promoting the real mission of education, which is to provide the student-athletes with educational experiences and develop them athletically simultaneously. Taking what the athletes learn in competition and teach them to use it in everyday life."[1] His goals are to make sure student-athletes recognize what they've learned from competition, to be a positive window for the university by doing the right thing the right way, and to help the campus be engaged in the athletic department.

These beliefs and goals have been instrumental in helping Smith gain acceptance and respect among the inner circle of collegiate athletics. Keith Tribble, the first African-American CEO of a Bowl Committee, and first Bowl Committee CEO to move into the role of athletic director, says that Smith "is a role model for all of us that aspire to be great at what we do. He has definitely set the standard on how to be a successful Athletics Director in today's ever challenging environment. He is truly a pioneer!"[2]

As a reflection of his outstanding expectations and achievements, Smith has received numerous nominations, awards, and appointments in various positions. Smith has held positions as first vice president of the Division I-A Athletics Directors Association as well as the NCAA Men's Basketball Committee. He has also been a member of the NCAA Management Council, the NCAA Committee on Infractions, the Rose Bowl Management Committee, and the NCAA Football Rules Committee. In 1994, Smith became the National Association of Collegiate Directors of Athletics' (NACDA) first African-American president and has been affiliated with the NACDA Executive Committee, Division I-A Executive Committee, and the NCAA President's Commission Liaison Committee. In 2005, *Black Enterprise* named Gene Smith one of the "50 Most Powerful African-Americans in Sports."

With such honors and positions come many challenges, a fact that Smith has readily accepted. His biggest challenge thus far is his role as a director of athletics centers on managing the student-athlete environment. In an era in which student-athletes are constantly changing, Smith has made it a priority to manage their environment because of diverse backgrounds and the constant pressure to fit into the culture of both school and society. For Smith, being a pioneer is more than just a title. He firmly believes that the title warrants paving the way for others to follow. Smith understands that many people who look at him see his race very distinctly, so he makes an extra effort to do his job well and do it the right way in order to demonstrate that athletic directors of color can do the job. For many people this kind of scrutiny would create pressure; for Smith it's simply his responsibility as a collegiate director of athletics and pioneer of social change.

Notes

1. Gene Smith, interview with author, November 14, 2006.
2. Keith Tribble, interview with author, February 27, 2007.

Craig Littlepage

First African-American Athletics Director in the Atlantic Coast Conference

by Jessica Bartter

Courtesy of the University of Virginia.

While driving late one night during a family summer vacation in 2001, Craig Littlepage came close to tears when he overheard a conversation between his then-15-year-old daughter, Erica, and 12-year-old son, Murray. Upon hearing Erica ask her younger brother what he wanted to do when he grew up, Craig Littlepage carefully listened to Murray's answer, fully prepared that he would say "I want to be an NFL or NBA player." To Littlepage's surprise, Murray's response was "I want to be an athletics director." Littlepage's heart sank for several reasons. First, he knew Murray was not completely aware of what an athletics director did but that he simply wanted to follow the footsteps of his father. Secondly, Littlepage was concerned with the lack of opportunities his son would face in the future, knowing all too well about the scarcity of African-American athletics directors. In addition, Littlepage was intimately familiar with the competition in the business.

At the time, Littlepage was serving the University of Virginia as the interim athletics director and anxiously awaiting a decision as to who would fill the post permanently. Littlepage was concerned that his son would be devastated if his father was not hired. Fortunately, Littlepage was named athletics director and says, "Now five and half years later and after some significant hirings of other African-Americans at major college positions, Murray Littlepage can realistically pursue his dream of becoming an AD, having some great role models to follow."[1] But in Murray's mind, his dad is likely the only role model necessary.

Craig Littlepage's accomplishments as athletics director of the University of Virginia have been numerous, yet one of his major accomplishments, one that will go down in the history books, was achieved before Littlepage had to make any executive decisions. Just by being named athletics director, Littlepage integrated that position in the Atlantic Coast Conference (ACC). Never before had an ACC school had an African-American athletics director. In fact, when he was appointed, most conferences and schools across the country still had not had an athletics director of color. Prior to Littlepage's appointment, Gene Smith made change happen for the Big 12 when Iowa State hired him as AD in 1993. Littlepage kept the ball rolling with his hiring in 2001. Eventually Damon Evans was named AD at the University of Georgia, which integrated the SEC in 2004, and Daryl Gross did the same for the Big East while at Syracuse in 2005. At the time of Littlepage's hiring, he was one of only six black athletic directors at all of the NCAA Division I-A institutions. While this number increased to 12 as of July 2007, the ratio of African-American athletics directors to student-athletes is alarming. While 24.8 percent of Division I NCAA male student-athletes are African-American, only five percent of athletics directors at NCAA institutions, excluding historically black colleges and universities, are African-American. Littlepage is a much needed agent for social change.

When Littlepage faced the daunting color barrier at the University of Virginia, the community, athletic department, and university offered nothing but support. He "never felt that color was a factor as far as senior University leadership and our institutional decision-makers were concerned."

Littlepage stresses that it is important to realize that a successful "Division I athletics leader can come in all shapes, sizes and colors." To achieve greater diversity in athletic administrations, Littlepage reflects on his own hiring process. Like himself, other "athletics directors are being hired after having had successful stints as associate AD's, senior associates or executive associates." Littlepage adds, "We need to get more talented ethnic minority administrators hired in these positions where they have the fiscal responsibilities, and are involved in decision-making, hiring and personnel supervision. Also, we need to get more ethnic minorities involved in some of the other less represented areas in college athletics programs like development and facility management. People that are appointed to the position of athletics director are people that can be organizational decision-makers; candidates need to have experience in these types of roles."

As with the other administrators in Littlepage's position, he was hired because he was the best candidate for the job, not because of the color of his skin. Littlepage's experience with collegiate athletics dates back to his stardom on the basketball court for the University of Pennsylvania. He was a member of three Ivy League Championship teams at Penn when they went to three consecutive NCAA Eastern Regional Playoffs. Littlepage earned an economics degree from the Wharton School at Penn while playing and upon graduation was asked to assist the coaching program at Villanova. Littlepage did so for two years before assisting Yale University for a year and then starting his career at the University of Virginia in 1976. Littlepage was the assistant coach at Virginia until 1982, when he became head coach at his alma mater. After three years at Penn, Littlepage served Rutgers as head coach before returning to Virginia for good. Following his tenure as the assistant coach for two more years, Littlepage became a member of Virginia's administration as an assistant athletics director in 1990 and continued to work his way up the ladder until his athletics director appointment in 2001.

Littlepage credits his intercollegiate athletics experience as a student-athlete for teaching him the importance of networking and working as part of a team in his professional life. Littlepage says, "Success in the college athletics enterprise has everything to do with relationships and relationship building. You have to know people, and know how to find comfort in working with a wide range of people to have any level of success. Further, you have to work collaboratively, that is as a team, in order to make the most of the cumulative talents of those within your organization."

Littlepage inherited a strong 24-sport athletics program and quickly made it a 25-sport program by adding women's golf on just his second day. An advocate for change, he outlined an ambitious 10-year plan in 2002. Although the University of Virginia is already ranked among the top Division I-A public universities for student-athlete graduation rates, Littlepage strives for perfection. His goals to be completed by 2012 include the graduation of 100 percent of his student-athletes, winning 12 national championships and 70 conference titles, adding and maintaining the highest quality facilities, and fully complying with Title IX, among other things. Though lofty, Littlepage's expectations did not surprise many. Upon his hiring, University President John T. Casteen III noted that during Littlepage's previous 10 years with the department, he "stood out for his commitment to the overall well-being of our student-athletes, particularly their academic progress, and for his thoughtful, collegial approach to complex issues."[2]

With such a successful, determined, and well-respected father, it comes as no surprise that Murray Littlepage doesn't have to look farther than the driver's seat when considering his career aspirations. Craig Littlepage has set an example of excellence that is sure to be followed, not just by his children, but by all those with whom he has come into contact.

Notes

1. All the quotes by Craig Littlepage in this article are from an e-mail message to author, January 4, 2007.

2 "Littlepage Is Named New AD," *Inside UVA Online*, Aug. 31–Sept. 6, 2001, http://www.virginia.edu/insideuva/2001/26/littlepage.html

Damon Evans

First African-American Athletics Director
in the Southeastern Conference

by Richard Lapchick

There was a time when it was hard to imagine an African-American athlete in the SEC. Then after some of the barrier breakers mentioned in this book took the field and the courts, the coaching ranks seemed impenetrable. Once that began to open up, the position of athletics director seemed to be a far-away goal. Former University of Georgia football letterman Damon Evans was selected as the University of Georgia's director of athletics in December 2003, and assumed the duties of succeeding long-time and legendary athletic director Vince Dooley on July 1, 2004. The door was finally opened when Damon smashed that barrier.

Evans was an intern with the Southeastern Conference (SEC) in 1993 as a compliance and academic affairs assistant, then served as director of compliance and operations at the University of Missouri in 1994. In 1995, Evans returned to the SEC as the director of compliance and was promoted to assistant commissioner for compliance in 1997. I got to know Damon when he worked for the Southeastern Conference. From the time I met him it was obvious that he was a special person and a leader. He returned to UGA as an associate athletics director in 1998.

Damon Evans has deep Georgia roots. Born in Omaha, Nebraska, Evans went to Gainesville High School in Gainesville, Georgia, where he was a three-sport star, excelling in football, basketball, and track. Evans was the basketball MVP, set the school record for the 200 yard dash, and earned first team all-state honors as a wide receiver.

Evans played football for four years and earned two degrees at the University of Georgia. He was a starter for four seasons and played in the 1989 Peach Bowl, the 1991 Independence Bowl, and the 1992 Citrus Bowl. He was also a member of the 1991 and 1992 teams, which won nine and ten games, respectively. He played on Vince Dooley's last team in 1988. Evans played in eight games as a redshirt freshman at UGA and was named the "Most Improved Receiver" and "Biggest Offensive Surprise" following his first spring practice.

He was hired as an intern at the SEC in 1993 and then continued to climb up the athletic ladder. After earning his master's degree, Evans took the job with the University of Missouri. When he returned to the University of Georgia, his career accelerated. From 1998 to 2000 he was associate athletic director for internal affairs and then was senior associate athletic director for internal affairs from 2000 to 2004. From 1998 to 2001, Evans served as a member of the NCAA Division I-A management council, the highest governance committee attainable by an athletics administrator. He was chair of the UGA academic task force charged with reviewing academic credentials of prospective student-athletes.

The SEC had been criticized for the pace of its minority hiring. The appointment of Evans came less than three weeks after Sylvester Croom was hired as the first African-American football coach in the SEC at Mississippi State. When Evans was asked about his position as the SEC's first African-American athletics director, he said, "My goal was always to be an athletics director, not an African-American athletics director. However, I do understand the significance associated with being the first African-American athletics director in the SEC."[1] Evans also became the youngest AD at 34 years old.

The University of Georgia has excelled under Evans' leadership. As of 2006, the University of Georgia Athletic Association is composed of 19 intercollegiate teams, over 500 student-athletes, a $65 million budget, and a 250-person staff.

Evans is extremely active within the university and the NCAA. He has served as vice-chair of the NCAA Division I Management Council and on the NCAA Division I Oversight and Monitoring Group. Evans has overseen the largest capital campaign in the history of the University of Georgia Athletic Association, topping $60 million. Not only has Evans been an instrumental factor in the significant growth of the university, which boasts an athletic association budget of $50 million, but he has also been active in ensuring the student-athletes' successes as well.

His first years with the University of Georgia Bulldogs have been enormously successful. During his initial year with the Bulldogs, Georgia won three national championships and earned a 7th place finish in the 2004–05 NACDA Cup. He also aided in deals between UGA and ISP Sports, a leading sports marketing firm, to outsource marketing rights, and he gained a record amount of logo-licensing revenue, making UGA branding among the best in the country. In his second year, the Bulldogs set a record of seven conference titles and won another national championship. They were also recognized as "the most profitable intercollegiate athletic department in the country" when, for fiscal 2005, the Athletic Association had the largest operating profit among collegiate athletic programs at $23.9 million.

Evans has received several honors, including the Street and Smith's Sports Business Journal "40 Under 40 Award," the UGA Terry College of Business Award as the "Outstanding Young Alumnus," and being listed in *Sports Illustrated*'s "101 Most Influential Minorities in Sports."

He is married to the former Kerri Budd of Atlanta. They have a son, Cameron, born November 18, 1998, and a daughter, Kennedy, born July 5, 2001.

Note

1. "Damon Evans Is First Black Athletic Director at University of Georgia," *Jet*, January 19, 2004.

10

SOUTHEASTERN CONFERENCE, ATLANTIC COAST CONFERENCE, BIG 12, BIG TEN, AND IVY LEAGUE PIONEERS: STUDENT-ATHLETES PLAY WITH COURAGE

Introduction by Richard Lapchick

Just as in pro sports, in which African-American athletes broke the barriers long before coaches and administrators were able to do so, so it has been in college sport. Those professional athletes were generally a few years older and, perhaps, more worldly than 17- and 18-year-olds who came to our institutions of higher education to face the unknown world of previously all-white athletic departments and classrooms.

Most were chosen because a coach thought their great athletic gifts would win over the student body and faculty. Often it was the first time for the African-American student-athlete to be together with whites on an equal plane. There were tensions to be felt, threats to be encountered, and hateful crowds to be faced. There were teammates who did not want to be in the huddle together. And then there were all the Rebel flags flying in the stadiums. And more, much more. In part, the history of the Civil Rights Movement was played out on some of our fields and in our campus arenas.

This chapter, the longest in *100 Pioneers*, chronicles the stories of the first African-American student-athletes in the Southeastern Conference, the Atlantic Coast Conference, Big 12 Conference, Big Ten Conference, and the Ivy League. The Ivy League was chosen because several early African-American student-athlete pioneers played at their member institutions.

A game in Stillwater, Oklahoma, involving Oklahoma A&M (now Oklahoma State), a Big Eight team, and Drake in 1951 must have sent a chill into any African-American athletes who were thinking of being racial pioneers.

Drake's Johnny Bright, an African-American running back, was the nation's top rusher. Drake was unbeaten. Wilbanks Smith was an Oklahoma A&M defensive tackle and was white. He went after Bright twice. The second time he broke Bright's jaw with a punch that was captured by a *Des Moines Register* photographer. Down at the time, A&M came back to beat Drake, who was forced to play without its star player. Bright attended Drake although African-Americans could not live on campus. Segregation was the law in Oklahoma.

The SEC was the last conference in America to be integrated. Some member schools not only fought to keep African-Americans off their own teams but refused to compete against teams with African-American players. In 1956, the State of Louisiana passed a law banning interracial sports competition, which was overturned by the United States Supreme Court in 1959. In Mississippi, legislators threatened to stop funding schools that competed against integrated teams. Mississippi State skipped the NCAA tournaments in 1959 and 1961. The University of Mississippi refused to play Michigan in a 1961 bowl game. Mississippi was number two and Michigan was the top-ranked team. Mississippi, in effect, forfeited a shot at the national title rather than play against African-American athletes.

The Supreme Court had mandated the integration of schools in its landmark *Brown vs. the Board of Education* decision in 1954. Five years before Brown, the University of Kentucky admitted its first African-American students. Not until 17 years later did Kentucky sign Nat Northington and Greg Paige, two African-American football players in 1966. They were the first student-athletes in the football-dominated SEC. It was slow going from there at Kentucky and the others SEC schools. But by 1971–72, every SEC school had at least one African-American student-athlete. It should not have surprised anyone that it was nearly four decades before Sylvester Croom was hired as the SEC's first head football coach, at Mississippi State, and Damon Evans was named athletics director at Georgia.

The big breakthrough for the SEC was the now widely discussed game between the University of Southern California, coached by John McKay, and Alabama and its legendary coach, Bear Byrant. USC not only had superstar Sam "Bam" Cunningham but had an all-African-American backfield, the first in Division I football. Cunningham was joined by quarterback Jimmy Jones and running back

Clarence Davis. After USC whipped the Crimson Tide 42-21, full integration was only a matter of time.

While football was king in the SEC, basketball was number one in the ACC. The first African-American basketball player in the ACC was Maryland's Billy Jones in the 1965–66 season. That was nearly a decade after Jackie Robinson had retired! The Maryland football team had been integrated a few years before with Darryl Hill. Basketball great Charlie Scott was not the first African-American athlete at the University of North Carolina at Chapel Hill, nor was he the first who played basketball. But Scott became the first to receive an athletic scholarship from UNC-Chapel Hill.

Case-by-case there were still obstacles for the student-athletes who integrated the Ivy League, Big 8/Big 12 (this covered the Southwest Conference and the Big 8, which merged into the Big 12) and Big Ten schools. But the dates go far back into history. Harvard had an African-American All-American football player in William Henry Lewis in 1892 while he attended Harvard Law School. William Edward White played baseball on Brown's 1879 team.

Preston Eagleson played football at Indiana University in the 1890s and became the first African-American to earn a post-baccalaureate degree from Indiana University. Julian V. Ware and teammate Adelbert R. Matthews, both African-American, led the University of Wisconsin to its first Big Ten baseball championship in 1902. Tackle Gideon Smith helped the Michigan Agricultural College (now Michigan State University) have an undefeated season in 1913, in which they beat archrival the University of Michigan for the first time by a score of 12-7.

From 1891 to 1894, George Flippin was enrolled at the University of Nebraska as the first African-American student-athlete at the university. At the time, Flippin was just the fifth African-American student-athlete in the entire nation to compete for a predominately white university.

Sherman, Grant, and Ed Harvey were brothers who all played for Kansas, starting with Sherman in 1888. They were sons of slaves and went on to become an attorney, a doctor, and a civic leader, respectively.

The student-athlete pioneers written about in this part of the book had remarkable lives. Those who entered college in the 19th century were the sons of slaves and heard of the horrors of that institution firsthand. But all encountered various forms of racism in their college days that could have stopped less courageous men. Almost all had successful professional careers: doctors, lawyers, documentary film makers, elected officials, professional athletes, coaches, college professors, university presidents, high school teachers and administrators, and entrepreneurs. Many served our nation in the military. A substantial number earned advanced degrees.

My original goal for this chapter was to have the first African-American male and female student-athlete at each of the schools in the respective conferences. After exhaustive attempts by my graduate assistants in The Institute for Diversity and Ethics in Sport at the University of Central Florida, very few schools could identify the first African-American female student-athletes. In several cases, there was not much information even about the male pioneers. Surprisingly, many schools were not in contact with those pioneers. We could tell from the responses at some of the schools that the idea of African-American pioneer student-athletes had not been on their radar screens. I hope that these discussions and the publication of *100 Pioneers* will begin to change that in the years ahead and that these men and women will be brought back to campus and acknowledged for their part in the history of the schools.

In this chapter, we were not able to gather enough of their stories to talk about Robert Bell at Mississippi State, Ansel "Jackie" Brown at the University of South Carolina, Nat Lucas at the University of Virginia, Clifford Evans at the University of Colorado, Curtis Mills, Sidney Chachere, and Edgar Harvey at Texas A&M University, Danny Hardaway at Texas Tech University, George Henry Jewett at Northwestern University, John Henry Weaver at Purdue University, and Howard M. Smith at the University of Pennsylvania.

The roles of all these student-athlete pioneers created paths of enormous opportunities for future African-American student-athletes. In the *2005 College Racial and Gender Report Card*, the percentages for African-American student-athletes were listed at 21 percent, 18 percent, and seven percent in Divisions I, II, and III, respectively. The percentage of African-American male basketball players in Division I was 58 percent, and it was 45 percent in football and 6.5 percent in baseball.

The percentage of African-American female basketball student-athletes was 44 percent; 26 percent of the female track and field/cross country student-athletes were African-American.

In Division I, African-American male student-athletes make up 25 percent of all male student-athletes. In Division II, they comprise 22 percent, and in Division III, nine percent. In Division I, African-American female student-athletes comprise 15 percent of the total female student-athletes. In Division II, they make up 12 percent, and in Division III, only five percent.

I hope that these great current student-athletes in particular will read *100 Pioneers* and see the contrasts in what their predecessors had to face compared to today's African-American student-athletes.

Chapter 10

SECTION ONE

Southeastern Conference Student-Athlete Pioneers

Nat Northington

First African-American Student-Athlete at the University of Kentucky and in the Southeastern Conference

by Stacy Martin

Sometimes the first one to walk the path receives all the bruises of the journey. In the fall of 1965, the University of Kentucky was the first school in the Southeastern Conference to integrate its athletic teams. Unfortunately, tragedy struck both of the young men who signed those national letters of intent. Nat Northington was officially the first African-American to sign with UK as well as the Southeastern Conference, but Greg Page quickly followed Northington on the journey toward equality.

Edward "Ned" Breathitt, then the governor of Kentucky, took a vested interest in the integration of UK's athletic teams. Politically focused on passing a strong civil rights bill, he thought that the integration of the athletic teams would support his efforts and serve as an example for the rest of the state. Breathitt acknowledged that integration had a certain moral value that he wanted his state to portray, but another real concern was the threat of federal assistance funding for the university being cut off during a crucial time of growth on campus. The University of Louisville and Western Kentucky University had integrated their athletic teams in 1962 and 1963, respectively, but the University of Kentucky was the state's principal educational institution at the time.

The governor became hands-on in the recruiting process when he personally telephoned Northington and Page to request their attendance at UK to play football. Page was from Middlesboro, and Northington from the larger city of Louisville. Coach Charlie Bradshaw was able to sign both players to national letters-of-intent to play for the University of Kentucky. Again, Breathitt had to personally insure the fate of integration at UK by visiting Nat Northington's home as he signed his letter. Northington became the first African-American to sign with UK and the Southeastern Conference in December 1965.

Both young men came to the university and played on the freshman team during the fall of 1966. During that era, freshmen were ineligible to play for the varsity squad. Page and Northington paid their dues, waiting for their chance to play. Kentucky had integrated as a result of a lawsuit filed by Lyman T. Johnson in 1949, but even 15 years later hatred and exclusion ran rampant on campus. One of the African-American students attending UK during the same time, P. G. Peeples, recounted that it was not unusual to hear the "N" word or various other racial epithets as you strolled by some of the fraternity houses on campus. Apparently some of the students would even let their dogs loose on African-Americans walking nearby. There were decades of overt racism to overcome for both the students and the student-athletes who braved the struggles of the integration process.

After a year of surviving stereotypes and epithets, Page and Northington finally got their chance on the varsity field. Page and Northington had become close while rooming together at UK, despite playing on opposite sides of the football. Page was a defensive end and Northington a wide receiver. They had been sharing the burden of being pioneers, until the third day of varsity practice. Page participated in a standard defensive drill that is still practiced on most football teams today, the pursuit drill. Unfortunately, Page's pursuit of equality ended tragically during that drill.

A pursuit drill is meant to instill toughness and aggression in a defensive player, so that all players will converge on an offensive player carrying the ball during the game. Page was among the eleven defensive players that pursued an offensive player that third day of practice. Somewhere in the pile of football players, Page's neck was severely injured. He didn't get up and was paralyzed. He died from complications stemming from his injury 38 days later. Thirty-nine days later, Nat Northington changed history, becoming the first African-American to play in a Southeastern Conference game.

Northington played in the game between UK and Ole Miss in Lexington on September 30, 1967. He played in only three more games after that fateful day. The hardship of Page's death was too much to bear. In their shared dorm room, all of Page's belongings haunted Northington. They reminded him that he was alone and of what could be lost through his endeavor to play for the University of Kentucky. Some thought that Page's injury was intentionally inflicted with malice. Speculation surrounded the circumstances of Page's death. Looking back now, one of the former players recalled that a white player, Cecil New, suffered a broken neck during practice too. Sometimes it is difficult to see through the dense clouds of circumstance and mayhem. In the same season that Northington carved out his place in UK history he left the proving ground.

Before Northington left, he called together the three remaining African-Americans on the freshman team whom he'd had a hand in recruiting the previous year. Wilbur Hackett, Houston Hogg, and Albert Johnson agreed to Northington's request for them to stay and finish what he had started. His journey as a pioneer would end early due to the pain and heartache of his fallen brother, but he could still envision the integrated UK and wanted to ensure its future. Northington transferred to Western Kentucky but sustained an injury that subsequently ended his football career. Northington graduated from Western and now works for the Louisville Housing Authority. He doesn't speak of his time at UK because he would rather forget those painful days and focus on the positive changes that he can make in this world.

Northington was the unsung pioneer who dramatically altered Kentucky football for the better. Now he is the quiet pioneer who carries the price of integration and equality with class and dignity.

Lester McClain

First African-American Football Scholarship Student-Athlete at the University of Tennessee

by Stacy Martin

Lester McClain was originally cast merely as the roommate of the African-American pioneer at the University of Tennessee in the fall of 1967, but he jumped at the opportunity to play for the Tennessee Volunteers. Playing for the Vols was his childhood dream. It seemed as if destiny had a hand in crafting Volunteer history, because if the UT staff had had their choice, Albert Davis, a tremendously talented running back from the area, would have run through the color barrier for Tennessee. McClain was not selected because the recruiter could not be certain that he was good enough for the college football ranks. In response, McClain willingly put in the extra time to improve and never feared hard work. Achieving success was just a matter of time for McClain, but first he needed to be given a chance. His fortunes relied on the talents of Albert Davis, because during that time recruiting an African-American football player meant recruiting a roommate for him. Some thought that placing African-American athletes as roommates would ease the struggle and strife of the integrated college experience. McClain was not concerned about the reason but simply celebrated the opportunity.

Bill Garrett, a UT alumnus, became an advocate of McClain, helping secure McClain's place in history even when Davis was unable to attend due to difficulty with the entrance exam. The plan that UT had in place, selecting two African-American football players in 1967 to offer support and solace to one another during the long tumultuous journey, had failed; now McClain would walk alone. Not only did he have to prove himself on the field with his football skills, but he had to prove himself worthy of the position through his conduct so that he would not be thought of as simply a token of integration. Bill Garrett must have seen a great strength in McClain to encourage him in this enormous undertaking, and surely future African-American student-athletes are thankful for Garrett's insight and support.

McClain credits others with his development and inspiration; these individuals include Coach Doug Dickey, who committed to integration and signed McClain to a scholarship. He fondly recalls the moment when Dickey offered the scholarship to him and says that nothing will ever match that excitement. The dream came true for McClain and the reality of hard work followed. He remembers being impressed by a teammate, Jack Reynolds, the very first week of practice. Reynolds was an athlete who went full speed, hard-hitting from the time he set foot on the practice field to the second that he stepped off of it. McClain followed Reynolds' lead with the thought that if he demonstrated that level of intensity and passion daily, he would not be denied playing time.

McClain put in lots of extra time with Bill Battle, the receiver's coach for three years and his head coach his senior year. McClain once described Battle as a man "who came from a place where they believed in hard work."[1] Reaching one's goals requires determination and is usually accompanied by some degree of difficulty, but McClain had an additional, deep-rooted, Southern kind of difficulty to face regarding integration. When taking on a challenging task, people often look to leaders and peers for support and illumination of the best path. McClain certainly gained strength by looking to Garrett, Dickey, Reynolds, and Battle.

The path was tumultuous and lonely at times, but that is the nature of the trail a pioneer blazes. According to McClain, there was no occurrence of racism, only a bit of "awkwardness." McClain refers to the worst offense of awkwardness as a discourteous remark in casual passing. He was mature enough to realize that individuals from two different worlds would have two different perspectives. Occasionally, he would let slip an inappropriate remark as well. He and his teammates would merely apologize and move on with the conversation. They had a much greater purpose to focus on. Instead of the fear of Deep South segregation and ignorance, they had football games to win. Even if McClain felt alone at times, he never felt slighted.

McClain worked hard and moved past the awkwardness with determination and fortitude. He was a man influenced by other leaders crying out for equality and opportunity. He held fast the teachings of Dr. Martin Luther King, Jr., and Malcolm X and followed in the footsteps of Jackie Robinson. His parents had admired Robinson from afar and were fanatic baseball fans, becoming almost disappointed that their son, Lester, had chosen football. However, they were proud of their son's vision of playing at a predominantly white school and changing people's perceptions of black athletes.

McClain changed views with every step he took on the football field. His first step in his first varsity game was unforgettable and foreshadows the progress he would make over his career. He did not score a touchdown that game; he simply showed up and dared to defy the limits previously oppressing him. Neyland Stadium applauded his efforts that day with a standing ovation when he entered the game. That was only the start of the applause that McClain would receive during his Volunteer career, as he broke through the color barrier, making 29 receptions during his first season alone. He went on to a storied football career totaling 70 receptions, 10 touchdowns, and over 1,000 yards. McClain did not just break the color barrier for the University of Tennessee Volunteers; he broke records. In 1969, he ran his customary long decoy pattern against Memphis State, but that game was destined to be anything but ordinary. McClain snatched the longest touchdown pass in Vols history at that time—82 yards. Later he rewrote the receiving records.

McClain, today a successful insurance agent in Knoxville, considers his football career as a tremendous learning experience that taught him about life, getting to know people, and working hard for accomplishments. He was just a kid who wanted an opportunity, but he left the UT as a man who was an advocate for equal rights and who passionately believed in uniting individuals through the power of teamwork. He also learned that change is not instantaneous, but rather it requires a daily effort and a vision.

More than 20 years after his endeavor to change negative attitudes about race through the power of sport, McClain was honored at a Tennessee-Auburn football game for his heroic efforts. The Maxwell House® Coffee/SEC Spirit Award was bestowed upon 10 SEC alumni athletes, including McClain, to honor the tremendous spirit they demonstrated in spite of the obstacles they faced during their playing careers. McClain accepted that award with great humility and respect for society's transformation and the other pioneers who followed his trail. McClain illuminated and cleared the path so that a new generation of African-American athletes could experience equality and pursue achievements. He continued to serve UT student-athletes through his appointment to the UT athletics board from 1987 until 1990.

McClain may not have been the first choice, but he certainly was the best choice for the first African-American scholarship football player at the University of Tennessee. He was a man who carried the pressure and unbearable burden of racism with class and dignity. Many described McClain as a proud man with a sense of determination; McClain was a pioneer for equality and opportunity.

Note

1. Ben Byrd, "Vols Didn't Really Want McClain," *The Knoxville Journal*, August, 19, 1986.

Perry Wallace

First African-American Student-Athlete at Vanderbilt University

by Stacy Martin

Courtesy of Vanderbilt University.

Perry Wallace's life is an impressive example of achievement earned despite enormous pressure from society. He grew up during the Cold War, in the height of the space race between Russia and the United States. Intrigued and enthralled by the era's technological advances, Wallace became interested in math and science at an early age. His patriotism led him to pursue degrees in electrical engineering and engineering mathematics when he enrolled in Vanderbilt University. Wallace would be influenced not only by America's tumultuous relationship with Russia, but also by the uproar and conflict brewing between the races on America's own soil.

Wallace wanted an education and typically that meant one of two choices for an African-American high school student-athlete living in the South. Wallace could follow his older sisters to one of the nearby historically black colleges and universities like Fisk or Tennessee State, or he could strive for a scholarship to a Northern institution like the University of Michigan. With segregation running rampant in the South, Vanderbilt was not even a thought for Wallace until the Civil Rights Movement spawned the efforts toward integration. Wallace was given the opportunity to be the hometown hero at Vanderbilt and to change the course of history.

Segregation was a rule in society's game that did not allow a particular group of people to compete. Integration provided opportunity and enhanced the game's fairness. During Wallace's 1965–66 basketball season at the predominantly African-American Pearl High School in Nashville, the school was finally permitted to participate in the state championship tournament with white high schools, resulting in the first true Tennessee basketball state championship. This change garnered a significant amount of publicity. When Pearl won the first integrated basketball state championship, the future of basketball in Tennessee was improved dramatically. That season Wallace exuded leadership through his remarkable talent on the court and his academic excellence off the court. This exceptional young man earned valedictorian honors from Pearl upon graduation. He was the epitome of the desired NCAA Division I student-athlete, with equal focus and commitment to both academics and athletics.

In the early days of the Southeastern Conference's integration process, many of its member institutions recruited Wallace for his combination of brains and brawn. Wallace was a strong choice to break the color barrier at one of the universities because of his will, determination, and talents. Vanderbilt recognized this immediately, and in turn Wallace recognized the university's most favorable attribute, discipline in both academics and athletics. Wallace had the foresight to know that his endeavors at a predominantly white institution would have a greater impact if he attended a major university in a large, reputable athletic conference. Furthermore, Wallace knew that attending Vandy would allow him the built-in support system of his family in his hometown of Nashville. Parents are often apprehensive when their children begin college, but Mr. and Mrs. Wallace must have experienced more than just mild anxiety. Their son would experience well beyond the average student's social acclimation challenges on a college campus. His displacement and feelings of being ostracized would stem from other students' stereotypes of his skin color.

Wallace is a self-described private person so he was content to be placed in a single dorm room his freshman year. He capitalized on his quiet time by dedicating it to his studies, creating a balance between academics and athletics that is often difficult for freshman student-athletes to achieve. Wallace had the added pressure of being a pioneer. In an oral interview with a Vanderbilt University student, Wallace described a pioneering situation as one that generates a lot of focus, interest, curiosity, and publicity. The bar was set higher for Wallace than for white students, but he credits the pressure-filled situation with his success, because it made him "work harder" and "work smarter." Wallace related his decision to enroll at Vanderbilt and the unexpected pressure to pioneer the unknown. Wallace dared to imagine something different, something beyond the norm, and set out on a journey armed with faith and courage, because no map existed.

Socially, Wallace's was often diverted to the campuses of nearby Fisk and Tennessee State, where he and the other African-American Vanderbilt students created a social network parallel to the Greek system so fervently in place on Vanderbilt's campus. Again, Wallace was influenced by the world surrounding him and decided to look beyond the norm. He sought out other social circles, including those which seemed foreign to him. Wallace befriended graduate students, medical students, fraternity and sorority students, alumni, and other individuals throughout the city. During that era, Nashville cultivated leaders like Congressman John Lewis (a divinity student); future mayor of Washington, D.C., Marion Barry (Fisk graduate student); and Ron Walter, who has worked with the Joint Center for Political and Economic Studies. The influences of Martin Luther King, Jesse Jackson, Julian Bond, Harry Belafonte, Leotine Price, and others created the fabric of the community in Nashville. Wallace matured socially as society experienced integration.

His growth was also influenced by the evolution of the game of basketball. Wallace was athletic and hard working and was able to soar over his competition by dunking the basketball. This changed, however, after Adolph Rupp's Kentucky team lost to an all African-American starting five at Texas Western. Many thought that Rupp helped outlaw the dunk to inhibit African-Americans, but the announced reason the rule changed was to protect players' safety. Society in the South in those days was not concerned with the player's safety. In fact Wallace could feel spectators' anger penetrating his ebony skin during most away games. Screaming, vicious yelling, and verbal hatred were commonplace. Vanderbilt's fans treated him with adoration only as long as he was playing well, amplifying the pressure.

Wallace's teammates also added to the pressure. On the court they appreciated his talent, but once they stepped off the court some refused to even interact with him. Wallace explains the treatment as a product of the world they played in and its divergence into two different worlds in which he and his teammates lived respectively. He never faulted them for being part of a social structure that was wide open for whites but not for African-Americans. But the pain and anguish that it caused did not diminish even when, on rare occasions, someone stepped away from the crowd to invite him in. Wallace received threatening letters from the day he signed with Vanderbilt until after he graduated. Today, he still wrestles with the question of whether or not he should have played the role of pioneer for student-athletes at Vanderbilt because of the danger and risk. Most would fixate on the risk of physical harm, but in hindsight Wallace ponders the post-traumatic stress response of that volatile situation, very similar to that of war veterans. He fought through the darkness that haunted his nightmares with support from close friends and family, and now is grateful that he persisted.

Wallace attributes his resiliency to a man named Vereen Bell who took the time to encourage students throughout that terrifying time. Wallace depicts his psychological scar as one caused by a whole world dominated by injustice and hurt, which made it difficult to find balance. He did find balance and solace in achieving perspective. Even the negative develops us into the people we become, and Perry Wallace's experience cultivated his passion for civil rights and community involvement. He has continued work in both arenas, and today he is a professor of law at American University in Washington, D.C., counseling and encouraging students much like Vereen Bell. Recently, Wallace was remembered for his contribution to Vanderbilt through a ceremony retiring his jersey, one of the greatest honors an athlete can receive. Now every athlete at Vanderbilt can look up, remember the past, and be inspired for the future.

Maxie Foster

First African-American Student-Athlete at the University of Georgia

by Stacy Martin

Courtesy of the University of Georgia Athletic Association.

Georgia had a troubled history with desegregation that began with Governor Herman Talmadge's refusal to comply with the *Brown v. Board of Education* Supreme Court decision. He did not fear federal authority or exertion of force, nor did he make any attempt to secede from the union that asked him to desegregate his state's schools. He simply refused, and the next governor, Marvin Griffin, supported his predecessor's decision. Next, Senator Richard Russell accompanied Strom Thurmond in writing what is best known as the "Southern Manifesto," which proposed massive resistance to integration. This document was considered the catalyst for the large-scale, defiant behavior of the white community in regard to integration. The abusive and demeaning actions of white adults directed at young African-American students walking to school are viewed as cruel and unusual today, but back then it was commonplace. One young African-American girl characterized the simple act of walking to school, down a street lined with angry white parents protesting her attendance, as a sport for the parents. Fortunately, sport was able to help elevate Maxie Foster from the depths of hatred and degradation into the spotlight of accomplishment and achievement.

When Maxie Foster transferred to Athens High School from the African-American high school of Burney-Harris in the tenth grade, it was a turbulent journey. After all, one of his fellow students was the son of the Grand Wizard of the Ku Klux Klan, and Foster endured numerous violent acts by him. Foster had enrolled under a "Freedom of Choice" plan, but it seemed that his only choice was in attending the school; nothing else seemed to be within his control. The assistant principal enrolled him in senior level classes the first semester of his sophomore year, setting him up for failure. Only later was he able to transfer to the proper academic level. At the young age of 16 he was forced to face the harsh reality of white students being given preferential treatment over African-American students. He was asked to assist in packing boxes of used textbooks for the African-American schools so that they also could have books to read. Most likely, he and the others used the same boxes that had just delivered new textbooks for the white students.

Sport carried enough influence and interest to provide hope of an equal playing field. Everyone had expressed enthusiasm to create a powerhouse athletic program at Athens, especially a football team. The coach allowed the African-American students to practice with the team in the spring season, only to omit them from varsity tryouts in the fall for fear that his KKK membership would be revoked. Foster was one of the students disappointed. He persevered and tried out for the basketball team in the winter, which he successfully integrated at Athens High School. Later that spring he also integrated the track and field team. Foster admired both teams' coaches, looking back with respect on the acts of their courage and kindness. His own commitment to his cause should be equally admired, because he had to fight through the angry, affluent white parents who abhorred his playing on the team. After he'd had an opportunity to prove himself, though, the white students elected Foster captain of both the basketball and track teams. Unfortunately, the taunting continued when they left Athens to play other teams, and sometimes Foster had to remain on the bus, hungry, because he was not allowed to join his team for a meal.

Foster graduated from Athens High School and enrolled in the University of Georgia in 1968. Once again he led the way for African-American student-athletes by integrating the Bulldog track and field team. The university had enrolled African-American students a few years previously, but the athletic program had failed to sign an African-American student-athlete. Foster's leadership and tremendous talent launched him into success once more. His teammates named him captain again, and with his incredible example of determination and fortitude, the team defeated Auburn for the first time in a 1972 dual meet. Maxie Foster dominated the quarter-mile race when he competed, but the distance he ran for the African-

American athletes that followed him is what made him a true champion. He earned his degree in education in 1972 from the University of Georgia and continued studying education for his Masters of Education in 1974.

By 1975, Foster had earned his first faculty appointment, one he held for seven years, with the Department of Health and Physical Education at Macon Junior College in Georgia. In 1982, he joined the faculty at Louisiana State University of Shreveport, where he remained for more than 20 years.

Henry Harris

First African-American Student-Athlete at Auburn University

by Stacy Martin

Henry Harris experienced his share of pain while attending Auburn University. He suffered because of his skin color and the inferiority others associated with it. He endured the pain that only a select few athletes know, the pain of injury that first removes them from their game and remains with them as they attempt to return and continue forward. He tolerated the imbalance between the team's wins and losses along with the coach, his teammates, the fans, and the campus. Harris persisted and refused to be beaten. He wanted something more, something better for himself and for others.

Every fated hero seems to have a humble beginning. It is the experience of this humility that likely develops their desires, talents, and courage to be great. Harris' humble beginning unfolded on the banks of the Tombigbee River in the small town of Boligee, Alabama. The town is simple and would likely be completely unknown were it not for the river and the fishermen it attracts. "Big Tom," as the locals call it, is considered a primary commercial route through the southern United States. Boligee offers its youth few choices and yet the river promises them a glimpse at what lies beyond the borders of small town life. Harris was to integration at Auburn University what the Tombigbee River was for the small town of Boligee. He came from an unknown place with unknown traits and brought waves of change and opportunity to a community.

Harris took part in the usual activities in Boligee: fishing, backyard basketball and football, and walking. Harris once recounted to the former sports information director and later athletic director of Auburn, David Housel, "My buddies and I used to walk all the time. . . . We would spend a whole Sunday afternoon just walking and shooting basketballs."[1] Harris enjoyed long walks so much that he continued to list "walking" as a hobby while attending Auburn. Although he loved to walk, it was his talent for shooting basketballs that earned him a scholarship to Auburn. Harris is quick to praise those individuals who had a hand in molding him into a successful young athlete. After his domination in the backyard, he developed his skills with the help of Coach P. H. Pettway at Greene County Training School. Coach A. W. Young, Jr., assisted in Harris' development as well by instilling persistence and drive in the young man as he played the game.

Harris had a storybook high school athletic career in Boligee. He owned every hardwood floor he stepped on, scoring a total of 3,220 points in his career at Greene County Training School. During his senior year alone, he scored 1,117 points, which is still the fifth highest in the history of the Alabama High School Athletic Association. Harris' prowess was not limited to basketball, as he was a leader on the football field too. He played quarterback and led his team to an undefeated season. Greene County narrowly missed the state championship.

Many heroes have confidants who push them beyond their limits. For Henry Harris it was his youngest brother, Carl, who pushed his game to the next level day in and day out. There is a competitive nature built into sibling rivalry that can rarely be duplicated. The drive created by this one-upmanship becomes ingrained and the results it produces are far greater than only one player's determination. Henry bestowed on Carl his own kind of MVP award, a thank-you from one sibling to another for making him better, for making a difference in his life.

After an impressive high school career, Harris went to Auburn University to become the first African-American athlete to play collegiate basketball in the state of Alabama and to make a difference for the African-American race. Auburn University is commonly referred to as "the loveliest village on the plains," but its journey through integration was far from lovely. The University of Alabama bore the brunt of pain caused by massive resistance to integration when *Brown v. Board of Education* was decided, offering Autherine Lucy a chance to attend graduate school under court order. Governor

George Wallace's "infamous stand at the schoolhouse door"[2] was a picture worth a thousand words in describing the climate of the conflict surrounding desegregation. While Auburn escaped such violent protests, former African-American students have referred to it as "Apartheid U." Even recently, there have been bias incidents and hate crimes on campus. Perry Wallace, the first African-American athlete at Vanderbilt University, described playing in and traveling to Auburn as "going to hell, going straight to hell"[3] during the time that Harris played.

If Harris was tormented and threatened by ignorant individuals who saw only the darkness of his skin and not his talent as a young person, then he must have internalized the pain and anguish. Change brings attention, but Harris did not believe his pioneering efforts warranted any acclaim. He remained focused on the task at hand, playing basketball and earning an education. He thought of himself as one of the guys; among his teammates and his coaches, he was simply a basketball player.

Harris was the kind of player who found a way to contribute in every conceivable play. He demonstrated leadership, being chosen as the captain of the 1972 squad during his senior season. Harris had scored 630 career points going into his senior year, despite having knee surgery his junior year. The mark was still high enough at the time to make him one of the best in Auburn's history. This made him an asset to the team offensively, but Harris maneuvered the court like a tiger with speed, agility, focus, and raw determination. His defensive skills stifled the offense of the other team, and when they did shoot, Harris rebounded as quickly as that Auburn cat. Coach Bill Lynn constantly praised Harris for being versatile and so valuable to the team.

Harris finished his senior year with another 294 points to add to his total, as well as an additional 160 rebounds. He was a great player because of his hustle and tenacity, but he was not a first-round draft pick. Harris was selected by the Houston Rockets as the seventh pick of the eighth round in the 1972 draft.

The impact that Henry Harris made cannot necessarily be measured by record books or basketball accolades. The difference he made lies within the hearts of young, African-American men and women attending Auburn University today as athletes. Harris had chosen vocational rehabilitation as his profession so that he could help others less fortunate than himself. He simply expressed to David Housel that he wanted to be remembered by others "as a basketball player who cared for other people."

Sadly, Harris jumped from a building in New York in 1974, without leaving an explanation for his actions.[4] Some guess that the unbearable pain he internalized had finally led him into death, but only Harris knew the factors that catalyzed his decision.

Harris will never be remembered as just a basketball player. He is remembered annually at Auburn through a basketball tournament over the Martin Luther King holiday weekend as part of a celebration of the freedom and equality to which he contributed so unselfishly. He changed the opportunities available for African-American people at Auburn University, and that is a gift given in perpetuity.

Notes

1. David Housel, "Growing Up in Boligee Henry Harris," Auburn University Basketball Program, 1972.

2. Susan Basalla, "Two Cheers for 'Apartheid U,'" *Journal of Blacks in Higher Education*, n5 Fall 1994:81–85.

3. Frank Fitzpatrick, *And the Walls Came Tumbling Down: Kentucky, Texas Western, and the Game that Changed American Sports* (New York: Simon & Schuster, 1999).

4. Ibid.

Ron Coleman

First African-American Student-Athlete at the University of Florida

by Stacy Martin

Ron Coleman's quiet footsteps through racial integration in the South led him to giant leaps at the University of Florida as a pioneer for racial equality. Coleman began his journey in Ocala, Florida, where he learned to run and perfect his swift steps. Coleman attended Howard High School, a segregated African-American high school, until the fall of 1965. In 1965, Coleman and others transferred to Ocala High School, the first big step for integration in the small Florida city. Ocala's integration process was calm and was not fraught with the hostility that was common to race relations at the time. Nonetheless, Coleman and his former Howard classmates did face isolation at times in their new surroundings. His athletic talent offered him a certain level of insulation and some of the Ocala High students even welcomed his prowess on their athletic fields.

Athletics was Coleman's launching pad for success. The track coach at Howard High was the first to discover Coleman's running talent and became enamored of his abilities. Coleman had a smooth stride, carrying his frame in a quick and graceful manner like an Olympic athlete winning gold without a competitor in sight. Not until the track coach asked Coleman to try the high jump, though, did his true talent shine. High jumping was only the beginning of Coleman's track and field career. His natural speed and jumping ability catapulted him to distances no other long jumper in the state had reached. Coleman was the first athlete to jump 24 feet in the long jump. He was breaking records and securing his place in history.

The 24-foot jump attracted the attention of major universities, and recruiters began visiting Ocala. Coach Jimmy Carnes of the University of Florida was one of the recruiters who visited the Coleman family. Carnes came to see an athlete with tremendous talent but quickly realized that he had met a tremendous person in Coleman as well. Within a few moments Coleman's leadership qualities were evident, and Carnes discovered that Coleman was also an excellent student. Carnes particularly admired Coleman's ability to bring contentment and easiness to any conversation. If anyone could handle the scrutiny and resistance that would accompany being the first African-American student-athlete at the University of Florida, Carnes knew it would be Coleman. Any strife surrounding the situation would be softened by the strength and love that Coleman's family provided him.

Despite receiving hate mail after the announcement, Coleman pursued the opportunity to become the first African-American scholarship athlete at the University of Florida. The University of Florida had integrated in 1958 when the first African-American student, George Stark, enrolled in the law school. The integration efforts were peaceful in relation to the turbulent times society was experiencing. There were very few demonstrations against Stark's enrollment, even though the University of Florida had rejected 85 African-American students' applications at all educational levels from 1945 until Stark was admitted in 1958. Although Stark enrolled, he did not graduate; the first graduate was Willie George Allen from the law school in 1963, just five short years before Coleman enrolled at University of Florida. During the time that Coleman attended Florida, there was significant dissent on campus. By 1970, there were only 343 African-American students. Objection and opposition were growing from both races and the circumstances ultimately led to a demonstration now known as "Black Thursday" in 1971. There is no doubt that Coleman's presence at the university set an example for what African-Americans could accomplish if provided an opportunity.

Coleman took little time to mark his place in school history. Within a year of his enrollment, he duplicated his 24-foot leap in the long jump. This time his efforts earned him an Indoor Southeastern Conference title. The next year, Coleman proved his talent in yet another field event, the triple jump. His history with the high jump and the long jump and his natural speed made him a perfect candidate for the difficult and very technical event. His dedication and countless hours of practice made him a champion. In 1970, Coleman captured both the long jump and triple jump Indoor Southeastern Conference Champion titles, earning him the Commissioner's Trophy as well. Coleman improved his long jump mark to 24 feet 8 inches and triple jumped 49 feet 11 1/2 inches. The Commissioner's Trophy is awarded at each Southeastern Conference Championship to the athlete who accumulates the most individual points throughout the competition. Coleman continued his success into the outdoor track and field season with an Outdoor Southeastern Conference Championship title in the triple jump with a leap of 49 feet $\frac{1}{4}$ inch. By his senior year, Coleman had advanced his triple jump mark to 52 feet $2\frac{1}{4}$ inches to earn yet another indoor Southeastern Conference Championship in the triple jump. He was able to capture the outdoor title with a jump of 50 feet $7\frac{1}{2}$ inches. Both of those jumps were far enough to hold his place yet today on the Gator top ten indoor and outdoor all-time mark lists.

Ron Coleman has left his mark on school history in more ways than one. He ushered in a new era of African-American athletes to the University of Florida during a time when the university itself was struggling to include these students in their classrooms. He set records and earned championships in a humble, quiet manner. His action spoke much louder than the words used to oppose his scholarship when he signed with Florida. Most of all, the person that Ron Coleman became represented the school and its athletic teams in a dignified manner.

After studying human resource management at the university, Coleman went into service for the United States Navy. He commanded the skies for 22 years as a naval aviator. Coleman once said that it had been a childhood dream of his to fly. By the end of his naval career, Coleman had earned the distinguished honor and post of commander. Today, he focuses on the next generation of aviators and athletes, his grandchildren. Coleman's story is proof that dreams come true with a little practice and determination. He continues to pass that story along to his grandchildren while encouraging them to believe in themselves and their own dreams.

Jon Richardson

First African-American Scholarship Student-Athlete at the University of Arkansas

by Stacy Martin

Understanding Jon Richardson's story requires an appreciation of the turmoil his community faced when the nation stood up to say that it was wrong to segregate. The University of Arkansas' School of Law integrated in 1949, and the Little Rock Public Library opened its doors to whites and blacks just two years later. Even the city's public transportation desegregated without incident in 1956. It seemed as if blacks and whites could live and socialize together amicably, but learning together seemed to be an insurmountable task. Arkansas had its share of notoriety and infamous imagery when the Little Rock School Board executed its desegregation plan in response to *Brown vs. Board of Education* in 1957. The plan involved interviewing eligible African-American students so that they might enroll in Little Rock's Central High. After a lengthy process, only nine remained to change the color of Central High; they became known as the Little Rock Nine. Their bravery and resolve in the face of denigration from their fellow students earned them congressional honors more than 50 years later. During desegregation, it seemed even more impossible to compete on an athletic field together or for the fans to cheer with one voice.

It was common for the African-American community in the state of Arkansas to cheer for either the local all African-American high school, such as Jon Richardson's Horace Mann High School, or Arkansas AM&N, the historically black college in Pine Buff, Arkansas. The Arkansas Razorback football team had fielded all-white football teams throughout its 76-year history. According to the memory of a native Arkansas novelist E. Lynn Harris, there was only one brave African-American pioneer who attempted to walk on to the team in 1966 during the years of segregation. Darrell Brown did not receive a scholarship from the Razorbacks. He tried out for the freshman team out of love for the game of football and his beloved "Hogs."

As a result of the tumultuous race relations and hostile times, Brown's experience was characterized by hate and harassment. He walked through the threats and condemnation by fellow students on campus with a stoic presence. He held steadfast to his goal to play and gave every effort when given an opportunity. Eventually, his teammates acknowledged his contributions and undying exertions to earn his spot on the team. Although some of those teammates remained silent contributors to Brown's misfortune and anger, there were others who provided solace and encouragement throughout his struggles on and off the field. His outward confidence may have hidden the sadness and the damage to his self-esteem. Brown came to Arkansas first for an education and secondly a football career, the converse of most of today's collegiate athletes. He had proven himself as a football player despite the horrific circumstances, but after his experience he demonstrated his character and class by deciding to concentrate on the education he valued so much. The wounds already ran too deep, so he left the team. Brown laid a priceless foundation for Jon Richardson.

Richardson flew over the color barrier once posed by the Arkansas Razorbacks and became the first African-American scholarship athlete for the university. He enrolled in 1969 and became varsity eligible after his freshman year. Richardson's scholarship may have insulated him from some of the same growing pains that Brown endured. Although he received hate mail and ignorant threats, he was seasoned and strong enough to endure most anything placed in his path. Richardson had learned the harsh realities of football and life in the sandlot with his older brother.

The Richardson family has an athletic bloodline rich in successful history and local fame. Grover Richardson, Sr., Jon's father, had earned his stripes on the sandlot baseball field playing for the Little Rock Cubs after his high school and junior college triumphs in baseball, track, and football. Grover's father and Jon's grandfather, Lenoy Richardson, had become synonymous with local baseball folklore. Lenoy was talented enough to play in the Negro Leagues but opted to raise his family instead. Even Jon's brothers, Grover Jr., and James, were athletically inclined. The family members were as dedicated to sports as they were to one another, creating a close bond in spite of wins or defeats. It was Grover Jr. who took young Jon to play tackle football in the sandlot with high school boys, and it was James who defended Jon when fans booed him after a fumble. The Richardson boys were brothers and teammates, two bonds which are rarely broken.

The University of Arkansas had recruited Grover Jr., but he had too many reservations about what he might endure[1] and instead accepted a scholarship from Southern University in Louisiana. Jon Richardson followed in his brother's talented footsteps and became a recruiting sensation. Coach Frank Broyles of the Razorbacks knocked at the Richardson house once more and offered Jon a scholarship. The recruiting did not stop there. The postal route of Grover Sr. included an affluent neighborhood housing several influential Arkansas alumni. They persuaded him to send his son to Fayetteville with a promise for his safety. Grover Sr. was convinced that this opportunity would be too great for Jon to miss and thus encouraged his son's decision to become a Razorback.

Jon Richardson's arrival on campus was mild compared to Brown's three years earlier. It is likely that Richardson won people over with his personality. His brothers and his teammates characterized Jon as a guy who lightened the mood with a smile or friendly conversation. His days on the sandlot had taught him how to take a hit and survive, but also how to get to know others regardless of race. Richardson was not isolated entirely from the anger of racist individuals, but, like Brown, he walked away from any hateful altercations with dignity and character rather than perpetuate the violent behavior. He also had the comfort of another African-American athlete on campus when Almer Lee became the first African-American basketball player for Arkansas.

Richardson's dazzling footwork on the field quickly caught the eye of most Razorback fans who cheered with delight when he pushed the ball toward the goal line. They stood up with pride for Richardson when he took a hit from the opposing team, but also sat down when he fumbled a run or pass. Eventually, he was accepted and gained their loyalties. He had an accomplished career at Arkansas despite serving as a backup. By the end of his tenure he had inked his name on several of the team's top performance lists, such as all-time rushing yards, touchdowns, and kickoff returns.

During Richardson's debut in the Arkansas red and white against Stanford he soared into the end zone as he caught a 37-yard touchdown pass just before the half. The crowd roared because their beloved Razorbacks went up six points. Richardson firmly established his place in school history and led the way for change. With one touchdown reception, he was able to bring an entire stadium together in one voice—the beginning of uniting a once broken Arkansas community through sport. Sadly, Richardson passed away at the age of 50.

Note

1. Darren Ivy and *Arkansas Democrat Gazette*, Sports, *Untold Stories: Black Sports Heroes before Integration* (Little Rock Arkansas: Wehco Publishing, 2002). (Courtesy of University of Arkansas Libraries Special Collections.)

Coolidge Ball

First African-American Student-Athlete at the University of Mississippi

by Stacy Martin

Coolidge Ball began his basketball career at Gentry High School in Indianola, Mississippi, where he averaged 20 rebounds and 28 points per season. Rumor of his skills attracted the attention of recruiters from all over the country. New Mexico had made a great impression on him and he had an early interest in setting out on a trail toward the west. Before he settled on that journey, Coach Kenny Robbins at the University of Mississippi, or "Ole Miss," encouraged Ball to visit the university. Coolidge Ball's visit to an Ole Miss basketball game is a moment that changed history.

In those days the freshman played their own game before the varsity because they were not eligible for varsity until their sophomore season. Ball arrived in February of 1970 at the Rebel Coliseum, now known as the C. M. "Tad" Smith Coliseum, to see the Ole Miss Rebels take on the famed University of Kentucky Wildcats. The venue was electric with energy. He watched the freshman play, and then the players joined him in the stands during the varsity game to talk with him about their experiences at Ole Miss. They answered all of the typical athletic recruiting questions. What were practices like? How did Coach Robbins treat the team? How were the classes and coursework? Did they like the campus and the students? They even asked a few questions of their own. What were Ball's stats from high school? Where was he from? What did he like about Ole Miss? Who else was recruiting him? Halftime came and Ball experienced that prophetic moment that made a lasting impression on him.

They announced "Coolidge Ball" with all the clamor of a starting lineup introduction. It wasn't just hearing his name called over the loud speakers and echoing in the corners of the gymnasium that changed him. It was the constant stream of applause that followed his name. When he began to look around the domed building, he gazed in wonder at almost 9,000 fans standing to applaud him—the epitome of southern hospitality. In those days, schools were allowed to welcome a recruit in that way, a tradition long since retired. Ball described it as one of the warmest welcomes he had ever received in his life. He didn't bother to see the rest of campus or the Oxford, Mississippi, community that night; his experience at the game was more than enough.

Coach Robbins visited the Ball family home and sat with Coolidge and Mr. and Mrs. Ball. Utilizing a recruiting style that was more conversation than sales pitch, Coach Robbins appeared sincere and honest in his interaction with the family. They, in turn, respected Coach Robbins for his demeanor. Coach simply stated that Ball would be the first African-American student-athlete to sign a scholarship for the Rebels. He had recruited other African-Americans, but they had chosen not to attend Ole Miss. Robbins expressed that he did not think that there would be any "problems" with Ball's presence as a student-athlete on the Ole Miss campus. His word was enough and the family trusted him. In the end, Ball still had a decision to make, as New Mexico State was still recruiting him.

When Ball finished his senior year of high school, he chose to move west to New Mexico in the spirit of youth and curiosity. Change is sometimes a solace for the soul, but at other times it can be too much to bear. Ball moved to New Mexico in the summer and began to work. The desert and mountains did nothing to soothe him, so he telephoned Coach Robbins to see if he still had a scholarship. Robbins did. Since Ball had never signed a national letter of intent with New Mexico, he was eligible to sign with Ole Miss. The path through life can be full of wrong turns, but sometimes it is the wrong turn that leads to the right way.

Ball moved home with the support of his family and enrolled in school at Ole Miss in the fall. He harbored the same fears and anxieties as most college freshman about moving away from the familiarity of home to a new world full of strangers. Ball was nervous also about being the first African-American athlete.[1] He had attended a predominantly African-American high school, and now he would be attending a school that had integrated just a short time ago. His trust in Coach Robbins helped him move past the fear and nervousness. The memory of that standing ovation was like having a personal cheering section giving him the confidence to pursue his dreams. He enrolled in classes and began practicing with his teammates, a group of young men with whom he became very close. They quickly formed a family-like bond from the shared blood, sweat, pain, and sometimes tears that came from practices. The team became protective of Ball, although protection was rarely needed.

Talking with Coolidge Ball for the first time is like chatting with an old friend—the conversation takes on its own calming rhythm. He is a very easy-going man with a conversation style that is honest and direct, while being gentle and temperate. When he spoke with white students on campus, he spoke with kindness and meaning. Ball says that at Ole Miss everyone was always so interested in athletes and athletics that students frequently approached him just to talk. The conversation may have started with athletics, but Ball often found a new topic in the discourse and transitioned with subtlety and skill. He usually found a way to talk with other people about their interests and studies and, eased by his manner, they began sharing their own stories. During conversations with white students, Ball sometimes would learn that they had never been allowed by their parents to talk with an African-American before. They would walk away from a conversation with Coolidge Ball with an indelible impression of honesty, gentility, and kindness.

During his time at Ole Miss, Ball changed minds with his basketball skills as well as his conversational skills. During his freshman season he amassed over 500 points and more than 300 rebounds to help the freshmen team to a 20-3 record. Those numbers did not count in his official statistics, but in the next three years on the varsity team Ball collected over 1,000 points and 750 rebounds. His team made Ole Miss history when it ushered in a new era of basketball success at Ole Miss by recording three straight winning seasons for the first time in 34 seasons. His basketball success led him to the International Basketball Association team in Hamilton, Ohio, after he finished his degree in recreation and the study of art. Though he played only one year, Ball cultivated relationships that would benefit his business, Ball Sign Company, later in life. Ball put his artistic studies to use by printing and hand painting signs and tags for his graphic design company located in Oxford. It seems fitting that a man who made a lasting impression on the University of Mississippi spends his days leaving his mark through artistic endeavors across the country.

Ball had a goal throughout his career at Ole Miss to make a difference in the lives of the students, for the school, and for the State of Mississippi. His induction into the Ole Miss Athletic Hall of Fame, being recognized as a Southeastern Conference Living Legend and the place that he will forever hold in history as the first African-American at Ole Miss, speaks volumes to the difference Coolidge Ball made. He believes that sport is the biggest and best thing to happen to race relations. With humility, he realizes that his actions helped mend the wounds torn open by the tumultuous integration process that the first African-American student at Ole Miss, James Meredith, experienced. Ball's good-natured, serene personality opened the door wide to an overall improvement in race relations at the University of Mississippi. He simply changed minds one conversation at a time. The world would be a much better place if more people conversed with the ease, candor, and care of Coolidge Ball.

Note

1. Coolidge Ball, e-mail message to author, April 2, 2007.

Collis Temple, Jr.

First African-American Student-Athlete at Louisiana State University

by Stacy Martin

Louisiana State University faced a tumultuous battle throughout the integration process, one that involved court orders, demonstrations, and even violence. Change toward social diversity on campus was unwelcome, and the impetus for such a change was met with fierce resistance from leaders and students alike. Although many African-American pioneers attempted to settle the uproar and propel the campus into a more tolerant time, one man was chosen to change the appearance of the athletic program to reflect a more equal playing field. That man was handpicked by one of the university's esteemed coaches, Press Maravich, and former Louisiana governor, John McKeithen. Collis Temple, Jr., was chosen to lead the Tigers to victory, in basketball and integration.

Collis Temple, Sr., and Shirley Cross Temple had invested heavily in education, both obtaining master's degrees. This was an anomaly during that era, as it was difficult for African-Americans even to enroll in college. Moreover, it is remarkable that both of Shirley's parents had graduated from college at the turn of the century. Both generations certainly had to overcome their share of obstacles. When Collis Temple, Jr., was attending a segregated high school in Kentwood, Louisiana, the thought of attending LSU was a remote possibility, but times were changing. During his senior year the local schools desegregated so that black and white students attended classes and basketball practices together. Temple dominated the court with his statuesque (6-foot-8-inch) physique, and he matured into one of the best high school players in the country. Familial support and the value his family placed on education were what really elevated his game to the next level on the collegiate stage.

Temple moved into the LSU dormitories in the 1971 fall semester without another African-American student-athlete to roam the halls with him. The athletic programs had remained astonishingly white despite President Johnson's signing the Civil Rights Act into law seven years earlier. There was the promise of one other

African-American athlete on the track team, but in the revenue-generating sports it was a lonely walk for Temple. He faced the racial overtones that colored most of the school supporters during those times, and acclimating to the team was not a tranquil task. Nevertheless, Temple quickly learned how athletics could bridge the gap between divided societies.

It seemed as if the purple hue of LSU would shade the negativity and racism, while the golden hue of LSU would illuminate the possibilities and opportunities that would accompany this broken color barrier. The racial stereotypes and biases dissipated for the most part when Temple donned the LSU purple and gold uniform on the court. The LSU fans worshiped their players fighting for a Cajun win, so if supporting Temple meant supporting a win, the fans were willing to oblige. A similar truth was evident on the court with his teammates. Once Temple proved to them that he played the same game with the same ball, they were willing to judge him only by his ability instead of by preconceived notions about his race. Temple once characterized his teammates as some guys with less than desirable attitudes and some nice guys, but they ultimately found a way to respect the game and transcend race.

Sadly, the purple and gold insulation could protect him from the pandemonium surrounding integration for only so long. When visiting the other Southeastern Conference schools that had not yet integrated, fans vigorously defended their school's pride and colors and rallied against LSU's only African-American player. Unfortunately, Temple's tremendous ability did not level the playing field with the opposing team as it did his own. In fact, it might have helped to incite chauvinistic, obscene remarks from the opposing team's players in their efforts to defeat Temple and his Tigers. The turbulent times and aggressive nature of basketball led to at least three fights during Temple's career when opposing players called him a "nigger." One such fight broke out in his haven of Baton Rouge. Traveling brought more serious dangers, including death threats for Temple and even his coach, Dale Brown, during one away trip. Temple could not be deterred from his destiny and remained determined to play. He continued to be resolved to make the sacrifice for others, intent on making a difference.

Temple remains committed to LSU even today. After he finished his eligibility and earned his master's degree, his loyalty to

Baton Rouge and LSU remained true. In 1978, he created and began operating Harmony Center, Inc., a non-profit organization that benefits those less fortunate in the community—from foster children to developmentally disabled adults. He also devoted himself to providing assistance to the mentally ill and chemically dependent through Louisiana Health and Rehabilitation Options, which he co-owns. His dedication to others is apparent, but it is within the walls of the Sports Academy in Baton Rouge that his true passion can be seen.

The Sports Academy creates the opportunity for young athletes to develop their skills and talents. Temple has become a patriarch of the Baton Rouge community to many youths seeking guidance and instruction. His own sons have heeded his advice and developed into Division I basketball talents. Collis Temple III played for LSU from 1999 to 2003. He followed his father's hallowed footsteps into the LSU record books by being the first Ph.D. student to be a Division I basketball player. He had quickly earned his undergraduate degree in business, followed by a master's degree in kinesiology with a focus on sports management, and finally he achieved the academic slam dunk, a doctorate in educational leadership.

Garrett Temple is the second son of Collis Temple, Jr., to play for LSU. He wears number 14, the reverse of his father's number 41, as a tribute to the sacrifices his father made for him to have this opportunity. The inverse of the number seems to symbolize the about face in society's perception of African-Americans. Whereas one Temple had to fight for equality, now his son and four of his African-American teammates run the court without giving a second thought to racism lurking in the stands. Four of the starting five for the 2005 LSU Final Four team had played together for years on AAU teams under the tutelage of Collis Temple, Jr., at the Sports Academy.

Collis Temple, Jr., goes beyond the game of basketball with his players; he becomes a friend, a man that they feel comfortable confiding in when times are hard. Glen "Big Baby" Davis was the son of a drug-addicted mother, but he found stability and comfort in Temple. Davis moved in with the Temple family and prepared for college with the rest of his AAU teammates and newfound brother, Garrett. Temple created a foundation for these young men to achieve greatness at an early age, but not merely on the basketball court. His time and involvement in the youth of the community are ensuring that they grow up knowing nothing but equality and possibility.

Wendell Hudson

First African-American Student-Athlete
at the University of Alabama

by Stacy Martin

The true story here? There is no story. The University of Alabama faced some of the most tumultuous conflicts regarding integration in the Deep South, a fact that has been portrayed in history books with shocking and poignant imagery. The torment that the first African-American students suffered remained vivid for years in the minds of many Americans. Given this climate, it would seem almost certain that the first African-American student-athlete to enroll at the University of Alabama would suffer a similar fate of torturous nightmares and daily harassment. Fortunately, that simply was not the case.

The legendary C. M. Newton was the coach at Alabama at the time, and the athletic director was the legendary football coach Paul "Bear" Bryant. When Newton accepted the head basketball coaching job at Alabama, he managed only four wins in his first season. When it came time to recruit for the following year, Newton went to the Bear and proposed a new perspective. He wanted to recruit the best talent from within the state and that talent included African-American players. Bryant agreed, and so Newton went on the recruiting trail looking for a pioneer to cultivate the athletic program at Alabama. He first spoke with Henry Harris, who later became the first African-American to sign a scholarship at Auburn, and Bud Stallworth, who pursued his athletic career at the University of Kansas. Then Newton followed Alvin McGrew and his basketball team all the way to the state championship with a 33-1 win loss record. Although he lost McGrew to a baseball contract, Newton found a star in his teammate Wendell Hudson. Hudson became a force during the first integrated Alabama state high-school tournament, which took place on Alabama's campus.

Hudson's offensive talents interested Newton, but his academic record was the reason Newton selected him to change history. Newton had always had the academic welfare of his student-athletes as a priority and created a strict environment for his players' studies. So it is no surprise that he wanted the first African-American student-athlete at Alabama to also be the first African-American student-athlete to graduate from Alabama. Hudson would lead the way for the Alabama coaches that would follow in his and Newton's footsteps in recruiting African-American athletes. He would serve as a role model for the African-American student-athletes who would come to Alabama in the future.

Hudson came from a single-parent home, and his mother had her share of reservations about the journey on which her son was about to embark. She asked Coach Newton point blank how her son would be treated and he answered with honest uncertainty. He readily admitted that he had not experienced the stares and loathing comments typically directed toward African-Americans from the white race because he was not African-American. He could only promise Hudson's mother that he would treat him with respect like he would any other ballplayer.

Newton and Hudson grew close on this journey together. Most athletes and coaches have a bond built upon respect for each other's talents, but the trying circumstances of competition sometimes form a tighter connection between teammates and coaches. As with most things in life it is not just the celebrations that bind people to one another but also the moments of hardship and doubt. Newton loved Hudson's dominant playing ability and leadership on the court, but he also was personally concerned for his well-being. Newton even gave Hudson driving lessons. Later in life, when Newton's beloved wife Evelyn passed away, it was Hudson who organized phone calls from former players to Newton encouraging him through his tribulations as he had once done for all of them. Their bond is closer than family and surely that provided the foundation for Hudson's good experience.

Hudson braved his share of threats and insults, especially during away games. While playing for the University of Alabama Crimson Tide, he realized that crimson was the only color that mattered. His teammates followed the same train of thought, and they became so attached that they vehemently defended their teammate as a brother. Hudson always responded respectfully and with class to intense situations by calming his teammates and walking on with his head held high.

When Hudson recounts his experience at Alabama, only one awkward memory surfaces—the day that he and his teammates moved into the athletic dorms. They had all bonded through the game of basketball, but Hudson was still a stranger to the athletes from other sports. He walked into the athletic dining hall that evening where 150 football players were sitting down for dinner. The clamor of forks collecting food from the plate and the boisterous showmanship following a hard day's practice suddenly ceased, and quiet stares filtered throughout the hall. Hudson was the first African-American to eat in that dining hall, and it appeared that just the sight of him had caused a rowdy team of football players to lose their appetites. Hudson simply stepped into line like everyone else. He walked through the line with 300 eyes burning a hole in his t-shirt, but at the end of the line he collected comfort food with a serving of solace. A wall had separated him from the kitchen servers but, much like the situation of the color barrier he had broken, it ended in empathy. The kitchen servers were all African-American, and their smiling faces spoke a thousand words of encouragement and pride. His plate had twice the servings of any other athlete in the dining hall. From that moment on, the noise began to escalate and so did his self-confidence. Wendell Hudson was going to make a difference at the University of Alabama.

Hudson's play overshadowed any negative thoughts brought about by the team's integration. The three years that Hudson played varsity for Newton resulted in accolades for the program. During his junior and senior seasons his outstanding scoring and rebounding led the team and earned him All-Southeastern Conference honors. He also was named Southeastern Conference Player of the Year, another first for Alabama. No other player, African-American or white, had ever achieved that honor in school history. Hudson also led the team to its first National Invitational Tournament (NIT) appearance in school history in 1973. That was such a feat that Bear Bryant rescheduled spring football practice to fly up to New York and attend the game. Hudson still remains in the school record books on all-time lists and has left an indelible mark on the University of Alabama.

Newton credits Hudson's demeanor and integrity as the major catalyst for the successful integration of Alabama athletics. The focus and the emphasis that the community and region placed on sports and the commitment that Hudson displayed encouraged the fans to think about the success of the team instead of the skin color of a player. That desire for success united a group of people with a common goal instead of dividing them over race. Hudson shared his gratitude for his experience with incoming recruits, enabling Alabama to recruit its first African-American junior college transfer and sign its first African-American player for football the next season.

In youth, we are sometimes blinded by ambition. Hudson was thrilled at the opportunity to play for Alabama, and so he did not fully grasp what his decision meant. He knew that he would be first, but he did not understand the depth of his choice. Even at 18 years old, Hudson knew that "this was the opportunity people had marched for and been beaten for and died for."[1] He took an opportunity and created a better life for those who came after him. Hudson currently serves as the associate athletic director for alumni relations at the University of Alabama, where he helps create a better environment for today's student-athletes.

Note

1. Tommy Deas, "Trail Blazer," *Tuscaloosa News*, August 3, 2003.

Chapter 10

SECTION TWO

Atlantic Coast
Conference
Student-Athlete
Heroes

Lou Montgomery

First African-American Student-Athlete at Boston College

by Horacio Ruiz

Boston College's Jesuit tradition emphasizes to its students the need for intellectual and spiritual development for the benefit of the poor. In 1937, the apparent beneficiary of those values was a young man who was attending Boston College as the first African-American athlete in the school's history.

Fast forward two years to 1939, when BC had earned a trip to its first-ever bowl game—a New Year's Day match-up, no less, in the fourth annual Cotton Bowl against Clemson. Lou Montgomery, the only African-American player on the football team is standing alone, watching his teammates board a train headed toward Dallas without him, because he is African-American and Clemson will not play a team with African-American players. When his name is announced at the train station, it receives the loudest, heartiest cheers because the 5,000 BC fans in attendance know there would have been no Cotton Bowl for them without Lou Montgomery.

Boston College originally had been slated to play Duquesne University in the Cotton Bowl, but BC administrators expressed their hesitation, stemming from fiscal concern, about a game featuring two northern schools being played in the south. In deference to this concern, Duquesne was dropped from the contest and Clemson was chosen as BC's opponent, thus assuring a bigger paycheck to Boston College. Clemson then refused to play against African-American athletes, causing BC to drop Montgomery from the trip. The Jesuit promise of intellectual and spiritual development for the benefit of others failed Montgomery miserably, giving way to the temptation of the American dollar.

The trend had started earlier in the 1939 season when the University of Florida refused to play against BC if Montgomery played in the game. Not wanting to jeopardize the payday they would have garnered from the anticipated crowd at Fenway Park, the Jesuit administration informed Montgomery he would not be playing against Florida. The decision to keep him off the field was twofold. Not only was Montgomery African-American, but he also was one of the best, if not *the* best player for BC. Opposing teams used race as a motive to keep Montgomery, one of the most talented players, off the field.

The African-American newspaper, *The Boston Chronicle*, wrote as its sports page headline: "Lou Montgomery Is Made Jim Crow Victim." The white media did not act so urgently in response to Montgomery's exclusion. There were mentions of his not playing in the game, but the newspapers did not address the underlying reasons. The *Chronicle* was able to speak with then-athletic director Reverend Patrick H. Collins, who was quoted as saying, "We do this for the sake of Lou."[1] Montgomery was made aware he would not be playing by Coach Frank Leahy only after the media had already broken the story. There was no need to look out for Montgomery as the school administration claimed; Montgomery had always been the target on the field, regardless of whether he was playing a northern or southern school. Florida, considered to be a mediocre team, beat BC 7-0.

A pattern quickly emerged. As Montgomery's star was beginning to rise, BC looked outwardly at the financial benefits it would gain from keeping Montgomery out of games, instead of looking inwardly at its values as a Jesuit institution. It would also blame the southern institutions for having to sit out its African-American player, rather than deciding to fight such injustice. Similarly, it was Montgomery who was judged outwardly because of his skin color and not considered for his character as a man and for the football ability that he wanted everyone to see.

Prior to the Florida game, several of Montgomery's teammates stated they would not play if he did not play. Montgomery exhorted them to put the team first by participating in the game. The following week, Montgomery was back to help guide the football team past Temple by returning an interception 98 yards. The week after that his playing time was significantly reduced against St. Anselm because Coach Leahy, fully aware that Montgomery would not be able to play against Auburn, opted to give playing time to others in anticipation of Montgomery's absence. Boston College was able to pull out a 13-7 victory, and this time Montgomery's absence was not as noticeable due to the Eagles victory.

The *Chronicle* continued to be critical of the BC administration, prompting Father Collins to write, in a letter to the newspaper, "at Boston College, Christian ideals have not been neglected when the question of race or creed arise, and it is to be regretted that we are misunderstood and are judged of being unjust in our dealings with the Negro boy." Father Collins' words held little weight. While saying that they had done everything to be fair to Montgomery, the administration was trying actively to schedule southern schools for upcoming seasons. Boston College was willing to allow Montgomery to travel with the team to Dallas, but he instead declined, saying he did not want to run into any confrontations while in town. The truth is he did not feel he would have had the support of his coaches should any problems have arisen.

At the train station, Montgomery stood on the platform as the crowd implored him to make a speech. He tried to resist, but the cheering was too much. His speech was five words long. "I hope the fellows win," he said. The train carrying his teammates soon departed and he was left alone. On New Year's Day, Montgomery traveled to Philadelphia and sent the team a telegram wishing them good luck. Montgomery's telegram was not enough, as BC lost to Clemson 6-3. When the team returned from Dallas, Montgomery awaited the team's arrival at the train station, whereupon Coach Leahy told him they would have won if Montgomery had been there.

The following year proved to be more of the same for Montgomery, playing in certain games and being barred from others. Boston College played in the Sugar Bowl that year for a shot at the national championship, which they won with a 19-13 victory versus Tennessee. Montgomery traveled but he did not play.

Looking back at his career in a 1987 interview, Montgomery stated he probably would not have attended BC given another chance. Although he felt he was doing what was right for the team at the time, the injustice of his situation began to hit him in the years after his 1941 graduation. He felt that if he had stood up for himself more vehemently, he may have helped pave the way for something to be done much sooner for other athletes.

In 1997, 60 years after he first broke the athletic color barrier at Boston College, Montgomery was elected into the Boston College Hall of Fame.

Note

1. K. Gregg, "Tackling Jim Crow: Segregation on the College Gridiron between 1936–1941" (B.A. thesis, Boston College, 2005).

Irwin Holmes

First African-American Student-Athlete at North Carolina State University

by Richard Lapchick and Horacio Ruiz

When he enrolled at North Carolina State University in 1956, Irwin Holmes did not care that there were no African-Americans attending. A 1955 court case had given him that right and he wanted to exercise it. In 1955, three black undergraduate students sued for and won the right to attend the University of North Carolina at Chapel Hill in *Frasier vs. the Board of Trustees of the University of North Carolina*. The decision applied to the entire Consolidated University of North Carolina school system. African-Americans now had the legal right to attend universities previously closed to them for their undergraduate educations. The legal right, however, did not make for an easy passage for teenagers confronted by racist acts and surrounded by symbols of segregation

Holmes had graduated third in his high school class and enrolled at NC State as an electrical engineering major. All students had to take a physical test as part of a required physical education course. The students were divided into three skill levels, with the top level reserved for athletes. The vertical jump and the standing broad jump were two standards used to determine the level where students would be placed. Holmes had the highest scores for both.

The track coach was impressed with how high and far Holmes could jump and offered him a spot on the track team to run the quarter mile. However, Holmes, who had been ranked as high as the number two African-American tennis player in the country in high school, decided to join the tennis team, thus becoming NC State's first African-American student-athlete. The next semester, he integrated the track team, but competed for only one semester so he could play tennis exclusively. He was co-captain in his senior year.

In spite of his accomplished years in high school, the times bred feelings of inferiority in too many African-Americans, and Holmes was no exception. Although his mother tried her best to convince him he was as good as anybody, there were simply too many signs around him saying otherwise. Holmes never even had a conversation with a white peer until his senior year in high school, and that one lasted less than five minutes. Then there were the "whites only" signs for almost every public facility. The segregated water fountains, waiting rooms, and entrances of Raleigh, North Carolina, had a not-so-subtle way of undermining the confidence of Irwin Holmes and anyone else who looked like him.

"But you had to feel inferior to some degree," Holmes said. "The old South was two civilizations living in the same place. Back in my head somewhere, I wasn't sure I was able to compete [academically] until I met so many dumb people. Brains have nothing to do with race. The dumb white people were just as dumb as the dumb black people."[1]

Tennis itself was overwhelmingly segregated at the time Holmes competed. African-Americans could compete only in tournaments sponsored by the American Tennis Association, the association for African-American tennis players. At one point, Holmes was runner-up at the national ATA tournament and was eligible for a qualifier position at the U.S. Amateurs, now known as the U.S. Open. He declined because he knew his skills were not as developed as those of other players. He greatly admired Althea Gibson and Arthur Ashe for pioneering the integration of such all-white tournaments.

In spite of many supportive white students, including his teammates, it was lonely on campus. In his four years at NC State, Holmes never had another African-American student in his classes, and he never played against another African-American tennis player.

His teammates did their best to stop the segregated south from crushing Holmes. On the drive back from a match against North Carolina at Chapel Hill, the team stopped to eat at a highway diner. Holmes was the only NC State player to win a match that day. The entire team ordered burgers, hot dogs, and drinks. After the players had waited longer than expected for their orders, the store manager approached the head coach and said he would not serve the team unless Holmes ate outside. When the coach informed the team members, they immediately departed, leaving the burgers cooking on the grill.

The professor scheduled for Holmes' very first class as a freshman forced the university to find someone else to teach it, because she refused to teach an African-American student. Holmes recalled another professor who publicly criticized him for his grades although he actually had excellent grades. That all changed after a white student stood up to the professor for him. At the end of the year, when the students had the option to drop one grade, Holmes decided to write completely off-topic on his final quiz. He received an A. He knew then that the professor had not bothered to read his work the entire semester.

Holmes said his dorm hall was so small that it had to combine with another dorm hall in order to put together a team to compete in the intramural touch football league on campus. He and his roommate, an All-State football player, were the only two African-American players on the combined dorm team. Neither Holmes nor his roommate entered the first game, and the team lost. The team had co-captains, one from each dorm. The captain from Holmes' dorm, who had not attended that particular game, complained bitterly to the co-captain about his not having played either of them. He then went to the intramural office and saw to it that the intramural schedule be redone and that the team be split up into two. Holmes' dorm sought out non-athletes to complete their teams for the intramural competitions. Holmes said the racism encountered "riled up" his teammates to play harder, and they finished second overall in intramurals that year. Holmes said, "The racism riled up not only the blacks in the dorm, but also the whites. Before then, most of the guys were friendly when they ran into you, but they were not actively involved until they got riled up."[2]

Holmes was knocked down hard in one game and the referees did not call a penalty. Two of his teammates told him they would take care of it themselves. On the very next play, the man who had hit Holmes was carried off the field with a broken leg. Although they had not intended to break the man's leg, it was clear they would defend Holmes.

In 1960, Holmes became the first African-American student to receive an undergraduate degree from NC State. He then earned a master's in electrical engineering from Drexel University and worked for IBM from 1969 to 1988, when he retired. Holmes is currently semi-retired, serving in a chief financial officer role for his wife's staffing company.

In the spring of 2006, Holmes was invited back to the campus to speak to a group of 300 African-American students who had been identified for their academic achievement. Holmes told the students that "Integrating the schools—the classroom—was far more significant than integrating the playing fields."[3] Holmes did both. That same year, the NC State Alumni Association acknowledged his contributions of 50 years earlier when it named a room in the alumni building after Holmes.

A circle had been closed. Holmes had arrived at North Carolina State as the first African-American student and returned to speak to a large gathering of academically gifted African-American students. When he walked the campus as a student, all the roads and buildings were named after white people. Now there is a room named after him. We surely have a long way to go on the issue of race in America, but Irwin Holmes is a measure of how far we have come.

Notes

1. Irwin Holmes, interview with author, October 3, 2006.
2. Ibid.
3. Ibid.

Darryl Hill

First African-American Student-Athlete at the University of Maryland

by Richard Lapchick and Horacio Ruiz

No African-American athlete had ever played for a service academy. No African-American football player had ever played in the Atlantic Coast Conference. Activists were literally dying, fighting for civil rights in an era that most young people today have no idea about. That is why Black History Month is so important. We put history in the face of young people who make assumptions about entitlements that others had sacrificed for them to get.

It is strange how society makes people famous. This story is mainly about Darryl Hill, whom most of the readers will not know. Playing a crucial role in his life and the history Darryl made was a young assistant coach who is now a media megastar with ESPN. Another who did the same was a white player for Wake Forest who would later make such a warm and dramatic display of his openness on the racial issue that a movie would be made about his life and death.

Darryl first made history when he enrolled at the Naval Academy in 1961. It was not long before he realized that life in the Navy was not for him. Hill had played freshman football for the academy before he made the decision to leave, and he'd had a great game playing against the Maryland freshman team. At that time Maryland had an assistant coach named Lee Corso, who asked Hill to become a Terrapin.

Hill had Notre Dame and Penn State on his radar screen, but he had never thought about playing in the South. Hill told Corso, "You must have forgotten that you're in the ACC." Corso responded, "We've decided you're the guy we'd like to have to break the racial barrier in the ACC. If you don't do it now, it might be another three or four years before it happens."[1] That was both a challenge and a heavy burden placed on Hill's shoulders.

Was Hill the right person? He had already been the only African-American football student-athlete at Navy and at his high school. Although that experience would be helpful at Maryland, it was not really the same thing, because he would have to play in the deep South. Nonetheless, Hill liked Maryland's offense, which had a wide-open passing game. In 1962, Darryl Hill took the plunge and enrolled at Maryland.

The University of South Carolina and Clemson University vowed not to play against an integrated Terrapin team in their home stadiums. Darryl Hill didn't like it but thought he knew why. "Southern college football at the time was king. There were no other football teams. In the South, fans were really attached to their teams, fervently so. They worshipped the game of football and the stadiums were their temples. So to have an African-American in their temple, it desecrated it for them."[2]

Like all transfers, Hill sat out the first year, making for a difficult transition to Maryland's campus, where he received a chilly reception. There were only 32 African-American students on the College Park Campus. Those 32, along with teammates, became the nucleus of his campus social life.

His teammates bought into the mission and were helpful in Hill's move to the team. The team refused to stay in hotels that would not accommodate him. The hotels where they did stay eventually had to screen his phone calls after callers threatened to aim their high-powered rifles at him during the game. The team would not eat in restaurants that would not serve him. Jerry Fishman, a 230-pound middle linebacker, threw his plate of food to the floor when the team was walking out of a diner because it refused to serve Hill.

It all came to a head in his second game, which was in Columbia, South Carolina, where Maryland was scheduled to play against the University of South Carolina. The game that many had threatened would never be allowed to be played was, in fact, taking place. Hill put the Terrapins ahead with a 13-yard touchdown run. By the half, Maryland led 13-0, outraging Gamecock fans. On the way to the locker room, one of them dumped a drink on Hill. Fishman reached into the stands and smashed the man with his helmet.

"I never had an opposing player be disrespectful," Hill said. "But the fans were nasty. They had racial cheers and they would throw stuff at you. I told Jerry, 'If a riot breaks out, at least you can blend in with the rest of the players. I would have nowhere to go.'"[3]

The chilly reception in College Park turned warm after winless (0-4) Maryland hosted the undefeated Air Force Falcons. The score was 14-14 with only seconds remaining. Hill had caught a touchdown pass early in the game. As the clock ticked down, Hill caught a pass in the middle of the field, eluded two tacklers, and then dove from the five-yard line into the end zone. Maryland students poured onto the field in celebration, making Darryl Hill one of them for the first time. "My hometown's attitude changed," Hill said. "They warmed up to me soon after that."[4]

But the road games were rough. In spite of Clemson's threat not to play an integrated team, Hill entered Clemson's stadium on game-day.

In those days, African-American fans were sent to watch the game from outside the stadium on a mound of dirt. Before the start of the game, Hill found out that his mother was refused entrance into the stadium. Palestine Hill had been told not to travel alone if Darryl's father could not leave his business that day to accompany her. Hill's father could not make it to watch his son play, but Mrs. Hill traveled alone anyway and attempted to go inside the stadium with her ticket. Hill was ready to leave the team and escort his mother safely back home. However, Robert C. Edwards, then Clemson president, invited Mrs. Hill to watch the game from his box. Mrs. Hill was a teacher, and she and President Edwards began a friendship that lasted for years.

During warm-ups before a game at Wake Forest, Hill was the target of racist remarks and taunts. Brian Piccolo, later to play in the NFL and become the subject of the movie *Brian's Song*, was Wake Forest's captain. That day Piccolo showed the crowd a preview of his feelings on race, which would later be depicted in a movie that focused on his profound friendship with the great African-American running back Gale Sayers. In a remarkable gesture for that era, Piccolo walked over to Hill and apologized for the fans' racist behavior. Piccolo then put his arm around Hill and led him toward the Wake Forest fans, silencing their taunts. Hill recognized Piccolo as hero long before America did.

Hill was a quiet celebrity in the African-American community. Often invited to visit local black colleges, Hill was once approached by Stokely Carmichael, chairman of the Student Nonviolent Coordinating Committee. Carmichael wanted him to get involved in protests. Hill convinced him that he was involved in the Civil Rights Movement by playing football. He fought a lonely battle; it would not be until his senior year that another African-American football player would be recruited.

Hill broke his foot that year and was never drafted into the NFL. After a brief time with the New York Jets, Hill realized he had no future in pro football and went back to school. Ultimately he earned a master's degree in economics at Southern Illinois University. Having left the world of sports, he was ready to enter the business world.

As an entrepreneur, his vision went global, and he set up businesses in Russia and China. Back home, Hill led the Metropolitan Washington Business Resource Center and the Greater Washington Business Center. He headed for California, where he launched the Pacific Energy Corporation, an energy-management company.

Nearly four decades after he entered the University of Maryland, Hill was approached by Ralph Friedgen, Maryland's football coach, who asked him about returning as an administrator. Hill became director of major gifts. "It's wonderful," he said. "I'm doing a lot for a university that's done a lot for me."

Maryland gave Hill the chance to be a pioneer for other African-American athletes in the ACC. Corso, the assistant who helped get him there, is before ESPN audiences each college football Saturday. Viewers discover Brian Piccolo on late night reruns of *Brian's Song*. Many people know their names. As with other figures who made history, most people could not tell you who Darryl Hill is. But the seven African-American ACC basketball coaches, Virginia athletics director Craig Littlepage, and the nearly 58 percent of ACC football players and 67 percent of ACC basketball players who are African-American should all salute this lesser-known giant who paved the way for them to work and play without having to encounter the in-your-face racism that Hill endured.

Notes

1. John Greenya, "Black Man on a White Field: Darryl Hill's Run to History," Black Athlete Sports Network, http://www.blackathlete.net/artman/publish/article_0810.shtml (accessed October 8, 2006).

2. Darryl Hill, interview with author, October 30, 2006.

3. Ibid.

4. Ibid.

William Smith, Robert Grant, and Kenneth Henry

First African-American Student-Athletes at Wake Forest University

by Horacio Ruiz

The story of Wake Forest's athletic integration begins with the image of the late Clemson coach Frank Howard on television. He was told by a reporter that Wake Forest had recruited several talented African-American players, including a player named William Smith. Smith, who would join Robert Grant and Kenneth Henry in becoming the first African-American players to integrate Division I-A college football below the Mason-Dixon Line, happened to be watching the interview on local television. "I'll never have a nigra at Clemson," Smith remembers Howard replying.[1]

The response on Wake Forest's campus was not much more inviting. On Grant's first day of class in 1964, a school administrator stopped to inform Grant that he was not welcome there. The experiences the three freshmen endured galvanized them to nickname themselves the "Junior Jim Crow Killers" as they headed to take on Clemson as members of the freshman football team. Smith, a member of the Baha'i Faith, had fellow members of his congregation travel to Death Valley to watch him play. Smith hugged and embraced his family and members of his congregation, composed of both African-Americans and whites. Freshman coach Joe Madden, seeing Smith hug white members of the church and fearful of the tense environment, ordered him to stop and refused to play Smith in the game. Earlier in the season, Smith had asked that Madden address him as William and not "Willie," a request that prompted the freshman coach to cut all verbal interaction with Smith, using an assistant as a middle-man for any communication.

In the spring, Smith decided to leave the team and transfer to the University of Massachusetts, where he would go on to earn his bachelor, master's, and doctoral degrees. "Wake's decision to integrate was less about social justice than athletic prowess, and nobody should confuse the two," Smith told *Sports Illustrated's* Alexander

Wolff. "That experience showed me the value placed on my life. Without sports, it was clear I had no value. So I chose to assert my humanity in another way."[2]

Grant would stay the rest of the way, conscious of his contribution as an African-American but also fully aware he was doing so for his own reasons, desiring a spot in the National Football League. Before their freshmen seasons ended, Grant, Smith, Henry, who passed away in 1996, and basketball prospect Jim Carter woke up to their dorm room filled with smoke. Someone had flooded the room with smoke from the crack in the door, sliding a note underneath saying, "Next time we're going to bring the matches niggers." The incident would force the four athletes to take turns sleeping, with one person always on watch. One night, they awakened to a burning cross in front of the dorm.

"We did not report it because when we first arrived on campus we were told by a higher up official that we were not welcome here," Grant told WFMY News 2 in Greensboro, North Carolina. "He could have been behind it, but we really had no way of knowing who was behind it."

Football fields became virtual stages of war, with racists trying their best to intimidate the football players with death threats. There was no staying in the town where the team members were to play— the threat of violence often had them staying in hotels far away from the game location. On the team bus Grant, Smith, and Henry would have to sit in the aisles so as to keep people from throwing a rock or firing a shotgun into the bus. Walking onto the field and then off it, they would try to ignore the death threats while ducking from bottles being thrown at them from the stands.

Grant would earn All-ACC and Playboy All-American honors while at Wake Forest, going on to be drafted by the Baltimore Colts and earning the team's Rookie of the Year honor in 1968. "We beat anyone on the field," Grant told WFMY2. "We had no choice but to excel on the field." Grant would play in two Super Bowls; Super Bowl III in the Jets' upset of the heavily favored Colts and Super Bowl V, in which the Colts defeated the Dallas Cowboys. He would later be the Los Angeles Rams strength and conditioning coach and was president of the World Football League's players' association. He also is a managing member of Uncle Moki's Kahana Bay Trading Company and president of North Shore Traders, Inc.

Smith was inducted into the Piedmont Athletic Association Hall of Fame and worked as a civil rights activist. He was drafted into the U.S. Army, in which he served as a decorated combat platoon medic in Vietnam. Currently, he is engaged in education and media, having made the nationally acclaimed documentary *The Invisible Soldiers: Unheard Voices*. After being broadcast on the Public Broadcast System, the documentary spurred the 2000 Joint Resolution of Congress, establishing the Day of Honor, which formally acknowledged the role of minorities in World War II.

In 2005, 41 years after arriving on the field in Death Valley as freshmen, Grant and Smith returned to the Clemson campus to promote the Call Me MISTER program, which was based out of Clemson's Eugene T. Moore School of Education. The program's aim is to recruit, train, certify, and find employment for 200 African-American males as elementary school teachers in South Carolina's public school system.

Although Wake Forest has yet to formally acknowledge Grant, Smith and Henry as the first African-American football players, Smith and Grant still get together annually in May, holding a private reunion in which they walk the campus in anonymity, conscious of the barriers they shattered.

This story ends as it began—with Clemson coach Frank Howard. Howard, who once stood in front of the ACC's first African-American football player, Maryland's Darryl Hill, smoking a cigar during pre-game warm-ups in an attempt to intimidate him, approached Grant when the two were at a fundraiser several years after Grant's career ended. "Back when you were playing, you thought I didn't like you," Howard told Grant. Grant replied he thought Howard hated him. "I wanted some colored players, too," Howard replied. "I was really glad to see you out there. One day, Clemson is going to have plenty of colored players."

The honesty of Howard's statement may be debatable, but there was an obvious change in attitude, even from one of the most die-hard segregationists. Grant, Smith, and Henry made people think and provoked changes, whether or not Greensboro and Wake Forest were ready for them.

Notes

1. Alexander Wolff, "Breaking Down Barriers," *Sports Illustrated*, November 2005.
2. Ibid.

C. B. Claiborne

First African-American Student-Athlete at Duke University

by Horacio Ruiz

Dr. C. B. Claiborne is a busy man. Talking on the phone 20 minutes before a scheduled meeting on the Texas Southern University campus, the marketing professor with the cool, calm voice and direct manner speaks of his experience as the first African-American athlete in Duke University's history. Claiborne has done these interviews and stories before, but there is no forgetting why he is asked to do them.

As an 18-year-old entering college in 1965, Claiborne knew he was in a unique and historical position, but the true impact of what he was doing as he enrolled at Duke was, at the time, beyond his grasp. "It wasn't just about going there and playing basketball," Claiborne said. "It was about integrating the campus—it was about integrating the social scene. A whole world opened up at Duke."

Once on campus, Claiborne became one of only 15 African-American students. The people he encountered at Duke were generally pleasant and cooperative, at least more so than those in his hometown of Danville, Virginia. As a young boy he would walk along the railroad tracks that divided the African-American and white parts of town, making sure to pick up rocks in case he might be attacked by a group of white boys. Although better than what he had experienced in Danville, race was certainly still an issue at Duke. Claiborne was harassed by older players on the team and was not notified of an end-of-the-year banquet for athletes because it was being held at a segregated country club. A professor of engineering told Claiborne, a future professor and holder of three advanced degrees, that he could not receive an A in the professor's class because he was African-American. Although he never missed a day of class or practice on the Duke campus, Claiborne gravitated toward the social scene at North Carolina Central University, a historically black university also located in Durham. He spent so much time at NCCU that he had his own meal card.

In his first year as a guard on the freshman team in 1965, Claiborne was assigned to play against future Hall-of-Famer "Pistol" Pete Maravich of Southwood College in Salemburg, North Carolina. A player from the opposing team continually jabbed and pushed Claiborne as he tried to set screens for Maravich. Claiborne pleaded with the officials to call a foul on the player but to no avail. When the pushing continued, Claiborne lost his patience and swung at the opposing player. A brawl broke out at half-court with some spectators joining, eventually leading the game to be suspended out of fear for the players' safety.

Claiborne's basketball career was not spectacular. He had his best season as a senior, when he averaged 6.3 points and 2.3 rebounds per game. He does not hold race accountable for his lack of playing time, although he did want to be a starter for his team. Claiborne argues that coming from a strong high school team where he concentrated on becoming a strong defensive player and assist man, he was not a good fit for Duke's offensive system, which relied heavily on scoring in a three-guard scheme. He was often assigned to play out of position as a forward even though he stood 6 feet 2 inches tall. His greatest memory comes from his senior year when he sank two free-throws to seal a victory, in triple overtime, over rival North Carolina. "Almost everyone else had fouled out by then," he has said. "So that's why I was in there."

His basketball feats may have been less than stunning, but there is no doubt that Claiborne excelled in the classroom. He remembers his high school teachers taking a personal interest in him and his fellow classmates, although they had only second-hand textbooks and no lab supplies. It was not uncommon for teachers to hold classes on Saturdays because they were concerned the students were not learning the skills they would need to succeed in college. In fact, it was expected that most of them would attend college.

His senior year, Claiborne was one of two students in Virginia to be named a presidential scholar. He won a scholarship and a trip to the White House, where he met President Lyndon Johnson. At Duke,

Claiborne majored in engineering and would go on to earn a master's in engineering from Dartmouth, an MBA from Washington University in St. Louis, and his Ph.D. in marketing from Virginia Tech.

While at Duke, Claiborne became involved in the school's Black Student Alliance as a way of unifying the small African-American student population at Duke. He took part in a famous sit-in at the Allen Building when the Associated Students of Duke University passed a statute prohibiting Duke organizations from using segregated facilities. When it was passed on to the student body vote, however, it was defeated, prompting the BSA to stage a daylong "study-in" in the president's office. Three days later, the original statute was amended by Duke's administration.

It would take four years after Claiborne's graduation for the Duke basketball program to graduate another African-American player. He thinks part of the delay has to do with the high academic standards, but he also acknowledges it was a difficult time of transition for both African-Americans and whites. "We were all in this together," he said. "So when [the crowd] was yelling obscenities, those guys were dealing with those things. We were all learning to adjust. When you put it in perspective, we were all dealing with social change. It's not about what I did—it's about what everyone did."

Claiborne remembers receiving a letter from a woman who had worked on the Duke campus while he was a student. The woman wrote how sorry and regretful she was for not being aware of what he was going through. His forgiveness was immediate. "Somebody is touched on a personal level," he says, "and that's part of bringing change, just touching people on a more personal level."

Fred Flowers

First African-American Student-Athlete at Florida State University

by Horacio Ruiz

Outside the Flowers & White law firm in Tallahassee, Florida, is an oak tree that is part of the National Registry. No one is sure of the giant oak's age, but the man who made sure the tree was part of the law firm's backyard knows of its significance. Fred Flowers, attorney and partner of the firm and Florida State University's first black student-athlete, tells of how once upon a time people of his skin color were lynched from the very oak that stares into his office.

History is not lost on Flowers, whose firm now specializes in personal injury cases from automobile accidents and also works with wills and guardianships. As salutatorian of his high school class and as a distinguished pitcher, Flowers had high hopes of attending FSU and starring all four years as a member of the baseball team. After one year, however, he had seen enough. Flowers felt disconnected from his coach, who rarely, if ever, spoke to him. The racial indignities he heard on the field stung badly enough, but in the summer of 1966, when the head baseball coach helped the white players find summer leagues across the country, Flowers found he didn't have a league to go to.

"At the end of the season, I just got completely ignored by the coaches," Flowers said. "I know I wasn't being treated the way other people were being treated."[1]

As a young boy, he could never understand why his next-door neighbor, a lady he calls Ms. Perkins, would sit in the backseat after being picked up by the white woman whose children she would baby-sit. Flowers figured that if Ms. Perkins was good enough to take care of that woman's children, she certainly was good enough to sit in the front seat.

Flowers encountered the same situation at FSU. He knew he could play with the rest of his teammates, he just couldn't understand why his coaches didn't communicate with him—not even enough to be sent to a summer league, which would have benefited Flowers as well as the team. It was difficult for Flowers to walk away from the team and game he loved so much. When asked if he would have walked away again given a second chance, there was a slight pause, and then a moment of hesitation. He responded that the real question is whether he would have attended FSU all over again.

"I was filled with a certain amount of rage and anger because of what was taken from me," Flowers said. "It took me 25 years to get over it. It seems the first often times becomes the sacrificial lamb."[2]

Flowers turned his attention to school work, expressing the anger and bitterness he felt from his playing days into his academics and participation in campus politics. He was active in setting up the Black Student Union and in helping to establish a house for the organization. But racism was not isolated to the baseball team. In the classroom, Flowers says he was stared at by classmates and some professors in an attempt to intimidate him. Some students would cross the street to avoid walking past him. Flowers dismisses those incidents, saying they pale in comparison to what his mother, father, grandmothers, and grandfathers had to go through. He considers the first black students at FSU to be a part of the Talented Tenth, a notion started by the African-American scholar W. E .B. DuBois, which states that the best ideas and actions were undertaken by the top 10 percent of the black community.

Flowers graduated from FSU in 1969 with a bachelor of arts degree as a philosophy and pre-med major and later received a master's in urban and regional planning. He would later enroll at the University of Florida, where he earned his law degree. He calls himself a "Seminole liti-Gator."

In 2002, then-FSU president Dr. Talbot "Sandy" D'Alemberte struck up an idea to commission a sculpture honoring the university's first black students, including Flowers. When he caught word of the plan, Flowers did not believe it would happen, still skeptical after so many years. But behind the scenes, D'Alemberte continued his plan, commissioning renowned sculptor W. Stanley "Sandy" Proctor to create a piece symbolizing the integration of FSU. The first plan, one in which three black students were to be shown tearing through a brick wall, was rejected because it was said to be too dramatic. The planned sculpture's rejection was music to Flowers' ears, convincing him the university was serious about the project. The university unveiled the sculpture, entitled "Integration," on January 30, 2004, in a ceremony honoring the black students who helped integrate the FSU campus. FSU's current president, Dr. T. K. Wetherell, took the reins from D'Alemberte and saw the project through to completion.

Three individuals are depicted in the sculpture: Doby Flowers, FSU's first black homecoming queen and Flowers' sister, Maxwell Courtney, FSU's first black student, and Flowers himself in a baseball uniform as the first black student-athlete. The figures all have their backs turned to one another as they stand in a circular formation. Flowers said the positioning of the figures is significant because it represents how the black students watched one another's back.

"I walked up to [Dr. "Sandy" D'Alemberte] and asked him why he did this," Flowers said. "He said, 'This is recognition of a very important time in the history of the university.' I'm still dealing with it. I'm still digesting the significance of it all. I do know it is very significant to other people."

In his speech at the ceremonial dedication of the statue, Flowers focused his honor on his parents, his main support system when he was a student at FSU. He commended FSU for its efforts in recognizing that period in time and in recognizing the struggle he, and so many others like himself, had to endure. Flowers may have mixed feelings about being immortalized on the FSU campus, but his views and ideas have changed as he now is 59 years old. He no longer is the fearless kid who integrated Seminole athletics.

"Time has a way of making a mountain look like a mole hill,"

Flowers said. "Everything happens for a purpose. Sometimes you don't know what that purpose is."

Today, he has a grandson he's training to become "the world's greatest hitter."

"I tell him, 'If you could hit the ball out of the park, they would have no choice but to play you," the former pitcher said.

Flowers also is looking to start up a program in which young men charged with a crime can avoid prison time by being diverted to a community service program. There they could learn a skill or a trade such as carpentry to prepare them for a career when they get out of the program. Flowers said the program would be privately funded by those who are in it, which would be possible because of the money they would save by not having to pay lawyer fees.

Flowers still struggles with the idea of racism, a concept he has never been able to grasp. He asks himself how and why African-Americans have been exposed to so much violence and hatred from a different race.

"If you studied slavery you'd have the same questions," Flowers said. "It is surprising to me how the young people of today have so little connection to history. Too many African-Americans have no appreciation of how things are today. Too many believe, naively I think, that racism doesn't exist today."[3]

Surely the oak tree outside his office makes it hard to ever forget.

Notes

1. Fred Flowers, interview with author, September 27, 2006.
2. Ibid.
3. Ibid.

Ray Bellamy

First African-American Student-Athlete at the University of Miami

by Horacio Ruiz

Growing up as the son of migrant workers in Bradenton, Florida, in the 1960s, Ray Bellamy thought life would be better if he enlisted in the Army, stayed in the Army, and died in a hail of gunfire. Anything, Bellamy thought, had to be better than spending winters crammed in a tent with his parents and eight siblings as they constantly relocated to find work in Florida's vegetable fields.

While his family was working in the fields picking tomatoes, cucumbers, and sweet potatoes, he would go to school without shoes or lunch. "It's not about football," Bellamy said. "It's about being the fifth son and seventh child. People are interested in what I did—my father and mother are responsible for that."

Bellamy signed a football scholarship with the University of Miami on December 12, 1966, to become the first African-American player to sign with an historically white institution in the southeastern United States. Ironically, Miami had in the past canceled games because of its refusal to play against African-American players, due to a Florida law prohibiting African-Americans and whites from playing on the same field. In 1946, Penn State canceled its game versus Miami because many of its war veterans refused to play without African-American halfback Wally Triplett. Miami once refused to play a football game against UCLA solely because of UCLA's African-American student-athletes, a group that included Jackie Robinson, who would later go on to break Major League Baseball's color barrier.

In 1962, the University of Miami, under the direction of newly appointed president Dr. Henry King Stanford, underwent a search for the school's first African-American football player. While receiving a courtesy visit from then-football coach Andy Gustafson, Stanford said it would please him very much if Miami recruited an African-American football player. It would take four years, but the president, who was raised in Americus, Georgia, the heart of the South, felt it was time for the school to do something about its segregated athletics department. Stanford remembers that as a young boy going home from a trolley ride after finishing his paper route, he felt embarrassed because African-American women had to wait for him, a little boy, to get on and find a place in the trolley before they could board. From the very moment Stanford set foot on the Coral Gables campus, the president made it clear that he wanted to see change.

In the five years Bellamy would spend at the University of Miami, Stanford would be Bellamy's biggest supporter. "Dr. Stanford stood up for me when it wasn't popular to stand up for African-American men," Bellamy said. "That man's my everything. He did a great thing for blacks when nobody else would."[1]

Bellamy was just the player the university had been seeking. He was a good student who had been elected student-body president at Lincoln Memorial High and was one of the top recruits in the nation. Bellamy nearly signed with Southern California, a school that was beginning a four-year run of Rose Bowl appearances. However, Bellamy decided to attend Miami because of the proximity to his home and the opportunity it would give his parents to watch him play.

While he was growing up, football became an escape from poverty for Bellamy. He remembers a man named Melvin Rutledge, who went on to play college football, as being someone who inspired him to become an even better athlete. As a teenager, with a football in his hand, Bellamy would slip into high school football games by sneaking underneath the fence. "I went from the [outhouse] to the penthouse," he said.[2]

Bellamy said that at Miami he paralyzed a lot of people, because they did not know how to react to him. Once he nearly was run over when a car swerved toward him. On the football field, he threw his body around recklessly to prove he could play and wanted to win as badly as his white teammates did.

It was with that desire to prove himself and his passion for football that fueled his football ability. In a game against the Florida Gators, whose coach had said previously that he would never play an African-American player, Bellamy took a swing pass 67 yards for a touchdown. It was personal. "Whenever I played against [the Gators]," Bellamy said, "I made sure that whenever I broke a run, unless they had a black player, nobody was going to catch me."[3]

Although Bellamy broke barriers on the field with the help of a few loyal supporters, he reinforces that "it wasn't always a picnic." Bellamy once was arrested for riding in a car with a white woman. Bellamy used his one phone call to contact Stanford, who promptly showed up at the jail and took Bellamy out without signing any papers. Stanford confronted the police, as Bellamy watched him in secret. It was something Bellamy would remember as a moment of true sincerity, one in which he knew how Stanford truly felt, by confronting the police without the pretense of simply keeping up appearances. "It just seemed completely wrong," Stanford said. "To challenge a person's potential, that they should be relegated because they were black."[4]

At Auburn in 1968, Miami officials had to notify the Federal Bureau of Investigation of a death threat against Bellamy. The sophomore slept that night with an FBI agent guarding his hotel room door. The next day, as he entered the field, a rock struck him on the head, prompting an anger that propelled him to an eight-reception, 121-yard day. Although memorable to Bellamy, incidents like these were rare, as he actively sought to avoid conflict on campus and on the road by remaining low key.

Bellamy had a stellar three-year career as wide receiver before crashing his car while driving to Miami from his home in Bradenton. He suffered massive injuries that effectively ended his football career and forced him to stay in the hospital for four months. His athletic tenure at Miami had finished, but his capacity as a student certainly had not. Before graduating in 1971, Bellamy ran for student-body president under the slogan "It ain't a black thing or a white thing; it's a people thing." He won.

Bellamy currently serves as a student advisor for the Florida

A&M football team, passing his knowledge, experience, and passion to the next generation of athletes.

Notes

1. Ray Bellamy, interview with author, January 29, 2005.
2. Ibid.
3. Ibid.
4. Henry Stanford, interview with author, January 31, 2005.

Charlie Scott

First African-American Scholarship Student-Athlete at the University of North Carolina, Chapel Hill

by Horacio Ruiz

Courtesy of University of North Carolina Athletic Communications.

Charlie Scott was so good that Lefty Dreisell, the legendary basketball coach who retired with 786 career wins, argued that if Scott had gone to Davidson, where Dreisell was coach from 1960 to 1969, Dreisell would have been known as the Dean Smith of the South.

Instead, it was Smith who landed Scott's commitment to attend the University of North Carolina at Chapel Hill. What followed him was a pipeline of great players that started with Bill Chamberlain and Bob McAdoo, and continued with Phil Ford, James Worthy, Michael Jordan, and a successive stream of future stars.

Scott was not the first African-American athlete at the University of North Carolina—that distinction belongs to Edwin Okoroma, of Nigeria, who integrated the soccer team in 1963. Scott wasn't the first African-American basketball player, either, but rather it was a man named Willie Cooper who played on the freshman squad in 1964–65 before deciding to leave the team. In 1966, however, Scott did become the first African-American scholarship athlete in North Carolina's history. Scott became the first great African-American player in the history of the Atlantic Coast Conference. To this day, African-American and white fans approach him, remembering him not only as one of the few African-American basketball players in the ACC, but also as one of the best of his time.

Just as he was ready to sign a national letter of intent to play for Dreisell's Davidson team, Scott was redirected and became sold on Smith and the Tar Heel program. Upon his hiring at North Carolina in 1961, Smith was persuaded by the assistant pastor at his church to actively pursue and recruit an African-American player. It was tough, however, to find a player who met the academic standards at North Carolina. Smith has been quoted as saying that was partially due to what he believed was a biased SAT exam. Smith planned to keep Cooper on the team no matter what, but after Cooper left, Smith found his gem in Scott. As valedictorian of his high school class and after being recruited by the likes of Duke, North Carolina State, and Wake Forest, Scott was more than ready to help begin defining the modern-day UNC basketball legacy being built by Smith.

Scott's decision to attend North Carolina was based on the comfort level he felt during his recruiting trip. Scott said yes when Smith asked if he wanted to attend a church service. What Scott found was that Smith's church was one of the few fully integrated churches in the area. Smith also made it a point to address Scott as "Charles," the more formal name he preferred, rather than "Charlie," the name by which most casual acquaintances and fans knew him.

By his sophomore year, Scott became a bona fide superstar. He would hear racist remarks from opposing fans on the road, but those seemed to matter little to Scott, whose career at North Carolina was stellar enough to silence even the darkest jeers. In his first season with the varsity squad as a sophomore, in 1967–68, Scott led the Tar Heels to their second consecutive NCAA Final Four and their fourth appearance in school history. The following year, he would again lead UNC to the Final Four. During the NCAA Tournament in 1969, Scott drained a jumper at the buzzer to beat Dreisell's Davidson team and send the Tar Heels to their third consecutive Final Four. The buzzer-beater would be Scott's 32nd point of the game.

Although masked by his success, that year also marked perhaps the biggest slight of Scott's career: even though he was widely regarded as the best player in the ACC, he was not given Player of the Year Honors. The same oversight occurred during his senior year, in 1970, when he was again passed over and the award was given to the same player as the year before, though Scott would somehow win the league's Athlete of the Year award.

"That was about the only time in college that I felt things were done in a prejudicial manner," Scott told a North Carolina newspaper, the *News & Record.* "And what concerned me more was how the media handled it. Nobody ever said anything about it, never challenged what took place. To me, that's just another form of hypocrisy."[1]

Scott was sensitive to his status as an African-American in the United States. In 1964, as a junior at Laurinburg Institute, his high school in North Carolina, Scott and two of his friends went for a walk off campus. Some police officers stopped the group and took them in a squad car to the house where a white woman claimed she had been the victim of a gang rape by three African-American men. When the police took the boys out of the car, Scott could remember bystanders holding their shotguns, possibly ready to fire at them if the woman gave a positive identification. Luckily, the woman said that these three young men were not the ones who committed the crime and they were released.

In 1968, Scott had the opportunity to join an African-American players' boycott of the 1968 Olympics in Mexico City, but he instead felt that such a move would have been counterproductive. He went on to become the second Tar Heel in history to play on the Olympic basketball team and helped capture a gold medal for the United States.

At the end of his career at North Carolina, Scott had averaged 22.1 points per game and had been an All-America selection twice and an All-ACC selection three times. To date, he is the fifth all-time leading scorer in Tar Heel history and was one of 12 North Carolina players selected to the ACC 50th Anniversary Team.

Scott went on to play for the Virginia Squires of the American Basketball Association, where he was selected to the All-Star team twice in his two seasons in the league. He also was ABA Rookie of the Year in 1971. Scott left the ABA for the National Basketball Association in 1972, where he played 10 seasons, making the All-Star team his first three seasons and winning a championship with the Boston Celtics in 1976. Scott finished his basketball career in 1980 and went on to sell high-end shoes to celebrities before joining the sports apparel company Champion as a marketing director.

In 1999, Scott was inducted into the Hampton Roads African-American Sports Hall of Fame, joining such legendary inductees as Julius Erving and George Gervin. To this day, Scott is on the home page of Laurinburg Institute, putting up a lay up in his Squires uniform. He currently is in business for himself as a sports marketer.

Notes

1. Scott Fowler, "Great Scott: Lefty's Big Loss," *The Charlotte Observer*, November 2005.

Jerry Gaines

First African-American Scholarship Student-Athlete at the Virginia Polytechnic Institute of Technology

by Richard Lapchick and Horacio Ruiz

Jerry Gaines was a heavy lifter all his life, someone always willing to take on life's big challenges. But he never made the choices lightly. His first major decision was to leave segregated Crestwood High to compete at predominantly white Churchland High in the 1966–67 school year so his athletic prowess would be showcased. However, he carried a heavy burden for decades after he chose to leave his friends behind.

That decision paid off. While his former classmates at Crestwood were shackled by segregation's cruel restrictions on life opportunities for African-Americans, Gaines became the first African-American scholarship athlete in Virginia Tech history. But Gaines never forgot those he left behind. He knew that there were many more talented athletes at Crestwood who never got the chance for a better educational opportunity by displaying their own athletic gifts. Gaines said he was "a dime a dozen" athlete at Crestwood who became a star athlete in his new integrated world.[1] In the back of his head, Gaines worried that his former classmates and teammates considered him a traitor to his race for leaving them behind.

In the fall of 1967, Gaines didn't know what to expect as the first African-American scholarship athlete entering Virginia Tech. Track Coach Martin Pushkin made Gaines feel as comfortable as possible, and he had faith in the athletes he had met during his recruiting trips. Nonetheless, Gaines said, "It was never a thing of pure comfort. There were a whole lot of factors I had to balance. I didn't have any intention of going to Tech to be anyone's pioneer, at least not initially."

He quickly developed a constant routine at Tech. He would attend classes, go to practice, eat a meal, and then either study or rest after the day's activities. Gaines did not feel as welcomed in the classroom as he was on the track. There were professors who seemed to show disdain for Gaines as a student. "African-American students were so few and far in between that you rarely ran into them," Gaines said. "There were the usual stares and in 90 percent of classes I was the only black face in there."

An English professor made comments on Gaines' papers that he thought were inappropriate. Gaines had befriended James Jarrett Owens, another English professor who was a former basketball player at Tech. Gaines shared the papers with the negative comments with Professor Owens, who knew about the other professor's "ideologies." Owens, who became a huge influence on Jerry Gaines, assured him that his papers were well written.

A student in one of the Tech dorms threw an egg that landed just in front of Gaines as he was walking across campus in his ROTC uniform. The egg splattered on his shoes and pants. Gaines saw a student ducking down when he looked up to see who threw the egg. He would later gain a better perspective, but at the time, he was ready to let the student know he had discovered his cowardice. Gaines "paid him a visit" inside the dorm to let him know he did not appreciate having egg on his uniform. When the perspective came, Gaines regretted his reaction. "Things like that taught me that you don't need to go there," Gaines said. "I wasn't the one with the problem, they were."

Gaines worked hard both in the classroom and on the track. In his freshman year he was the collegiate state champion in the long jump. When Gaines qualified for the NCAA Indoor National Championships, Coach Pushkin asked the athletic director for new sweats for Gaines since he was representing the school in the championships. Pushkin was not surprised when the AD offered Gaines only one of the basketball team's sweats. Pushkin felt as if the athletic department was forced by the government to take Gaines into Virginia Tech in order to receive federal funding. Gaines wore his old sweats, refusing to acknowledge the offer by the athletic director. Gaines simply saw it as another slight to overcome. "It was motivation to get good," Gaines said. "It was not a nice gesture, but it was part of what you had to deal with. It was character-building stuff in the long run. It was hard work, but during those years when we grew up, it was all we knew. You could always work a little harder no matter how talented."

Gaines worked hard to ignore the prejudice that surrounded

him to be the best athlete and person he could be. Gaines still holds the Virginia Tech record for the outdoor long jump, the oldest track record on the Tech books, dating back to 1971. He also has the best record in the 120-yard hurdles and is fourth all-time in the indoor long jump. After his eligibility in track was up and he had earned his degree in Spanish, Gaines received one more year of eligibility to play football. He had wanted to play football very badly while he was running track, but Pushkin would not allow it because he recognized the dangers Gaines would face on the football field.

Pushkin told Gaines, "I have your legs tuned like fine Stradivarius violins. I'm not going to let them destroy my work." Gaines realized that Pushkin was referring to people who wanted to deliberately hurt him on the football field, possibly including his teammates. Some people did attempt to take him out with cheap shots to the legs, but Gaines proved to be an effective defensive back and punt returner.

He entered the Army as a second lieutenant. After his tour in the Army, Gaines was hired as a Spanish teacher in 1972 at Western Branch High School in Chesapeake, where he taught and coached both football and track. Gaines led the cross country team to eight straight district titles and three regional titles. He was named high school coach of the year by the Portsmouth Sports Club in 1987, and in 1990 he was selected as the Teacher of the Year in Chesapeake. Gaines taught Spanish with the same passion and enthusiasm he had for everything he did. That engaged him with and endeared him to his students.

Gaines loves the holidays. Beginning in the first week of December and going through the holiday season, cards arrive from different parts of the world from former students wanting to wish their former teacher the best for the holiday season. "Those are just reminders that, yes, you did make a difference. I did not train to be a teacher. But there are certain characteristics that make for good teachers. You have to have a heart for it—you have to have a passion for kids. It's a matter of creating what I think is the most important thing in life, which is building relationships."

In 1996, he moved to Great Bridge High School to become an assistant principal, where he still works today.

No matter how successful and happy he was, he never forgot those students he felt he left behind at Crestwood. He went to his

25th high school reunion in 1992 with trepidation, unsure of the reception he would receive. His former schoolmates could not have known he never forgot them and that he worked harder than others to somehow represent the Crestwood athletes who never got a chance. He worried that they would view him as a traitor who left his past behind and sold out for greener pastures at the predominantly white Churchland High School. It was a great relief to discover they were rooting for him through all those years. Gaines was succeeding for the ones whom a segregated school system might have stopped 25 years before. He had the backing of his old schoolmates. Although it took 25 years to find that out, Gaines was very happy the moment finally came.

Gaines has always believed the events in his life were laid out for him by a power above him. A humble man, he gives credit for any successes to others and to a heavenly power. While he was searching for his role in life, he got a sudden jolt with the birth of his first daughter in 1981. His vision went global. Now Gaines hopes to work with a friend to construct shelters for refugees in African countries. He questions how a continent with gold, oil, and diamonds can have so many countries in dire need of basic necessities. "I would like to expand my horizons as far as helping people," Gaines said. He is negotiating with government authorities in America and Africa to gain clearance.

Africa is far away from Virginia. The shackles of a segregated society that might have held Gaines back had he remained at Crestwood were real, and he broke loose by attending Churchwood and Virginia Tech. But he knew that the original shackles were placed on his ancestors somewhere in Africa. Jerry Gaines, a humble man who seized opportunity and became a servant for children in an integrated America, is ready to close the human circle and work to help those in dire need in Africa.

Note

1. All of the quotes in this article are by Jerry Gaines, from an interview with the author on November 27, 2006.

Eddie McAshan

First African-American Scholarship Student-Athlete at the Georgia Institute of Technology

by Richard Lapchick and Horacio Ruiz

Georgia Tech's starting quarterback was sitting in a white limousine outside the Liberty Bowl in Memphis, Tennessee, next to civil rights activist Jesse Jackson. The problem was Georgia Tech's game versus Iowa State, in front of a then-Liberty Bowl attendance record of 50,021, had already begun. An NAACP picket line was formed outside the limousine in protest of the move that had McAshan sitting in a luxury vehicle rather than under center for his team's bowl game.

Jackson was a witness to the era during which African-Americans began to integrate predominantly white institutions; and by the 1970s, he was an activist in many of that drama's major happenings. In 1972, Memphis was in the national spotlight when it played host to the Liberty Bowl between Georgia Tech and Iowa State. The NAACP picket lines outside the stadium were in protest of Tech first-year coach Bill Fulcher's suspending starting quarterback Eddie McAshan, the first African-American scholarship athlete in Georgia Tech's history—and the one who was playing the biggest position in the biggest sport. Up until the suspension, McAshan had passed for 32 career touchdowns, which still leaves him fourth-best in Tech history 34 years later. His five TD passes against Rice in 1972 set a school record, and he is seventh on the Yellow Jackets' career passing list—all in spite of the fact that he played only three years. He'd helped lead Georgia Tech to a 22-9-1 record and two bowl appearances before Fulcher suspended him. Prior to the game that day, five of McAshan's teammates were on the picket line to protest the suspension, but eventually went into the stadium to play, wearing black armbands to signal their solidarity.

The suspension ostensibly grew out of a disagreement over a request by McAshan for four extra tickets for the season-finale game against archrival Georgia so his family could attend. When Fulcher denied the request, McAshan skipped a practice; and in response, Fulcher suspended his quarterback for the next two games. This was an era in which a handful of black athletes protested against actions by what they saw as the white establishment. McAshan believed there was a double standard being applied to African-American athletes.

McAshan had become all too familiar with the double standards that existed in his world. In 1966, he'd become the first black high school quarterback in Florida to play for a predominantly white school when he helped integrate Gainesville High's football team. He did not know it at the time, but the Ku Klux Klan, enraged with his playing quarterback from as early as his junior varsity days, would burn crosses in front of his coach's yard.

"They would happen all the time," McAshan said of the cross burnings. "It was really terrible. But they never told me anything about it until afterward, which I appreciated and could understand."[1]

By the time he came out of high school, McAshan's athleticism was unquestioned. At Gainesville High he threw for 61 career touchdowns, which still puts him in the top 20 all-time for touchdowns scored by Florida preps. He led his basketball team to the state championship primarily by driving to the basket from his left side and utilizing his left hand, in direct contrast to his right-handed throwing as a quarterback.

During his final three years in high school, McAshan had to be escorted onto the football field by bodyguards because of threats made on his life. At the time, though, he did not understand why bodyguards were escorting him; the coaches didn't dare tell him about the threats.

"I would stay up all night as a child thinking that a vampire or a zombie or something you'd see on TV was going to come in the room and get me," McAshan told the *Augusta Chronicle*. "So I always told people, 'This is nothing.' What could live people do that could spook you?"[2] McAshan would soon find out. At Georgia Tech he found his tires slashed and his dorm room burned by a suspicious fire. He saw his effigy hanging from a tree as the team bus went through the Auburn campus. Later in his career, McAshan would not be allowed into the Auburn stadium because the security guards at the gate could not believe that any black men were part of the team. This came with being the first African-American quarterback for a major southeastern university, but he never lost his composure.

Breaking barriers was part of McAshan's football career. Today, nearly 50 percent of college players and nearly 70 percent of NFL players are African-American, but few of them are aware of what athletes like McAshan went through to pave their way.

In the limousine at the Liberty Bowl in Memphis that day, sitting next to Jackson, McAshan knew his career at Georgia Tech was finished. A few months later, he entered the draft, where he was taken in the 17th round by the New England Patriots, and he had a short, injury-riddled pro career in the NFL. McAshan resurfaced with the Jacksonville Sharks of the World Football League during the 1974–75 season until the WFL folded. His football dreams shattered, he showed his strength of character by completing his degree in industrial management at Georgia Tech in 1979.

As changes came about in the South, history twisted itself into a different ending. Eddie McAshan was inducted into the Georgia Tech Hall of Fame in 1995.

Notes

1. Allison Clark, "Breaking Down Barriers," *The Gainesville Sun*, May 26, 2004.
2. Larry Williams, "Eddie McAshan," *The Augusta Chronicle*, August 23, 2002.

Craig Mobley

First African-American Scholarship Student-Athlete at Clemson University

by Horacio Ruiz

Courtesy of Clemson Sports Information.

Craig Mobley remembers getting his spot back as one of Clemson University's disc jockeys two weeks after a program director pulled him off the air. In his show, Mobley played top-40 hits while mixing in a number of black artists. The program director objected to these additions and removed Mobley from his duties. Two weeks later, the student body signed a petition to get him back on the air. Back in the booth, Mobley made sure to play more of the black artists—he even threw in some heavy metal. "It had nothing to do with music—it had to do with inclusion," Mobley recalled, more than 35 years removed from his days at Clemson. "You need to make sure you have everyone represented."[1]

Mobley is especially familiar with the importance of representation. He represented Clemson as its first African-American scholarship student-athlete when he signed on to play basketball in 1969. At the time he signed, it seemed like no big deal. "I didn't know I was the first black athlete," he said. "But once I got there, it was obvious."

Mobley grew up an avid fan of Atlantic Coast Conference basketball. He wanted to attend North Carolina, but Coach Dean Smith had only a partial scholarship to offer. Clemson, another ACC school, jumped in with a full athletic scholarship offer. Mobley's status as the first black scholarship athlete was not discussed—he didn't care. Mobley wanted to play in the ACC and pursue a degree in chemical engineering; a scholarship from Clemson would allow him to do just that.

As his career at Clemson developed, Mobley found that his naivety as a black player integrating athletics would forever mold his experiences as an individual. His freshman year, the black students on campus protested a black-face skit that was going to be held as part of Clemson's homecoming festivities. All of the black students walked off campus and drove to their own homes or the homes of their friends. Mobley, though different by virtue of being an athlete, took a stance with them. "Even though I was an athlete," Mobley said, "I didn't feel I was in any different situation than the other black students." Clemson president R. C. Edwards responded by canceling the skit, prompting the students to return to campus.

Oddly enough, it was the student body at Clemson that was Mobley's biggest supporter on the court. One night, the Clemson freshman team beat Furman University behind Mobley's 20-point, 11-rebound effort—the best game of his career. Mobley figured he would have a lot more opportunities to play, but his hopes came to an end when Clemson coach Bobby Roberts left and was replaced by another coach. The basketball program instantly changed. Practices were held at 5 a.m. and in the afternoon. Mobley's schoolwork began to suffer, as did his playing time. "Some coaches have their systems and have people fit in them," Mobley said. "I tried my best to adjust to that system, but it probably hurt me. When you put in that much effort, you want to be able to show it. I was there to practice."

The students at the game would call out Mobley's number and his name in an attempt to get him playing time, but they seldom had reason to cheer. Some of the assistant coaches thought he should have seen more playing time—even the players above him thought Mobley was not getting a fair chance. His sophomore year he averaged 0.5 points per game. He hung around for part of his junior year, but by then, he was spending his time sitting on the bench. It would not be until 1973 with Tree Rollins, a 7-foot-1-inch center, that the Clemson basketball team would regularly play a black player. Rollins would go on to have an 18-year NBA career.

The community surrounding Clemson was not as welcoming as the students. During Mobley's freshman year, a black man was stabbed for entering an all-white nightclub. Six African-Americans were arrested for trying to "incite a riot," though Mobley says they were merely standing on a street corner. There was nowhere to eat off-campus because the restaurants surrounding the campus, as Mobley puts it, might as well have had "whites only" signs.

Mobley didn't walk away from the team, he says, he was pushed away. By the time he ended his playing career, he no longer saw race as an issue. It simply became a matter of good people and bad people, race be damned. Mobley concentrated on earning his degree in chemistry with a minor in physics. He helped form a black student association called the Student League for Black Identity whose mission was to improve opportunities for black students. He also participated in the school's ROTC all four years. Upon graduation, he went to the Institute of Paper Chemistry, a nonprofit research and educational institute, whereupon he was hired by Minnesota Mining and Manufacturing (3M) as an industrial tape research chemist. After working at 3M for one year, Mobley began a commission as a second lieutenant in the United States Air Force. As an officer in the Air Force, Mobley continued to encounter racism. "People were not used to having a person of color leading them," he said. "There were times when no one wanted to hear what I had to say." In the Air Force, Mobley joined the recreational basketball leagues, averaging 30 points per game and winning league titles. "My best playing days came when I was in the military," he joked. "I must have learned something at Clemson."

In 1991, he pursued a civilian life after leaving the Air Force as a major. In 1993, he formed Magna Enterprises Construction, a construction company he currently owns, as sole proprietor and owner. His company designs and builds one-story single family residences and is also involved in public works projects, including contractual work with the City of Los Angeles. In 2001, Mobley was named chairman of the LA Watts Summer Games, started in 1968 in response to the racially charged Watts riots in 1965. The Watts Games, the largest high school athletic competition in the United States, includes more than 7,000 athletes participating in 18 different sports. High school athletes from different parts of California, various ethnic and economic backgrounds, and numerous states compete every year as part of what Mobley calls "building bridges of understanding. The Watts Summer Games gave me a chance to do something I wanted," Mobley said. "It gave me a chance to incorporate all the different things I believe in."

In 2003, Mobley was invited back to Clemson to conduct a ceremonial jump-ball in a string of festivities held by Clemson to celebrate Dr. Martin Luther King Jr. Day. Clemson played against Morris Brown, an historically black college, in order to give them more exposure as they played against an ACC opponent. "I will always hold that experience closely and dearly in my heart," Mobley said.

He has mixed feelings about being the first African-American scholarship athlete, not having left much of a playing legacy, although he tried his best considering the circumstances. He will forever hold the memory of Dean Smith and his North Carolina players standing and applauding him when he entered a game against the Tar Heels. It was an act that has endeared him to Smith, the coach he wanted to play for all along.

"My heart goes to Clemson," Mobley said. "I have no regrets, except I wish I could've been a better player. Clemson was a great experience, it taught me that when isolated you can still survive. Being the first, you almost have to be twice as good to be half as good."

Note

1. All of the quotes in this article are by Craig Mobley, from an interview with author on October 8, 2006.

Chapter 10

SECTION THREE

Big 12
Conference
Student-Athlete
Barrier
Breakers

Sherman, Grant, and Ed Harvey

First African-American Student-Athletes at the University of Kansas

by Horacio Ruiz

Ed Harvey stands with his arm on a teammate's shoulder, looking off somewhere into the distance with a proud gaze. The picture of the University of Kansas' 1893 football team looks like a Goya painting. The men are posing, looking in different directions, inviting the viewer into their world but offering little else. There is no telling what they are thinking. This was a different age and, whether or not he knew it, Harvey was fortunate to be playing football. African-American men were being excluded from playing professionally and subjugated to the racial prejudices of the time, with many athletic programs refusing to play teams with African-American participants.

Although Ed participated as an athlete for both the football and baseball teams, he later would grow disenchanted with his beloved university's treatment of African-Americans and athletics. Ed was not the first African-American athlete at Kansas; his brothers Sherman and Grant had lettered earlier in baseball, in 1888 and 1889 respectively, earning their "K" letters and the card that would subsequently allow them to attend any Kansas sporting event free. Ed was the first African-American to play football, and his disenchantment

University Archives, Spencer Research Library, University of Kansas.

Ed Harvey with the 1893 Kansas University football team.

with the school's position on race was documented in letters he wrote to the school's administration.

The Harveys' parents were born into slavery. Their father, David Harvey, enlisted in the Federal Army in the Civil War. After he was released in 1863, he was sent to Lawrence where he met up with his family. The Harvey family began to sharecrop for the sheriff of the town and after five years had managed to acquire a few acres of land, adding land continually until 1893 when David Harvey died. By that time, the Harvey family had acquired 100 acres of improved land, and the Harvey brothers had all attended the University of Kansas, participating in athletics in one form or another.

Upon his graduation from Kansas, the oldest of the three Harvey brothers, Sherman, took up farming on family land before becoming a teacher in Lawrence and then being elected to two terms as clerk of the district court of Douglas County. In 1898, soon after the outbreak of the Spanish-American war, Sherman organized and became captain of the Twenty-Third Kansas, an African-American regiment. The company was sent to Cuba, where it served guard duty. In 1902, Sherman passed the state bar and in the same year moved to the Philippines to start a law partnership with one of the officers of the Twenty-Third Kansas. He stayed overseas for nearly 19 years in what would become a lucrative law firm. In 1920, he returned home to Lawrence to work on the family farm until his health failed. He died on September 9, 1934.

Grant Harvey spent one year at Kansas and then took the preparatory medical courses Kansas offered before completing his education at McNarry Medical College in Nashville, Tennessee. He joined the Twenty-Third Kansas along with his brother Sherman, and in the winter of 1888–89 he traveled to Cuba, where he was enlisted as a surgeon. By 1903 he had moved to Lawrence, where he was active as a physician and in civic affairs until his death in May 1923.

Ed Harvey, the youngest of the three brothers and the young man staring out in the team photo, went to work directly on the family farm following his graduation 1894. He would become secretary of the Douglas County farmer's institute, secretary of the tax payer's league, and a member of the school board of his district. In 1944, he was honored when the University of Kansas' chancellor presented him with the university's Gold Medal, an honor bestowed upon him as recognition for being a 50-year graduate.

What is most interesting to note about Ed is a letter he wrote on January 15, 1914 to the Board of Control in which he stated: "My understanding is that negroes are barred from participating in athletics at KU. Not by any rule of the school but by "common consensus" they are kept off the various teams. . . . Now if these things be true, and I think they are, is it fair? Has not the negro student the same rights to show his prowess on the athletic field as the white student? Athletics are not social organizations. I am not asking for social equality."

Perhaps though, in an attempt to be political, deep down inside Ed knew he was asking for social equality. He would write one more paragraph in the letter to the Board. He made sure to include the role he and his brothers had played in athletics at Kansas and that he had earned three K's for his involvement in football and baseball. A reply was sent one week later with the administration's thanks to Ed for writing his letter, but it stopped there.

The chancellor replied in three sentences, the first and third sentences mere formalities served for introduction and farewell. The second sentence of the letter reads, "I was directed to say that the Board will do its best to see that the athletics at the University are administered to the best interests of the University and of all concerned."

In 1921, the three brothers sent a letter to the chancellor on a Harvey Farms letterhead. At the top, part of the letterhead's heading reads Ed S. Harvey, Manager. The brothers voiced their concern away from athletics this time and questioned whether attempts to segregate Kansas students at the cafeteria and at theatres in the Fine Arts department had been approved by the highest figure on campus, the chancellor. No records were received regarding a reply, but it is obvious that this time, in direct contrast to the letter Ed had written six years before, the three brothers were asking for nothing less than social equality.

In a feature article written about the Harvey brothers, Ed said that what he is most proud of is that his parents, born slaves, were able to acquire a job, earn their own land, and put their three sons through college. The three brothers were donors of the David and Rebecca Harvey Scholarship, in honor of their parents. Even if the school was not always able to honor the Harvey brothers who paved the way for so many, at least the Harvey brothers could honor the loved ones who paved the way for them.

George Flippin

First African-American Student-Athlete at the University of Nebraska

by Marcus Sedberry

In the late 1800s, football was very different from the game we consider a national passion today. Each time players stepped onto the field, they risked serious injury due to a lack of adequate equipment and rules that made helmet wearing optional. African-Americans were few and far between in the collegiate realm, both academically and athletically. Ultimately, 19th-century football had a significantly different look than the modern version to which we are so accustomed.

George Albert Flippin was born on February 8, 1868, in Port Isabelle, Ohio, to Charles and Mary Flippin. His father, Charles, was a freed slave who had fought in the war for emancipation. Within the community, Flippin's parents were well-respected physicians and surgeons who eventually opened a medical office and drug store in Henderson, Nebraska, in 1888. The strength, courage, and intelligence of both parents helped to pave the way for young George Flippin.

From 1891 to 1894, Flippin was enrolled at the University of Nebraska, eventually becoming the first African-American student-athlete at the university. At the time, Flippin was just the fifth African-American student-athlete in the entire nation to compete for a predominately white university. At Nebraska, Flippin played baseball, wrestled, and threw the shot put, along with playing tackle and running back on the football team. In Flippin's freshman year, he led the team against the University of Iowa, a major rival, in hopes of reversing defeats the team had suffered in previous years. Over the course of the game, some Iowa players became frustrated and ultimately violent, leaving Flippin with cuts on his hands and face. Nonetheless, the Bugeaters, now Cornhuskers, squeaked out a 20-18 victory on the back of Flippin, who provided both the aggressiveness and finesse needed for the win. This victory gave Nebraska its first win over an out-of-state opponent.

As a result of the prejudices and racism in the 1890s, many teams declined to play against teams who had African-American

players on their roster. On November 5, 1892, Nebraska was scheduled to play the University of Missouri. Missouri, however, refused
to play Nebraska because of Flippin's presence on the team, thus
forfeiting the game. Despite a lack of respect from the opposing
teams, Flippin persevered to reach even greater heights. In his senior year, Flippin led the Bugeaters to be co-champions of the Western Inter-State University Football Association.

Not only did Flippin face prejudice from other teams, but he
was also subjected to it from his own coach. Though Flippin was
elected captain by his teammates, Nebraska Coach Frank Crawford
overruled the decision. Crawford explained, "It takes a man with
brains to be captain: all there is to Flippin is brute force . . . I don't
take exception to him because he is colored, but it takes a head to be
a football captain."[1] Although Flippin did not meet the "intellectual"
standards set by his coach, Crawford perhaps motivated Flippin to
achieve bigger and better things off the field because of his tough
love on the field. While at Nebraska, Flippin became an accomplished orator and president of the campus Palladian Literacy Society; yet, this was only the beginning of Flippin's success.

Although most people knew Flippin for his on-field play, immediately following his graduation from Nebraska, Flippin attended
the University of Illinois in order to study medicine. Following in
his parents' footsteps, Flippin received his medical degree from Illinois' College of Physicians and Surgeons in Chicago. In 1893, Flippin married Georgia Smith, a student at Nebraska Conservatory of
Music. Georgia and George had two children, Dorothy May and
Robert Browning Flippin, before divorcing. Flippin later married a
woman named Martina Larson.

After completing his education, Flippin traveled the world,
learning new medical techniques and methods in order to better
serve his patients. In 1907, he opened the first hospital in Stromsburg, Nebraska. As expected, Flippin grew to be one of the best in
his field, becoming a noted, respected physician. His passion for
helping others was evident in his work. Flippin prided himself on
making house calls regardless of the location of his patients. He is
credited with assisting to save the lives of more patients with polio
than any other doctor.

As a pioneer, Flippin's accomplishments did not end on the
football field or in the hospital. During his lifetime, the acceptance

of African-Americans was rare, and Flippin often experienced this rejection. While trying to dine at a restaurant in Nebraska, he was denied service because of his race. As a result of this incident, Flippin became a part of the first civil rights lawsuit in the state of Nebraska. Throughout Flippin's lifetime, he also saw the transformation of transportation. Flippin holds the title of being the first owner of a car in Stromsburg, Nebraska. George Flippin died in 1929 and was the first African-American buried in his hometown cemetery.

Many years have passed since George Flippin traveled the world in an attempt to be the best physician and surgeon, and even more since he roamed the football field terrorizing opponents as both an offensive and defensive threat. In 1974, Flippin became the first African-American to be inducted into the University of Nebraska Hall of Fame. Despite the timeline, George Flippin's accomplishments and accolades are ones that cannot be changed or tarnished. Flippin paved the way for others on the field, in the classroom, in the office, and in everyday life. Although the game of football has evolved significantly, the lessons that we can glean from George Flippin about strength, perseverance, and barrier-breaking are as relevant and fresh today as they were in the 1890s.

Note

1. "George Flippin," http://net.unl.edu/sportsFeat/pioneer/hc_mvp/hc_players/flippin.html (accessed October 10, 2007).

Johnny "Jack" Trice

First African-American Student-Athlete at Iowa State University

by Marcus Sedberry

Some people devote their lives to performing great deeds, in turn garnering the praise of others. Some people are blessed with great wealth and choose to donate a portion of that money to others, again garnering recognition. Johnny "Jack" Trice is not "some people." Trice lived his entire life without recognition, which did not come until more than a half a century after his death.

In the sports world, it is an unspoken rule that you have to break long-standing records, win numerous prestigious awards, or be loved by the masses in order to be eternally remembered. This makes Trice's story phenomenal.

Jack Trice was born in 1902 in Hiram, Ohio, and grew up hoping to be nothing less than the best. As a child of a former slave and buffalo soldier (a term first used by Native Americans to describe African-American soldiers' "combat prowess, bravery, tenaciousness, and looks on the battlefield"),[1] it was evident that life was not going to be a crystal stair. Nonetheless, Trice persevered and began to distinguish himself athletically. Before he entered high school, Trice's mother sent him to Cleveland, Ohio, to live with his uncle. There he attended East Technical High School, where he participated in football and in track. Following his high school graduation in 1922, Trice and five other teammates sought a post-secondary degree. The six young men followed their high school coach to Iowa State College, now Iowa State University. This made Trice the first African-American athlete at Iowa State and one of only 20 African-Americans on the entire campus.

While attending Iowa State, Trice participated in track as well as football. Athletic excellence was only one dimension of Trice's interests and skills. He also studied animal husbandry and received a 90 percent average in the 45 college credits he completed. His dream was to one day be able to help African-American farmers in the South.

Because of the lack of athletic scholarships during this time, Trice worked different jobs in order to pay for his education. During his freshman year, Trice played on the freshman team and had wonderful success, causing him to be touted as a potential all-conference performer for his second season. The summer following his freshman year Trice married Cora Mae Starland and added "family provider" to his already numerous roles.

The next season began and Trice was indeed ready to excel on the field. On October 6, 1923, Iowa State was scheduled to play the University of Minnesota in Minneapolis/St. Paul. The night prior to the game, Trice stayed in a racially segregated hotel. In his hotel room, he wrote a letter expressing his plans for the following day, as well as the implications his first "real" college game had for society. Trice wrote, "My thoughts just before the first real college game of my life: The honor of my race, family & self is at stake. Everyone is expecting me to do big things. I will. My whole body and soul are to be thrown recklessly about the field tomorrow. Every time the ball is snapped, I will be trying to do more than my part. On all defensive plays I must break thru the opponents' line and stop the play in their territory. Beware of mass interference. Fight low, with your eyes open and toward the play. Watch out for crossbucks and reverse end runs. Be on your toes every minute if you expect to make good." This letter was later found in Trice's jacket pocket.

The following day would change Trice's life forever. In the first half of the game, Trice suffered an injury to his collarbone, but insisted he was healthy and returned to the field. In the third quarter, Trice attempted to tackle the opposing runner and was trampled by three Minnesota players. Although he claimed he was fine, Trice was forced to go to the hospital. Minnesota doctors examined Trice and deemed him healthy enough to travel back to Iowa with the team. Upon his return, Trice was sent to the hospital and examined once again. Doctors found that Trice's collarbone was broken and he was suffering respiratory complications from the vicious hit in the third quarter. On October 8, 1923, Johnny "Jack" Trice died from hemorrhaged lungs and internal bleeding as a result of the injuries suffered in the game. The following Tuesday, classes were postponed and the funeral services were held on the Iowa State campus.

Trice's name and honor have been remembered. Fifty years after his passing, Iowa State began searching for names for the new stadium, and the legacy of Jack Trice was brought to the forefront. After long consideration, however, the stadium was named Cyclone

Stadium. Ten years later, Iowa State's student government began gathering support from faculty, parents, state politicians, and public figures to keep the name of the stadium, Cyclone Stadium but to change the name of the playing field to Jack Trice Field. Their perseverance paid off and Iowa State accepted the name change. The student government raised funds in an attempt to honor Trice in a greater fashion. In 1987 after three years of planning and development, a 1,000 pound statue of Trice was erected, paid for by student government funds. This statue depicted Trice with his collegiate wear from the 1920s, books to symbolize his accomplishments as a student and bronze shoes beside him in remembrance of the fatal game he played in 1923. It was originally placed on campus for all who visited to observe. In 1997, the statue was restored and placed at the north entrance of Iowa State University's newly named Jack Trice Stadium.

Jack Trice was a pioneer and hero, not because of the many things he accomplished over a long life, but for what he championed in the time he was allotted. Being the first African-American student-athlete at Iowa State was a feat in itself, but his character, integrity, and goals on and off the field speak volumes about his contribution to humanity. Although his own journey was short, Johnny "Jack" Trice paved the way for many to follow, making him a true American pioneer.

Note

1. "Buffalo Soldiers," http://www.buffalosoldiers.com (accessed September 21, 2007).

Harold Robinson

First African-American Student-Athlete at Kansas State University

by Marcus Sedberry

One man's desire to "just play ball" became an historical event in 1949 as he became the first African-American male athlete at Kansas State University. Harold Robinson, a football student-athlete at K-State, opened the doors for the demise of color barriers in sports.

Robinson was born and raised in Manhattan, Kansas, where he was member of his varsity football team. Following graduation, Robinson tried out for the Kansas State Wildcats. Robinson was undeterred, although in 1949 there were no African-Americans on any of the teams in what was then the Big Seven Conference. In fact, Ralph M. Graham, KSU's coach at the time, welcomed Robinson with open arms and acted as a major key to Robinson's success.

Coach Graham was no stranger to having African-American student-athletes on his teams. As a coach of the Wichita State University Shockers, he was responsible for several African-American

Courtesy of Kansas State University Sports Information.

players. "People have to give him credit for letting black players on the team," Robinson told the *Kansas State Collegian*. "Jackie Robinson had Branch Rickey who brought him into Major League Baseball. If it wasn't for Ralph Graham, I wouldn't have been playing at K-State."[1]

Robinson's success at tryouts generated a great deal of publicity and word reached baseball sensation Jackie Robinson. Jackie Robinson, who is credited with breaking the Major League Baseball color barrier just two years prior in 1947, wrote Harold Robinson a letter of congratulations and mailed it to K-State Athletics.

Although some triumphantly supported his inclusion, Robinson still encountered many obstacles during his tenure at Kansas State. He was unable to enjoy many of the luxuries that his teammates experienced. For safety reasons, Robinson was often expected to stay in private homes while his teammates stayed in hotels during road trips. Robinson only missed one game due to segregation. Memphis State, he recalled, "didn't even allow blacks in the stadium, much less players."[2]

The reality of his unequal treatment resounded in his life and was a situation that he could not overlook. His physical separation from his teammates played a huge role in his perception of people. However, this separation did not affect his relationship with his teammates. Amazingly, Robinson and his teammates were able to overcome the racial barriers formed by society. His fellow players developed an indestructible bond as they protected Robinson and stood by his side through adversity.

At the time that Robinson began playing for Kansas State, the United States Supreme Court was still five years away from the landmark *Brown vs. Topeka Board of Education* decision, which enabled whites and blacks to legally attend the same schools. Although segregation was the social norm, it did not hold Robinson back as he excelled as a center for the Kansas State Wildcats. Robinson earned first team All-Big Seven honors in 1950, despite playing on a 1-9-1 team.

After his football career, Robinson went on to serve in the Army during the Korean War, in which he was injured and received a Purple Heart. In 2004, Robinson was inducted into the Kansas State Athletics Hall of Fame.

Robinson's persistence and determination paved the way for many athletes to follow. One of those he inspired was Earl Woods, the late father of Tiger Woods, who would become the first African-American baseball player at Kansas State in 1952. Robinson's life is an example of perseverance brought to fruition. He fought for the equality of all African-Americans in society and in sports. He did not allow the outside world to tear down his internal drive to success as he strode the roads less traveled.

Notes

1. Associated Press, "Big 12 Trailblazer; Robinson Broke Color Barrier as Player at K-State," *Columbia Daily Tribune* (accessed September 20, 2006).

2. Associated Press, "Athlete Who Broke Big 12 Race Barrier Dies," http://www .cstv.com/sports/m-footbl/stories/051306aaa.html (accessed September 20, 2006).

Al Abram

First African-American Scholarship Student-Athlete at the University of Missouri

by Horacio Ruiz

Although the youngest members of his family were robbed of the opportunity to meet him, it is still Al Abram whom they idolize. In 1982, Abram died of a heart condition at the age of 43, leaving his wife, Glenda, to ponder the death of someone so young and full of life. The legacy he left behind as the first African-American to earn an athletic scholarship at Missouri and also as a family man driven by a compulsion to educate himself has been passed down to even the youngest generation of his relatives. Abram's spirit permeates his family.

It was not Abram's intention to become a pioneer after having a standout career at Charles Sumner High in St. Louis. While Abram was fielding a number of scholarship offers, Missouri Coach Wilbur "Sparky" Stalcup offered him a basketball scholarship in 1956. Figuring it would be close enough for his family to watch him play, Abram accepted both an athletic and an academic scholarship. He would go on to have a standout career for Missouri, competing on the varsity team from 1958 to 1960.

The realities of being the first African-American athlete at Missouri would soon hit Abram. Although he was often met with stares and uneasy glances on campus, it was his separation from the basketball team that bothered him most. Because of the segregated communities the team would travel to, it was routine for Abram to spend a night with a black family away from the team hotel or to eat at a separate dining facility. When Missouri traveled to Houston to play Rice in December of 1958, the team walked into a hotel where a man asked if Abram was with the team. Coach Stalcup said he was and the man immediately refused to let Abram stay in the hotel. Since it was too late to make other arrangements, Stalcup arranged for Abram to stay at a dorm on the nearby Texas Southern campus. It was an experience so painful that Abram did not mention it to his friends or family for many years.

"Al was always a very mild person," his wife said. "He wasn't at the time a person that would make a big deal about it because he just accepted it as the way things were. But he was not a pushover by any means. He would take on issues head on."[1]

With the hotel incident fresh in his mind, Abram would go on to score 23 points to lead Missouri to a 68-62 victory. His first year was the most difficult for Abram, living alone in the athletic dorms without a roommate. The next year he would room with Norris Stevenson, the first African-American to play football at Missouri. The two had known each other from high school as they played against each other for rival high schools in the St. Louis area. They would vent about their frustrations in their dorm room and then play cards to clear their heads.

Abram's junior season would be his finest. He led the Tigers in scoring and rebounding during the 1958–59 season, averaging 16.1 points and 9.3 rebounds per game. That season he scored 404 points, becoming only the fourth player in Missouri history to reach 400 points for a season. Midway through his collegiate career, Abram changed majors from engineering to business. After completing four years at Missouri, he was still one year away from completing his degree in business because of his change in major. Realizing that he could not afford to stay in Columbia to finish his degree, Abram went to try out for the NBA's Cincinnati Royals and ended up playing for the Buchanan Bakers, a team based out of Seattle in the old National Industrial Basketball League. He played professionally for the Bakers until the Industrial League folded.

That December, he married Glenda, and the two eventually found their way back to St. Louis, where Abram completed his business degree at Washington University. He worked for the city of St. Louis for several years while attaining a master's degree at St. Louis University. Abram then worked for the Internal Revenue Service until 1975, when he was forced to retire because of the discovery of his heart ailment. In 1978, Abram started a consulting firm for minority business owners, where he worked until his death. In all that time, he continued to educate himself for the sheer pleasure of it. "Al never stopped going to school," Glenda said, "because there was always something he needed to know."

From an early age, Abram's daughter, Gayle, knew she was going to college because it was instilled in her that there was no other option. Abram also was very much into probing and asking questions, curious about the opinions other people held on current events and other topics.

"We talked all the way from St. Louis to California," Glenda recalled about a road trip she took with Abram. "It was always a debate but that's what he enjoyed. Al was always reading or going to lectures."

In 2004, Abram was inducted into the Missouri Athletics Hall of Fame. A committee reviews all nominees, who must then be approved unanimously. Two years earlier, Abram had been nominated but fell one vote short of the unanimous induction requirement. His eventual induction was a gratifying moment for Abram's family. More than 60 members arrived in Columbia, many of whom had taken a chartered bus from St. Louis. At the ceremonial dinner, Gayle accepted a plaque on behalf of the family. "I really felt good about it," Glenda said. "When I first knew of the inductions at Missouri I was just wondering why he had never been recognized. But I never made a big deal about it."

It was not the first time Abram had been recognized for his accomplishments. In 1992, Charles Sumner High inducted him into its Hall of Fame, and in 1996 St. Louis University dedicated a book in its business department in his name. In 2007, Abram's alma mater Charles Sumner High, established in 1875, recognized him as one of the top 100 basketball players in school history.

"Al was a very humble and wise person. People liked being around him," Glenda said. "I don't know how he would even react now to the inductions. He would have taken it in stride, but he was not one to be boastful. He was pretty much always on the money, but I wouldn't always let him know that."

Note

1. All of the quotes in this article are by Glenda Abram, from an interview with the author on May 28, 2007.

Prentice Gautt

First African-American Football Student-Athlete at the University of Oklahoma

by Horacio Ruiz

You are a young Prentice Gautt, an all-star high school running back attending your first team meeting for Bud Wilkinson's Oklahoma football team. Already you have been denied a scholarship because people surrounding the Oklahoma football program have pressured Coach Wilkinson into not dedicating money to an African-American athlete. It seems you will not be playing football for the program and the coach you love so dearly, but at the last minute a group of African-American doctors and pharmacists raise enough money for you to attend Oklahoma and walk on to the football team. You see Wilkinson walk into the room and begin to address the team.

He tells the team that you, Prentice Gautt, will be a full-fledged member of Oklahoma football and that if anyone has a problem with you, they are more than welcome to leave. Two or three players walk out, a fact you will recall years later. There are more players, you are sure, who feel the same way but who do not walk out. It is 1956. Welcome to the University of Oklahoma, where football is king and like a religion; it is a way of life, and you are the first African-American to ever play football there. In your senior year in high school, you were the first African-American player to ever play in the Oklahoma All-State game, earning MVP honors. This is different—this is college football on a huge stage, and you know it.

It was under these conditions that Gautt began his playing career at Oklahoma. After two weeks of practice, Wilkinson returned the private funds donated by the local African-American professionals and awarded Gautt the scholarship he deserved. After playing on the freshman team in 1956, Gautt would become the starting fullback for the next three seasons, from 1957 to 1959. The team eventually learned to support Gautt. Wilkinson backed Gautt's every move, and the players soon followed their coach's lead. In his freshman year, Gautt was denied service in a Tulsa restaurant. The team promptly stood up and left. "If it hadn't have been for Bud, there wouldn't have been any way that I'd have made it," Gautt said at a 1991 tribute to the coach. "His talking and believing in me was probably the biggest thing that helped me get over even the thought of being the first black."

But the players and coaches couldn't leave every segregated restaurant and hotel that Gautt was forced to leave. During his entire career, Gautt was unable to stay in the Oklahoma City hotel his teammates and coaches frequented. Gautt endured much frustration, feeling the pressures of being the first African-American player on the team. As he would later say, he was afraid to fail and afraid to succeed. Through it all, he succeeded far more often than he failed. "The opportunity to participate in athletics took some of that pressure off," Gautt told George Zabloski of the *Oklahoma Daily.* "Any frustrations or anger I had I could deal with on the football field."[1]

In his final two years, Gautt was an All-Big Eight selection, and in his senior year he was named an Academic All-American. He was named the 1959 Orange Bowl MVP after rushing for 94 yards on six carries, helping lead the Sooners to a 10-1 record. The Oklahoma football team had made it to the Orange Bowl the previous year, and although Gautt was allowed to stay in the team hotel in Miami, it was negotiated that he would not be allowed to use the pool.

After finishing his career at Oklahoma, Gautt went on to play in the NFL, spending one season with the Cleveland Browns and six with the St. Louis Cardinals. During his seven-year career, Gautt appeared in 89 games, rushing for 2,466 yards on 629 attempts while accumulating 901 receiving yards on 79 receptions.

After his playing career had come to an end, Gautt coached football at Missouri while earning his Ph.D. in psychology. Soon after, he embarked on a career in collegiate athletic administration in which he exhibited a compassion for student-athletes that went above and beyond what was expected. In 1979, he took a position as an assistant commissioner for the Big Eight Conference until he later became an associate commissioner working in education, eligibility, and enforcement. He then transitioned into an associate commissioner role in the Big 12.

Gautt's career as an administrator was marked by a constant stream of praise for the way he carried himself and the way he touched the lives of others. In 1996, the Big 12 created a post-graduate scholarship in his honor by beginning the Dr. Prentice Gautt Scholarship Program for student-athletes. In 1999, he was officially recognized and honored during a football halftime ceremony when Oklahoma named its expansive academic office for student-athletes the Prentice Gautt Academic Center. One year later in 2000, a former teammate and traveling roommate, Jakie Sandefer, introduced Gautt at his induction into the Oklahoma Sports Hall of Fame, an enshrinement that put him in the company of his former coach, Bud Wilkinson. "Was Prentice different?" Sandefer recalled saying in his introduction. "Yeah, Prentice was different. He had more class than the rest of us, and he was a better student."[2]

Dr. Gautt died suddenly of flu-like symptoms on March 17, 2005, but his death did not stop the flow of honors. To commemorate his passing, his jersey number 38 was not issued for Oklahoma's 2006 football season, and a No. 38 sticker was put on the back of all helmets. He was honored posthumously by the National Football Foundation with the 2005 Outstanding Contribution to Amateur Football Award. "A true pioneer in his day, Prentice showed remarkable will and determination, which allowed him to break the color barrier at Oklahoma," said Jon F. Hanson, chairman of the National Football Foundation & College Hall of Fame. "As Jackie Robinson did for baseball, Prentice left a civil rights impression on the school and sport of football that will never be forgotten."[3]

Near the end of his administrative career, Gautt oversaw the Big 12 Life Skills Program, working with the Student Athlete Advisory Committee and the Big 12 board of directors. The Life Skills program involves the participation of more than 4,000 Big 12 students in community and charity work within the students' respective communities. Gautt credited Wilkinson with much of his success, developing a close friendship with his former coach as he embarked on his professional career. If you were Prentice Gautt, you would know you owed much of that credit to yourself. "Prentice was such a remarkable human being," said Oklahoma athletic director Joe Castiglione at the time of Oklahoma's commemoration of Gautt's jersey number. "Knowing the quality of humility Prentice possessed, he probably would have shied away from the recognition, but it is important that we remind ourselves and other generations of his wonderful contributions."[4]

Notes

1. George Zabolski, "Gautt Overcame Obstacles, Changed Face of Oklahoma Football," *Oklahoma Daily*, February 8, 2002.

2. *Sooner Magazine*, "Prentice Gautt Just Wanted to Play Football and Get An Education—Then Hate Took Him By the Hand," Spring 2005.

3. Matt Sweeney, "Prentice Guatt Named 2005 Outstanding Contribution to Amateur Football Awardee," National Football Foundation, May 5, 2005.

4. SoonerSports.com, "Sooners to Commemorate Gautt," http://www.soonersports .com/sports/m-footbl/spec-rel/081906aab.html (accessed August 19, 2006).

Orlando Hazley

First African-American Student-Athlete at Oklahoma State University

by Marcus Sedberry

In 1956, the Oklahoma State University football team went 3-5-2, and the men's basketball team went 18-9. The men's track and field put up similarly impressive statistics, but perhaps the most notable achievement is the lettering of Orlando Hazley.

While at Oklahoma State, Hazley was a remarkable athlete on the track and an exceptional student in the classroom, graduating with degrees in science and physical education. Among a plethora of stellar athletic performances, there are a few that stand out. One of them came from Hazley and the Cowboys when they attended the Clyde Littlefield Texas Relays.

The Texas Relays is a track and field event named after legendary University of Texas athlete and coach Clyde Littlefield. While at the University of Texas in the 1910s, he lettered in track, football, and basketball. As a coach, Littlefield led teams across the nation to remarkable achievements. His teams had 11 individual NCAA honors, setting four world records and five national records. Littlefield started the Texas Relays as a way to get the top athletes from across the country to come and compete on one stage prior to the NCAA championship. In 1958, Hazley and his teammates showed up to compete with the best from across the country. While at the meet, Hazley competed in a highly competitive 100-yard dash. In spite of the stiff competition, he pushed ahead to win the event in 9.5 seconds. The following year, Hazley won the Big Eight Championship in the 220-yard dash and the mile relay. Many people referred to Hazley as a multi-talented pure sprinter, and he proved them right.

Hazley's experience on campus was different than many others. Being a successful African-American student-athlete on a predominantly white campus was difficult enough, but Hazley also had to deal with teammates and their prejudices on a normal basis. Hazley's interaction with faculty and staff was positive overall. Nevertheless, he remembers two specific racially charged situations involving students and teammates. When Hazley entered college, one of his teammates discriminated against him often, unable to understand why Hazley would want to come to a predominately white institution. The other encounter was at a social event. He saw one of his white teammates at the event and attempted to speak to him, but his teammate would not speak back because he was with his date.

As with any college experience, there are many lessons that resonate across one's life. The student-athlete experience offers the backdrop for many of those memories. Hazley recalled, "My most memorable experience as a student-athlete was traveling across the country to track meets and being denied a place to eat or lodging in the south or southeast of Oklahoma. Of course Oklahoma was no exception. I once had to stay in Mexico because of poor in-state conditions."[1]

Although Hazley was not accepted in many places, he found comfort at home. To date, he is thankful for two men who truly cared for him, Lee A. Ward, a school principal, and Ralph Higgins, a track coach at OSU. Higgins was the Cowboys track coach for 32 years and had much success, including 17 straight Missouri Valley Conference team championships before the team switched to the Big Eight, a conference which eventually became the Big 12. Higgins was inducted into the USA Track and Field Hall of Fame in 1982.

After Hazley graduated from college, he went on to work for over 30 years with Oklahoma Public Schools as a track coach and science teacher. Hazley also spent time as the assistant principal at Booker T. Washington High School and principal at Tulsa McClane. Growing up, Hazley considered Jesse Owens and the great singer Paul Robeson to be his role models. Today, Hazley is a role model for many young people, African-American and white, athletes and non-athletes.

The impact Orlando Hazley made on the Oklahoma State University campus and athletic department will never be forgotten, as he persevered through racial prejudices and discrimination to become the first African-American to letter at OSU. Although Hazley may not have known the significance of this accomplishment at the time, African-American student-athletes at OSU would do well to thank him for paving the way for them to follow.

Note

1. Orlando Hazley, interview with author, November 18, 2007.

James Means

First African-American Student-Athlete at the University of Texas

by Horacio Ruiz

The University of Texas was the trendsetter, the leader of the Southwest Conference (SWC) in the liberal state capital of Austin. In keeping with that role, the university announced on November 9, 1963, that all extracurricular activities would be open to all students, regardless of race. In the following months, Baylor, Southern Methodist, and Texas A&M followed Texas' lead. Housing and the faculty at Texas were integrated in May 1964.

In 1962 Bertha Means, a mother concerned for her son, placed a call to a Texas regent named Frank Erwin. Mrs. Means, a school teacher and activist, protested to Erwin that her son James, an above-average student and track athlete, would not be able to run track at Texas because of its segregated athletic teams. UT dropped its ban on students of color participating in extracurricular activities only six months later. Soon after the ban ended, James Means, Cecil Carter, and Oliver Patterson were the first to integrate Texas athletics when they joined the track and field team.

Although the team did not resist integration, Carter quickly left the team. On February 29, 1964, Means and Patterson competed for the first time at a track meet in College Station, Texas. When Patterson also dropped off of the team, Means was the sole remaining African-American on the team.

Means excelled on the track, running the 100-yard dash in 9.5 seconds and the 220 in 21.7. He became the first African-American varsity letterman in SWC history and was awarded a scholarship in 1966. Although it appeared as if Texas was on the verge of a major integration movement in its athletic department, there was little real progress. On February 13, 1968, linebacker Leon O'Neal became the first African-American athlete to sign a football scholarship. Means was about to graduate.

"Look, we walked on in 1963. 1964—nobody. 1965—nobody. '66—nobody. '67—nobody. '68—O'Neal. One guy? What kind of consciousness is that? If you're a recruiter and you sign only one guy, you ought to get fired," Means said to author Richard Pennington. "Texas was so long in getting a black football player, I couldn't believe it. What took them so long? It was probably in the back room, at the Faculty Club, where the decisions were made. In 1963, if UT had integrated football, it would have been a whole different scene. Texas should have been the first one and gone ahead and bitten the doggone bullet."[1]Means was frustrated about the lack of progress. Even if Texas had been first among a number of SWC schools to integrate its athletic teams, the progress to fully integrate all sports came at a disturbingly slow pace.

In any case, Means avoided any large confrontations as an athlete, but could only think that even if he didn't see any signs of racism, perhaps as soon as he turned his back it was always there, hidden from his eyes. "I didn't have any problems, nothing sensational," Means told Pennington. "Once a restaurant in Lubbock wouldn't let us go in and we had to go somewhere else. Maybe I wore rose-colored glasses in those days because if people were saying derogatory things, I didn't hear it. No telling what their real response was back in the coffee shop."

Former Texas football coach Darrell Royal, a college football legend, was viewed as both a hero and a symbol of the unhurried progress of integration on the Texas football team. There is no doubt that Royal was under pressure from some Texas regents to deliberately slow the pace of integration for the sake of keeping the status quo. To a certain extent the process did take longer than most would have thought reasonable, especially given the rich football talent in the state of Texas.

In the book *Coach Royal*, co-authored by Royal and John Wheat, the former football coach is quick to point out that Means, not the great Southern Methodist running back Jerry LeVias, was the first African-American letterman in the Southwest Conference. Although Royal may have been taking undue credit for a historic moment that took place outside his sport at his own school, it's important to note that even a storied football coach recognizes the historical importance of Mr. James Means.

Note

1. All quotes in this article are from Richard Pennington, *Breaking the Ice: The Racial Integration of Southwest Conference Football* (Jefferson, North Carolina: McFarland & Company, Inc., Publishers, 1987).

John Westbrook

First African-American Student-Athlete at Baylor University

by Horacio Ruiz

It was his "psychological suicide"—grabbing a handful of aspirin and swallowing it all at once to see what would happen. It turns out when you're as large as John Westbrook, a running back for Baylor University in the mid 1960s, death requires more than a handful of aspirin. One night when Westbrook had nothing to do but drive around Waco alone, he stopped at a lake and contemplated driving his car into the water, sinking to the bottom to end a life once so full of optimism. Westbrook put the car in gear and returned to the road, driving to the home of a local minister to spill his heart and seek guidance as a deeply devout Christian.

In the fall of 1965, Westbrook walked onto the Baylor football team, joining the freshman squad without a scholarship and without any promises. In enrolling at Baylor, he was poised to become the first African-American football player in Southwest Athletic Conference history. (The conference was dissolved in 1996 when Texas, Texas A&M, Texas Tech, and Baylor left to join the Big Eight Conference, ultimately forming the Big 12 Conference.) On September 10, 1966, in Westbrook's sophomore year, he became the first African-American football player to appear in a Southwest Athletic Conference varsity game.

Westbrook's father was called a "fighter," a preacher who goes into churches with problems, fixes them, and then moves on to assist another church in need. Occasionally, his father would be paid for his work in chitlins, or cooked pig entrails. Westbrook took an early interest in the church, preaching as a kindergartener to his schoolmates, thus earning him the nickname "Little Preacher." By the age of 15, he had become a fully ordained minister, shortly thereafter presiding over his first funeral. Westbrook undertook his hobbies with the same fervor and passion he gave to religion. He learned to play the piano and coronet, took up ballet, and participated in debate classes. In the tenth grade he joined the football team because, as he said, growing up in Elgin, Texas, you were considered a sissy if you didn't play football, especially if you had a frame like Westbrook's. Throughout his athletic career at Washington High School, Westbrook served as captain of the football, basketball, baseball, and track and field teams.

Westbrook excelled as a running back, but his fundamentals suffered because Washington High could afford only one coach and an assistant who had never played football. Although a natural and prolific runner in high school, scoring 35 touchdowns his junior and senior seasons, Westbrook was not an adept blocker. Coaches at Baylor would use Westbrook's undeveloped blocking skills as an excuse to stunt his playing career.

Prior to the beginning of his senior year in high school in 1964, Westbrook was considering enrolling at Baylor, which was admitting African-American students for the first time that fall semester. Many discouraged him, warning him of the obstacles and hardships he would have to endure, but he reasoned that a religious-oriented university like Baylor would be a fitting place to take part in the integration process. That summer Westbrook drove to the Baylor football offices and introduced himself to assistant coaches Jack Thomas and Clyde Hart. Westbrook let them know that he was interested in playing for Baylor and ran down his list of athletic accomplishments. The coaches, curious and somewhat bewildered by Westbrook's approach, promised to send scouts to his football games. No one ever came.

The following summer, still unsure of whether he would attend Baylor or decide on an historically black college that had offered a football scholarship, Westbrook again drove to Waco and spoke with Thomas. The assistant coach told him a scout had not been sent because his last name started with a "W." Westbrook took the explanation at face value, but after Thomas called Washington High to ask about Westbrook's background, he immediately offered Westbrook a spot on the team without a scholarship. Westbrook needed a few minutes to consider the offer, retreating to a men's bathroom and sitting on a toilet to have privacy to think.

Ultimately, Westbrook chose Baylor. "I did it to prove to people in Elgin and at Baylor that I could make it, because a lot of people had discouraged me," Westbrook told author Richard Pennington.

In the fall of 1965, Westbrook became one of seven African-American students on the Baylor campus. He walked onto the Baylor football team, full of an optimistic teenager's enthusiasm for changing the world, changing attitudes, and changing his standing in life. He expected the transition into college life would be easy, but not even a college campus with a religious affiliation could make things easier. "I thought it would be a little better than it was since it was a Baptist institution and I figured, well now, this ought to be the ideal place . . . maybe my expectations were too high," Westbrook said.

On the freshman squad his first season, Westbrook played a total of three minutes. Everyone quickly realized that he was the third fastest player on the team and a talented athlete, but coaches had much more money invested in the other 27 scholarship athletes. Coach Catfish Smith played a joke on Westbrook when he sent him in for the final play of a game. By the time he had reached the huddle, time had expired. In the locker room an assistant named Corley cried for Westbrook, knowing of the unfair situation and pleading with him not to quit because he wanted to see Westbrook succeed on the field one day. The gesture moved Westbrook, who vowed not to quit. The practices were difficult. One coach called him "Sambo," a racist term referring to the character in Helen Bannerman's *The Story of Little Black Sambo*. He would walk out of the locker rooms to the practice fields alone and walk back after practice alone. The solitude changed him. "I'm the kind of guy who in high school was the talker of the spirit," Westbrook said. "Here I changed completely. I didn't say anything unless anybody said something to me. I felt alone in a room of people."

In the spring of 1966, Baylor head coach John Bridges told Westbrook he would have a fair chance to compete for a spot on the varsity team and gain the scholarship he coveted so much. He needed the scholarship, because it was unlikely Westbrook would have been able to attend Baylor another year without financial assistance. In the spring, he averaged nine yards per carry and played well as a defensive back. His play was more than worthy of making the varsity squad and earning a scholarship. Still, some assistant coaches did not want to put Westbrook on scholarship. Bridges overrode all of them.

On September 10, 1966, wearing his Baylor uniform, Westbrook made his debut against the seventh-ranked Syracuse Orangemen. Prior to the game, a teammate put his arm around Westbrook's shoulder and said, "Our nigger is going to play better than theirs," referring to Syracuse All-American Floyd Little. Late in the fourth quarter, with Baylor safely ahead, Westbrook was put in. On the first play, he carried the ball for nine yards, and then gained two yards on the next play to make a first down with Baylor 11 yards from a touchdown. He was then taken out of the game and another player scored the final touchdown of the game. Westbrook finished his sophomore year with 99 yards on 20 carries, but he suffered a serious knee injury against Texas Christian in a game in which he gained 32 yards on six carries. The injury was unfortunate, because it came at a time when the Baylor program and opponents were recognizing Westbrook as a significant offensive threat. He should have carried more than 20 times in his sophomore year, and just as race was beginning to give way to talent, his injury would forever limit his abilities as a football player.

The following year, ten pounds heavier and not completely healed from his knee injury, Westbrook had carried the ball 25 times for 90 yards midway through the season when he suffered a concussion in practice that sidelined him the rest of the season. That season he had to contend with teammates calling him a "coon," coaches trying desperately to intimidate him, and a loneliness that pervaded his entire life. It was that year he turned to the aspirin bottle to see what would happen if he swallowed just enough pills. It would do nothing more than put him to sleep. By all accounts, Westbrook always remained upbeat, confident, and smiling. He continued to preach at churches, sing in the Baylor men's choir, and take care of a bear cub, the school's mascot. Putting on such a masquerade of happiness can weigh anyone's spirits down. Westbrook made a valiant effort to appear positive, but he felt his dreams fading away with every moment at Baylor.

During his senior year, he played sparingly once more. In May 1969, Westbrook finished his college experience and graduated with a degree in English. "I was just glad it was over more than anything else," he said. "I wanted to put it behind me as much as possible."

He married and then moved to Kansas City, Missouri, where he received his master's degree in English from Southwest Missouri State University. In 1978, he moved to Houston to lead the historic Antioch Baptist Church, founded by 12 former slaves in 1866 in an area that is now in the heart of downtown Houston. During his tenure, attendance at services increased. Westbrook helped shelter and feed the local homeless, sometimes with the expenses coming out of his own pocket.

In 1978, running against a millionaire incumbent and with a campaign fund of just $10,000, Westbrook ran for Texas' lieutenant governor post, surprising many by garnering 23 percent of the total vote to finish second in the 1978 Democratic primary. Westbrook continued his speaking engagements, sometimes secular ones delivered at Waco churches and the Baylor chapel, always preaching the importance of education and intellectual stimulation.

On December 17, 1983, already hobbled by poor health, Westbrook collapsed, while playing the piano for his three children, and died of a blood clot in his lung. His funeral was attended by Houston's mayor and Texas' governor in an overflowing funeral procession. Ronnie Allen, a star track and field sprinter at Baylor, best described Westbrook's legacy in a simple anecdote. "I had a voice impediment. I slurred my words and stuttered," Allen told author Richard Pennington. "He worked with me and took time to help me. He spent more time helping others than he did himself. If anybody called him, he'd go."

It turns out when you're as large in both stature and influence as John Westbrook, dying does not have to end life. Westbrook's legacy of good works and concern for others continues, just as he would have wanted it.

Note

1. All quotes in this article are from Richard Pennington, *Breaking the Ice: The Racial Integration of Southwest Conference Football* (Jefferson, North Carolina: McFarland & Company, Inc., Publishers, 1987).

Chapter 10

SECTION FOUR

Big 10
Conference
Student-Athlete
Trailblazers

Moses Fleetwood Walker

First African-American Student-Athlete at the University of Michigan

by Stacy Martin

Moses Fleetwood Walker was a jack-of-all-trades and a master of baseball. Along his journey, Walker faced incredible misfortune. He was born in Mount Pleasant, Ohio, a town of silent train whistles and peaceful salvation, in 1857. Mount Pleasant's Quaker population was an important proponent of the Underground Railroad, delivering freedom to the men and women escaping slavery in nearby West Virginia. This pleasant beginning, full of amicable race relations, built a powerful platform for Walker at an early age.

His family moved to Steubenville, Ohio, where his father, Dr. Moses W. Walker, took on prominent roles in the community, becoming one of the state's first African-American physicians and later serving as a spiritual leader through ministry. Dr. Walker was a powerful and highly respected leader who had wealth to accompany his social stature. He learned the game of baseball from Civil War soldiers after the war in Steubenville and taught the game to his children in their youth. His children were educated in black schools as well as the integrated Steubenville High School and went on to pursue higher education after graduation. Fleet Walker's perception of the African-American race and its relationship with its white counterparts grew stronger and more favorable because of his upbringing and experiences in the bustling community of Steubenville.

In turn, he selected a college that supported the values of equity that had become a part of him throughout his life. By 1878, Oberlin College valued the contributions of women and African-Americans so highly that it had become nationally renowned for its open admission policies. Walker began his academic career with solid achievements in the classroom, but college opened his eyes to interests outside of the studies to which he was accustomed. The game of baseball captured more and more of his interest and time. During Walker's early years, Oberlin College fielded intra-squad games. Walker took the game of baseball to places it had never been on Oberlin's campus with his powerful homeruns, namely through a window of Cabinet Hall hundreds of feet from the meager field where the team played. In the spring of 1881, Oberlin decided to form the first intercollegiate team in school history, a baseball squad led by Walker.

Walker hit homeruns with ease and played impeccable defense. In the early days of baseball, catchers caught pitchers' fastballs bare handed. Walker, with his hands of steel and rocket arm, was the best catcher in his day. He attracted the attention of the University of Michigan, which had suffered defeat at the hands of the Oberlin team. The Wolverines needed a catcher, and Walker needed to transfer from Oberlin, the school he loved. He had studied a variety of disciplines while at Oberlin and, given his flawless oratory skills, thought that he might pursue law at Michigan. Law school, however, was not the sole reason for leaving Oberlin. Walker's girlfriend, Arabella Taylor, was pregnant, and although Oberlin was liberal, it was not liberal enough to accept a child conceived out of wedlock. They both transferred to Michigan after deciding that the school would be a better fit for their family. Fleet's brother, Weldy, transferred to Michigan to play as well.

Walker's transfer was not easily orchestrated and seemed to have an undertone of racial prejudice. One thing was clear: outside influence was necessary to ensure his future in baseball. Soon after Walker's arrival on the Ann Arbor campus, the university president asked Walker to stop taking classes. Rumors had surfaced that Walker might not have honestly prepared for a test, and so President Angell at Michigan requested a character assessment of Walker from Oberlin's President Fairchild. Luckily, Arthur Packard, the Oberlin pitcher who had transferred with Walker to Michigan, took it upon himself to write a letter persuading President Fairchild to offer his support to Walker. A student's opinion rarely speaks so loudly to a university president. Packard's word carried the volume of his father, Jasper Packard, a distinguished Civil War general and United States congressman. Although the words spoken between Angell and Fairchild are unknown, Walker resumed classes and began his baseball career as a Michigan Wolverine. The team was grateful and gained significant favorable press in the student newspaper throughout the season, including several positive remarks on the impact Walker had on the win-loss record. Strangely enough, Walker's race was rarely mentioned. Whether it was omitted because it lacked importance or out of fear that it would matter too much to segregationist baseball supporters is only speculation.

The lines between college and professional play were blurred during those days just as the lines between amateur and professional are in some cases today. Walker's talent in baseball earned him the money he needed for tuition at Michigan, but he did not earn it in the traditional means that student-athletes know today. During the summer of 1883, Walker had to play ball for the Toledo Blue Stockings to earn enough money for law school tuition. The next year, the Blue Stockings became sanctioned by the American Association of the Major Leagues, so Moses Fleetwood Walker broke the color barrier almost 63 years before Jackie Robinson played for the Dodgers.

Walker's career followed a tragic path. He played for several teams between 1884 and 1889. When he was ready to leave the game in 1889, he was the only remaining African-American player. This period of integration in the game lasted briefly, and while it lasted the players faced horrible situations, including some white players' refusal to play, boos and trash thrown by fans, denial of hotel service, and the general disparagement that accompanied any person of color during that era. Despite his outstanding play, Walker was no exception, and these circumstances took their toll on the first and last African-American of baseball's early days. He caught for pitchers like Tony Mullane, who never threw the pitch Walker called. In the days without baseball gloves, a pitcher choosing his own pitches made a catcher's job extremely difficult. In 1887, for the New Jersey team, Walker caught for one of the all-time great African-American pitchers, George Stovey, a lefthander who was almost impossible to hit. He played in front of visiting fans who cheered for Walker despite their own team's white players refusing to play against Walker. Walker also played in front of fans that hissed and spit at him as he strode to the plate. He became disillusioned with the game he had come to love, and even his hope for peace between the races had faded into oblivion. Finally, the end came when the owners realized their power. A gentleman's agreement was made that resulted in a diamond full of white players for the next 63 years, until Jackie crossed the line that Walker had breached decades earlier.

Walker's disillusionments and brilliant talents led him down a different path after baseball, one that was successful and tormented at the same time. After ending his baseball career in Syracuse, Walker remained in the city and was admired by most for his career with the Syracuse Stars. One evening a group of white men confronted Walker as he was walking home. Hostile words were shouted by the men and Walker believed that an altercation was looming. Walker feared for his life because he was so outnumbered and pulled a knife out to defend himself. After taking a blow to the head, Walker fatally stabbed one of his attackers, Patrick Murray, in the groin. Walker was able to escape the rest of the men, but the police caught up to him, placing him under arrest. Walker stood trial for second-degree murder charges. Once again a number of people stood up on his behalf to affirm the goodness of his character. An all-white jury cleared Walker of all charges against him. The crowd roared just as it had when he swung the baseball bat for a homerun. Unfortunately, this experience would only support Walker's jaded feelings and resentment about race relations.

Walker returned to the serenity that he knew in Steubenville and the support of his brother Weldy. The brothers purchased the Union Hotel in Steubenville and several movie theatres in the surrounding area. Walker was an intelligent man who could apply unique thought to most any situation, and his experience with the motion picture industry led him to apply for patents on some of his ingenious designs. His thoughtful but tormented nature also led him to the innovation of a type of artillery shell for which he also received a patent. His thoughts spurred not only inventions, but also newspapers and a book full of suggestions on race relations. Walker and his brother Weldy published a newspaper, *The Equator*, which told the stories of the African-American community, addressing both its causes and challenges. Sadly no copies of the publication survive in their original form.

In 1904, Walker moved to Cadiz, Ohio, with his wife, Ednah, and purchased an opera house on West Market Street, a building that remains standing today. He still suffered from the despair he felt regarding race relations in America. He felt that racism was an intrinsic trait and thus any harmony would be defeated by this inevitable hatred. In 1908, he bound his determined thoughts into a 47-page book titled *Our Home Colony: A Treatise on the Past, Present, and Future of the Negro Race in America*. The conclusions set forth by Walker included thoughts such as, "The only practical and permanent solution of the present and future race troubles in the United States is entire separation by Emigration of the Negro from America," and "The Negro race will be a menace and the source of discontent as long as it remains in large numbers of the United States."

Walker's peaceful childhood and friendly experiences with his white classmates set a stage for a man to embrace the differences and celebrate the human race no matter the skin color. The torment he suffered throughout his travels and baseball career only crumbled those idealistic thoughts. At the end of his life, Walker was a desperate man who thought the only right answer would be mass emigration—or rather no answer at all, just a removal of the problem from within the borders. Although Walker lost hope for a progressive, amicable solution to American race relations, the improvements that exist more than 100 years later are a tribute to his vision, heroism, and pioneering spirit.

Frederick Douglass Patterson

First African-American Student-Athlete at The Ohio State University

by Stacy Martin

Not only was Frederick Douglass Patterson the first African-American student-athlete at The Ohio State University but he also subsequently started and owned the country's first and only African-American automobile manufacturing company.

Although The Ohio State University has long been known for its dominance on the football field, history was truly made when Frederick Douglass Patterson played football for the Buckeyes in 1891. The football program had gotten off to a humble beginning in 1889 with practices and friendly intra-squad match-ups. Ohio State slated its first real game, against Ohio Wesleyan University, for the 1891 season. After Fred Patterson joined the team that year, the Buckeyes set a precedent for the winning history they would eventually achieve. They easily defeated Ohio Wesleyan in the inaugural game. Patterson played for two more seasons and completed his education after just three years. He left Ohio State and, ironically, taught history in Kentucky for three years. Patterson undoubtedly left a lasting impression on The Ohio State University athletic program, but it was not the first time in his life that he changed history, and it was certainly not the last.

Patterson's story really begins in Greenfield, Ohio, with the roots of his family and their many accomplishments. Charles Rich Patterson, Fred's father, escaped slavery in West Virginia, where he practiced the craft of blacksmithing for his white owners. The details of his attempt at freedom are unknown, with the exception that it occurred just before the Civil War. Greenfield, Ohio, was a harbor of safety for runaway slaves during that time and had several ties to the Underground Railroad. C. R. Patterson put his blacksmith skills to use at a local carriage company, and his knowledge of the craft soon earned him leadership responsibility. By 1873, C. R. Patterson had entered into a business partnership with a white gentleman by the name of J. P. Lowe. His partnership with Lowe ended almost ten years later, as a result of Lowe's death. Lowe bequeathed his share of their business to Patterson, thus making him the carriage company's sole proprietor. The Patterson family had established a tremendous legacy, from slavery to business ownership, through hard work and the kindness of others. Patterson went on to produce 28 types of horse-drawn carriages. His sons Frederick Douglass and Samuel became fine mechanics, contributing to the design and construction of several vehicles. The company became known as C. R. Patterson and Son Carriage Company.

Fred not only contributed to the family business, but also found time to study and play a new game called football. He followed the family example of hard work and made his own place in history by graduating high school in 1888, becoming the first African-American to do so in the small town of Greenfield. Three years had gone by before he played at Ohio State, but he spent that time perfecting his craft and dedicating his time to the family business. After leaving Ohio State and then Kentucky, Patterson returned home to Greenfield and the family business in 1897.

The Patterson family had suffered the loss of their son Samuel in 1888, so Fred was the likely successor. He began to direct the company more as time passed. The company had secured its place in the carriage market and performed quite well, but automobiles were becoming more prominent. Fred Patterson took notice of this trend and took steps to move the company into position to compete with the changing times and new competitors. His first step involved a sales trip with his sales manager to understand the needs of consumers. It was evident to him that the company needed to manufacture automobiles. He reported to the board his bold recommendation for change. Patterson dared to build a vehicle that was easily driven and superior to any other automobile in comfort.

The company differentiated its product lines with the automobile manufacturing process, but it continued to remain profitable in the carriage line of business. The early advertisements characterized the car as far superior to Henry Ford's Model T with cantilever springs, electric starting, and a split windshield. Continental provided the 4-cylinder engine, with power equal to 40 horses, which could carry the horseless carriage at speeds close to 50 miles per hour. The Patterson-Greenfield model made history for its quality and earned the Patterson family another first; they became the country's first and only African-American automobile manufacturer. Patterson produced two passenger automobile models, a two-door coupe and a four-door touring model. Each could be purchased for $850.

Although Patterson's models were advertised to be better than Henry Ford's, Ford capitalized with his invention of the assembly line and dominated the market with mass production. Patterson again diversified his product line by producing custom bodies for school buses and delivery trucks. The Patterson bus and truck bodies were mounted on other manufacturers' chassis, until the company shifted to an all-steel body model in 1930. C. R. Patterson and Son Carriage Company had come a long way in its history, from slavery to success, and from carriage to automobile. In the 1930s the Patterson vehicles lined the streets of Cincinnati, Ohio, and traveled all the way to Haiti as public transportation. Unfortunately, the Great Depression and Detroit's dominance over the market finally became too much for the Pattersons' company to bear, and they closed their doors in 1939.

Although the company's doors may have closed, Fred Patterson and his family opened many doors throughout their history. The Patterson family capitalized on an opportunity through hard work and commitment. Fred brought a unique sense of innovation to the family and the company. His forethought and creativity enabled the company to offer several designs in the carriage line, and they ushered in a new line of business with automobiles to help the company compete. It is likely that his impetus for change led him to excel in other aspects of his life, such as becoming the first African-American to graduate from the local high school and the first African-American student-athlete at The Ohio State University. His experience at Ohio State might not have been enough to change minds immediately, but it may have helped to set the stage for Ohio State's Jesse Owens and his daring feats against racism on a worldly scope.

Preston Eagleson

First African-American Student-Athlete at Indiana University

by Stacy Martin

Preston Eagleson came from a common man's lifestyle, yet he pondered extraordinary thoughts and accomplished feats during his brief life that would change the common lifestyle for every African-American. Eagleson's meager childhood in rural Indiana could not have foretold the powerful legacy that he would leave. His father, Halson V. Eagleson, moved the family to Bloomington so that his children would be educated and have the chance to attend Indiana University (IU). A barber by trade, Halson raised his five children to believe in the power of education. Preston Eagleson graduated from Bloomington High School and pursued his educational advancement at IU in the fall of 1892.

Eagleson began studying philosophy but thoughts and concepts alone were not enough to satisfy him. After his freshman year, Eagleson tried his athletic talents on the football field. He thrilled the Hoosier fans with his versatility and skill as an athlete. Primarily he played left halfback, but he also could play right halfback, dodging defenders as he ran for a touchdown. Additionally, Eagleson showcased his talents on special teams as a punter.

American football in 1893 was a sport for the macho and daring at heart. In those days a player donned his school's colors on his back, but wore nothing for protection on his head. The National Football League did not mandate helmets in their present-day form until the 1940s. A few players who were tired of head injuries fashioned their own headwear to protect their ears or covered their hair with some form of leather. It was decades before someone decided to add padding for protection from concussions. As a halfback, Eagleson would have taken a brutal number of hits, since the object of the game is to defend the goal line from the other team's ball carrier. Eagleson's aptitude for thought likely aided his performance on the athletic field since he would gather a deep understanding of the opposing team's defense and pair it with a winning strategy for his team. His speed helped him execute his plan in a quick, decisive manner.

Eagleson's playing time lasted three years, and it was not without challenges. He first faced adversity on his own practice field from white players who thought that they could remove Eagleson from their game with a perfectly timed hit. They planned to coordinate their hits, to be executed during practice, so that Eagleson's body could not withstand the impact of both a high hit and a low block simultaneously. Another of Eagleson's teammates, however, had a conscientious and compassionate nature, and he warned Eagleson before practice. These ill-mannered men were no match for Eagleson's swiftness, and they hit each other instead.

Eagleson's torment only escalated when the team traveled outside the soft-rolling hills of Southern Indiana. Crawfordsville, Indiana, was located northeast of Indianapolis and, according to the census, has had a dominant white population. An elevator service operator there denied Eagleson access to the elevator during the Indiana University football team's hotel stay. Although this injustice may not seem surprising, it was actually so unexpected locally that a judge later fined the elevator operator, awarding Eagleson a compensation of $50. The resolution was remarkable, but no amount of money could make a man feel whole after being denigrated in front of his peers.

Eagleson was befriended by many of his teammates and respected for his talents and commitment to education. The comfort of friendship could offer only so much protection from threatening remarks on team road trips, though. During one away game at Butler University, Eagleson drew a significant number of hard hits from the defense and faced even greater bodily harm, according to the threats shouted from the stands. Prejudice prevailed during that game, but Eagleson maintained his composure and his teammates remained protective.

The experiences that Preston Eagleson faced on the athletic fields had a significant impact his daily life, allowing him to gain a deeper understanding of his fellow man and the society in which he lived. Eagleson may have run for touchdowns on the football field but his success did not end at the goal line. He was an accomplished student, as well, and entered philosophical and educational battles to demonstrate his oratory talents. In 1895, Eagleson entered The Primary Contest in which individuals demonstrated their oratory skills and speech-writing capabilities. Eagleson dominated his competition with a pristine oration regarding Abraham Lincoln. The judges complimented Eagleson on his well-thought-out preparation and supreme conveyance of the topic at hand. He was The Primary's winner and went on to attend a statewide competition in Indianapolis, where he placed fourth. His talents earned him a bachelor's degree in philosophy in 1896. Eagleson became the first African-American student-athlete to graduate from Indiana University and only the second African-American to graduate from IU following Marcellus Neal.

Four of Eagleson's five siblings followed him to IU; three graduated and two went on to earn their PhDs. One of his siblings, Halson Eagleson, earned his PhD in physics. He also survived a terrifying kidnapping by three white university students nearly 26 years after Preston played for Indiana. The students admitted that they wanted to keep Halson off the football field during the marching band's performance at the halftime of the Indiana-Purdue rivalry game. A jury acquitted the white students of kidnapping.

In 1906, Preston Eagleson earned another prestigious honor from his alma mater when he became the first African-American to be awarded a master's degree. Eagleson delivered his thesis, "Emerson's Wider View of the Education of Man," to earn his master's in philosophy. Preston Eagleson's pursuit of education predates by more than a century the ignorant claims made by xenophobes that African-Americans lack intelligence.

An African-American man from a small farming community in Indiana, Eagleson attended a university, helped his siblings gain an education, and continued to impress upon his own children the importance of education. His daughter, Elizabeth Eagleson Bridgewaters, graduated from Indiana University in 1930, and his son, Wilson V. Eagleson, graduated from IU and strengthened the family's academic legacy by marrying the first female African-American IU graduate, Frances Marshall. Preston Eagleson's descendants are still heavily involved in the Neal Marshall Education Center, honoring the countless contributions that African-Americans have made to Indiana University over the years. Marcellus Neal, Preston Eagleson, and Frances Marshall struggled to forge a path to enlightenment, and more than 13,000 African-American youths have followed their trail through Indiana University's doors. Eagleson demonstrated a belief in education, a commitment to preparation, and an attitude of determination. Society would do well to follow "Eagleson's Views Concerning the Education of Man and Pursuit of Equality" into the future.

Carleton W. "Kinney" Holbrook

First African-American Student-Athlete at the University of Iowa

by Jenny Brenden

There may be a question as to how Carleton Holbrook became a member of the Iowa football team, but there is no question as to the vital role he played in bringing the first conference championship to the University of Iowa. Holbrook was born in 1874 in Tipton, Iowa, and would eventually become a star athlete in his home state. He reached this status through his role as the first African-American student-athlete at the University of Iowa. Holbrook pioneered as a dual-sport athlete, participating in both football and track and field. Although the Iowa football program had experienced some difficult years, Holbrook was able to help them achieve some measure of success.

The University of Iowa football program has a very long history, dating back to 1889. As is often the case, the program experienced some growing pains early on. Eventually, though, it was able to overcome obstacles and become a Big Ten football powerhouse. In the Hawkeyes' first three seasons, the team was not affiliated with any particular conference and played as an "independent." In addition to being an independent team, the squad had no official head coach. The 1892 season introduced Iowa's first official head coach, E. A. Dalton, and also introduced Iowa into the Western Inter-State University Football Conference.

The 1893 and 1894 seasons each saw new head coaches, but in 1895 the Iowa Hawkeyes football team, in an attempt to save money, was without a coach once again. Being coach-less, however, was not the greatest concern for the team. The school came close to not fielding a football team at all because of a lack of funds. The school's athletic board required that the team pay off its debts before it would be recognized officially as a school entity. Emergency fundraising actions were taken, and there was an official Iowa football team in 1895. This was the year that Carleton Holbrook had the opportunity to join Iowa football.

The highlight of that season was the team's mere existence, as the squad's 2-5 record didn't give Iowa fans much to cheer about. This embarrassing display prompted Iowa officials to hire A. E. Bull, a former Ivy League star from Pennsylvania. The new coach lived up to expectations, and in his first year as head coach he brought home the Western Inter-State University Football Conference championship, largely due to his senior super-star, Carleton Holbrook. Holbrook may have possessed these skills the previous year, but the order and discipline of a head coach was needed to allow the young man to reach his full potential.

In his senior season in 1896, Holbrook was Iowa's best ball carrier, but he was also known as one of the best halfbacks in the west. Holbrook was a stellar sprinter, and the speed that he gained by participating in track and field only made him a better football player. His speed was a benefit on both sides of the ball, as Holbrook was also Iowa's best defensive man. Opposing teams knew that Holbrook was the star of the Iowa team, but not all were accepting of his race.

Iowa started off the season strong by defeating Drake 32-0, which included four rushing touchdowns for Holbrook. A few games later the Hawkeyes beat conference rival Kansas to break their conference losing streak. The Hawkeyes had been winless in conference games the previous year. The 1896 contest against another conference rival, Missouri, would prove to be a very hateful game. Before the game was even played, Missouri alumni demanded that Iowa play without their star player because he was African-American. Coach Bull refused to adhere to the demand and insisted that Holbrook would be in the line-up on game day. Although the alumni were not able to force the issue, they made their voices and their opinions heard loud and clear when Iowa came to play in Columbia, Missouri. People mobbed the hotel where the Iowa football team was staying, and they seemed to follow team members wherever they were in public. There were shouts of "The Tigers will kill the Negro" among other things. This hatred was also evident in the game. With encouragement from the crowd, the Missouri players proceeded to play a brutal, unsportsmanlike game, with plenty of late hits and cheap blows. After disagreeing with a call, one Missouri player even went so far as punching one of the officials.

With all of the tension and rough play, the Iowa teammates remained cool and collected. They restrained themselves from retaliation and let skillful play do the talking. The Hawkeyes rallied behind their leader as Holbrook continued simply to dominate the game, unshaken by the harsh treatment. Iowa got its revenge by winning that game 12-0, with Holbrook rushing for one of the two Hawkeye touchdowns. In the following years, Iowa refused to play Missouri. The two teams would not face each other again until 1902.

The last game of the 1896 season pitted the Hawkeyes (6-1) against Nebraska for the conference championship. The big game was postponed for two days due to bad weather, but Iowa went on to defeat Nebraska 6-0 and earn the school's first conference championship. It seemed fitting that Carleton Holbrook scored the game's only touchdown, bringing his season total to 12.

Carleton Holbrook joined a list of amazing pioneers at Iowa, one of the first schools to have an African-American on a varsity athletic team—in 1895. The university was founded in 1847 and in 1855 Iowa became the first public university to admit men and women on an equal basis. It was also one of the first institutions in America to grant a law degree to a woman, Mary B. Hickey Wilkinson, in 1873, and to an African-American, G. Alexander Clark, in 1879.

Regardless of Iowa's pioneering status, not all of these African-Americans were treated with the respect that they deserved while attending the university. African-American athletes were allowed on collegiate playing fields years before they were fully welcomed to participate in the professional ranks. The University of Iowa was one of the first pubic institutions to integrate their athletic teams. However, in those early years the African-American athletes had to sleep in the Field House, because the housing administration would not allow them to stay with the white student-athletes and would not provide them with their own housing.

The fact that African-Americans were allowed to participate in athletics at the University of Iowa was a very positive step, but those athletes still lacked many of the privileges common to other student-athletes. Holbrook was strong enough to overcome the additional obstacles that were placed before him because of his skin color. Ted Wheeler was another African-American athlete who ran track at Iowa, over 50 years after Holbrook had broken the color barrier.

Unfortunately, half of a century had not drastically improved race relations at the university. He recognized what those who came before him had to endure in order to represent the school athletically. "All these guys played in spite of the difficulties of being in the classroom under pressure, being in football, sleeping in the Field House, not being able to live in the dorm, getting good grades and were good citizens," Wheeler said. "It's a battlefield of sorts."[1] Carleton Holbrook waged that battle and gave many others the strength to do the same.

Note

1. Alex Johnson, "Breaking Through the Barriers," *The Daily Iowan*, May 1, 2007, http://media.www.dailyiowan.com/media/storage/paper599/news/2007/05/01/Sports/Breaking.Through.The.Barriers-2889432.shtml (accessed on June 20, 2007).

Julian Ware and Adelbert Richard Matthews

First African-American Student-Athletes at the University of Wisconsin

by Horacio Ruiz

Baseball is a dead sport at the University of Wisconsin. In 1991, the university dropped the baseball program to become the only Big Ten school not represented in the sport. Considering the historical significance the program has played in the university's athletic development, the loss of the baseball program is certainly a great one. Baseball was the first intercollegiate sport at the university and also became the first varsity sport at Wisconsin to field African-American players. Julian Ware and Adelbert Richard Matthews were the first African-American student-athletes in Wisconsin's history, playing baseball at the turn of the 20th century, only 35 years removed from the end of the Civil War and 60 years before the American Civil Rights Movement.

Ware would go on to become the first African-American to captain a Big Ten team when his teammates elected him to carry the honor in both 1902 and 1903. Ware's career and life after 1903 are unknown, but it's well established (in spite of the fact that schools at that time did little record keeping) that Ware was widely respected as both a leader and an athlete by his peers. Playing in his first year in 1900, Ware won the first base job and particularly stood out with his offensive power. Ware would normally bat clean-up and, in an era without fences, he led the team in triples in 1901 and 1902. In a game against Dixon College during his first season, Ware slid for third base on his way to collecting another triple when he suffered an injury severe enough to keep him out for the remainder of the year. He came back in 1901 to reclaim his spot at first base. In 1902 he was elected team captain, becoming not just the first African-American captain in the Big Ten but one of the first in the country in any intercollegiate sport.

The 1902 season would be the most remarkable of Ware's career as the newly elected captain led Wisconsin to its first Big Ten base-ball championship. Ware was not alone in leading his team toward the championship that year. Adelbert Matthews started that champi-onship season by pitching the Badgers to a victory versus Milwau-kee's professional minor league team in an exhibition game. That year, Wisconsin would go 8-4, including a Big Ten record of 5-1 to capture the conference title. Matthews had developed into one of Wisconsin's most reliable arms. Although student newspapers doc-umented that he sometimes struggled with his control, when Matthews put his game together he was nearly untouchable. In a 1901 game against Northwestern, the student newspaper, the *Daily Cardinal*, commented that Matthews was "almost invincible." Later that year he would strike out 10 batters against the University of Chicago. The year of the Big Ten championship, Matthews was on the mound for two of the Badgers' conference victories, also picking up a win on the road against Notre Dame.

Ironically, the championship year would be the pinnacle of both men's collegiate baseball careers. Matthews moved to Chicago and did not finish what would have been his senior year in the 1902–1903 academic term. Matthews caught the attention of a baseball promoter and manager who hired him as a pitcher for the Union Giants, an all African-American team. His most notable appearance came when he pitched an entire 16-inning game that finished in a 0-0 tie for a semi-pro team in Kanakee, Illinois. Matthews pitched until after the 1905 season when he opened up his own barbershop. He worked in his shop until 1924, when he was appointed as an inspector by the Illi-nois State Department of Education and Registration. He worked in this capacity until 1938, when he died in his home in Chicago.

Unlike Matthews, Ware returned to Wisconsin in 1903 with high hopes. He was again elected captain, and in his first game of the year versus the University of Dubuque, he starred by hitting a homerun. It would, however, be the final game of his career. Ware was behind on his school work and sacrificed his playing time in order to catch up with his "shop work" and complete his electrical engineering de-gree. The baseball team waited for him, but reluctantly replaced him as captain midway through a losing season. Frustrated by the way the season had unfolded, several players refused to travel to a sched-uled game in Illinois late in the year. Ware, no longer playing but still concerned about his teammates, heard that players were refusing to travel. He quickly rounded up nine players to make the trip to Illinois and fulfill their obligation.

The *Daily Cardinal* documented the event, "This action so disgusted former captain Ware that he hustled out nine ball players and led them to Coach Bandelin's room at 606 Frances Street. It was long after the midnight hour that the Coach was awakened by the call: 'Bandelin, here are nine men for you to take to Champaign.'"[1]

Unfortunately, Ware was not able to complete his school work and did not receive his degree in the spring of 1903. Nothing is known about what he did after leaving Madison. Wisconsin would not have another African-American baseball player until infielder Frank Burks joined the Badger squad in 1960.

In February 2007, the University of Wisconsin created a web site and ran commercials featuring prominent Badger athletes in celebration of Black History Month and in honor of the first African-American athletes at the school. Women's basketball player Janese Banks read a script during the commercial that recognized both Matthews and Ware, cementing a connection among Wisconsin's African-American athletes, both male and female, spanning more than 100 years.

Note

1. UWBadgers.com, "Julian Vivian Ware," Celebrating Black History, http://www.uwbadgers.com/history/cel_bhist/matthews_bio_331.html (accessed May 1, 2007).

Roy Young and Hiram Wheeler

First African-American Student-Athletes at the University of Illinois

by Stacy Martin

Athletics participation proved difficult for African-Americans as society struggled to accept them as equal members of the human race. There were times when society's perceptions dictated the acceptance of African-Americans on playing fields, and there were times when athletics exerted its own influence. In the early 1900s, society's opinion often mattered heavily. African-American athletes had enjoyed early success in some of the professional leagues, but it was the liberal minds at some educational institutions that opened many of the doors to African-American athletes. Oberlin College helped Moses Fleetwood Walker start his career in baseball, and there were many other such colleges in the North. The University of Illinois opened its locker rooms to Roy Young and Hiram Wheeler in 1904 as they prepared to play football for the Fighting Illini that season.

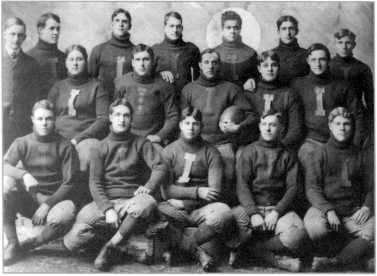

Roy Young with the 1904 Illinois University football team.

Courtesy of the University of Illinois.

Young was a skilled football player and quickly proved his talent during the 1904 season. He played tackle, and his dominance of the position quieted most of the racial comments. However, he still faced his share of society's ills. Young attended Illinois from 1903 to 1907 and pursued a degree in civil engineering, but unfortunately he fell short of that goal. He earned two varsity letters for his performance on the football field in 1904 and 1905. Young also had a teammate, Hiram Wheeler, to share both the burden and the celebration of becoming the first African-American athletes at Illinois.

Wheeler competed on the same 1904 and 1905 squads as Young, but he served only as a second-string quarterback or halfback. His performance is unknown, but his time was likely as turbulent as any other African-American athlete challenging a white man on the athletic field during those times. Wheeler earned distinction at Illinois for becoming the university's first two-sport athlete. In the spring, Wheeler demonstrated his speed on the track, since he wasn't provided the opportunity on the football field. In 1904, he also became the school's first African-American athlete to win the 100-yard dash. His winning time was 10.6 seconds, and the winning points earned him a varsity letter that year. Wheeler studied agriculture while at Illinois, but no degree was awarded.

Young and Wheeler were the first African-American athletes at the University of Illinois, and while their experiences failed to earn prestigious awards or educational degrees, it is still important to recognize the path that they identified for other African-Americans. George Thomas Kyle followed their blazing trail in 1924 when he competed on the track team in the 75-yard dash. His performance did not break records, but did earn him second place in the Notre Dame Relays. He earned a bachelor of arts in liberal arts and sciences in 1926. In 1930 he completed work for a master of arts in psychology. Thus, he joined Young and Wheeler as being among the first African-American student-athletes at University of Illinois. Kyle was the first African-American student-athlete to earn a college degree for the Fighting Illini. Being first usually requires a great deal of strength and bravery and yet sometimes returns little other than heartaches and difficulty. It is this selfless act that earns individuals such as Young, Wheeler, and Kyle the admiration of all who follow.

Bobby "Rube" Marshall

First African-American Football Player at the University of Minnesota

by Jenny Brenden

Bobby Marshall, more affectionately known as "Rube," was an all-star athlete at the turn of the 20th century. Marshall was a standout on the University of Minnesota football team. He also played first base on the baseball team and lettered in track, as well as participating in hockey and boxing. One hundred years later this list of involvements and accomplishments would be an impossible feat. Not only was Marshall a phenomenal all-around athlete, he also broke barriers by being the first African-American to play football for the Gophers and in the Big Nine Conference, which would later develop into today's Big Ten Conference.

Marshall's individual ability and success directly contributed to the success of any team he played for. The years that Marshall was a part of the Gopher football team, 1904–1906, the squad went 13-0, 10-1 and 4-1, for a combined record of 27-2. In addition, the team outscored its opponents 1,238-63. In the 29 games in which Marshall participated, the average score would have been 42-2. Although such an average is uncommon, Minnesota was a powerhouse football team. Marshall excelled at his end position on the field, and he also had quite an impressive kicking leg. In the days when field goals were worth four points, Marshall once kicked a 60-yard field goal to beat the Gophers' opponent 4-2.

Born in Milwaukee, Wisconsin, Marshall moved to Minneapolis and attended Central High before moving on to the University of Minnesota. The university—and college football as a whole—honored Bobby Marshall in 1971, when he was officially inducted into the College Football Hall of Fame. Marshall passed away in 1958, so he was represented by his family when he was inducted during halftime of a Gopher football game.

When Marshall attended the university, segregation had yet to be enforced by law, allowing African-Americans both to attend the school and to participate on its athletic teams. The full fury of racism had not yet emerged, but Marshall and his fellow African-American students still endured racial stereotyping and degrading racial slurs. Even his status as a standout football player did not protect Marshall from insult and ridicule. In one of the Gophers' annual publications, Marshall was described as a "lank-limbed child of sunny Ethiopia." Because of the limited number of African-Americans attending the university, racial problems were fairly isolated, but as the number of African-American students grew over the years, so did the tension. Even though Marshall was the only African-American on the football team, the team did exhibit some diversity, with a Jewish quarterback and a Native American lineman accompanying the rest of the typically white roster.

Marshall was not only a great athlete, but an outstanding student as well. He studied law at the university and graduated with his law degree in 1907, but there was not a great demand in Minneapolis for African-American lawyers. He did open a law office but decided to turn his focus to sports, an arena that afforded him many more opportunities than his legal work.

After college, Marshall stepped away from football and began playing baseball for the all-black St. Paul Gopher baseball team, along with another great player of that era, William Binga. This team would eventually be known as the greatest African-American baseball team in Minnesota history. Marshall also had short stints with two other Minneapolis professional teams—the Deans and the Marines. After a few years, Marshall had the opportunity to play baseball nationally and traveled all over the country after accepting an offer to play with the Chicago Leland Giants. His time spent on the Chicago team was brief. He soon moved back to his home state, where he joined the Otto A. Pitzke and Franklin law firm and later practiced with the office of Nash and Armstrong.

After resettling in Minnesota, Marshall married. He and his wife, Irene, had four children. Sports continued to be an important part of his life, and from 1912 to 1930 Marshall played, administered, or coached baseball teams. He retired from the sport in 1938 and was arguably the best athlete to come out of the state of Minnesota. In the midst of his baseball-playing and coaching career, Marshall pursued a career in professional football. He continued to follow the trail of opportunity, making history in every stage of his life.

Professional football originated in 1869, and the league had teetered back and forth on the issues of integration and segregation.

In the beginning, African-Americans were not permitted to play in the league. That changed in 1902 when Charles Follis played for the Shelby Athletic Club. In 1919 the league developed its first governing body, the American Professional Football Association (APFA), which would evolve into the organization that exists today, the National Football League (NFL). Also in 1919, Bobby Marshall signed to play tight end for the Rock Island Independents. Another African-American, Frederick "Fritz" Pollard, also signed with the Akron Pros. Because both men were on teams when the league made the transition to the NFL, both are known as the first African-Americans to play in the NFL. Marshall also played one year for a team in Duluth, Minnesota. Throughout the 1920s, many African-Americans played and excelled in the AFPA and the NFL, but in 1933, the league banned African-American players. Thirteen years later, in 1946, the league was integrated once again and African-American players made an immediate impact on professional football.

In the mid-1920s, Marshall retired from the game of football at the age of 44 but came out of retirement six years later to play in an exhibition game at Nicollet Park in Minneapolis. Playing in a professional football game at the age of 50, regardless of whether it's an exhibition or regular-season status, is a very impressive feat. His retirement from baseball came a few years later. One can't help but admire and appreciate the athletic career that Bobby "Rube" Marshall forged, as well as the advancements that he was a part of in both college and professional sports.

Cumberland Posey, Jr.

First African-American Student-Athlete at The Pennsylvania State University

by Jessica Bartter

He was a standout basketball and baseball player, manager, and team owner. Eventually he was inducted into the Baseball Hall of Fame. Some may know him as Charles Cumbert, others as Cum Posey; some know him as the great Penn State basketball player, and others remember him as the great Duke of Duquesne University baseball. All consider him invaluable to the Negro Baseball Leagues. He was born Cumberland Willis Posey, Jr. but opted to use an alias in order to integrate both Penn State and Duquesne universities.

Posey was born a year and a half before the birth of basketball, but he learned at a young age to embrace the sport and is even credited with helping to make it popular in Pennsylvania's African-American community. After "basket ball" was invented by Dr. James Naismith, a physical education instructor at a YMCA in late 1891, the indoor game spread from gymnasium to gymnasium, garnering popularity.

In 1897, Penn State University adopted basketball as its first indoor, intercollegiate sport. That season consisted of two games; one away game and one home game, both against Bucknell University. They split wins. The following years saw the season grow to three games in 1898, five in 1899, and 14 in 1908. In 1910, Penn State athletics saw its first African-American student-athlete when Posey joined the basketball team.

In his first year, Posey led the freshman basketball squad to an interclass league victory when they overpowered the sophomores 27 to 5. The December 16, 1909 issue of the Penn State newspaper, *The State Collegian*, mentioned that "Mauthe and Posey, of the freshman team, excelled in gathering the points, each being credited with four baskets." After the varsity team was set with 13 members, including Posey, for the 1910–11 season, the December 8, 1910 issue of *The State Collegian* described the future of the season: "From now on, scrimmage for the team will take place three times a week, the remaining two nights will be devoted to handling the ball on the floor and running." This schedule prepared the athletes for their 14-game season. As sophomores during this season, Posey and his classmates defeated the seniors 26 to 11. Posey and teammate Rogers were again described as leading the team's scorers with three baskets each. Such interclass competitions were common, with Posey's team often emerging victorious.

The intense scrimmages and ball-handling practice paid dividends to the team's success. In their season opener, the Nittany Lions trounced Susquehanna University 41 to 9. Even though Posey did not enter the game until he was substituted in at the beginning of the second half, he led the team with four baskets. Two months later Posey earned a starting position, and Penn State crushed Albright College 50 to 9. Again, Posey led the team in scoring.

Although Posey's basketball skills were celebrated, he left Penn State after one season with the freshman squad and one year on the varsity team. The Nittany Lions suffered from the loss of their great forward, but Posey found himself following a passion for baseball. He began playing with a the Negro Leagues' Homestead Grays in 1911. He even began splitting his time as player and manager. He negotiated so many bookings for the Grays that the players were financially able to devote all of their time to the team rather than just playing weekends.

After two years on the field, Posey returned to school, closer to his hometown of Homestead, Pennsylvania, this time attending the University of Pittsburgh. Posey was already a hometown hero after leading Homestead High School to the 1908 city championship, and he continued to make a name for himself while playing for the Homestead Grays and studying chemistry and pharmacy at Pitt.

Posey's transition preceded yet another college sports career. From 1915 to 1918, Posey used the alias Charles Willis Cumbert to play baseball at Duquesne University—formerly Holy Ghost College—just a few miles away from the University of Pittsburgh.

It is not known exactly why Posey chose to use an alias at Duquesne, but historians believe it was common practice in those days to play professionally and collegiately, forcing many to use assumed names in order to compete in both realms. Collegiate sport rules have since changed accordingly, preventing such practices in modern collegiate athletes. In 1973, Posey's daughter, Ethel Posey Maddox, attributed the alias to the fact that "the Posey family was known to be black in race if not in color,"[1] referring to Posey's fair skin. Posey's light appearance and fickle residence was noted by W. Rollo Wilson in the *Pittsburgh Courier* on January 20, 1934. Wilson said, "Because he was born beyond the pale of want, Cumberland has had every educational advantage and at various times he was a student at Penn State, Holy Ghost, and Pitt. But an adventurous and turbulent spirit brooked no faculty interference with his desires and he never stayed anywhere long enough to get the recognition which might have been his."[2]

When Posey did finally decide to leave college in 1918, he returned to basketball. Since there was not a black professional basketball league for him to compete in and since the NBA was still three decades away from integration, Posey and other African-Americans started their own teams with inter-league play. Posey played with the Monticello Delaneys before organizing his own team, the Loendi Big Five, in 1919. The Loendi Big Five, named for the original term used for basketball teams because they consisted of five players, competed on a nationwide barnstorming circuit. Posey formed, operated, and played on the team, learning a great deal about the structure of organized competition. All the while, Posey continued to juggle his two passions, basketball and baseball. From 1911 to 1919, Posey remained affiliated with the Homestead Grays, first as a player, then as a field manager, and eventually in a front office position. In 1920, Posey became the principal owner. The Loendi Big Five won four straight "Colored Basketball World Championships" from 1919 to 1923. In 1925, Posey finally ended his juggling act when he chose to leave his basketball career to devote his full attention to the Homestead Grays.

The innovative owner had specific plans on how to run his franchise and is remembered for his industry smarts and entrepreneurial talent. Much of Posey's leadership skill can be attributed to the influence of his father, Cumberland Willis Posey, Sr., a prominent river man who owned several steamboats. A pioneer in his own right, Posey Sr. was the first black man in the United States to become a licensed chief engineer of a steamboat, when he was just 20 years old. Behind the strict rules and tremendous business skills of Posey Jr., the Homestead Grays dominated the Negro Leagues for years. He built an empire out of the Grays, consistently collecting a record that exceeded an .850 winning percentage including 140-13 in 1926, 163-23 in 1931, and 152-24 in 1947. The Grays were often compared to the powerhouse New York Yankees.

Posey had several future Hall of Famers on his team at all times. In 2006, 17 Negro Leaguers, including Posey himself, were inducted into Baseball's Hall of Fame. Of the 18 that had previously represented the Negro Leagues in the Hall of Fame, 11 of them had played for Posey at one time or another. He earned a reputation for invading his opponents' squads and persuading their best players to come to the Homestead Grays. In order to prevent the same from happening to him, Posey instituted set wages for his players in 1922. In a league where costs and profits were typically shared by the owners, managers, and players, Posey's guaranteed salary was revolutionary.

In charge of the schedule, Posey secured dates and opponents in communities regardless of color lines. The action of the Grays was so highly demanded that they split home games between Pittsburgh on Saturdays and Washington, D.C., on Sundays. In D.C., the Grays often garnered crowds of 25,000 to 30,000, exceeding the fan draw of the major league's Washington Senators. With the help of their hefty financial backer and co-owner, Rufus "Sonnyman" Jackson, Posey was able to initiate night games with the Grays before the major leagues did. His innovative ownership kept his bench full of talent, his stands full of fans, and his scoreboard full of wins. Posey's team won eight of nine Negro National League pennants from 1937 to 1945, including three world titles.

The year of 1945 brought much joy and sadness to the American pastime of baseball. Jackie Robinson began his breakthrough into the major leagues by signing with the Brooklyn Dodger's farm team, but that event also signaled the end of a prosperous time for the Negro Leagues. In addition, Posey's health began to deteriorate. After suffering for more than a year, and after three weeks of bed rest, he died of lung cancer on March 28, 1946, at Mercy Hospital in Pittsburgh. His death ended the 35 years—two-thirds of his life—he had spent with the Homestead Grays.

The great basketball player, great baseball player, great manager, great owner is, most importantly, remembered as a great pioneer.

Notes

1. Ocania Chalk, *Black College Sport* (New York: Dodd, Mead, January 1976), 25.
2. Ibid., 26.

Gideon Smith

First African-American Student-Athlete at Michigan State University

by Stacy Martin

There are heroes that inspire legends. These legends become a part of our culture, our history, and the fabric of our folklore. Gideon Smith was merely a student from Virginia who enjoyed playing the new sport of football in America in 1913. His academic career began at a historically black university, Hampton Institute in Virginia, which is now known as Hampton University. After graduation he still yearned to further his education and enrolled at Ferris State University in Big Rapids, Michigan. After a brief stay at Ferris, he decided to enroll at Michigan Agricultural College (MAC) in 1913 so that he could play football while attending school. Michigan Agricultural College later became Michigan State University, and Gideon Smith became the hero, the legend, and the pioneer of the university.

In 1913, the country was still segregated in many places as a result of the United States Supreme Court upholding *Plessy v. Ferguson*, giving states the right to mandate racial segregation in a separate but equal manner. Of course, the separate was never equal. Race divided people in a way that was common to the era of segregation, dictating separate sleeping quarters, hospitals, public schools, eating facilities, and most prominently, transportation. President Woodrow Wilson segregated the military service in 1913 and gave credence to separate but equal on a national level. The National Football League had not yet been formed, but the sport of football was slowly growing into the game we know today. It was a time referred to as the Progressive Era. Although some would debate the progression that occurred, there is no doubt that those years set the stage for change and societal evolution in this country. One quiet man sought a change in his life. He sought out the opportunity to play sports and further his education. Gideon Smith was the man who stepped forward and broke new ground at a then-small, Midwestern agricultural school by becoming the first African-American to play the game of football at MAC.

In a collection of writings offered by Michigan State University, a teammate of Gideon Smith tells how difficult it was for Smith to even begin practice at MAC because of his skin color. He went to the old armory to "suit up" and officials refused him. At first, Coach Macklin refused to give Smith a chance and did not allow him a "suit," or uniform. Subsequently, Chuck Duffy, a veterinarian and admirer of Smith's untapped talent, loaned Smith his suit from high school football. Smith proved his worth to Macklin and earned a spot on the team.

Smith conquered the gridiron, controlling the opposing team when he played defense. His size and work ethic were his assets. Smith had not completed any introductory traditional skills training in preparation for his first major football practice. He arrived at school determined and with raw strength from a long summer of back-breaking work in the Adirondack Mountains.

Teammates characterized his wingspan as wide enough to wrap up his whole side of the offensive line in one tackle. He seemed never to let a play get through him. Offensively, Smith was a sure thing. His size allowed him to carry the ball and defenders down the field with him toward the goal. His quiet confidence evoked a sense of calm and trust. His teammates knew that if they trusted Smith with the ball that he would score and lead them to victory when time expired.

Fans and sports writers were equally enamored with Smith's style of play and skillful execution during those games. Statistical calculation of play is a relatively new tool of the game. Almost a century ago, fans were captivated by the action and the team score rather than by individual contributions. Smith would surely have dominated the statistical leader board in tackles and touchdowns, but he did lead the headlines and news stories in his time.

His endurance was awe-inspiring. Much like a marathon runner, he kept going mile after mile. In several games, Smith never rested, defending touchdowns and scoring them in equal parts, resulting in favorable outcomes for the MAC "Aggies." His athleticism allowed him to accomplish legendary feats. His play contributed to shutout wins against Carroll College and Olivet. He also ensured his team's place in school history with its first win over the powerhouse University of Michigan Wolverines in 1913 with a 12-7 victory.

He had earned the respect of his teammates, but it was difficult for him to earn the respect of his opponents. According to papers archived in the Michigan State University Athletic Department, one of his teammates remembers how horrifying the threats against Smith were at the line of scrimmage. It never outwardly affected Smith, as he only continued his outstanding play. Luckily, football is a sport that rewards aggression and rarely punishes it, so Smith could exact his anger on the opposing team through his monstrous defensive tackles. His former teammate also marveled at how lonely and quiet Smith's struggles were when the team traveled for away games. Smith would ride in a separate car of the train and meet Coach Macklin on the platform to learn practice, game, departure times and to receive money for a hotel room and food. Coach gave him a few dollars and the schedule and sent Smith on his way alone into a strange city. No one knows what Smith's experience on away game trips was like because he walked that journey by himself. He would return to the field the next evening for the game and, for those on-field minutes, his exceptional play would overshadow his skin color. He would be equal and included, but after the final whistle blew he would return to his isolated life.

Toward the end of his career, a watch was presented to Smith by the citizens of the newly formed town of East Lansing, Michigan, for the prestige that he had brought to the university. Smith continued this dual existence, winning more football games and capturing more headlines throughout his career at Michigan Agricultural College until 1916, when he graduated. Smith earned the unique place in Michigan State University history of being both the first African-American athlete and the first African-American male student to graduate from the university then known as Michigan Agricultural College.

He later played for the Canton Bulldogs professional football team with Jim Thorpe and against the legendary Knute Rockne. The Bulldogs' coach, John Cussack, believed that Smith was the first African-American pro football player in the years before the National Football League. However, a well-known author of African-American sports history, Ocania Chalk, lists Smith as the third African-American pro football player. Regardless of whether or not he was the first, he definitely was an early leader on the path. The Canton Bulldogs won what was then referred to as the "Championship of the World" in 1916. Smith's pro football career was cut short by his enlistment in the military during World War I, but it still earned him a place in history and a charter membership in the National Football Foundation Hall of Fame.

Smith returned to Hampton University to educate African-American youth and coach football. Smith taught these young men the game of football, simultaneously providing them with the tenacity necessary not only to approach the game but also to overcome the ignorance of others. In addition to promoting learning in his facilitator role, he demonstrated his lifelong commitment to education. Smith was a man who sought out knowledge and growth. In later years, he returned to Michigan State for additional graduate classes. He then returned to Hampton to serve as an assistant athletic director until his retirement in 1955.

The walls Gideon Smith broke through did not crash loudly but, rather, they crumbled quietly in reflection of Smith's calm demeanor. He was not an outspoken advocate for equity and race relations like some; he preferred a more subtle approach that included teaching and coaching students who would shape the world in the future with their thoughts, ideas, and actions. His determination and courage in 1913 began a path at Michigan State that opened doors for African-American students and athletes. Smith quietly began the growth in enrollment of African-American students to Michigan State University by simply planting a seed in 1913, as one African-American student who enrolled in Michigan Agricultural College to play football. In 1992 Michigan State University Athletics Hall of Fame inducted Gideon Smith for his lifetime of quiet, but heroic, efforts.

Chapter 10

SECTION FIVE

Ivy
League
Student-Athlete
Leaders

William Edward White

First African-American Student-Athlete at Brown University

by Horacio Ruiz

Jackie Robinson's image is emblazoned in our minds. Jackie sliding just beneath Yogi Berra's mitt to steal home during the 1955 World Series is one of the defining images of Robinson, a reminder of his greatness as the first African-American baseball player in major league history. But just as Larry Doby, the first African-American to play in the American League, remained in Robinson's shadow despite his role in integrating the major leagues, it was believed for decades that a man named Moses Fleetwood Walker and not Robinson was in fact the first African-American major leaguer when he played for the Toledo Blue Stockings in 1884. Walker was an advocate for civil rights and became so disillusioned with race relations in the United States that in 1908, in his book, *Our Home Colony*, he advocated that all African-Americans should move back to Africa.

In 2003, though, there came a new and surprising twist: Information had come to light that a man of mixed races posing as a white man, not Moses Fleetwood Walker, was the first African-American to play Major League Baseball. The man's name was William Edward White. Although he may never have known about his achievement, recent research indicated that baseball historians knew about him but not about his racial background. On June 21, 1879, White entered a game for the Providence Grays of the National League as a substitute first baseman going 1-for-4 with a run scored and fielding 12 plays without an error. The *Chicago Tribune* reported that White "played the position with remarkable activity and skill for an amateur."[1] Despite the Grays' regular first baseman being out for a month with a broken finger, it would be the last major league game White would ever play.

At the time, White was also a first baseman for Brown University's baseball team. In that era, it was fairly common for professional clubs to borrow collegiate or amateur players as substitutes for injured regulars.

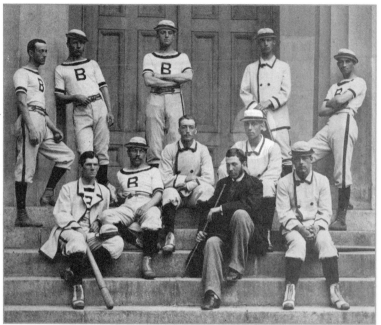

William White with the 1879 Brown University baseball team.

White's achievement may never have been known without re-search conducted by a group of individuals whose hobby is complet-ing the biographies of obscure baseball players. They are members of the Society for American Baseball Research, also known as SABR. Considered to be amateur historians, they are independent from Major League Baseball but are very much involved in devel-oping the game's history.

Peter Morris, a well-known member of SABR, contacted Civil War historian Bruce Allardice, who was from White's home state of Georgia. Allardice found that White's father was a former slave owner and his mother was one of his slaves. Brown University records indicate that White was from Milner, Georgia. In the 1870 census, the only person of his name listed was a 9-year-old mulatto boy who was one of three children living with his mother, Hannah White, listed as a mulatto woman. A. J. White, William White's fa-ther, stated in his 1877 will that his three children born from Hannah White be educated in the north.

While SABR members had known about White, they were not able to complete his profile until Allardice brought up the possibility that White may have been part African-American. In an 1880 census, White, who was at the time living in Rhode Island and attending Brown, listed himself as white. He was also listed as white in 1900 and 1910 census records, during a time when he was living in Chicago as a bookkeeper.

Soon the pieces of the puzzle began to come together. In those years, Brown University was affiliated with the Baptist church, and A. J. White had built the first Baptist church in Milner. Further, Morris remembered that another SABR colleague, John Husman, had a great-grandfather who played for Brown. Husman happened to have a photo of Brown's 1879 baseball team, which shows White behind the manager. White's skin, according to Morris, looked darker than that of his teammates. In January of 2004, Morris wanted to find a definitive link between William White and his father A. J. Already armed with census records and Husman's photograph, Morris found the link through A. J. White's will. The fourth item of the will reads: "All the balance of my Estate, both Real and Personal of Every Kind and description . . . I do hereby . . . bequeath unto William Edward White, Anna Nora White, and Sarah Adelaide White, the children of my servant Hannah." A. J. did not directly identify William as his son, but that would not be a surprise in the South, considering the times.

White's activities after 1880 remain obscure, and members of SABR have actively tried to find out more about him. Many questions remain unanswered. Why, for example, did White play in only one game? Was it because his racial background was discovered? What happened to White in those years after Brown? In any case, he was the first of a few African-American players to enjoy the freedom of playing in the major leagues before the modern, post-Jackie Robinson era.

And what about Moses Fleetwood Walker's historical significance? Walker and another pitching great named George Stovey were the initial targets of the Color Line when Cap Anson, the first professional baseball player to accumulate 3,000 career hits and one of the first men inducted into the National Baseball Hall of Fame, refused to play against any men of color.

In a July 14, 1887 game, Anson refused to play against a Newark club of the International League that had both Stovey and Walker on the roster. That day, International League owners agreed not to sign any African-American players, and the American Association and National League soon followed. By 1897, all African-American players were banned from playing in minor or major league games.

What William White began, Moses Walker could enjoy only briefly, and then it was up to men like Jackie Robinson and Larry Doby to pick up where White had started and where men like Walker left off.

Note

1. Stefan Fatsis, "Mystery of Baseball: Was William White Game's First Black?" *Wall Street Journal*, January 30, 2004.

William Henry Lewis

First African-American Student-Athlete at Harvard University

by Marcus Sedberry

In 1868, the 14th Amendment was ratified giving citizenship to ex-slaves, the first African-American, John W. Menard of Louisiana, was elected to Congress, and William E. B. DuBois was born in Great Barrington, Massachusetts. These events would shape the melting pot the United States has become. Although the other happenings were notable, 1868 would not have had the same significance without the birth of William Henry Lewis. Lewis used racial barrier breaking in sports as a transformational vehicle to pioneer in the venues of politics and law.

Between Portsmouth and Norfolk, Virginia, lies the small town of Berkley, birth place of William Henry Lewis. Born to two former slaves, Lewis grew up immediately following the American Civil War in a time when America was coping with the return of the seceded states and the status of newly freed slaves. As Lewis grew older, his father worked on the docks of Berkley and later as a Baptist minister after moving the family to Portsmouth. Ashley Henry Lewis, Williams' father, was an affranchised slave from North Carolina prior to joining the Union Army during the Civil War. He was married to Josephine Baker.

Despite his background as the son of former slaves, Lewis exemplified extraordinary educational competency. At the tender age of 15, Lewis was accepted into Virginia Normal and Collegiate Institute, Virginia's first college for African-Americans, now Virginia State University. The president of the institution was John Langston, an African-American abolitionist and lawyer. Under Langston's guidance, Lewis transferred to Amherst College in the fall of 1888. African-American students were rare in those days. However, Lewis' class had two additional African-Americans, William Tecumseh Sherman Jackson and George Washington Forbes. At Virginia Normal, sports and exercise were very limited. However, Amherst required its students to participate in athletics, and Lewis selected football, despite having to wear his street clothes in lieu of a proper uniform.

Football during this time was nearly exclusively white, as no other football team at a predominately white college had African-American players. In Lewis' sophomore year, William T. S. Jackson joined the varsity team as halfback, while Lewis was a roving center. Amherst did not win many games, so they looked for other victories, such as scoring points or trying to keep the opponent's score low. In Lewis' junior year, Amherst stunned Harvard by scoring first, and Harvard responded with 74 unanswered points. Then Amherst shocked Yale by holding it to 10 points.

During the 1890s, the captain called the plays and led the team, as coaches could not participate once the game had begun. Lewis' teammates elected him captain in his senior season, making him the first African-American to lead a predominately white football team. The 1891 season, under Lewis' leadership, brought an amazing change for Amherst. At the end of the season, Amherst tied Williams in the championship game, after tying in the regular season for the league title.

Nearly all of Amherst's Class of 1892 was white, but Lewis' race did not affect his popularity among his classmates, which included the future 30th president of the United States, Calvin Coolidge. In his junior year, Lewis' peers elected him to the student senate, and in his senior year, he was elected to give the class oration and was the president of the Hitchcock Society of Inquiry. His address was centered on a strong statement: "The Amherst Idea of liberty, fraternity and equality in the state, of purity, honesty and honor in politics, carried into life, is a panacea for every national ill." Amherst prided itself in "letting the world at large know that the color of a man's skin has no bearing whatever on the part he may take in the student or social life at Amherst College."[1]

Several African-Americans, including W. E. B. Dubois, one of the nation's most prominent African-American scholars, traveled to Boston for Lewis' graduation from Harvard Law School. Along with DuBois was Elizabeth Baker, who later became Lewis' wife and who had influenced him to attend law school at Harvard.

At this time, there were no eligibility rules in place, and Lewis subsequently became a part of the Harvard football team. During his time at Harvard he earned the respect of Caspar Whitney. Whitney selected the All-American teams, choosing Lewis for the 1892 and 1893 seasons. In his last season as a member of the Crimson, Lewis was elected captain and led his team to a surprising victory over a superior University of Pennsylvania squad. After his graduation from Harvard Law School, Lewis stayed with the football team as a defensive and line coach until 1907. As a Harvard assistant coach, Lewis wrote one of the first books about football entitled *A Primer of College Football*. A few years later, he contributed a chapter on defense to Spalding's *How to Play Football*.

Many coaches transitioned from alumni athlete to coach, but none were paid. As with most things, Lewis was the exception. In 1901, Lewis became the first Harvard coach to be compensated, receiving $500 for two years, which was later increased to $1,000.

In 1905, there was talk across the country about eliminating football because of its brutal nature. As a result, Lewis proposed a "neutral zone" rule. This rule would change the game of football as it mandated that opposing teams remain apart by the width of the football before each play. The rule was enacted in 1906.

Sports are an avenue observed by many people from many different backgrounds, a point proven through Lewis. A young politician named Theodore Roosevelt followed Lewis' Harvard career as an athlete, law student, and coach. As the young man grew into the vice president and then president of the United States, he and Lewis became close friends. Roosevelt eventually helped Lewis pioneer into yet another arena.

In 1899, Lewis was elected to the Cambridge Common Council, and in 1901, Cambridge sent him to the Massachusetts House of Representatives, where he served one year. After losing his race for re-election, Lewis became the first African-American assistant U.S. attorney for Boston, appointed by President Theodore Roosevelt. This was only the beginning of his political triumphs. In 1907 Lewis was promoted to assistant U.S. attorney in charge of New England for the newly formed Bureau of Naturalization. Lewis was elevated as President William Taft named him assistant attorney general of the United States in 1911, making Lewis the first African-American to hold that lofty federal office. His appointment did not sit well with many, and he was asked to resign from his post because of his race. Lewis refused. When Woodrow Wilson became president, one of his first acts was to segregate federal employees by race, primarily because of his status as the first Southern president since the Reconstruction Era. Subsequently, Lewis was fired.

Lewis' political involvement was not stopped. He continued to practice law and eventually went into private practice. In 1924, Calvin Coolidge won the presidential election. At that time, most African-Americans were unable to vote, mostly because of Jim Crow Laws in the segregated South. When the Republican Party did not support a change, Lewis became an avid proponent of converting the African-American vote to the Democratic Party. By 1936, the majority of African-Americans identified as Democrats, which they do to this day. Lewis practiced law for the rest of his life and in 1930 became the first African-American to argue a case before the U.S. Supreme Court alone and win.

Lewis had a tremendous impact on America. He also left a silent but powerful legacy on college football. Lewis' life is a prime example of using sports as a vehicle to enact social change. In both sports and politics, William Henry Lewis was a pioneer for justice, equality, and love for all humankind.

Note

1. Evan J. Albright, "Blazing the Trail," http://www.amherst.edu/magazine/issues/07winter/blazing_trail/index.html (accessed June 9, 2007).

Matthew Washington Bullock

First African-American Student-Athlete at Dartmouth College

by Marcus Sedberry

On November 6, 1869, Princeton and Rutgers met to play in the first-ever intercollegiate football game. Rutgers defeated Princeton. Neither of the squads had an African-American on either the team or the coaching staff. It was not until 20 years later that African-Americans had a presence on the field. Amherst College is recorded as the first college to have African-American players on its teams, William H. Lewis and William T. S. Jackson. Years passed as African-Americans slowly began to appear at predominately white institutions across the country. The University of Nebraska, Harvard University, Williams College, and Oberlin College of Ohio were among the next schools to have African-Americans on their teams throughout the 1890s. As the new century began, Dartmouth College was blessed with an African-American star of its own.

Matthew Washington Bullock was born on September 11, 1881 to slave parents who could neither read nor write. His father moved to Boston in 1889 with a wife, seven children and a $10 bill after being forced out of the South. Bullock began attending Boston Public School at eight years old in 1890. Four years later his family moved to Everett, Massachusetts, where Bullock graduated from Everett High School in 1900. Immediately following Matthew's graduation, his father gave him $50 and told him he would be on his own. He set out on his solitary journey, enrolling at Dartmouth College in the fall of the same year.

Bullock became Dartmouth's first African-American football player, playing from 1901 to 1903. He did not limit his involvement to football, though. Bullock was also a star high jumper and broad jumper on the track team for four years. He was a member of the college choir and glee club for all four years of his collegiate career, as well as Palaeopitus. (Palaeopitus in its present state is a society that encourages working harmony among various campus organizations and communities, facilitates communication between undergraduates and the college administration, fosters positive traditions at Dartmouth, promotes her welfare, and protects her good name.)[1] Bullock was named a Walter Camp honorable mention All-American in 1903. In his senior year, Bullock was elected the captain of the football, baseball, and track teams. Beyond a shadow of doubt, Bullock was an excellent athlete and had an equally impressive voice, but he also found a way to balance and excel in his coursework. Bullock graduated from Dartmouth College and entered Harvard Law School in 1904, graduating with his LL.B. degree in the class of 1907.

When Bullock had entered law school, he had immediately become involved with more than just his school work. Still on his own, he paid his way through law school as a coach at Massachusetts Agricultural College (MAC), now known as the University of Massachusetts, Amherst. He became the first African-American head coach at a predominantly white institution. Upon his appointment as the new head coach of MAC, the Athletic Board gathered a collection and raised $251.03 to be used as payment for Bullock's services. In his first year as a coach, Bullock won the support of the student body, as he led his team to a 5-2-1 record. Although he had led MAC to its best record in years, he was only there for one year. The following year, Bullock became the coach of Malden High School, where he stayed for the next two years. Neither of his two seasons there resulted in a winning record, as he was 3-7 and 1-7-1, respectively. However, that did not have an effect on the people who still solicited his services. Bullock was considered "a student of football and fine conditioner of men" and one who put his "heart and soul into his task."[2]

In 1907, Massachusetts Agricultural College was successful in getting Bullock to return as coach. The editor of the MAC *College Signal* wrote, "Coach Bullock is fast rounding a mass of rather unpromising material into a strong football machine." Bullock did not disappoint as he did another masterful job at leading his squad to a 5-3-1 record. The 1908 season found Bullock having to rebuild his team once again and the taxing nine-game schedule resulted in a 3-3-3 record.

At the end of the 1908 season, Bullock moved on to become a teacher and coach at Atlanta Baptist College (now Morehouse College) in Atlanta, Georgia. While at Atlanta Baptist, Bullock teamed with Edwin Henderson to be among the few who selected the Negro college all-star teams. He became a very well respected faculty member at Atlanta Baptist and began teaching courses in economics, history, Latin, and sociology.

In 1912, Bullock was admitted to the Georgia Bar and practiced law in Atlanta for three years. Following those three years, he was the dean of Alabama Agricultural and Mechanical College at Normal, Alabama, before returning to Boston where he was admitted to the Massachusetts Bar. In 1917, Bullock attempted to enlist in the army but was rejected because of an "athletic heart." However, during World War I Bullock served for 15 months in the American Expeditionary Forces as a physical director. Shortly after the war, he was selected to represent the organization at burial services for unknown soldiers. He was then asked to serve as special assistant attorney general and was later the chairman of the Board of Parole of Massachusetts.

After his retirement from state service in 1949, he began traveling what would total 100,000 miles at his own expense in service of the Baha'i World of Faith. These travels took him to places in Europe, Asia, Africa, the West Indies Islands, the Hawaiian Islands, and the Philippines. In 1953, Bullock was elected to the Baha'i National Assembly. Bullock was also a member of the Knights of Pythias, the Masonic order, and Omega Psi Phi Fraternity, Inc.

In addition to his already impressive educational background, he was given two honorary degrees. He received an honorary degree from Harvard Law School and in 1971 was awarded an honorary doctorate of laws degree from his alma mater, Dartmouth College.

There are many types of barriers one may face in life. Matthew

Washington Bullock was forced to sift through life on his own. Transitioning from a family of seven children with parents who could neither read nor write, to becoming the first African-American student-athlete at Dartmouth College, the first African-American head coach at a predominately white institution, receiving a law degree from Harvard, and becoming dean of a college is a life well led and widely admired. Bullock passed on December 17, 1972, at the age of 91, but will forever be known as a pioneer.

Notes

1. Palaeopitus, "Palaeopitus Senior Society," http://www.dartmouth.edu/~palaeop /about2.html (accessed June 3, 2007).

2. Martin Kaufman and Michael Konig, "Education in Massachusetts: Selected Essays" (Westerfield, Massachusetts, 1989).

John Howard Johnson

First African-American Student-Athlete at Columbia University

by Horacio Ruiz

The Reverend John Howard Johnson, one of the best basketball players of his day, was the first African-American student-athlete at Columbia University in 1918. It is argued that before African-American
men could play on the same courts as white men, it was the African-
American men who had to continually prove themselves as superior
athletes in a kind of perpetual audition. African-American athletes
could not be just good enough. If they were to play with whites, they
had to be exceptional.

Johnson stepped in as a sophomore and caught the eye of *The
Spaulding Guides*, a magazine that noted "Johnson of Columbia occasionally showed flashes of form."[1] In his first season he was cited
along with a teammate for contributing the most to a 48-15 Columbia victory versus St. John's College. In that game, Johnson scored
12 points. Only a few days after the victory against St. John's, Johnson got into a fight with an opposing player from Penn and was
ejected from the rest of the game. Columbia would go on to lose 31-
18. By the end of the season, there was no doubt that Johnson was
the best of Columbia's 25 players. *The New York Times* mentioned
his name in the headlines after a victory versus Yale: "Yale five
beaten by Columbia . . . Johnson wrenches game from five with
brace of goals in final minutes."[2] Johnson, who played center, scored
the game-tying and winning shots with less than two minutes remaining in the game.

Johnson would go on to prove himself as one of the most
skilled players in the Eastern Intercollegiate League, playing virtually every position on the floor with a rugged style. In his junior year
he scored 14 points in Columbia's 28-25 victory over Dartmouth,
and in his senior year he scored 11 points in a 15-14 victory versus
cross-town rival CCNY. It is reported that Johnson was talented
enough to have played for the Harlem Rens, the legendary all-black
team that is one of only six teams to be inducted into the Naismith
Memorial Basketball Hall of Fame.

Johnson had other plans in life. He was ordained in 1923, two years after graduating from Columbia, and worked as an assistant minister to his father before founding what would become his life's work—St. Martin's Parish on Lenox Avenue in New York City. By the late 1940s he had built a congregation of more than 3,000. Johnson also was heavily involved in politics and was committed to integration, insisting that his church was not a "black church" but one open to all people. He worked to build relationships with the diverse ethnic groups in New York City.

Johnson was the first African-American in other ventures as well. In 1935 he became the first African-American to be appointed as a member of the Emergency Relief Bureau, an agency that worked to provide relief to needy families in their homes at the time of the Great Depression. Four years later he was elected as the first African-American police chaplain in New York. In addition to his work for St. Martin's, he pushed his "Don't Buy Where You Can't Work" campaign during the 1930s and soon became a central figure in Harlem.

In 1947, the same year Jackie Robinson and Larry Doby integrated Major League Baseball, Johnson was named commissioner of the Negro National League. Johnson had his own ideas of how to run the Negro Leagues and was open about sharing those ideas. He was often criticized for being a committed integrationist, specifically encouraging the integration of the major leagues. Even with his commitment to integration, Johnson wanted to improve the lives of the Negro Leagues players, give more financial security to the owners, and give the fans a better product on the field. Johnson's role with the Negro Leagues came to an end after the 1948 season. It was clear the league was undergoing a rapid demise. During his brief tenure, Johnson was still able to address the on-field violence as well as unruly fan behavior.

Throughout his different appointments, Johnson stayed true to his life's work, St. Martin's Parish in Harlem. In 1966, the church was declared a New York City landmark during the leadership of the Reverend David Johnson, one of Johnson's three sons.

Notes

1. Ocania Chalk, *Black College Sport* (New York: Dodd, Mead, January 1976).
2. Ibid.

Jerome "Brud" Holland

First African-American Football Student-Athlete at Cornell University

by Jessica Bartter

Lying on his bed in his dorm room like many present-day collegiate student-athletes, Jerome "Brud" Holland juggled in his mind the many rigors of his coming day. Thoughts of balancing his daily practice schedule with having to wait tables to pay his tuition so that he could earn his bachelor's degree probably cost Holland some valuable sleep. More disruptive was the flimsy cot he called his bed and the boiler room that was his dorm room. Probably most distracting was the fact that he was burdened with the tuition of an Ivy League School, Cornell University. The year was 1935.

Holland was one of 13 children and the only one to attend college. It would seem, though, that Holland could not escape his brotherly ties anywhere he went. After a younger sibling called him "Brudder" when they were younger, the nickname stuck outside the family and was shortened to "Brud" most of his life. With his bachelor's and master's degrees from Cornell and a doctorate in sociology from the University of Pennsylvania, Holland went on to earn enough degrees for each of his 12 siblings to have two. Beyond his degrees from Cornell and Penn, he received 22 honorary degrees from colleges and universities across the country.

Holland was a special person not just in the field of education. He was a difference maker in the sports arena. After being a standout basketball and football player at Auburn High School in New York, Holland made a big difference at Cornell University by being the Big Red's first African-American student-athlete on the football field.

Like other freshman of his time, he was ineligible to play on the varsity squad. After his freshman year, Holland spent his remaining three years of eligibility starting for the Big Red in 1936, 1937, and 1938. Holland was known for his quickness, and his coach designed plays especially for him. One of his famous plays was known as the end-round. Often times, Holland capitalized on his speed and was able to turn the same play into a touchdown multiple times per game. He earned All-American honors in 1937 and 1938 at the end position. Holland was just one of five African-American players to be named All-Americans in the first half of the century. According to Ivy League Office records, Holland was the second-leading vote-getter for the 1937 All-American team, a remarkable achievement, considering many Southern newspapers would not run his photo with the other 10 players for fear of offending their readership.

The team leader helped guide Cornell football through its glory days. On September 30, 1938, Holland and his team attracted 14,000 fans to watch the gridiron battle against Colgate University. Among the 14,000 fans at Schoellkopf Field was a sportswriter from *The Cornell Daily Sun*, who recalled Holland's potency on the offensive and defensive sides. "Holland came through with his specialty on three occasions—tackling the ball carrier behind the line of scrimmage." Offensively, "Brud Holland drew first blood with his famous end-round play. With Cornell on its own 43-yard line, Holland tucked the ball under his arm and streaked across the Crescent side of the field 57 yards to go over standing up. Halfway on his jaunt, the fleet Brud turned without breaking his stride to stiff-arm two of the Raiders who were in hot pursuit."[1] That is just a small window into the epoch of an All-American career.

When Holland graduated in 1939 with high honors, the American workforce did not greet him with the open arms that Cornell had. Job recruiters covered the Ivy League campus at the end of the academic year, but Holland received little attention and no interviews. The American industry was not welcoming to an educated black man in 1939. The color of his skin even prevented him from the opportunity to continue playing football in the NFL, despite his celebrated talent. His time at Cornell showed Holland he could prosper in the world of education, so that is where he stayed. At a young age, Holland had realized education was the best escape from poverty. First, Holland earned his master's degree in sociology from Cornell. He then taught sociology and physical education at Lincoln University while coaching football. In 1950, Holland furthered his education by attending the University of Pennsylvania for his Ph.D. In 1953, Delaware State College made Dr. Holland its president until 1960, when he was named president of Virginia's Hampton Institute. Holland remained the Institute's president for 10 years and became one of the nation's most distinguished educators in the 1960s.

Holland's appointments outside education shed even more light onto his passion for people. In 1970, President Richard Nixon appointed Holland the American ambassador to Sweden. American and Swedish relations were at an all-time low. In 1968, Sweden had begun granting asylum to U.S. Army deserters. Shortly thereafter, Sweden became the first Western country to officially recognize North Vietnam. Tensions escalated when Premier Olof Palme marched in a protest against American war policies. The United States returned the cold shoulder when The Apollo 11 astronauts' world tour blaringly excluded Sweden. Just two months before Holland's appointment, Sweden promised Hanoi $45 million in reconstruction aid, forcing the United States to close their consulate in the Swedish town of Goteborg. When Holland bravely accepted President Nixon's appointment, he was the first U.S. Ambassador in Stockholm in a year. Holland and his family remained in Stockholm until 1972.

Upon Holland's return to the United States, he earned appointments on the boards of several key American companies, including AT&T and General Motors, and chaired the Salvation Army, the American Red Cross, and Planned Parenthood boards. Holland's effectiveness in facilitating good relations between the American Red Cross and the Red Crescent, the Red Cross' Islamic counterpart, is still celebrated today. He was also active with the United Negro College Fund and the Boy Scouts of America. From 1972 to 1980, Holland sat on the board of the New York Stock Exchange (NYSE). He was the first African-American to become director of the NYSE.

Holland's football performance in the 1930s was so memorable, he received several prestigious accolades in the subsequent decades, including the most recent, in 2006, when former NCAA president Joseph Crowley named Holland 24th on the list of the 100 Most Influential Student-Athletes in honor of the NCAA's 100th anniversary. In 1963, he was one of 25 men to receive the *Sports Illus-*

trated Silver Anniversary All-America Award, which is given for successful performances in life off the gridiron. He was inducted into the 1965 National Football Foundation's Hall of Fame. In 1972, he was the recipient of the National Football Foundation's Distinguished American Award. Holland was awarded the Presidential Medal of Freedom in 1985. President Truman established the Medal of Honor in 1945 to honor service during World War II. President Kennedy revived the honor in 1963, and it was expanded to recognize individuals who have made "an especially meritorious contribution to the security or national interests of the United States, world peace, cultural or other significant public or private endeavors." For his work, Holland received the nation's highest civilian award. Crowley's honor wasn't Holland's only mention in 2006. Holland was named as the greatest player ever to wear number 86 in ESPN.com college football columnist Ivan Maisel's 2006 list of the greatest players to wear each jersey number 1 through 100. Holland was the only Ivy Leaguer to grace Maisel's list.

The Auburn, New York, native lost his battle with cancer in 1985. Dr. Jerome "Brud" Holland was 69 years old. In the same year, Cornell's International Living Center was named in Holland's honor. Before he died he was able to watch his son, Joe, go on to Cornell and enjoy a successful football career like his storied father. The high school fields where "Brud" first made a name for himself have since been named in his honor, but forgetting Jerome Holland would be hard to do regardless.

Note

1. Archives, "Black Student Athletes Overcome Adversity," *The Cornell Daily Sun*, February 11, 2004.

Arthur Wilson, Jr.

First African-American Student-Athlete
at Princeton University

by Horacio Ruiz

A list of Princeton's graduates would include former presidents of
the United States, Nobel laureates, Supreme Court justices, a multi-
tude of chief executive officers, Pulitzer Prize winners, and award-
winning actors. With alumni of this caliber, one is bound to wonder
whether great talent makes up a great university or whether a great
university inherently molds great talent.

Art Wilson, Jr., a man who is nearly unrecognized on an
alumni roster that includes James Madison, Woodrow Wilson, and
Robert Johnson, has nevertheless made important contributions to
Princeton. His enrollment at Princeton made him Princeton's first
African-American athlete and only the second African-American to
receive an undergraduate degree from the Ivy League school when
he earned an economics degree on June 9, 1947.

Wilson wasn't the only one in his family with exceptional
achievements. His grandfather, Maynard Wilson, was a prominent
figure for the African-American community in Omaha, Nebraska,
where he was a secretary to the mayor for more than 20 years. His
father, Arthur Sr., was one of the nation's first African-American
certified public accountants. When Illinois passed a law requiring
that accountants complete an apprenticeship before becoming CPAs,
several African-Americans were left without opportunity because of
racial considerations. Arthur Sr. took it upon himself to take young
aspiring CPAs under his wing so they could fulfill their apprentice-
ships under his supervision. By 1945, half of the United States'
black CPAs were in Chicago near Arthur Sr.

With a history of family pride behind him, Wilson Jr. took a
lengthy path to Princeton, first attending Morris Brown University
in Atlanta before heading to Southern University in Baton Rouge,
Louisiana. At Southern he was a member of the black college
national championship basketball team before joining the Navy to
become a member of a skilled construction unit. During World War
II he spent 14 months in the Pacific, where his superiors recom-

mended he enroll in an officer training program. He enrolled in that program at Princeton.

At Princeton, Wilson, known as "Pete" around campus, was a two-time captain of the basketball team and also participated in 150-pound football and ran track. He was mostly noted for his ability to create plays for his teammates by constantly passing the ball. *The Harvard Crimson* noted that his speed created a number of scoring opportunities for his teammates in a match up between Harvard and Princeton. He was, however, capable of scoring outbursts, as he once scored 12 points in a game against Villanova.

After receiving his degree, Wilson returned to his hometown of Chicago, where he found work as a Cook County deputy sheriff. It would be the beginning of a remarkable professional climb that saw him take a job as clerk in the U.S. Marshals office in 1965 after 18 years of working for Cook County. He then worked as an administrator in the witness relocation program and became a court-appointed U.S. marshal for the Eastern District of Illinois in 1975. In 1976, he received a special commendation for outstanding service.

"I would say it is an amazing bottom-to-top approach. It is rare, extremely rare," U.S. Marshals historian David Turk told writer Brett Hoover. "He would have to have had a phenomenal range of knowledge of the U.S. Marshals program to elevate from an administrative assistant to become a marshal. It does not happen very often."[1] After retiring from the U.S. Marshals Service, he served as director of public safety and chief of police for East St. Louis, Illinois.

He died of a massive stroke on December 28, 2000 at the age of 77. In an interview for his obituary, Wilson's wife, Marcella, attested to Wilson's perpetual love of sports. Marcella recounted that while she was pregnant and going into labor, Wilson, an avid Chicago Bears fan and season-ticket holder, dropped her off at the hospital one Sunday and returned home so that he would not miss the televised kickoff to the second half. "The Bears won that game," she told the *Chicago Sun-Times* writer, who noted that she said so with a laugh.[2]

Although Wilson was not active in class affairs after graduating from Princeton, he did attend his 50th reunion in 1998. In a memorial in the Princeton Alumni Weekly, his class wrote a tribute to Wilson saying "The class is poorer at the death of an accomplished, courageous man who was a fine scholar and gifted athlete." While

Wilson's name may not stand out in a list of Princeton's famous politicians, academicians, or artists, there is no doubt he left his fingerprint on the university.

Notes

1. Brett Hoover, "Art Wilson," Ivy League Black History, http://ivy50.com/black History/story.aspx?sid=1/7/2009 (accessed April 24, 2007).

2. Lon Grahnke, "Arthur Wilson Jr., Law Enforcement Officer," *Chicago Sun-Times*, January 3, 2001.

Jay James Swift

First African-American Student-Athlete at Yale University

by Jessica Bartter

Courtesy of Yale Athletic Department.

In the early 1940s, college sports took a hard hit. Many athletes were drafted to fight in World War II, forcing the temporary hold on or end to their collegiate athletic careers. Nonetheless, with smaller rosters and ever-changing line-ups, college sports persevered. Many athletes got breaks when team stars were shipped overseas, but as quickly as the opportunities came, they left when the GI's returned home.

Although Jay James Swift managed to avoid the draft, he had his own battles to fight on the home front. Like many African-Americans, Swift was fighting for equality in a "separate but equal" society. In a flag-raising sign of victory, Swift stepped onto the hardwood of Yale's gymnasium where he would fight his own war to integrate college sports.

In the fall of 1944, the New York City native entered Yale University, fresh from Townsend Harris High School. The English major became Yale's first African-American student-athlete when he joined the basketball team that season. The "Basketball Dope Book," referred to as a media guide today, for 1944–45 introduced the freshman: "Tall and fast, he is a good ball handler and shows great possibilities for defensive operations."

Swift was an impact-player right away, playing in 11 of the team's 18 games his freshman season. He totaled 48 points that year, with a game high of nine points against the University of Connecticut during only 12 minutes of playing time. The team went 14-4. The Bulldogs enjoyed even more success during Swift's sophomore year when they went 14-1, winning the New England Basketball Collegiate Championships. Again, Swift played in most of the games, but did not score much. His top point production was four points, but he had a strong defensive impact.

Students of Yale University are assigned to a residential college at the time of admission. Swift was a member of Timothy Dwight College, one of 12 colleges at Yale today. The colleges engage in competitions in a variety of sports for pride and bragging rights. Some of the sports are even challenged by teams from the Harvard University houses. Swift was active with Timothy Dwight College's football and crew teams in addition to his varsity basketball participation.

The 1946–47 basketball roster listed Swift, but records show he only played in six games, going scoreless in all six. It is quite possible his position was relinquished as veterans returned home from war and took their old spots back. Why Swift dropped off the team before graduating is unknown, but there is no doubt he went on to accomplish great things in his professional life.

Swift returned to New York City where he held several city positions under Mayors John V. Lindsay, Abraham D. Beame, and Edward I. Koch. From 1968 to 1970, he headed the community development department of the New York City's Addiction Services Agency. He had a three-year stint as deputy city administrator before being named executive director of the Environmental Control Board from 1974 until his retirement in 1983. Even into his retirement, Swift was called upon by the Queens District Attorney as a special consultant. The Ad Hoc Review Committee of the National Institute of Mental Health also utilized Swift's knowledge after he retired from the city's work.

On June 23, 1988, cancer took the life of Jay Swift. He was just 62 years old. He died at the Roosevelt Hospital in Manhattan. Theodore Roosevelt once said, "There are good men and bad men of all nationalities, creeds and colors; and if this world of ours is ever to become what we hope some day it may become, it must be by the general recognition that the man's heart and soul, the man's worth and actions, determine his standing."[1] Judging by Roosevelt's words, Jay James Swift should stand in high regard in the minds of a nation that owes him our appreciation. His "heart and soul, worth and actions" were truly honorable.

Note

1. Theodore Roosevelt, letter, Oyster Bay, NY, September 1, 1903.

Student-Athlete Epilogue

"Ball Like Paul": Paul Robeson, the Triple Threat

by C. Keith Harrison

Paul LeRoy Robeson, considered by many to be one of the great Americans, was born in New Jersey. He took the concept of pioneer to a whole new level in his life from 1898 to 1976. Robeson was a 20th-century renaissance man and excelled as an athlete, scholar, lawyer, and Broadway and film star who became a major activist in the fight against racism in America.

In terms of education, Robeson scored the highest marks in competition with his high school peers for the New Jersey statewide exam. This is extraordinary, considering that three parts of the exam were excluded from Robeson's preparation; he did not have access to the information in comparison to the other students. This would be a theme throughout his life—barrier plus perseverance equals success.

After winning an academic and athletic scholarship to Rutgers University, Paul competed in football, basketball, baseball, and track and field for a total of 14 varsity letters. On the football field, he faced challenges that were commonplace for the few African-American athletes competing against whites in those days. Robeson's teammates felt threatened by his presence at school and on the team. Because of these fears he was abused and attacked in his first week of practice. Robeson fought back later in the week and went on to become a two-time Walter Camp All-American.

Courtesy of Dr. Keith Harrison and Dwight Williamson.

These athletic accomplishments were hardly all he achieved. Robeson majored in political science and took the concept of scholar-athlete to a new level. Robeson knew the importance of interacting with faculty and gaining all the knowledge he could while his education was paid for. One example of his passion for learning outside the classroom was a visit to his first Broadway play in New York. Professor Whitman from the Rutgers English department exposed him to the acting culture, which had a serious impact on his life. Robeson went on to act in numerous plays and films and was part of the longest-running stint of the Shakespeare play *Othello*.

Robeson perfected the synergy of mind, body, and soul. He is what Harvard scholar Professor Howard Gardner referred to as "bodily kinesthetic intelligence," with his brilliant performances in education, sport, and entertainment. All these accomplishments were done in the face of society's institutionalized and personal racism. How did Robeson manage to achieve all of this?

Paul Robeson's life and career are paradigms of resistance to racial stereotyping. His life as a black athlete with a powerful intellect was a living example of how to shatter the stereotype.

While lettering in four sports and earning All-American honors in football, Robeson was also a member of the Cap and Skull Society, Phi-Beta Kappa, Philocean Society, Mathematics Club, and the champion each of his four years on the debate team. Yet his peers looked at him primarily as an athlete, as is shown by the inscription in his senior yearbook in 1918:

> *Paul LeRoy Robeson*
> *All hats off to the Robie men;*
> *All honor to his name;*
> *On the diamond court or football field*
> *He's brought old Rutgers fame.*

The omission of Robeson's intellectual achievements was not necessarily a racial slight, but was rather a stereotypical neglect of the value of education when connected to athletic individuals. Robeson paved the way for thousands of African-American students and student-athletes to experience higher education, not only at Rutgers, but at other traditionally white campuses around the country.

Paul Robeson endured both personal and broader cultural struggles while an athlete at Rutgers University. His triumphs serve as a testament to the courage, perseverance, and dignity that Robeson modeled each day of his life. Our nation's rich history has provided us with many men and women who have served as torchbearers for change and accomplishment. Yet there have been few who have done so in such a multi-talented way as Robeson did academically, athletically, and socially. Therefore, in many ways, he serves as the ideal model, particularly for children.

Robeson was much like many early black pioneers involved in school and intercollegiate athletics—they all used sport as a means to an end. Robeson best illustrated this concept while playing professional football for Akron, Indiana, and Milwaukee in the early days of the NFL. His earnings went toward his education at Columbia Law School. He used the system, rather than allow the system to drain him.

Robeson kept his ethnic and cultural ties and was recognized by W. E. B. DuBois in *The Crisis* for his academic and athletic achievements. He was well recognized and praised by the black community in New York during his scholar-athlete days. His circle of friends included some of the most respected and distinguished African-Americans during that period of time: Rudolph Fisher, Gwendolyn Bennett, Countee Cullen, Langston Hughes, Aaron Douglas, E. Franklin Frazier, Charles Johnson, William L. Patterson, and Hubert T. Delany. Paul concluded his eclectic undergraduate days by extending to the black middle class at the Carlton YMCA in Brooklyn, where the program "Four Negro Commencement Speakers" was presented. Paul was balancing not only academics and athletics, but the black and white worlds! As an adult he would become a powerful voice against racism in America—and thus become a target of racism aimed directly at him.

Robeson set a standard of excellence for all to follow. He would not accept the narrowly defined position for African-Americans in society created by whites at that time. Instead, he fought for progress every step of the way. A triple threat is something that merits pioneer status even today by all people in the 21st century. This is why the Paul Robeson Research Center for Academic and Athletic Prowess was started on April 9, 1998 at the University of Michigan in his honor. His legacy continues today with various research projects, as we continue to investigate how stereotypes affect athletes, entertainers, and the public at large.

OLYMPIC
SPORT

II

WORLD STAGE PIONEERS:
AFRICAN-AMERICAN OLYMPIANS

Introduction by Richard Lapchick

When I first thought about writing this introduction on African-American athletes and the Olympics, I thought mostly about the first African-American male and female to win gold medals in both the summer and winter games. African-Americans have had a history of great successes in the Summer Games and have been so unrepresented at the Winter Games that Bryant Gumbel opened up a wound and hit a nerve when he commented, on *HBO's Real Sports With Bryant Gumbel*, that the lack of African-Americans made the Winter Olympics "look like a GOP Convention."

George Poage and Joe Stadler were the first African-American Olympic participants in the 1904 Games. Four years later, John Baxter Taylor made history for being the first African-American to win a gold medal in the 1908 Olympic Games. He died unexpectedly from typhoid pneumonia in December of 1908 at the age of 26, only four months after achieving this momentous feat. Taylor helped his team win the gold medal in the 1,600-meter relay event. Sadly he did not live to see even the first of the great African-American athletes who succeeded him in the Olympics.

After the absence of any Olympics in 1940 and 1944, Alice Coachman made the 1948 team where she became the first African-American woman to win the gold medal. She was also the first American woman to win a gold medal in a track and field event and the only American woman to win a gold medal in the 1948 Games. Talk about a pioneer! She led the way for literally hundreds of African-American women who subsequently competed in the Olympics.

If there is to be a history for African-Americans in the Winter Games, it is in the future. Vonetta Flowers was named the partner of

Jill Bakken and became the brakeman for the USA-2 bobsled in the 2002 Winter Games. The sport was new to her after a distinguished career in track and field. Not only was Flowers the first-ever African-American to win a gold medal in the Winter Games, but she and Bakken carried the American flag in the closing ceremonies.

The Winter Games in Torino in 2006 had 211 U.S. Olympians. Including Shani Davis, five were African-Americans. Regardless, it was at those Games that Davis became an Olympic champion at the 1,000-meter speed skating event, becoming the first African-American male athlete to win an individual gold medal in Olympic Winter Games history.

Upon reflection, I felt that there had to be other athletes included here because of the drama of their extraordinary stories. They include Jesse Owens, who won four gold medals in the 1936 Berlin Olympics, throwing an icy chill on Adolf Hitler's presumed Nazi triumph. In 1960, Wilma Rudolph won three Olympic titles and now is mentioned in the same breath as Jackie Joyner-Kersee as the greatest female Olympians of all-time. Joyner-Kersee won three gold, one silver, and two bronze Olympic medals in four different summer games. The stories of Owens, Rudolph, and Joyner-Kersee are also in this part of the book. But there were also great political stories that involved African-American Olympic athletes in Berlin in 1936 and in Mexico City in 1968, when John Carlos and Tommie Smith took the victory stand with black gloves and clenched fists in their dramatic protest of racism in America. There is a story on that event in this part of the book, and the importance of the Nazi backdrop is covered in the Jesse Owens story.

Hitler's Nazi regime did its best to conceal its racist, anti-Semitic, militaristic character as the host of the 1936 Summer Olympics. The Nazi propaganda machine tried to sell an image of a peaceful, accepting nation. Before the Games there was a proposed boycott by the United States and several European nations. United States Olympic Committee president Avery Brundage made the case that politics had no place in sport and defeated the boycott attempts. When the Games ended, Hitler rapidly proceeded toward the extermination of the Jews across Europe and the start of World War II. Some historians believe that if we had boycotted the Games there might have been more international resistance to German intentions, and World War II and the Holocaust might have been avoided.

But Hitler's showcase of the Aryan master race fell apart with the great performances by the 18 African-Americans on the U.S. team. The four-gold-medal triumph of Owens was only part of the story. Among the other stories is that of Matthew "Mack" Robinson, the older brother of Jackie Robinson—who is thought by many to be the greatest racial pioneer in the history of sport. Mack won the silver medal in the men's 200 meters, finishing just 0.4 seconds behind Owens.

African-Americans won 14 of the 56 medals earned by the United States team. They dominated the popular track and field events. American correspondents touted the victories of the African-Americans as a crushing blow to the Nazi hype of Aryan supremacy.

In an ironic end to their triumphs, the African-American Olympians returned home and faced the same social and economic discrimination as before the Olympics. There was more history to write, about both racism in American society and about a still-segregated American sports system. Mack Robinson could hardly have foreseen the role his brother would play.

John Baxter Taylor

First African-American to Win an Olympic Gold Medal

by Jenny Brenden

Courtesy of University of Pennsylvania Athletic Communications.

"It is far more as the man [than as the athlete] that John Taylor made his mark. Quite unostentatious, genial, kindly, the fleet-footed, far-famed [Penn] athlete was beloved wherever known . . . As a beacon light of his race, his example of achievement in athletics; scholarship and manhood will never wane, if indeed it is not destined to form with that of Booker T. Washington." These were the words that Harry Porter, Acting President of the 1908 American Olympic Team, wrote in a tribute letter to the parents of John Baxter Taylor.

John Baxter Taylor, who is most well-known for being the first African-American to win a gold medal in the Olympic Games, died unexpectedly only four months after achieving this momentous feat. He succumbed to typhoid pneumonia in December of 1908 at the age of 26. Although he had accomplished more in his short lifetime than most people do over an average lifespan, he did not have the opportunity to reach his full potential and achieve everything of which he was capable. This was unfortunate not only because Taylor was such a great athlete with much more to prove, but because society lost an upstanding human being who had the ability to touch many lives and serve as a role model to other aspiring athletes.

Born in Washington, D.C., Taylor spent most of his life in Philadelphia, Pennsylvania. He attended a school that was not only academically highly acclaimed, but also known as a track and field powerhouse. Taylor was the star of the Central High track team, and by his senior year he had become the best quarter-miler in the city.

A year at Brown Prep prepared Taylor both academically and athletically to attend the University of Pennsylvania (Penn) in Philadelphia. Taylor was a freshman at the University of Pennsylvania in 1903 and he wasted no time putting his name in the record books, as he won the Intercollegiate Association of Amateur Athletes of America (IC4A) championship in the quarter-mile with a meet record of 49.2 seconds.

Even by the time Taylor entered college, he had very few African-American runners to look up to as role models. He, in fact, was the role model for others to aspire to emulate. Although there were surely hardships being the only African-American on the team and on the track, he did not let them hold him back from greatness. Taylor was forced to acclimate to the situation on his own, evidenced by the fact that in each of his team photos from Penn, he was the only African-American on the team.

Early in the century, the young Olympic Games had not evolved into the global craze that it is today. It has grown from 14 countries and 241 participants in its inaugural year to over 200 participating countries and over 10,000 athletes. In the two Olympic Games preceding the 1904 Games, as well as the 1904 Games itself, participants did not represent their home countries or wear a national uniform. They entered individually or by clubs or colleges. One change that came about in the 1904 Games was the awarding of gold, silver, and bronze medals to event winners and runners-up.

Taylor did not participate in the 1904 Olympic Games, although the games were held in America and Taylor was certainly fast enough. The winner of the 400-meter race ran the same time that Taylor had run in the IC4A in an event that was three yards longer. Had he competed, Taylor would have joined George Poage and Joe Stadler in being the first African-American Olympic participants.

Athletics were not the only realm in which Taylor was proving to be impressive. At the end of his sophomore year he was invited to be a part of Sigma Pi Phi Boule, a fraternity of professional African-Americans. He was one of three undergraduates to be admitted to the prestigious fraternity.

While at Penn, Taylor matured both as a person and as an athlete. The 1907 season was a good one for the star, when his 5-foot-11-inch, 160-pound frame and eight-and-a-half foot stride helped him to drop his all-time best 440-yard time to 48.8 seconds and become the greatest quarter-miler in the world. When Taylor ran in the National Championships in Norfolk, Virginia, the following event occurred and was written about in the *Philadelphia Inquirer*. "While running the race Taylor was deliberately fouled by one of the contestants, but he refused to fight back and after winning the race was so loudly applauded that hundreds of Southern gentlemen rushed up and shook him by the hand, an almost unheard-of thing for a white man in the South."[1] This incident was simply another testament to both the maturity and good character that Taylor possessed, features in him that everyone recognized and appreciated.

Taylor continued to dominate his senior season, when he won his third quarter-mile title, becoming only the third runner to achieve such a feat in the 33-year history of the IC4A. To prove how much faster than his competition Taylor was, his winning time was 52.2 seconds, almost four seconds slower than his all-time best. In his defense, he was running during a downpour, which slowed most runners down on that particular day. He ended his collegiate career on top, despite being bothered by a hernia all season. Taylor also graduated from Penn's School of Veterinary Medicine in 1908.

After graduating, Taylor was ready for the real world, but he still had plenty to prove on the track. He qualified to participate in the Olympics and with the newly structured international event, Taylor became the first African-American to represent his country and wear his American team uniform, rather than a club or college uniform. Rome had been the initial host site of the 1908 Games, but because of the eruption of Mount Vesuvius, the International Olympic Committee moved the event to London. Taylor's first race, the 400 meter, ended up being one of the most controversial events in Olympic history.

There were four finalists in the 400-meter race, three Americans and an Englishman. American Carpenter was leading going into the final leg of the race and then swerved to the other side of the track, making it impossible for the Englishman to pass. The race was immediately called a "no race" and rescheduled for the following day. To protest the decision and in support of their American teammate, Taylor and the other two American runners did not participate in the rescheduled race, so the Englishman won as the only participant.

The second event Taylor participated in had a much different outcome. Taylor was the third leg of the first-ever Olympic relay race, a sprint medley. He ran a 49.8 second, 400-meter third leg, which was good enough to help his team win the gold medal in the 1,600-meter relay event, making him the first African-American ever to win a gold medal in the Olympic Games.

His tragic death just four months after winning the gold was very sudden, but the front-page story that ran as a tribute to John Baxter Taylor repeatedly stated how well-liked he was on campus, how hard he worked, and what a gentlemen he was. Although his time in the spotlight was sadly short, Taylor made an impact on Olympic sport and will always be remembered with the greatest respect.

Note

1. David Johnson, "John Baxter Taylor Profile," Profiles from the Ivy League's Black History, http://ivy50.com/blackHistory/story.aspx?sid=12/27/2006 (accessed May 10, 2007).

James Cleveland "Jesse" Owens

First American in Olympic Track and Field History to Win Four Gold Medals

by Marcus Sedberry

From the son of a sharecropper to an Olympic champion who changed the face of the Olympic Games in track and field and inspired millions to strive for their dreams, Jesse Owens was the epitome of a pioneer.

James Cleveland Owens was born in 1913 in small town Alabama to Henry and Emma Owens. When J. C., as he was known then, was eight years old, he and his parents moved to Cleveland, Ohio, in hopes of a more prosperous life. They were met with disappointment. Upon arrival in Cleveland, Owens was enrolled into public school. During his first day at school, Owens was asked his name by the teacher and he responded, "J. C." The teacher, mishearing the name, began referring to him as Jesse and the name stuck. The Owens' family continued to struggle throughout Jesse's childhood. The young Owens took jobs as a grocery deliverer, shoe repairman, and freight car loader. As Owens began to recognize his love for running, he began to train in the mornings; he could not participate in after-school practices because of work.

Owens' work paid off as he became a track and field star at Cleveland East Technical High School. In his senior year, he tied the world record in the 100-yard dash with a time of 9.4 seconds, leapt to a six-foot-high jump, and soared to 24 feet $9^5/_8$ inches in the broad jump. Owens graduated high school as a highly touted track star, enrolling in The Ohio State University and becoming a member of the track team. Unfortunately, Owens was not awarded a scholarship, so he was forced to work part-time through college in order to survive. Owens was a vital part of the team; however, he was not treated as such because of the color of his skin. First, he was required to live off campus with other African-American student-athletes instead of on campus with his white teammates. When the team traveled across the country, Owens was forced to eat at "blacks-only" restaurants and stay at "blacks-only" hotels. "Whites-only" hotels would sometimes allow African-American student-athletes to stay but would require them to come in through the back door and to use the stairs instead of the elevator.

In 1935, he attended the Big Ten conference meet and excelled. Owens set three world records and tied a fourth during a phenomenal performance in a span of 45 minutes. During the entire week leading to the meet, Owens' ability had been questionable because of a back injury. He exemplified extreme resiliency, though, as he competed like a champion in spite of the injury. After persuading his coach that he was able to run, Owens put in a time of 9.4 seconds in the 100-yard dash, tying his own world record. Fifteen minutes later, just prior to his first and only attempt at the long jump, Owens placed a handkerchief at 26 feet $2^{1}/_{2}$ inches to mark the world record distance. Although many people saw the gesture as bold and flamboyant, Owens used the marker for motivation. His motivational tactic worked, as he met and surpassed the world record by nearly six inches, jumping 26 feet $8^{1}/_{4}$ inches. This record would last for 25 years. Shortly after, Owens competed in both the 220-yard dash and the 220-yard hurdles, winning and setting world records in both, with times of 20.3 and 22.6 seconds respectively.

In his sophomore season, Owens decided to further pursue his dream of attending the 1936 Olympics. Although his 1935 performances had proved remarkable, Berlin, Germany, would be the place where Owens truly put on a show. In Germany, Owens encountered tough competition not only on the track but also in his surroundings. The 1936 Olympics in Berlin, Germany, were known as "Hitler Olympics" and the "Nazi Olympics," because it was Adolph Hitler's goal to show the world that German "Aryan" people were the dominant race and that all others were inferior. With red and black swastikas flying all around him, Owens rose against the odds to prove to the world that the color of one's skin and that one's national origin had no bearing on the ability to excel. Owens put on a stellar performance, winning gold medals in the 100- and 200-meter dashes, the broad jump, and the 400-meter relay. He was the first American in the history of Olympic track and field to accomplish such a feat. In the end, Owens stood proudly in the center of the cheering Olympic crowd and accepted his gold medals with pride, not only for himself but for all of those for whom he would pave the way.

Upon his return to the U.S., little had changed. There were no major endorsement deals or presidential visits awaiting his return.

He recalled, "When I came back to my native country, after all the stories about Hitler, I couldn't ride in the front of the bus. I had to go to the back door. I couldn't live where I wanted. I wasn't invited to shake hands with Hitler, but I wasn't invited to the White House to shake hands with the President, either."[1] Those injustices didn't stop Owens from going forth with his desire to make a difference in the lives of young people. Owens went on to become a public speaker, sharing his athletic experiences and inspiring youth and adults alike to follow their dreams. Eventually he opened his own public relations company. Owens sponsored youth programs all over the country and spent his life working with underprivileged youth, serving as a board member and director of the Chicago Boys Club.

Many years after his unprecedented accomplishments, Owens was finally honored by his native county. In 1976, he was awarded the highest honor a U.S. civilian can receive when President Gerald Ford presented him with the Presidential Medal of Freedom. Owens' impact was not confined to just the U.S. In Africa, the American Embassy is located on Rue Jesse Owens. In Berlin, Germany, a location so hostile to his presence in the 1936 Olympics, lies a street named Jesse Owens Allee.

Before Owens' death on March 31, 1980, he left a lasting legacy. Along with Ruth, his high school sweetheart and later his wife, and their three daughters Gloria, Beverly, and Marlene, he left his thriving spirit in youth and adults across the globe. Owens expressed, "We all have dreams. In order to make dreams come into reality, it takes an awful lot of determination, dedication, self-discipline and effort."[2] Owens practiced what he preached. He overcame racism, bigotry, and segregation to pave the way for others of all colors and national origins to follow. President Carter said it best when he remarked, "His work with young athletes, as an unofficial ambassador overseas, and a spokesman for freedom are a rich legacy to his fellow Americans."[3]

Notes

1. Larry Schwartz, "Owens Pierced a Myth," ESPN.com, http://espn.go.com/sportscentury/features/00016393.html (accessed July 9, 2007).

2. CMG Worldwide, "Quotes by Jesse Owens," http://www.jesseowens.com/quotes (accessed July 7, 2007.)

3. The Jesse Owens Foundation, "Jesse Owens," http://www.jesse-owens.org/about5.html (accessed July 7, 2007).

Alice Coachman

First African-American Woman to Win an Olympic Gold Medal

by Jenny Brenden

Alice Coachman was training to be a track star before she could even set foot on a track. Born in 1923 in Albany, Georgia, she was the fifth of 10 children born to Fred and Evelyn Jackson Coachman. With plenty of brothers and sisters to play with, Coachman was a very active child, although growing up in the segregated South did not allow her many opportunities to participate in organized sports and many other activities in school, or even at YMCAs. She was also discouraged from pursuing athletics because of her gender. Sports were not seen as proper activities for young ladies. Needless to say, Coachman's formative years were characterized by a lack of support for her athletic ability. Without a proper training facility, she was forced to train in fields and on dirt roads. Coachman created her own training routine, practicing her jumping barefoot at a neighborhood playground. Despite the less-than-ideal training conditions, Coachman was a gifted, natural athlete with the work ethic to succeed.

Two women openly supported Coachman's potential, encouraging her to use her gifts and talents as best she could: her fifth-grade teacher at Monroe Street Elementary School and her aunt, who supported and defended Coachman's dreams against her parents' will. This support was enough to keep her motivated until she reached high school. In 1938 Coachman attended Madison High School where the boys' track coach immediately took an interest in her. She hadn't received any formal training, so Coach Harry E. Lash was able to teach her and nurture her natural talent from the very fundamentals. Because her talent was so raw, even the slightest bit of coaching made a big difference. Just one year later, in 1939, Coachman was invited to attend the Tuskegee Institute in Tuskegee, Alabama, a big step for her both athletically and academically.

In her first Amateur Athletic Union national championship competition, prior to starting classes at Tuskegee, Coachman broke the AAU high school and college women's high jump records—barefoot. While competing at Tuskegee from 1940 to 1946, Coachman went on to win national track and field championships in the 50- and 100-meter dashes, the 4 x 100-meter relay, and the running high jump. She also led the Tuskegee basketball team to three consecutive conference championships as a guard. Coachman quickly developed into a very well-rounded athlete.

Following the immense success she achieved at the Tuskegee Institute and through the AAU championships, Coachman continued her education and her training at Albany State College in Georgia. Academics were very important to Coachman. She earned a degree in dress making from Tuskegee in 1946, before moving on to Albany State College, where she received a B.A. in home economics in 1949.

Coachman was a dominant high-jumper and sprinter for a decade. Her success came to a peak when she qualified for the 1948 Olympic Games, despite experiencing back problems. Had the 1940 and 1944 games not been cancelled because of World War II, it is likely that Coachman would have competed and succeeded in both. Coachman finally got the opportunity to showcase her talent to the world at the 1948 Olympic Games, which were held in London, England. One of Coachman's teammates, Audrey Patterson, was the first African-American to win a medal at the Olympic Games. She earned a bronze medal in the 200-meter sprint event. Not to be outdone by her teammate, Coachman jumped 5 feet $6^{1}/_{8}$ inches in the high jump event. Her biggest rival in the high jump was Great Britain's Dorothy Tyler, who seemed to be mimicking Coachman's every move. Coachman noticed her copycat and decided to alter her starting position on the runway just a bit; Tyler did the same, but she could not handle the adjustment and she had trouble with the height. Tyler did eventually jump the same height as Coachman, but only after several jumps, making Coachman the champion. King George VI personally presented the medal to Coachman at the awards ceremony. She was not only the first African-American woman to win a gold medal, but also the first American woman to bring home the gold in a track and field event. She was also the only American woman to win a gold medal in the 1948 Olympics.

After being awarded her medal by the King in her Olympic debut, Coachman returned to the U.S., where she was treated like royalty. Parties were thrown for her, and banquets were held in her honor. In the end, she decided to retire from athletic competition.

She was only 25 years old and in peak physical condition, and she decided to go out on top.

In addition to her Olympic gold medal, Coachman won a total of 25 indoor and outdoor AAU championships during her career. In retirement, she would continue to benefit from endorsements, a first for an African-American female athlete. In 1952, Coachman became the first African-American female athletic champion to sign a product endorsement for a multinational corporation, Coca-Cola.

Following her athletic career, Coachman gave back to many of the institutions that had offered her so many wonderful opportunities both educationally and athletically. She began teaching high school physical education in her hometown of Albany, Georgia. She also moved on to teach at South Carolina State College, Albany State College, and Tuskegee High School.

Building off of the experiences she had as a young child and as an Olympic athlete, Coachman founded the Coachman Track and Field Foundation, a nonprofit organization that provides assistance to young athletes and helps former Olympic athletes adjust to life after the Games. She wanted to make sure that every child who wants to participate in track and field and chase after their athletic dreams has the opportunity to do so.

At the 1996 Olympic Games in Atlanta, Coachman was honored as one of the 100 greatest Olympic athletes in history, a very fitting honor for a phenomenal athlete and pioneer. She led the way for many African-American female athletes to follow in her footsteps, leading to hundreds of African-American female Olympic competitors. Coachman was a great role model for the sport. With her diligent work ethic, dedication, and passion, she was able to overcome all obstacles and reach her Olympic dreams. Her sweat and toil did not go unnoticed, as she has been inducted into several Halls of Fame, including the National Track and Field Hall of Fame, the Black Athletes Hall of Fame, Bob Douglas Hall of Fame, Helm's Hall of Fame, the Georgia State Hall of Fame, and the Tuskegee Hall of Fame.

Coachman preached a message to people in all walks of life: if you believe and work hard to achieve, victory is yours to receive. Alice Coachman certainly worked hard for what she achieved, and for that she will always be remembered.

Wilma Rudolph

First American Woman to Win Three Gold Medals

by Marcus Sedberry

American comedian Bill Cosby once said, "In order to succeed, your desire for success should be greater than your fear of failure."[1] Although his statement was not directed at Wilma Rudolph, it is a true testimony of who she was and the things in which she believed.

In 1940, America was still recovering from the hardships of the Great Depression. Millions of people, including Ed and Blanche Rudolph, were poor and homeless as they struggled to live. Ed Rudolph worked as a railroad porter and handyman. His wife, Blanche, was a housekeeper for wealthy white families. In order to make ends meet in such trying times, Mrs. Rudolph often had to make her daughters' dresses out of flour sacks. In the midst of a difficult time for the Rudolph family, Ed and Blanche were blessed with their 20th of 22 children, Wilma Glodean Rudolph, in Clarksville, Tennessee. Rudolph was born prematurely, weighing only $4\frac{1}{2}$ pounds at birth and needing extra care. Clarksville at the time was not very conducive to an easy life for African-American families because of segregation. The local hospital was a whites-only facility. and there was only one African-American doctor in the city. The Rudolph family budget could not afford expensive medical treatment.

Over the next several years, young Wilma's mother nursed her through measles, scarlet fever, chicken pox, and double pneumonia. However, when her mother discovered that Wilma's left leg and foot were becoming weak and deformed, she knew the little girl had to be taken to the doctor. At a very young age, Wilma was diagnosed with polio, a crippling disease for which there was no cure. The doctor told her she would never be able to walk.

After that visit to the doctor, Mrs. Rudolph refused to give up on the well-being of her daughter and took Wilma for treatment 50 miles away at Meharry Hospital, the black medical college of Fisk University in Nashville, Tennessee. Mrs. Rudolph transported her young daughter to Nashville twice a week to seek treatment. After two years, little Wilma was finally able to walk with the assistance of a metal leg brace. To prevent the Rudolph family from incurring the steady cost of traveling miles to get treatment, the doctors taught Mrs. Rudolph how to administer physical therapy at home.

At the age of seven, Rudolph was able to attend a segregated school after being home schooled for the previous years. Finally, at the age of 12, she was able to walk normally without a brace or corrective shoes. While Rudolph was in junior high school, her older sister Yolanda joined the basketball team and Rudolph followed in her footsteps. The basketball coach felt Rudolph was not ready for the court, so she was forced to sit the bench for three years before being allowed to play. Rudolph earned the starting guard role, set the state scoring record for the most points in a game, and led her team to a state championship. During the championship tournament, the Tennessee State track and field coach, Ed Temple, was very impressed by her talent. As a result Temple asked Rudolph to train with Tennessee State's summer camp. She eventually earned a full scholarship as part of the Tennessee State Tigerbells.

Rudolph quickly became a track and field star. In 1956, at the tender age of 16, Rudolph earned a spot on the U.S. Olympic Team in Melbourne, Australia. In spite of her youth, Rudolph won a bronze medal as a member of the 4 x 100-meter relay. Even more impressive than the bronze medal she earned was her ability to overcome all of the hardships of her childhood and become an Olympian only four years after being freed from wearing leg braces and corrective shoes. Rudolph did not stop there, as she continued to shine on the track and field scene. In 1959, she qualified for the next year's Olympics by setting a world record in the 200 meters. At the 1960 Olympics in Rome, Italy, Rudolph became the first American woman to win three gold medals. Rudolph won the 100- and 200-meter dashes and then anchored the U.S. 4 x 100-meter relay to victory, despite an ankle injury. Because of her success, gender barriers in track and field began to fall.

After returning from Rome, Rudolph began to receive numerous awards. In 1960 she was awarded the United Press Athlete of the Year and the Associated Press Woman of the Year. The following year, Rudolph became the first woman to receive the James R. Sullivan Award for good sportsmanship. She was also the first woman to receive the European Sportswriters' Sportsman of the Year and the Christopher Columbus Award for Most Outstanding International Sports Personality. Her accolades only continued; in 1980 she was named to the Black Sports Hall of Fame and in 1983 she was inducted into the Olympic Hall of Fame.

Perhaps one of the most impressive awards and "firsts" associated with Rudolph occurred immediately after her return from the 1960 Olympics. The governor of Tennessee wanted to have a victory parade in honor of her tremendous accomplishments. Rudolph refused to participate in the parade unless blacks and whites were allowed to share in the event together. She was granted her wish and Clarksville, Tennessee, had its first racially integrated event with an integrated banquet to follow.

In 1962, Rudolph retired from track and field and returned to Clarksville to teach at her old school, Cobb Elementary School, as well as be a track coach at her alma mater, Burt High School. The following year, she married Robert Eldridge and later had four children, Yolanda, Djuanna, Robert Jr., and Xurry. Also in 1963, Rudolph received her bachelor's degree in English from Tennessee State. After a brief stint of teaching and coaching in her hometown, she moved on to coach in Maine and Indiana along with becoming a sports commentator on national television and co-hosting a network radio show. Rudolph traveled across the country sharing her story of overcoming misfortune by believing in herself and those around her. She would advise her listeners that, "Winning is great, sure, but if you are really going to do something in life, the secret is learning how to lose. Nobody goes undefeated all the time. If you can pick up after a crushing defeat, and go on to win again, you are going to be a champion someday."[2]

Rudolph is a true demonstration of someone who pioneered not only through racial and gender barriers but also through personal hardships. She is a living testament that adversity does not have to have the last word. Rather, she gave this advice: "Never underestimate the power of dreams and the influence of the human spirit. We are all the same in this notion. The potential for greatness lives within each of us." As a child, doctors told her she would never walk. They were right. She didn't walk—she ran. She ran through pain, discrimination, racial and gender inequity and became a role model and pioneer for all to follow. At the age of 54, Rudolph was finally caught. After several hospitalizations to receive treatment for brain cancer, Rudolph died on November 12, 1994. Nonetheless, Rudolph's legacy will last forever.

Notes

1. Study World, "Quotes by author; Bill Cosby," http://www.studyworld.com/newsite/quotes/quotebyauthor.asp?ln=Cosby&fn=Bill (accessed July 8, 2007).

2. Wilma Rudolph, "Wilma Rudolph Quotes," http://www.wilmarudolph.net/more.html (accessed July 10, 2007).

Tommie Smith and John Carlos

Shaking Up the Sports World

by Horacio Ruiz

Tommie Smith stands on the winner's podium, his country's national anthem booming through Mexico City's Olympic Stadium and his country's flag raised the highest. There is an Olympic gold medal dangling from Smith's neck—his reward for winning the 200-meter race in world-record time—but the medal is hardly the object of the moment's attention. Smith has his right fist raised, clenched in a black glove, with his head bowed down and eyes shut.

John Carlos stands a few feet below Smith on the winner's podium, the winner of a bronze medal in the same event. He is Smith's fellow countryman and his pose mirrors Smith's. He bows his head and lifts his left fist in the air, clenched in a black glove. He does not open his eyes. Neither man looks as the American flag is raised into the air. In that moment, Smith and Carlos create a lasting image for black power in the United States, demonstrating the impact two individuals can create in protest. Many interpretations have been made of the protest. At its broadest it is applied to international human rights and to a more specific point, the treatment of African-American people in the United States. Those moments during the playing of the national anthem of the United States would change the lives of Smith and Carlos forever—and the American sports scene.

Ten days prior to the beginning of the 1968 Olympics in Mexico City, a group of students protesting against the Mexican government was surrounded by the Mexican army and fired at in the Plaza of Three Cultures. An estimated 270 students died and more than 1,000 were wounded in what would be called the Tlatelolco Massacre. The preceding months had seen the assassinations of presidential hopeful Robert F. Kennedy and civil rights leader Dr. Martin Luther King, Jr. In 1967, before the assassinations of two of the most prominent leaders in the United States and the Tlatelolco Massacre of 1968, sociologist and civil rights activist Harry Edwards had asked a group of black American Olympians to boycott the Mexico City Games. Edwards was well aware that the Mexico City Games would be the first to be televised live to an American audience—

creating the perfect platform for a protest. Edwards created the Olympic Project for Human Rights with the intention of bringing to light the social injustices faced by African-Americans on the world's premiere sporting platform. As the Olympics approached, however, the boycott seemed less likely to occur as the majority of African-American athletes did not agree on a boycott being the best form of protest. Instead, each athlete was left to create his or her own form of protest.

A closer look at the protest of Smith and Carlos reveals intricate symbolism. Both Smith and Carlos went to the podium shoeless and wearing black socks to represent black poverty in the United States. Smith wore a black scarf to represent black pride. Carlos put a string of black beads around his neck to represent those who had been lynched. Smith would later explain that his right fist represented black power in America and Carlos' left fist represented unity in black America. Both fists together, represented an arch of unity and power. All three athletes on the podium, including Australian silver-medalist Peter Norman, wore Olympic Project for Human Rights badges on their jackets. Norman, knowing that Smith and Carlos would stage their protest, had asked if there was anything he could do. They handed him the human rights badge, and he became forever unified with them not just because of his place on the podium, but because of his show of solidarity. Smith and Carlos would reunite as pallbearers at Norman's funeral nearly four decades later.

Although the conservative Australian media pushed for Norman to be sanctioned, Julius Patching, Norman's team manager, refused to take any action against him. Smith and Carlos would become victims of a much more powerful political machine. Both were removed from the Olympic Village and banned from the Olympics by International Olympic Committee president Avery Brundage. "The basic principle of the Olympic Games is that politics plays no part whatsoever in them," read an IOC statement. "U.S. athletes violated this universally accepted principle . . . to advertise domestic political views."

Smith and Carlos returned home to San Jose—heroes to some and enemies to many others. They were subjected to death threats and hate mail, schoolyard insults and bricks smashing through their windows. For many years, they were relegated to the fringe of the track and field community, forced to alter their school schedule so that they had to take night classes, and had difficulty finding jobs. Neither man got a meaningful job in the United Sates until Smith was hired as a coach at Oberlin College by sports activist and Oberlin athletics director, Jack Scott. Despite the life-altering consequences, neither regrets his actions.

"I knew it was going to be big," Carlos told the *Orlando Sentinel* years after his stand on the podium. "I was prepared to face the repercussions. What I wasn't prepared for at all was how it would touch everything. I had only been thinking about me being John Carlos, not me being a young married man with a kid. It was hard for us. We still feel it today."[1]

It seemed as if Smith was primed to protest for black Americans and to be a symbol of the social movements of the 1960s. In his autobiography, *Silent Gesture*, he remembered growing up in a family of sharecroppers working to harvest cotton or grapes, only to see the major portion of their crop handed over to white landowners. But a particular event is etched into Smith's memory: watching his father pulling their family wagon filled with 10 children to the side of a road so that a lone white man could pass. It was an early lesson in Smith's life about his place in society.

Today, Smith is a faculty member at Santa Monica College, where he also is the head men's cross country and track and field coach. Carlos is working as the track and field coach and as an in-school suspension supervisor at Palm Springs High in Palm Springs, California.

Thirty-seven years and one day after their protest, San Jose State, Smith's and Carlos' alma mater, unveiled a statue of their famous pose in the 1968 Olympics. Back in 1968, San Jose State was the one place the two runners were well-received, as students cheered them on and then-president Robert Clark called them "honorable young men."

"It's an honor for us, but we also realize this isn't all about us anymore," Smith said at the ceremony. "The history of what happened will live on long after we're gone, and I'm just glad a part of it will live at San Jose State."[2]

Notes

1. Rick Maese, "Strike a Pose: Smith, Carlos Sent Powerful Message at '68 Olympics," *Orlando Sentinel*, July 27, 2004).

2. "Statue Honors Olympic Sprinters' Civil Rights Protest," *Jet*, November 7, 2005.

Jackie Joyner-Kersee

The "First Lady" of Olympic Track and Field

by Stacy Martin

Jackie Joyner Kersee and Richard Lapchick at the National Consortium for Academics and Sports Hall of Fame Induction Ceremony in 2003.

Jackie Joyner-Kersee has always had "a kind of grace" as an athlete because even though she is a tough competitor she has always demonstrated poise and charm on and off the track. Her race in life has been filled with obstacle after obstacle, but she breezed past each one with her head held high as if it was just another hurdle on the track. Her maternal grandmother, Evelyn Joyner, named her Jacqueline after former first lady of the United States, Jacqueline Kennedy Onassis, a woman known for her elegance. Evelyn knew that Joyner-Kersee would also be a first lady.

Joyner-Kersee quickly secured the title of "Greatest Woman Athlete of the Twentieth Century," assuring her place as the first lady of track and field for quite some time. She competed in the heptathlon, a two-day event composed of the 100-meter hurdles, high jump, shot put, and 200 meters on the first day, and the long jump, javelin, and 800 meters on the second. It's not simply that she was the first female to become so decorated in track and field, for as time passes her records will be passed on to future generations of runners. Rather, Joyner-Kersee will remain in our memories because of the way she conducted herself with such class.

Joyner-Kersee grew up in East St. Louis, Illinois, and spent most of her time at the Mary Brown Community Center, which offered sports to young people, as well as story time and painting. Joyner-Kersee's neighborhood was plagued with violence and drug abuse, so the community center was as much a safe haven as it was an opportunity for personal growth. Al and Mary, Joyner-Kersee's parents, had married young and were barely out of childhood themselves when they gave birth to Jackie. Mary Joyner was extremely conscientious about her daughter's future and so she pushed her in the classroom and on the athletic fields, to break the cycle of babies having babies that seems so compelling in a poor community. Her daughter was to know greatness, not poverty. Joyner-Kersee's trek to the top would start when she joined the track club at age nine without any financial resources. She sold candles to her elementary classmates to raise money for track meet travel expenses. She ran in a pair of shoes until the rubber wore out or they fell off. She didn't need shoes to race past her competition. She was a good student as well. Joyner-Kersee had it all from a young age.

Evelyn Joyner doted on Joyner-Kersee by playing dress up with her and painting her tiny fingernails so they would match her own. Joyner-Kersee felt like the first lady when her grandmother was around. She was the adult who always made her feel special as a child. Evelyn planned a trip from Chicago to visit her darling granddaughter, and Joyner-Kersee could barely contain her excitement anytime her grandmother planned a visit. One trip was only a few days away when the family received a call that Evelyn would be visiting the angels instead. Joyner-Kersee's step-grandfather was a destructive alcoholic. He had come home drunk from the bar and shot her grandmother, while she was sleeping, with a 12-gauge shotgun. Joyner-Kersee had it all, except her loving grandmother. She never drank or used any recreational drugs because she saw how their use often leads to violence. She is proud of the fact that her family never became victims of violence again, because they continued to expect great things from one another and encouraged one another's hopes and dreams, just as Evelyn had encouraged Joyner-Kersee to be the first lady of whatever her heart desired.

Joyner-Kersee became a talented high school athlete in track and field as well as basketball. She was so successful that she was offered a scholarship to the University of California at Los Angeles (UCLA), consistently one of the top track and field programs in the country. She was so capable that she was one of the few athletes who could handle the demands of two sports and her coursework. Her mother asked her to come home for Christmas her freshman year, but she declined and promised to come home in the spring. Unfortunately, she would return home sooner than that. Joyner-Kersee's mother died suddenly from meningitis just a short time after the Christmas invitation she had declined. Joyner-Kersee went home to attend her mother's funeral. Her three siblings were terribly grief-stricken. As the eldest child, Joyner-Kersee had to remain strong. She held her head high above the abyss of emotion drowning everyone else. Returning to school, she remained strong for nearly a year, but the wave of grief found her in Los Angeles the next Christmas, when she realized that she wouldn't be getting a call to come home that year. The tears flowed and she momentarily lost the resilience that she so elegantly had displayed on the athletic fields. Her indestructible façade may have cracked, but it would not crumble. She endured the almost insurmountable pain and continued on the path her mother had set her on all those years ago. She continued her education to set an example for her family, showing them that life would go on and they would not become victims of tragedy.

Often, when a door closes, a window opens; however, one can get seriously scraped climbing through. Joyner-Kersee saw her open window as an open lane on the track, but in 1982 she developed a condition known as exercise-induced asthma. As a woman who characterized herself as invincible, she was shaken to the core when she was told that she had limitations. Jackie Joyner-Kersee denied that she had a disease, but today she admits that she was scared to acknowledge it. She went so far as to hide her inhaler from people, even when her breath escaped her and she needed to use it. Eventually, she couldn't deny its existence any longer; she didn't take her inhaler with her to practice one day and ended up in an emergency room feeling suffocated and losing control. When she awakened, she had a deep awareness of her disease and realized that her medication was life-sustaining. However, her athlete persona had to realize that a new routine and workouts were part of that medication, and that she was not weak and vulnerable because of it.

Once again, doors seemed to be closing on her and her escape to the field or track, away from life's anxiety, seemed to be slipping away. Just then, someone special stepped in and helped her manage her disease, as well as her track and field career. Bob Kersee was the assistant coach at UCLA and had experienced the loss of his mother as well. He offered his support to Joyner-Kersee and then helped her gain control of her asthma. He encouraged her to continue in track and field as the same fierce competitor that she had always been, and helped her realize that the asthma was not a limitation, just something to contend with and be treated for. His compassion and reinforcement were invaluable to Joyner-Kersee, and they became good friends. Four years later, they became husband and wife. Bob has the same fire in him that Joyner-Kersee does when it comes to competition. He is her biggest critic and her biggest fan on the track. He will scream at her on the track and cook her dinner the same evening. They truly complement each other and their relationship has proven successful in life and in sport.

Joyner-Kersee became a household name because of her remarkable athletic achievements. Her willpower to compete with asthma enhanced her prestige. Her collegiate athletic career started her on the path to success when she set the NCAA record for the heptathlon twice. She continued to play basketball for UCLA during this time as well and was recognized as the UCLA All-University Athlete for three years. In 1984, Joyner-Kersee won the silver medal at the Olympics and finished fifth in the long jump. She won numerous heptathlon titles after that at the World Championships and Goodwill Games. She graduated from college, married Bob, and then in 1988, she struck gold. She set the world record in the heptathlon at the U.S. Olympic Trials and won the long jump. She traveled to the Olympics and won a gold medal for both the heptathlon and the long jump events. She beat her own world record in the heptathlon and set an Olympic record in the long jump. In 1992, she won gold once more in the Olympic heptathlon and stole silver in the long jump. Four years later, Joyner-Kersee won a bronze medal in the long jump after she had pulled a muscle and had to withdraw from the heptathlon. In fact, she did not lose a heptathlon for over 12 years from 1984 until the 1996 Olympic Trials.

Her success in track and field built the pedestal from which she so gracefully speaks today. She was a star female athlete during a time when girls who competed in sports were commonly referred to as tomboys. She challenged that perception by exuding what she calls "a kind of grace." She describes her definition of grace in her autobiography, aptly titled *A Kind of Grace*. She continues to promote women in athletics and encourages young girls to follow in her footsteps.

Her career came full circle around the track and finished at her starting line in East St. Louis. The community center that she enjoyed so much as a child had closed while she was traveling the world for track meets and publicity appearances. She took a percentage of all of her endorsements and raised $40,000 to reopen the center for the children of East St. Louis and give them some of the same opportunities that had placed her in such an advantageous position. It wasn't enough, but Joyner-Kersee would not be deterred. She explored other ways to finance a brand new 37-acre facility that will boast both indoor and outdoor tracks, basketball courts and state-of-the-art computer rooms. She is determined to create opportunities for children who are facing the same tough decisions and turbulent lifestyles that she did when she was their age. One such experience that she provided was a trip to New York City for the Macy's Thanksgiving Day Parade for 100 children through her Jackie Joyner-Kersee Community Foundation. The inspiration that she received at the Mary Brown Center when she was nine was so profound that all of her efforts are focused on her foundation today.

She also speaks out about asthma as her next great opponent. She says that she approaches fighting the disease as if it were one of her competitors, and her treatment is the training she needs to be competitive. According to Michael Letterlough of the *Philadelphia Tribune*, African-Americans "only represent 12 percent of our population, [but] they comprise 26 percent of the deaths related to asthma."[1] Joyner-Kersee was fortunate enough to have the proper medical treatment for her disease, but she realizes that so many do not have the availability of sound medical care that is needed to manage the disease properly. She knows that African-Americans are more likely to simply attempt to live with asthma, and she wants to use her status to draw attention to how tragedy can happen without treatment and how one can live a full and complete life with it.

She also speaks about the importance of goal setting and violence prevention. She challenges members of her audience to think about what could happen at their schools even though they have not experienced a violent act as of yet, and how they could prevent it. The loss of her grandmother had a profound influence on her life. She now wants to provide a positive influence for today's youth. She had goals and dreams that carried her out of an impoverished neighborhood and that brought her back to that same town with a renewed purpose. She emphasizes that having goals is a real antidote to violence. Her listeners may have come to hear Jackie Joyner-Kersee, the world's greatest female athlete, but they left having heard a message that challenged them to be serious about their future.

Joyner-Kersee has experienced the power that sport can wield, and she has done everything she can to utilize that power. She has even entered the business of sports, first and foremost through her endorsement money that she has funneled into the Jackie Joyner-Kersee Community Foundation. She ventured outside her sport to become certified as a sports agent with the National Football League Players Association from 1998 to 2001, a role that only five females had filled at the time. Her company, Elite International Sports Marketing, Inc., is designed to help athletes prepare for a career in athletics as well as to determine what they can do after their career is complete. She has been extraordinarily successful in the heptathlon in track and field, and she is becoming an exceptional leader in the heptathlon of life.

Note

1. Michael Letterlough, Jr., "Breathing Easy; Olympic Gold-medallist Jackie Joyner-Kersee Talks about Her Battle with Asthma," *Philadelpia Tribune*, April 3, 2005.

Vonetta Flowers

First African-American Female to Win a Winter Olympics Gold Medal

by Jenny Brenden

It takes an extraordinary athlete to make a successful transition from one Olympic sport to another. There are few athletes who possess the ability to make such a switch, and Vonetta Flowers is one of them. Flowers put her name in the Olympic record books by becoming the first African-American ever to win a gold medal in the Winter Olympics.

As a young girl, Flowers had aspirations of winning a gold medal in track and field and for much of her life all of her energy was spent trying to achieve that goal. Many might believe Olympic aspirations at such a young age to be unrealistic, but Flowers' innate athletic prowess made her hopes a bit more justified. In 1982, Coach DeWitt Thomas came to Vonetta's elementary school in search of talent for the Marvel City Striders, a youth track team which has since been changed to the Alabama Striders. The rest, as they say, is history. Vonetta had a lot of support and encouragement from her childhood coach, who watched as she developed into an incredible runner. Her athleticism was showcased as she participated in volleyball, basketball, and track in high school.

Flowers went on to be the first in her family to attend college when she was awarded a full athletic scholarship to the University of Alabama, Birmingham. She further developed as a track athlete during her college years and finished her collegiate career as a much-decorated star. She was the first seven-time All-American at UAB. In addition, she held 35 conference titles and victories at the Olympic Festival and the Penn Relays. Flowers seemed to be an Olympic track athlete in the making.

Her Olympic dreams were very much alive after college. Flowers competed in the Olympic trials in 1996 and 2000, but was disappointed in both outings. She was preparing to move on with her life and set aside her Olympic dreams, when her husband, Johnny Flowers, became aware that there was a push for Olympic track athletes to try out for the U.S. bobsled team. Although not sold on the idea right away, Vonetta's competitive nature eventually prevailed, and she agreed to try out. This scenario may sound familiar, as it is the basic plot of the movie *Cool Runnings*, which Flowers admitted was her initial source of knowledge when she first decided to convert from a track and field athlete to a bobsledder. Vonetta and Johnny both tried out for the team, but Johnny became injured and was unable to continue.

The simple concept, both in the movie and in Flowers' situation, is that speed is speed, regardless of the surface on which an athlete is running. It did not take her long to acclimate to the ice and cold. Flowers was named as Jill Bakken's partner and became the brakeman for the USA-2 sled, behind the USA-1 sled, which was a gold medal favorite in the 2002 Winter Olympics. This pairing came after Flowers was dropped by her initial partner and thereby forced to compete in a push-off with other U.S. brakemen. Flowers got the job only a few months before the games, but she and Bakken worked well together. As a duo, Bakken and Flowers broke a track record on their first run of the Olympics with a time of 48.81 seconds. Together, they were able to hold on and win the gold medal. For their achievement, Flowers and Bakken received the honor of carrying the Olympic flag into the closing ceremonies.

Life did not slow down for Flowers after her gold medal run at the Olympics in 2002. She found out she was pregnant shortly after the Olympics and gave birth to premature twin boys later that year. Flowers continued to train, but found a new partner in Jean Prahm. Flowers also found time to write a book, *Running on Ice: The Overcoming Faith of Vonetta Flowers*. She also received the Wilma Rudolph Athletic Olympian Award, as well as being named one of the "50 Most Inspiring African-Americans" by *Essence Magazine*.

Faith and perseverance have gotten Flowers a long way in her life, whether it pertained to her athletic career, her family life, or the health of her kids. Even in the beginning, Flowers faced many challenges with her twins as she went into preterm labor at the end of her fifth month of pregnancy. She had to be highly medicated in order to stop the contractions and even with all the medication, the boys were born almost three months premature. Jaden and Jorden each weighed less than four pounds when they were born, and Jorden's outer ears were severely underdeveloped.

Family is extremely important to Flowers and her husband. When she decided to continue to be a part of the American bobsled team, she took her whole family with her to both training and competition. She does more than carry their spirit with her. On her racing gloves, which she wears whenever she is on the track, she has written her two boys' names, Jaden on one hand and Jorden on the other. Physically, her entire family also travels with her when she is training on the European bobsled tour. She and her husband believe firmly in the importance of sticking together.

The family has been there for one another, especially as Jorden underwent surgery for his underdeveloped ears. The family knows how to communicate with Jorden through sign language. To give him the chance to hear, though, they wanted to try a surgical procedure called auditory brainstem implant (ABI), which is not yet approved in the United States. A doctor in Italy performed Jorden's surgery, in which microelectrodes were implanted on Jorden's brainstem. The process is a waiting game, as the microelectrodes must be given time before they can be activated.

The success of this procedure will not determine Jorden's or the Flowers family's quality of life. The hope is that the surgery will be successful, but regardless, they will continue to be a loving family who rely on one another for strength.

Vonetta Flowers intends to continue with her bobsled training and she has expressed some interest in learning how to drive the bobsled, a skill that can take years to master. With all that she has achieved, together with her great faith and familial support, there is no doubt that what Vonetta Flowers puts her mind to, she can accomplish.

Shani Davis

First African-American Winter Olympics Gold Medalist in an Individual Sport

by Jenny Brenden

At the age of three, when he was flying around the roller-skating rink at breakneck speeds, Shani Davis may not have known that he would be an Olympic gold medalist, but onlookers certainly recognized his potential. Speedskating has been described as a roller derby on ice, so it is easy to see how Davis made the transition from the sport with wheels to the sport with blades.

For many reasons, much of Davis' success can be attributed to his mother, Cherie Davis. Although speedskating is not a particularly common sport among young people, an employer of Davis' mother suggested that she get a very young Shani involved in skating. At age six Davis joined the Evanston Speedskating Club and began competing locally. Davis was coached by an African-American man in Evanston, and he skated with a diverse group of young athletes. It wasn't until later in his training that he came to realize that speed-skating was a predominantly white sport. Although the demographic make-up of the sport has changed little in 20 years, leaving African-Americans somewhat of a rarity on the ice, Davis remains as un-fazed as he was as a child. Davis did have to endure a lot of teasing from his peers, but that never deterred him from the sport.

Davis' mother was a single parent, and they lived on the south side of Chicago, so it was not an easy commute to the rink by train. After only a few short years, it was evident that Davis had a very special talent and he had the potential to go far in the sport. Taking his potential and opportunities very seriously, the family moved to the north side of the city to be closer to the rink when Davis was 10. It was also around this age that Cherie would wake the young man up in the morning to do dry-land training, employing a particularly rigorous training style. She was always pushing him to be better. To this day, Davis' mother continues to be an integral part of his speed-skating career. Whether it's encouragement or criticism, she always has her son's best interests in mind. "My mom never thought of herself first, and I credit most of my success to her. She continues to manage my career and is always there for me."[1]

Chicago is a city very rich in sports history and tradition. When asked about his favorite athletes, Davis named famous Chicago sports icons Michael Jordan and Walter Peyton, but he also mentioned the not-so-familiar name of Bonnie Blair. When he was younger, Davis would ignore the teasing and the looks he received as he proudly wore his Bonnie Blair sweatshirt. Davis knew that in order to achieve greatness, he had to admire greatness. Bonnie Blair, a five-time Olympic gold medalist in speedskating, certainly fit the bill. Not only was it rare for a child to have Olympic speedskating aspirations, but it was even more rare for that child to be African-American. Davis' mother always assured him that he could dream whatever he wanted. She encouraged him to go out and have fun.

Athletes in speedskating, like athletes in most other Winter Olympic disciplines, tend to be white, a phenomenon which has been explained by a lack of access and exposure to winter sports in Latino and African-American communities. In that respect, Davis is a pioneer simply by his participation in the sport, but his success goes far beyond just putting on his skates. Being the first African-American to dominate this sport is only part of the history he has made. Another factor that makes Davis unique to the sport is his 6-foot-2, 185-pound frame—a very large build for a speedskater. Typically skaters need to be smaller, with a lower center of gravity, but Davis' strength and speed overcome his size.

Although Davis was a speed demon from the start, he worked diligently on his technique as well, and the combination led him to dominate the sport at a very young age. When Davis was 16 he moved to Lake Placid to train for the Olympics, a major culture shock for a boy who had grown up in Chicago. He quickly acclimated to his new surroundings and the changes affected his racing only in a positive way, as he achieved more wins and more titles.

Breaking barriers in 2002, Davis became the first African-American to qualify for the Olympic short track speedskating team. The short track speedskating event is a fairly new event to the Winter Olympics, making its debut in 1992 at the Albertville games. It is a modified version of the speedskating events that have been a part of the Winter Olympics since they started in 1924. In the short track competition, skaters are racing against their opponents, as opposed to the long track competition, in which they are racing against the clock. As the names of the events would suggest, shorter distances are raced in the short track races and longer distances in the long track races. With the emergence of the short track events, many speed-skaters have been forced to specialize in their particular events, but Davis has proven that he can excel at any distance on the track.

When Davis made the short track team in 2002, it was the beginning of his chapter in sports history. In 2004, Davis became the first American to make two junior world teams in the short track and long track in the same year. Although he made his debut in the Olympics on the short track team, Davis has earned medals in a variety of events. In 2003, he was the U.S. long track 1,500-meters and 10,000-meters champion, and in 2004, he was the 5,000-meter champion and silver medalist in the 1,500-meters and 10,000-meters. In 2003 and 2004, Davis was the U.S. all-round champion, and in 2005 he was the world all-round champion, becoming the fourth American to achieve that accolade. He also set world records in 2005 in the 1,000- and 1,500-meter events.

The Winter Games in Torino in 2006 had the typical Winter Olympic racial make-up. Of the 211 U.S. Olympians, five were African-American. Regardless, it was at the 2006 Winter Games where Davis became an Olympic champion at 1,000-meters, becoming the first African-American athlete to win an individual gold medal in Olympic Winter Games history. In those same games, he also earned a silver medal in the 1,500-meter event.

Currently, Davis trains in Calgary for most of the year and takes summer courses at Northern Michigan University in Marquette. Most of his fellow U.S. speedskaters train in Utah, but Davis tends to keep to himself and focus on his individual training. He has aspirations of becoming a marine biologist after his speedskating days come to an end. Even when he is done competing, speedskating will always be a part of his life, and he would love to teach the sport one day.

Note

1. Shani Davis Speedskating Biography, http://shanidavis.org/shani_davis_biog raphy.php?i=1&sessionToken= (accessed April 15, 2007).

12

CONCLUSION

by Richard Lapchick

Although we celebrate the lives of these pioneers for being the first African-Americans in their respective categories, it is more important that they are not the last. In most cases, the doors they forced opened have allowed others to walk through; the footsteps of some have been followed in small numbers, and those of the student-athletes have been duplicated by countless more. Whether it be one additional individual to follow the athlete's path or 100, each should be equally celebrated and respected. How better to honor people's lives than by having someone want to follow in their footsteps?

The life of each pioneer should be celebrated for what he or she accomplished in the face of doubt and adversity. Each paved a path that had never before been walked by another African-American. To believe in what you cannot see is a powerful and daring feat. Today, African-Americans and sports fans of all ages and races have role models to emulate and look up to, but imagine picturing yourself in a world where no one looked like you and those with the power prohibited your participation because of the color of your skin. Had Buck O'Neil, Kenny Washington, Willie O'Ree, Eddie McAshan, Alice Coachman, and so many others chronicled in this book not let their imaginations and determination find their way onto the playing fields, who knows how much longer the United States would have failed to break the barriers for African-Americans. The bravery and fortitude they showed is so admirable.

My wish, and I am almost certain that our pioneers would concur, is that each individual feel the power sport has to bring people together. There are few feelings better than being part of a team. Whether it be in a gym, a schoolyard, or an office, professionally, recreationally, or politically, working together in effort to achieve one common goal is a beautiful feeling of strength and achievement. The success of a team working together as a "well-oiled machine" is more attainable than many realize. Keith Lee is a great colleague and special friend of mine. A former NFL player, Keith often compares society to football. If only society could better represent the team huddle of a football game, he dreams. When teammates step on the field in matching uniforms, their differences in race, religious beliefs, age, and sexual orientation disappear as they come together in the huddle. Their desire to win—their common goal—overpowers any superficial differences and discrepancies. Keith calls it the power of the huddle.

But there are obstacles to people of color that remain both in and out of sport, especially in the area of power. Who runs our teams? Our leagues? Our athletics department? Unless there is a keeper of the flame lit by these pioneers, it is possible that the flame could flicker and be extinguished.

In my mind, the keeper of the flame in 2007 is Floyd Keith. He might be considered a man whom society blocked from his early aspirations to become a head football coach in a Division I program. He paid his dues in the coaching ranks, while never getting a Division IA head coaching job. He hung up the coaching whistle after nearly three decades and was appointed to the position of Executive Director of the Black Coaches & Administrators on March 12, 2001. His dynamic leadership has brought the BCA back as the preeminent force for the social consciousness of race and ethnicity in sports. He has been a new kind of champion of the people ever since.

What I said in the first book of this series, *100 Heroes: People in Sports Who Make This a Better World* is still relevant for *100 Pioneers*. The 100 pioneers "described in this volume should serve as a light, indeed, as a beacon for us all. They followed their dreams and helped us dream as well. They served others even as they succeeded on the playing field. They found hope where others believed none existed. Let us cheer their accomplishments as we follow their example" and ensure no man, woman, or child is prevented from achieving a dream again.

Without dreams and determination, we would not have 700-career homeruns, multi-gold medal winning Olympians, or 28-foot long jumps. In the 1936 Olympic Games in Berlin, Germany, Jesse

Owens set two Olympic records and broke a world record while winning four gold medals—a feat that stood unmatched for almost 50 years. Records were made to be broken, because nothing is impossible.

In the 1960 Olympic Games in Rome, Italy, Wilma Rudolph won three gold medals on the track. As a child, she had polio and had been told she would never again be able to walk. Never say never, because nothing is impossible.

At the 1968 Olympic Games in Mexico City, Bob Beamon shattered the long jump record by $21^{3}/4$ inches with a jump of 29 feet $2^{1}/_{2}$ inches. The world record had been broken 13 times since 1901; each by an average of just two inches, with the most ever stretching it by six inches. Beamon nearly quadrupled that amount. His record has stood for 23 years and remains the Olympic record long jump distance today. "The perfect jump," as ESPN's Dick Schaap titled it, proved that nothing is impossible.

The "Great Bambino," Babe Ruth, is still thought of by many as the greatest baseball player of all time, more than 70 years post-retirement. His skills with a bat are best remembered. After his 21-year career, his homerun record of 714 was believed to be virtually unbreakable. The next closest number trailed by more than 50, with Willie Mays' record of 660 homeruns. Although it took almost 40 years for another athlete to rise to Babe's level, the great Hank Aaron tied his record in 1974. Aaron finished his career in 1976 with 755 homeruns. Breaking the unbreakable proves that nothing is impossible.

The stories of the 100 pioneers are a testament to the world-renowned Adidas ad campaign that claims, "'Impossible' is just a big word thrown around by small men who find it easier to live in the world they've been given than to explore the power they have to change it. Impossible is not a fact. It's an opinion. Impossible is not a declaration. It's a dare. Impossible is potential. Impossible is temporary." Temporarily, the posts held by African-Americans in this book were made impossible by "small men." Fortunately, bigger "men" came around and used their power to change society, with sport as their tool to do so. Thankfully, these 100 pioneers accepted the "dare" and sacrificed to better our world. If nothing more, they have proven that nothing is impossible.

These pioneers changed teammates, schools, communities and,

ultimately, the nation. In smashing such barriers, they helped speed up the healing process of the wounds of America's segregated past. Someday sports may help allow us to stop talking about a white America, a black America, a Latino America, and an Asian America and to see ourselves all as part of the United States of America. If they do, we should give profound thanks to these pioneers and the lives they led.

Epilogue

FLOYD KEITH: KEEPER OF THE FLAME

by Horacio Ruiz

His speech in the fall of 2006 stunned a number of University of Central Florida graduate students. "If you are black, you have a greater chance at becoming an Army general than a head football coach in Division I-A. The Army is 26 percent black and 8.3 percent of the generals are black. In Division I-A schools, 51 percent of the football players are black, but only four percent of head coaches are black."

The percentage has increased to five percent since his speech to the graduate students, and Floyd Keith, executive director of the Black Coaches & Administrators (BCA, formerly known as the Black Coaches Association) will continue to give such examples to prove his point. He is passionate about monitoring the hiring practices of colleges for people of color and trying to raise awareness in the disparity between the number of black football players and black football coaches. When he first took over the BCA in 2001, Keith found an organization that had fallen into a state of irrelevance. Immediately, Keith raised more than one million dollars annually and has increased the number of BCA corporate sponsors from one in 2001 to 26 in 2007. During his tenure, the BCA's "Hiring Report Card" was implemented and today has become the preeminent report on college football's hiring practices. The organization has grown from 172 paid memberships in 2001 to more than 2,800 paid memberships.

Naturally, Keith is not welcomed in all circles. He is not immune from the occasional racial attack via e-mail or phone. Keith and the organization are often accused of raising racial issues where there are none. But Keith knows firsthand about unfair and unequal hiring practices that have led to a surprisingly low number of African-

Americans in head coaching positions. Keith is the only African-American to have ever been the coach of a Division I football program in New England, where he was coach at the University of Rhode Island from 1993 to 1999. In 1995 he was named Coach of the Year for New England Division I/IAA when he led Rhode Island to the Atlantic 10 New England Division championship, its best effort since 1985. Keith also was head coach for Howard University from 1979 to 1982. He has held assistant head coaching positions at Indiana University, Arizona, Colorado, and Miami of Ohio. He was a two-year starter at Ohio Northern University until he suffered a career-ending injury during his sophomore year. Keith has centered his life around football and knows the business he now finds himself taking on.

In 2006, statistics for African-American head football coaches were grim. Excluding historically black colleges and universities, of the 616 football teams affiliated with the National Collegiate Athletic Association, 16 programs, or 2.6 percent, were led by African-American coaches, although an estimated 32 percent of players are African-American. So how does Keith plan on going about making social change to a profession he has devoted his entire life to?

It goes back to an anecdote and final point he made to the group of graduate students. He said that if ever one is looking for an answer as to why, all one needs to do is look for and follow the money trail. It was a lesson he learned early, he says, from his grandfather. With that early lesson in mind, Keith is looking to push forward into the federal courts to remedy the hiring situation by citing Title VII of the Civil Rights Act of 1964. The Act prohibits discrimination in employment. If a case is pursued, it could threaten the funds received by colleges and universities from the federal government.

"Sadly, based upon my direct experiences during my tenure as the Executive Director of the Black Coaches Administrators, I have become more convinced we will see some sort of legal action take place that will alter the current discourse in the equitable hiring of intercollegiate head football coaches within the next 10 years,"[1] Keith said.

Keith will continue to pursue his case and has stood on several platforms to get his message across. He is often invited as a guest panelist on television specials, documentaries, and radio shows. He frequently appears on ESPN and HBO sports documentaries. Even in pursuing his life's work, Keith maintains the motivational guidance he exhibited as a football coach. In 2007, as a recipient of the National Consortium for Academics in Sports' "Giant Steps Award," Keith delivered a message of believing in oneself and the importance of maintaining a sense of self-certitude. Keith also has been recognized by *Sports Illustrated* as one of "The 101 Most Influential Minorities in Sports" and *Black Enterprise* as one of the "50 Most Powerful Blacks in Sport." He was named the All-American Football Foundation 2004 "Executive Director of the Year" and the 2005 "Johnny Vaught Outstanding Head Coach Award." In 2003, Keith was inducted into the Ohio Northern University Athletic Hall of Fame.

Along the way Keith has spearheaded the BCA through partnerships with the NCAA. He has become closely allied with NCAA President Myles Brand, who has launched coaching academies for minority coaching candidates to help advance their careers, has supported the BCA's Hiring Report Card, and created the first vice presidency position for diversity and inclusion, appointing Charlotte Westerhaus to the position.

Keith collaborated with the NCAA by developing the BCA's Achieving Coaching Excellence Program for women's and men's basketball coaches, also known as A.C.E. The program was made possible through a matching grant from the NCAA's Committee on Women's Athletics and the Office of Diversity and Inclusion. It is designed to help further advance the careers of minority men's and women's basketball coaches.

On a personal level, Keith jokes about the cold weather in Indianapolis, headquarters of the BCA. He speaks of his family, his wife, Dr. Nicole Keith, and his four children running around their home with toys scattered across the living room. Keith's wife, Nicole, joined him when he accepted the NCAS "Giant Steps Award," the two of them creating a strong duo. As fervent as he is in his position with the BCA, Keith the football coach and the administrator is just as fervent as a friend, father, and husband.

There are many leaders fighting for more opportunities for people of color, and we believe that no African-American is more influential in that role than Floyd Keith. His work with the BCA will help other African-Americans to be future pioneers in sport. That is why we have made him the focus of our epilogue as the "Keeper of the Flame."

Note

[1] Floyd Keith, interview with author, July 9, 2007.

About the National Consortium for Academics and Sports

The National Consortium for Academics and Sports (NCAS) is an ever-growing organization of colleges, universities, and individuals. The mission of the NCAS is to create a better society by focusing on educational attainment and using the power and appeal of sport to positively effect social change.

The National Consortium for Academics and Sports evolved in response to the need to "keep the student in the student-athlete." The NCAS was established by Dr. Richard E. Lapchick, and since its inception in 1985, NCAS member institutions have proven to be effective advocates for balancing academics and athletics. By joining the NCAS, a college or university agrees to bring back, tuition free, their own former student-athletes who competed in revenue- and non-revenue-producing sports and were unable to complete their degree requirements. In exchange, these former student-athletes agree to participate in school outreach and community service programs addressing social issues of America's youth.

There have been hundreds of people who have worked in NCAS programs over the past 22 years to help us fulfill our mission. Each has helped because of his or her passion for combining academics, sport, and the way we use sport to bring about social change for our children.

The NCAS started with 11 universities in 1985 and now has more than 220 member institutions. Members of the NCAS have brought back 27,430 former student-athletes to complete their degrees through one of our biggest programs. The Degree Completion Program was just a dream in 1985, but more than 27,000 now say that dream has become a reality.

Returning student-athletes participate in outreach and community service programs in exchange for the tuition and fees they receive when they come back to school. They have reached over 14 million young people in urban, suburban, and rural America. Wherever there are college campuses, our student-athletes are in the community, helping young people face the crises of the last 22 years. Member institutions have donated more than $297 million in tuition assistance to these former student-athletes. With no athletic participation in return this time around, the biggest return possible is to the students who leave with the degrees they were told would be there for them when they first enrolled. The NCAS and its members have been able to work with children on issues like conflict resolution, improving race relations, reducing men's violence against women, stemming the spread of drug and alcohol abuse, and emphasizing the importance of education and the importance of balancing work in the classroom and on the playing field.

The NCAS has worked with organizations and schools to help them understand issues of diversity, not only as a moral imperative, but also as a business necessity. The NCAS utilizes the Teamwork Leadership Institute (TLI) to teach our colleges, professional sports, and all of the people that sport touches the importance and value of diversity which, in turn, reflects back on society as a whole. The mission of TLI is to help senior administrators, team front office, and athletic department staff, through the provision of diversity training services, to apply the principles of teamwork to all areas of athletic departments and professional sports organizations. Challenges that stem from cultural prejudice, intolerance, and poor communication can be aggressively addressed in intelligent, safe, and structured ways. TLI works with staff members to help them anticipate, recognize, and address the problems inherent to diverse teams and staff. Diversity training demonstrates that diverse people have a great deal in common. Rather than being divisive issues, racial, ethnic, and gender differences can serve as building blocks. Just as in sports, these differences can strengthen the group. TLI has provided workshops for over 150 athletic organizations, including college athletic departments, the National Basketball Association, Major League Soccer, Maloof Sports & Entertainment (Sacramento Kings), and the Orlando Magic.

The Mentors in Violence Prevention (MVP) Program, founded

in 1993 by Northeastern University's Center for the Study of Sport in Society, is a leadership program that motivates student-athletes and student leaders to play a central role in solving problems that historically have been considered "women's issues": rape, battering, and sexual harassment. The mixed-gender, racially diverse former professional and college athletes who facilitate the MVP Program motivate men and women to work together in preventing gender violence. Utilizing a unique bystander approach to prevention, MVP views student-athletes and student leaders not as potential perpetrators or victims, but as empowered bystanders who can confront abusive peers. The MVP approach does not involve finger pointing, nor does it blame participants for the widespread problem of gender violence. Instead it sounds a positive call for proactive, preventative behavior and leadership. MVP has facilitated sessions with thousands of high school and college students and administrators at dozens of Massachusetts schools, as well as with hundreds of student-athletes and administrators at over 100 colleges nationwide. MVP has also conducted sessions with professional sports leagues, including players and staff from the National Basketball Association (NBA), National Football League (NFL), and International Basketball League (IBL) as well as with personnel from the U.S. Marine Corps. MVP has also trained the rookies and free agents of the New England Patriots and New York Jets, minor league players of the Boston Red Sox, and Major League Lacrosse (MLL) players.

With the alarming rate of alcohol use and abuse among students, the NCAS, in collaboration with The BACCHUS and GAMMA Peer Education Network, sought a solution through education and developed the Alcohol Response-Ability: Foundations for Student Athletes™ course in 2004. It is a 90-minute, Internet-based alcohol education and life skills program designed specifically for student-athletes and those who work with them in the college and university setting. In this first program of its kind, student-athletes receive a customized educational experience that is interactive, interesting, and designed to help them reduce harm and recognize the consequences associated with alcohol abuse in their campus communities. In its first year on college campuses, results came back as overwhelmingly positive. Ninety three percent of the students who took the course said they learned something new, and 95 percent of them said they would try at least one of the strategies they learned to lower their risk. An impressive 83 percent said they would likely make safe decisions as a direct result of the course. These figures prove that much more needs to be done with alcohol abuse education.

Each of the 100 heroes whose lives you can read about in the first book of this series, *100 Heroes: People in Sports Who Make This a Better World*, was honored in celebration of National STUDENT-Athlete Day (NSAD). NSAD is celebrated annually on April 6, providing an opportunity to recognize the outstanding accomplishments of student-athletes who have achieved excellence in academics and athletics, while making significant contributions to their communities. In addition to honoring student-athletes, the Annual National STUDENT-Athlete Day program selects recipients for Giant Steps Awards. These awards are given to individuals on a national level who exemplify the meaning of National STUDENT-Athlete Day. Each year nominations are received from across the country, and the Giant Steps Award winners are chosen by a national selection committee in categories ranging from civic leaders, coaches, parents, teachers, athletic administrators, and courageous student-athletes. *100 Heroes* was a compilation of the inspiring life stories of the first 100 to be chosen in honor of the "giant steps" they have taken in sports, in society, and in life itself.

The NCAS uses sport as a vehicle for social change because so many can relate to sport. The racial history of the United States may be studied by young Americans but too many cannot relate. Yet, young people do relate to sport. By illustrating the history of America's racial barriers that were confronted and challenged by our 100 pioneers in sport, the picture may become clearer. *100 Pioneers* tells their courageous stories, our history, and the many ways in which sport had a positive impact on race relations in the United States.

About the Authors

Richard E. Lapchick

Human rights activist, pioneer for racial equality, internationally recognized expert on sports issues, scholar, and author Richard E. Lapchick is often described as "the racial conscience of sport." He brought his commitment to equality and his belief that sport can be an effective instrument of positive social change to the University of Central Florida, where he accepted an endowed chair in August 2001. Lapchick became the only person named as "One of the 100 Most Powerful People in Sport" to head up a sport management program. He remains president and CEO of the National Consortium for Academics and Sport and helped bring the NCAS national office to UCF.

The DeVos Sport Business Management Program at UCF is a landmark program that focuses on the business skills necessary for graduates to conduct a successful career in the rapidly changing and dynamic sports industry. In following with Lapchick's tradition of human rights activism, the curriculum includes courses with an emphasis on diversity, community service, and philanthropy, sport and social issues, and ethics, in addition to UCF's strong business curriculum. The DeVos Program has been named one of the nation's top five programs by the *Wall Street Journal*, the *Sports Business Journal*, and ESPN's *The Magazine*.

In December of 2006, Lapchick, his wife and daughter, and a group of DeVos students formed the Hope for Stanley Foundation which is organizing groups of student-athletes and sports management students to go to New Orleans to work in the reconstruction efforts in the devastated Ninth Ward. As of the summer of 2007, Hope for Stanley members have spent five weeks in the city in a partnership with the NOLA City Council.

Lapchick helped found the Center for the Study of Sport in Society in 1984 at Northeastern University. He served as director for 17 years and is now the director emeritus. The Center has attracted national attention to its pioneering efforts to ensure the education of athletes from junior high school through the professional ranks. The Center's Project TEAMWORK was called "America's most successful violence prevention program" by public opinion analyst Lou Harris. It won the Peter F. Drucker Foundation Award as the nation's most innovative non-profit program and was named by the Clinton Administration as a model for violence prevention. The Center's MVP gender violence prevention program has been so successful with college and high school athletes that the United States Marine Corps adopted it in 1997. Athletes in Service to America, funded by AmeriCorps, combines the efforts of Project TEAMWORK and MVP in five cities across the nation.

The Center helped form the National Consortium for Academics and Sports (NCAS), a group of over 215 colleges and universities that have adopted the Center's programs. To date, more than 27,430 athletes have returned to NCAS member schools. Over 12,200 have graduated. Nationally, the NCAS athletes have worked with more than 15.3 million students in the school outreach program, which focuses on teaching youth how to improve race relations, develop conflict resolution skills, prevent gender violence, and avoid drug and alcohol abuse. They have collectively donated more than 16.6 million hours of service.

Lapchick was the American leader of the international campaign to boycott South Africa in sport for more than 20 years. In 1993, the Center launched TEAMWORK-South Africa, a program designed to use sports to help improve race relations and help with sports development in post-apartheid South Africa. He was among 200 guests specially invited to Nelson Mandela's inauguration.

Lapchick is a prolific writer. This is his 13th book. He is a regular columnist for ESPN.com and *The Sports Business Journal*, as well as a regular contributor to the op ed page of the *Orlando Sentinel*. He has written more than 450 articles and has given more than 2,700 public speeches. Considered among the nation's experts on sport and social issues, Lapchick has appeared numerous times on *Nightline, Good Morning America, Face The Nation, The Today Show, ABC World News, NBC Nightly News*, the *CBS Evening News*, CNN and ESPN.

Lapchick also consults with companies as an expert on both managing diversity and building community relations through service programs addressing the social needs of youth. He has a special expertise on Africa and South Africa. He has made 30 trips to Africa and African studies were at the core of his Ph.D. work.

Before going to Northeastern, he was an associate professor of political science at Virginia Wesleyan College from 1970 to 1978 and a senior liaison officer at the United Nations between 1978 and 1984.

In 2006, Lapchick was named both the Central Florida Public Citizen of the Year and the Florida Public Citizen of the Year by the National Association of Social Workers. Lapchick has been the recipient of numerous humanitarian awards. He was inducted into the Sports Hall of Fame of the Commonwealth Nations in 1999 in the category of humanitarian, along with Arthur Ashe and Nelson Mandela, and received the Ralph Bunche International Peace Award. He joined Muhammad Ali, Jackie Robinson, Arthur Ashe, and Wilma Rudolph in the Sport in Society Hall of Fame in 2004. Lapchick won the Diversity Leadership Award at the 2003 Literacy Classic and the Jean Mayer Global Citizenship Award from Tufts University in 2000. He won the Wendell Scott Pioneer Award in 2004 for leadership in advancing people of color in the motor sports industry. He received the "Hero Among Us Award" from the Boston Celtics in 1999 and was named as the Martin Luther King, Rosa Parks, Cesar Chavez Fellow by the State of Michigan in 1998. Lapchick was the winner of the 1997 "Arthur Ashe Voice of Conscience Award." He also won the 1997 Women's Sports Foundation President's Award for work toward the development of women's sports and was named as the 1997 Boston Celtics' Man of the Year. In 1995, the National Association of Elementary School Principals gave him their first award as a "Distinguished American in Service of Our Children." He was a guest of President Clinton at the White House for National Student-Athlete Day in 1996, 1997, 1998, and again in 1999.

He is listed in Who's Who in American Education, Who's Who in Finance and Industry, and Who's Who in American Business. Lapchick was named as "one of the 100 most powerful people in sport" for six consecutive years. He is widely known for bringing different racial groups together to create positive work force environments. In 2003–04 he served as the national spokesperson for VERB, the Center for Disease Control's program to combat preteen obesity.

Lapchick has received eight honorary degrees. In 1993, he was named as the outstanding alumnus at the University of Denver, where he earned his Ph.D. in international race relations in 1973. Lapchick received a B.A. from St. John's University in 1967 and an honorary degree from St. John's in 2001.

Lapchick is a board member of the Open Doors Foundation, SchoolSports, the Team Harmony Foundation, and the Black Coaches & Administrators and is on the advisory boards of the Women's Sports Foundation and the Giving Back Fund.

Under Lapchick's leadership, the DeVos Program launched the Institute for Diversity and Ethics in Sport in December 2002. The Institute focuses on two broad areas. In the area of diversity, the Institute publishes the critically acclaimed Racial and Gender Report Card, long authored by Lapchick in his former role as director of the Center for the Study of Sport in Society at Northeastern University. The Report Card, an annual study of the racial and gender hiring practices of major professional sports, Olympic sport, and college sport in the United States, shows long-term trends over a decade and highlights organizations that are notable for diversity in coaching and management staffs.

In another diversity initiative, the Institute partners with the NCAS to provide diversity management training to sports organizations, including athletic departments and professional leagues and teams. The Consortium has already conducted such training for the NBA, Major League Soccer, and more than 80 university athletic departments.

In the area of ethics, the Institute monitors some of the critical ethical issues in college and professional sport, including the potential for the exploitation of student-athletes, gambling, performance-enhancing drugs, and violence in sport. The Institute publishes annual studies on graduation rates for all teams in college football bowl games, comparing graduation rates for football players to rates for overall student-athletes and including a breakdown by race.

The Institute also publishes the graduation rates of the women's and men's basketball teams in the NCAA Tournament as March Madness heats up.

Richard is the son of Joe Lapchick, the famous Original Celtic center who became a legendary coach for St. John's and the Knicks. He is married to Ann Pasnak and has three children and two grandchildren.

Jessica Bartter

Jessica Bartter is currently the assistant director of communications and marketing for the National Consortium for Academics and Sports (NCAS). At the University of California, San Diego, Bartter was a member of the nationally ranked NCAA Division II volleyball team and was elected team co-captain during her junior and senior years. The UC San Diego Tritons went to the playoffs every year, including a Final Four appearance her junior season. As an individual who values teamwork, Bartter considers her "Best Team Player" award one of her greatest accomplishments. Exercising her talent on the sidelines as well, Bartter coaches high school volleyball in Los Angeles. Bartter attributes many valuable lessons she has learned to her experiences in sport and works to apply them outside of the sports arena and in her professional life. Prior to working for the NCAS, Bartter worked for the UC San Diego Recreation and Inter-collegiate Athletic Departments while she earned her bachelor's degree in management science, with a minor in psychology. Born and raised in Orange County, California, Bartter attended Valencia High School of Placentia before becoming a Triton. Bartter is grateful to her father who first introduced her to sports and to her mother who taxied her to softball and volleyball practices and even dared to catch wild pitches in the backyard. Bartter is the eldest of four siblings including Jacqueline, Brian, and Kyle, all of whom have proudly donned jersey No. 13. Bartter currently resides in Los Angeles, California, and is engaged to her childhood sweetheart C.J. Duffaut.

Jennifer Brenden

Jenny Brenden is a recent graduate of the DeVos Sport Business Management program at the University of Central Florida, where she earned a master's in business administration, as well as a master's in sport business management. She served as a graduate assistant for Dr. Richard Lapchick in the Institute for Diversity and Ethics in Sport, as well as being a graduate assistant within Academic Services for Student-Athletes (ASSA,) where she mentored and advised UCF student-athletes. Jenny graduated from Penn State University in May of 2005 with B.A. degrees in public relations and media studies and minors in business and sociology. She was on the Dean's List eight of her ten semesters in school, and she earned several academic awards, including Academic All-Big Ten Honors in 2002, 2003, 2004, and 2005. She also spent five years as a member of the Penn State Lady Lion basketball team, serving as team captain for two of those years. Jenny's team had much success during her tenure on the team. They were two-time Big Ten Champions, in 2003 and 2004, and their play in March Madness brought them to the round of the Sweet-Sixteen twice and to the Elite-Eight once. Jenny worked with student-athletes at Penn State on the Student-Athlete Advisory Board, which she served as president her senior year. She was also very involved in the community at Penn State through Habitat for Humanity, Easter Seals, Lift for Life, and Lifelink. Although her days of being a student-athlete are over, Jenny wants to remain close to the world of the student-athlete, hoping to help them have the same great experience that she had. Basketball has been a part of her life since a very young age, and she wants basketball and athletics to remain an integral part of her life. She aspires to be an athletic director in the future and really work at connecting her school and her athletes with the community.

Jenny hails from the Land of 10,000 lakes—more specifically, Sauk Rapids, Minnesota. She finished her graduate school work in May of 2007 and recently moved back to Minnesota to be closer to her family.

Stacy Martin

Stacy A. Martin grew up in Bloomington, Indiana, where she began her athletic career at a young age. She credits her success to her parents, Maureen and Randy, both former coaches. She won two state titles her senior year with record-breaking performances, and she was named the Gatorade National Female Track & Field Athlete of 1999. Auburn University offered her a full athletic scholarship in track and field. As an Auburn athlete, Stacy set new school records in the shot put, discus, hammer, and weight throw. A condition called compartment syndrome had plagued her legs for eight years and finally required surgery and extensive rehabilitation that began with learning how to walk again. In spite of this obstacle, her numerous collegiate career accomplishments included an SEC Championship, Academic and Athletic All-American honors, and competition in the Junior World Championships. The pinnacle of her athletic career was qualifying for the 2004 Olympic Trials in both shot put and discus. In 2007, Martin was inducted into the Indiana Track and Field Hall of Fame for her athletic career accomplishments. She was named to the SEC Good Works Team, served as a NCAA Leadership Conference representative, held the position of president of the Student Athletic Advisory Committee, and was named to the SEC Academic Honor Roll during all of her years at Auburn. She graduated with honors from Auburn University with a bachelor's of science in education, health promotion and a bachelor's of science in business administration, human resource management. She has passed the torch on to her younger brother, Cory, who has already earned All-American honors for Auburn in the throwing events and competed at the Junior World Championships.

After her time at Auburn, Martin entered the sports industry to work for the NCAA Beyond the Game Tour Presented by CBS Sports, a promotional tour for student-athletes, and for ESPN on a summer sporting event production. She then earned a master's of sports business management (2007) and a master's of business administration (2006) at the University of Central Florida's DeVos Sport Business Management Program. She served as a graduate assistant to Dr. Richard Lapchick and The Institute for Diversity and Ethics in Sport (TIDES) and worked for the Orlando Magic during graduate school. Martin was a co-author on TIDES' *2005 Racial and Gender Report Card* and *100 Heroes* with Lapchick and other graduate students. She participates in the Deliver the Dream weekends, for families that suffer from terminal illnesses, and in other community service activities. Martin is now working at *Disney's Wide World of Sports*® on the Sports Event Management Team to create a magical environment for Amateur Athletic Union athletes during AAU championships hosted on Disney property. She thanks her husband, Anthony Tenney, for his tremendous support throughout all of her endeavors.

Horacio Ruiz

Horacio Ruiz is a student in the University of Central Florida's DeVos Sport Business Management Program. He is a graduate of the University of Florida, and his stories have been published on ESPN.com and in *The Independent Florida Alligator* and *The Miami*

Herald. He also has helped research and co-author the Racial and Gender Report Cards for Major League Baseball, the National Basketball Association, and the National Football League.

Raised in Miami, Florida, Ruiz was born in Managua, Nicaragua. His father, mother, and sister currently reside in Miami.

Marcus Sedberry

Marcus Ray Sedberry was born in Greenville, Texas on February 12, 1984, to Marvin and Jackie Sedberry as the youngest of 5 siblings—sisters LaDia, Erika, and Stacie and brother Marvin Jr. Growing up with a father who was a head football coach and athletic director, a mother who worked for the federal government, and a family reared in faith and service, Sedberry was destined to be an avid, socially conscious sports lover. Because of his father's profession, Sedberry moved all over Texas, but spent a majority of his time in Greenville. The family's moving, including a move just prior to his senior year in high school, was tough for the young Sedberry, yet proved very beneficial in his ability to communicate well across geographical, racial, and socio-economical backgrounds. Sedberry spent nine years in the Greenville Independent School District before transferring to David W. Carter High School, where he was a football and track athlete. On the field, he experienced success, as the Carter Cowboys were district champions. He also had tremendous success on the track, leading his team to a state championship as well as a nation-leading time for the 4 x 100 meter relay and the 4 x 200 meter relay. After graduating from Carter High School, Sedberry became a student-athlete at the University of Nebraska. After two brief years of track and field competition, Sedberry was forced to stop competing for the Huskers because of a back injury. However, Sedberry continued to work with the Husker track and field team as a student assistant coach, focusing on the sprints and hurdles, as well as nation-wide recruiting. While at Nebraska, Sedberry was very involved with community service organizations and student organizations. He was a part of founding Your Degree First (YDF), a campus-recognized student organization emphasizing the importance of student-athletes getting the degree of their choice. He was the president of YDF, as well as the Afrikan People's Union and the local chapter of Alpha Phi Alpha Fraternity, Inc. He was a member of Husker

Choices, the Big 12 Conference on Black Student Government, IN-ROADS and TEAMMATES. Sedberry was also awarded several awards and honors while at Nebraska, including the Dean's List twice, Big 12 All-Academic team, Big 12 Community Outreach Award, Nebraska Student Impact Award, and two-time inductee into the Scholars and Leaders of Distinction Hall of Fame.

After receiving his bachelor's degree in marketing, Sedberry turned his attention toward earning a master's of business administration (MBA) and a master's of sports business management (MSBM) from the University of Central Florida's DeVos Sports Business Management program. Sedberry has the responsibility of managing the graduate program's community service endeavors and was elected co-president of his class. He has spent time as a mentor for numerous UCF student-athletes through Academic Student Services for Athletes (ASSA) and is also a graduate assistant for the National Consortium for Academics and Sports and for UCF's Director of Athletics, Keith Tribble. Upon graduation, Sedberry plans to give back to the community as a sports and business leader for student-athletes and business professionals to follow.

Catherine Lahey—Editor

Catherine Lahey,—known to her friends as Kt,—is currently a student in the DeVos Sport Business Management Program at the University of Central Florida, where she is working toward master's degrees in business administration and sport business management. While completing her graduate studies, Kt works as a graduate assistant in the national office of the National Consortium for Academics and Sports (NCAS). Before entering the DeVos Program, she attended Stetson University on the J. Ollie Edmunds Distinguished Scholarship, earning her undergraduate degrees in English and sport management. In her years at Stetson, Kt spent time volunteering in the Sports Information Department, studying abroad at Oxford University, working as a sports reporter for the student newspaper, and hanging out with legendary English professor Michael W. Raymond. Kt has proudly served as an assistant softball coach at DeLand High School for the past five years. Although she attended Bishop Moore High School in Orlando, Florida, she happily considers herself an honorary DeLand Bulldog.